THE BIG GUY

Also by Miranda Devine

Laptop from Hell: Hunter Biden, Big Tech,
and the Dirty Secrets the President Tried to Hide

THE BIG GUY

How a President
and His Son
Sold Out
America

MIRANDA DEVINE

BROADSIDE BOOKS

HarperCollins books may be purchased for educational, business, or sales promotional use. For information, please email the Special Markets Department at SPsales@harpercollins.com.

Broadside Books™ and the Broadside logo are trademarks of HarperCollins Publishers.

FIRST EDITION

Library of Congress Cataloging-in-Publication Data has been applied for.

ISBN 978-0-06-337481-2

24 25 26 27 28 LBC 5 4 3 2 1

To the whistleblowers.

"You do a favor for me, and you are my friend.
You do a favor for my son, and you are a friend for life."

—JOSEPH ROBINETTE BIDEN JR.,
46TH PRESIDENT OF THE UNITED STATES

CONTENTS

CAST OF CHARACTERS

FAMILY

Hunter Biden, 54, the president's son, artist, one-time crack addict. His demons can be traced to the tragedy that defined his life, the death of his mother and one-year-old sister in a car accident, when he was 2 and his brother Beau was 3. Convicted in June 2024 in Delaware on felony gun charges, indicted for tax fraud in California.

Kathleen Biden, 54, Hunter's ex-wife, mother of their three daughters. Prosecution witness in Hunter's felony gun trial in Delaware in June 2024. Sued Hunter twice for unpaid alimony. In 2023 her lawyer told the DC Superior Court that Hunter owed Kathleen more than $2.9 million.

Naomi Biden, 30, Hunter and Kathleen's daughter. Married lawyer Peter Neal in 2022 at the White House.

Finnegan Biden, 25, Hunter and Kathleen's daughter.

Maisy Biden, 24, Hunter and Kathleen's daughter.

Beau Biden, Hunter's elder brother and protector, former Delaware attorney general and Iraq war veteran, dead at 46 of a brain tumor.

Hallie Biden, 51, Beau's widow, Hunter's former lover. Prosecution witness at Hunter's gun trial. Married wealthy Ohio financial broker John Hopkins Anning the weekend before the trial.

Natalie Biden, 20, Beau and Hallie's daughter.

Hunter Biden, 18, Beau and Hallie's son.

Joe Biden, 81, US President, former VP, known in Delaware as "Lunch

Bucket Joe" or "Quid Pro Joe," political career began with the tragedy that ultimately propelled him to the White House in the year of the coronavirus pandemic. Joe was sworn in as a US senator in his motherless sons' hospital room. Lied during the 2020 presidential campaign that Hunter's laptop was a "Russian plant" and that he knew nothing about Hunter's overseas business dealings. Contested the 2024 election against Donald Trump.

Jill Biden, 73, Joe's wife of 47 years, a former English instructor at Delaware Technical & Community College, likes to be called "Dr."

Ashley Biden, 43, Hunter's half-sister, the daughter of Joe and Jill. Like Hunter, has struggled with substance abuse. A woman who found her diary at a rehab center and sold it to Project Veritas was jailed in April 2024.

Dr. Howard Krein, 57, Ashley's plastic surgeon husband.

Jim Biden, 75, Joe's brother, has run the Biden influence peddling business for four decades. Under federal investigation.

Sara Biden, 64, Jim's wife, involved in the family business.

Frank Biden, 70, Joe's youngest brother, lives in Florida, multiple DUI charges, once arrested at age 49 for allegedly shoplifting two DVDs from a Florida Blockbuster by stuffing them down his pants. Said his phone had been hacked when his naked selfie was discovered on a gay porn site in 2024.

Caroline Biden, 37, Jim's daughter. Multiple DUI charges, Paris Hiltonesque, can't live on $80,000 a year.

Valerie Biden, 78, Joe's sister, ran his first campaign, moved in with Joe to bring up Hunter and Beau after the accident. Hunter regards her as his second mother.

Jack Owens, Val's husband.

Missy Owens, 47, Val's daughter, worked for Rudy Giuliani.

Jean Finnegan Biden, Joe's mother, known to her grandchildren as "MomMom," matriarch, ambitious for her oldest son, died in 2010, age 92.

Lunden Alexis Roberts, 33, former waitress at a Washington DC strip club, in a relationship with Hunter for a year until he "ghosted" her when she was pregnant. Agreed to reduced child support payments in 2023 in exchange for Hunter establishing a relationship with their daughter and giving her a painting. As of June 2024 he had only met the child on Zoom.

Navy Joan Roberts, six, Lunden and Hunter's daughter, born August 2018, lives with her mother in Arkansas.

Melissa Cohen, 38, Hunter's wife since May 2019. South African–born filmmaker. They married ten days after meeting in LA.

Beau, 4, Hunter's son with Melissa. Born March 28, 2020.

Neilia Hunter Biden, Joe's first wife, Hunter and Beau's mother. Died in a car crash December 18, 1972, age 30.

Naomi Biden, Hunter's sister, died in a car crash December 18, 1972, at age 1.

BUSINESS/FRIENDS

Devon Archer, 50, Hunter's Yale friend and business partner in Rosemont Seneca Partners, former Kerry campaign adviser, fellow Burisma board member, sentenced to one year in prison on fraud and conspiracy charges related to fraudulent tribal bonds issued through Burnham Financial Group. Hunter was vice president of Burnham but not considered a suspect, abandoned Archer during his legal travails. Manhattan federal Judge Ronnie Abrams declared an "unwavering concern that Archer is innocent of the crimes charged" when she overturned his conviction in 2018, before it was reinstated on appeal in 2020. In May 2024, Abrams quashed his sentence over a guidelines error. Archer testified to the House Oversight Committee in July, 2023, implicating Joe Biden in his family's influence peddling schemes.

Bevan Cooney, part-owner of the hangout the Viper Room in Hollywood, serving 30 months in prison over the Native American fraud.

Jason Galanis, serving 16 years in prison over the Native American fraud, has multiple felony convictions for securities fraud. Testified to the Biden impeachment inquiry that Hunter introduced Joe on speakerphone to Russian oligarch Elena Baturina.

Jason Sugarman, LA-based investor, part-owner of the Viper Room, was served with an SEC Civil Enforcement over the Native American scheme.

Chris Heinz, John Kerry stepson, heir to the Heinz ketchup fortune, Yale roommate of Archer, formed Rosemont Capital with Archer, then Rosemont Seneca Partners with Archer and Hunter. Quit after they joined Burisma board.

Eric Schwerin, Hunter's loyal partner at Rosemont Seneca Partners, managed his financial affairs and helped Joe with his taxes. Was rewarded with a plum Obama appointment to the Commission for the Preservation of America's Heritage Abroad.

Tony Bobulinski, 52, successful California businessman, former naval officer, nuclear submarine instructor and UPenn wrestler, CEO of SinoHawk, the CEFC venture, fell out with Hunter and Uncle Jim. Star witness at Joe's impeachment inquiry.

James Gilliar, Hunter's business partner in SinoHawk, British businessman, ex-military.

Rob Walker, Biden family representative from Arkansas, partner in SinoHawk, former Clinton staffer. Was the conduit for CEFC cash to the Bidens.

Betsy Massey Walker, Rob's wife, WH personal assistant of Jill Biden.

James Bulger, nephew of Boston organized crime boss Whitey Bulger, runs Thornton Group, formed Rosemont Seneca Thornton with Hunter.

George Mesires, Hunter's lawyer, friend.

Kevin Morris, Hunter's "Sugar Brother," wealthy Hollywood lawyer who paid the First Son's tax debts and bankrolled his lifestyle. Orchestrated his legal defense.

Abbe Lowell, high-priced DC attorney hired by Hunter in December 2022, after Republicans won control of the House. Has represented Bill Clinton and Trump son-in-law Jared Kushner.

Zoe Kestan, 24-year-old art school graduate and exotic dancer who met Hunter in December 2017 at a Manhattan gentlemen's club, prosecution witness at his 2024 gun felony trial, spent a year bouncing around hotels with him in New York and LA watching him smoke crack every 20 minutes.

Ye Jianming, Chinese oil tycoon, chairman of energy company CEFC, Hunter's main Chinese business partner. Vanished in 2018 in China after being arrested for "economic crimes."

GongWeng Dong (Kevin), Ye's "emissary," as Hunter calls him.

Patrick Ho, Ye's assistant, arrested in 2017 at JFK for money laundering and bribing government officials in Africa. Served a three-year prison sentence and was deported to Hong Kong in June 2020. Threatened to sue Hunter in 2024 for the return of $1 million in legal fees.

Andrew Lo, Ho's deputy who prepared the "gift boxes" containing cash bribes for African officials, questioned by the FBI after Ho's arrest, immediately returned to Hong Kong and died a few days later in mysterious circumstances.

Jonathan Li, entered agreement with Hunter and Devon Archer to create BHR Partners, an investment fund with $2.5 billion accumulated assets under management, in which Hunter had a 10 percent stake, which he transferred to Kevin Morris in 2021. Hunter introduced him to his dad in Beijing after flying to China on Air Force 2 in 2013.

Gal Luft, Israeli-American former partner of Patrick Ho, gave evidence of Biden corruption to the Southern District of New York, was arrested in Cyprus on charges of lying to the FBI, being an unregistered foreign agent, violating Iranian sanctions, and gun running, all of which he denies. The IDF lieutenant-colonel skipped bail and remains a fugitive.

Alexander Smirnov, Israeli-American long-term, trusted, paid FBI informant, who alleged Hunter and Joe Biden had been paid a $10 million bribe by Burisma, was later charged with lying to the FBI and remains in jail in California awaiting trial in 2025.

Elena Baturina, Russia's richest woman, wife of former mayor of Moscow, friend of Putin, wired $3.5 million to Rosemont Seneca Thornton account. Met VP Joe in Washington DC in April 2015 at Cafe Milano dinner.

UKRAINE

Mykola Zlochevsky, owner of corrupt Ukrainian energy company Burisma, paid Hunter $83,000 a month to sit on its board, sent emissary to meet Joe.

Vadym Pozharskyi, Bursima senior executive, met VP Joe in April 2015 at the Cafe Milano dinner.

Viktor Shokin, Ukrainian Prosecutor General fired at Joe's behest. Was investigating Burisma and Zlochevsky before he was ousted, had planned to interview Hunter and Archer. Has been the victim of two attempted assassinations. Retired to a village outside Kyiv. Still trying to clear his name.

Vitaly Yarema, Shokin's disgraced predecessor as Prosecutor General, fired over allegations that a $7 million bribe was paid to prosecutors in 2014 to stymie the UK Serious Fraud Office case against Zlochevsky. Invited to participate in an Atlantic Council "Anti-corruption" event in Washington six months after Shokin was fired.

Yuriy Lutsenko, Shokin's successor as Prosecutor General, praised by Joe Biden as "solid." Closed the Burisma investigation and let Zlochevsky off with a fine. After Trump became US President, met with Giuliani to offer dirt on the Bidens. Was fired by Zelenskyy.

Vitaly Kasko, Shokin's disloyal deputy, a favorite of Ambassador Pyatt, who installed him in the prosecutor general's office. Accused of corruption by Shokin.

David Sakvarelidze, another disloyal deputy of Shokin, from the country of Georgia, Kasko's ally, another favorite of Ambassador Pyatt. Accused Shokin of corruption.

Tatiana Chornovol, heroine of Euromaidan, journalist, ultranationalist member of parliament, anti-corruption crusader. An ally of Shokin against Kasko. With Shokin, led a team to retrieve $1.5 billion stolen by the Yanukovych regime. Joined the war against Russia in 2022 as commander of an anti-tank platoon and then drone pilot.

Jan Tombinski, Polish diplomat, European Union ambassador to Ukraine from 2012–2016. First-hand knowledge of Shokin.

Petro Poroshenko, Ukrainian president who succeeded Viktor Yanukovych after the 2014 Maidan Revolution.

Arseniy Yatsenyuk, Ukrainian prime minister after Maidan.

Volodymyr Zelenskyy, Ukrainian president who succeeded Petro Poroshenko in May 2019.

Igor Kolomoisky, thuggish oligarch believed to be secret owner of Burisma, appointed governor of Dnipropetrovsk after the Maidan Revolution, bankrolled President Zelenskyy's election campaign.

Victoria Nuland, Obama administration's Assistant Secretary of State for Europe, Russia hawk, pushed for Ukraine to join NATO, backed the overthrow of the Yanukovych government. Became undersecretary of state in the Biden administration before resigning in March 2024.

Geoffrey Pyatt, US ambassador to Ukraine, Nuland crony, turned on Viktor Shokin. Assistant Secretary of State for Energy Resources in the Biden administration.

Marie Yovanovitch, Pyatt's successor, fell out with Prosecutor General Lutsenko, who accused her of giving him a list of people not to prosecute. She accused him of being a corrupt opportunist, told Congress she never asked him to "refrain from investigating or prosecuting actual corruption." Fired by Trump in 2019.

George Kent, bow-tie-wearing deputy chief of mission at the US Embassy in Kyiv in 2015. Troubled by Burisma corruption. Ambassador to Estonia in the Biden administration.

Eric Ciaramella, CIA analyst, John Brennan protégé, Joe's Ukraine adviser in 2015–16. Sparked the first Trump impeachment in 2019 as the "anonymous" whistleblower to Democrat Adam Schiff, chairman of the House Intelligence Committee.

Amos Hochstein, Obama administration special energy envoy, was in Ukraine in December 2015 when Joe threatened to withhold $1 billion in aid unless Shokin were fired. Falsely claimed to Congress before the 2020 election that Shokin was responsible for the collapse of the UK Serious Fraud Squad case against Zlochevsky. Atlantic Council board member. On the supervisory board of Ukrainian state-owned energy company Naftogaz between 2017 and 2020. Deputy Assistant to the President and Senior Adviser for Energy in the Biden administration.

John Herbst, Atlantic Council senior director, former Ukraine ambassador. Forged lucrative sponsorship with Burisma a few months after Shokin was fired.

DIRTY 51

Antony Blinken, as Biden campaign advisor in October 2020, prompted former acting CIA director Mike Morell to write a group letter falsely claiming Hunter's laptop was Russian disinformation. The letter was signed by 51 former intelligence officials. Used by Joe to deflect criticism at the final debate against Trump. Blinken became Secretary of State in the Biden administration.

Mike Morell, aspiring CIA director and former acting director in October 2020 when he penned the Dirty 51 letter. Testified that he had no intention of writing the letter before Blinken called him. Never became CIA director.

John Brennan, Mike Hayden, Leon Panetta, John McLaughlin (acting), and Morell (acting) were five former CIA directors who signed the Dirty 51 letter, along with former Director of National Intelligence James Clapper, eight CIA intelligence officers, seven analysts, and four chiefs of staff; 41 of the 51 signatories were former CIA.

Andrew Makridis, CIA chief operating officer in October 2020 when he was sent a draft version of the Dirty 51 letter by the CIA's Prepublication Classification Review Board. Told congressional investigators he recognized it as a "political document" but cleared it for publication after running it by the CIA director.

Gina Haspel, CIA director in the Trump administration. Makridis showed her the Dirty 51 letter before it was approved, he told congressional investigators.

INVESTIGATIONS

Gary Shapley, IRS Supervisory Special Agent who blew the whistle on obstruction and slow-walking by prosecutors, the DOJ and CIA in US Attorney David Weiss' criminal investigation of Hunter in Delaware.

Joe Ziegler, IRS Special Agent turned whistleblower.

Joe Gordon, FBI Supervisory Special Agent who worked on the Hunter investigation in Delaware.

Elvis Chan, FBI Assistant Special Agent in Charge, San Francisco Cyber Branch.

James Baker, former FBI general counsel-turned deputy general counsel at Twitter, played a key role in censoring the *New York Post* in October 2020.

David Weiss, Special Counsel prosecuting Hunter, former US Attorney in Delaware. Accused by Shapley and Ziegler of slow-walking their investigation of Hunter. Allowed the statute of limitations to run out on the most serious 2014/2015 charges. Was made Special Counsel in August 2023, after Hunter's plea deal collapsed.

Lesley Wolf, Assistant US Attorney in Delaware, was accused by Shapley and Ziegler of obstructing their investigation, allegations she denied. She was removed from the case after Hunter's plea deal collapsed and left the DOJ.

Leo Wise, Principal Senior Assistant Special Counsel assisting Weiss, replaced Wolf. Former Assistant US Attorney in Baltimore.

Successfully prosecuted Hunter on gun felony charges in Delaware in June 2024. Also prosecuting Hunter on tax fraud in California, and Smirnov over lying to the FBI.

Derek Hines, Senior Assistant Special Counsel assisting Weiss, Wise's offsider from Baltimore.

Maryellen Noreika, Delaware district judge who presided over Hunter's gun trial in Delaware in June 2024. Rejected his sweetheart plea deal in July 2023.

Martin Estrada, US Attorney in Central District of California, declined Weiss' request to bring tax charges against Hunter in his district.

Matthew Graves, US Attorney in Washington, DC, declined to bring tax charges against Hunter in his district.

Scott Brady, US Attorney in Pittsburgh, PA.

James Comer, Republican congressman from Kentucky, chairman of the House Oversight Committee, leading the Hunter Biden investigation which became the Joe Biden impeachment inquiry.

Jim Jordan, Republican congressman from Ohio, chairman of the House Judiciary Committee.

Jason Smith, Republican congressman from Missouri, chairman of the House Ways and Means Committee.

INTRODUCTION

"You gotta be an expert in knowing the guy, and [Hunter]
was the guy that was the expert in knowing the guy."

—DEVON ARCHER, JULY 31, 2023

November 14, 2019

This book started out as a corruption story about presidential candidate Joe Biden. I began covering it for the *New York Post* in October 2020, the night that Rudy Giuliani's lawyer, Bob Costello, texted me four photos from Hunter Biden's laptop and offered me a scoop.

The abandoned MacBook was a window into the Biden family business, a secret international influence peddling operation that Hunter operated to great profit during his father's time as the globe-trotting vice president of the Obama administration who would become leader of the free world. Four years on, Hunter Biden has repeatedly and under oath denied the authenticity of that sordid MacBook, but it has been used by prosecutors as evidence against him in his felony trials.

Some of the revelations about Hunter's adventures in countries such as Ukraine and China were covered in my first book, *Laptop from Hell*. But the bigger story turned out to be the coverup, and that is what this book is about. It is the story of how the FBI, the CIA, the State Department, the IRS and the Department of Justice conspired to protect Joe, his crack addict son Hunter and his scandal-prone brother Jim from the consequences of their reckless greed. The extent and nature of their crimes are coming to light as the United States and the world it leads face grave dangers from the very countries where the Bidens made millions of dollars.

Time and again, when the Bidens were in peril, an invisible hand reached out to save them, whether by creating a false media narrative about the firing of an honest Ukrainian prosecutor, coopting social media to censor the oldest newspaper in the country, or sabotaging a criminal investigation in Delaware.

We now know that the national security agencies were involved in efforts to bury and censor the *Post*'s exclusive about Hunter's laptop in October 2020. That could be seen as amounting to election interference, which prevented the American people from doing the necessary due diligence on one of the two candidates for president.

Venal politicians are a familiar scourge in Washington, but the coverup of the Biden scandal was worse, since it involved the corruption of institutions that are supposed to keep us safe. The erosion of public trust will reap bleak dividends for years to come.

Devon Archer, Hunter's former "best friend in business," recalls one of Joe's favorite sayings, that he heard him repeat over the years to their clients and prospective business partners.

"You do a favor for me, and you are my friend," Joe would say. "You do a favor for my son, and you are a friend for life."

It left nobody in any doubt that paying money to Hunter was the equivalent of paying his powerful father.

In notoriously corrupt countries like China, Ukraine, Russia, Romania, and Kazakhstan, where the Biden family traded cash for Joe's good graces, it was implicitly understood that you don't pay bribes to government officials; you pay their family members. In China, the sons of high officials are called "princelings." Around the world, lavishing largesse on princelings is a classic hallmark of corruption.

And yet, as the evidence continued to mount that this was precisely how the Biden family did business, Democrats and their many friends in the media continued to insist that Joe had done "nothing wrong." The traditional news media, gripped by the delusion that Donald Trump was an existential crisis who necessitated a new form of oppositional journalism, were willingly duped by their intelligence sources. They collectively ignored the story and shunned colleagues who broke ranks.

The key to unlocking the scandal was the "Laptop from Hell," as Trump dubbed Hunter's manic machine. Anybody who scoured it for evidence of corruption was under constant threat of being ambushed by hundreds of selfies of Hunter's erect penis, sometimes adorned with M&Ms, or flanked by a ruler, or being massaged by a pair of dainty feet, or simply flopped into a pizza in a hotel room in Vegas. But it revealed that, despite Joe's protestations, he was intimately involved in his family's corrupt dealings with America's adversaries. He was the Big Guy at the heart of all Hunter's money-making deals.

Hunter consistently has refused to admit the laptop is his. "I have no idea," he told CBS. "There could be a laptop out there that was stolen from me. It could be that I was hacked. It could be that it was Russian intelligence. It could be that it was stolen from me."

His father went on national television and lied to the American people that the laptop was a "Russian plant."

Fifty-one former intelligence officials wrote the "Dirty 51" letter before the 2020 election, falsely claiming that the laptop was Russian disinformation.

Twitter falsely claimed it was "hacked material."

But four years on, that sordid MacBook has been authenticated by the FBI and was the backbone of the prosecution case against Hunter in the gun felony trial he faced in Delaware in 2024.

Hunter's "laptop is real (it will be introduced as a trial exhibit) and it contains significant evidence of the defendant's guilt," federal prosecutors told the court.

Now we know that the "Dirty 51" letter, signed by five former CIA directors, was alleged in former CIA Deputy Director Michael Morell's Congressional testimony to have been instigated by the Biden campaign.

We know that the then-CIA director and chief operating officer gave the letter the green light, and other serving CIA employees smoothed its passage, despite its overtly political nature two weeks before a presidential election.

As a result, on November 3, 2020, the American people went to the polls with the false impression that Hunter Biden's laptop was Russian disinformation.

We know that FBI officials met with executives at Twitter and Facebook in the weeks before the election to pre-bunk the *Post*'s story that Joe had enabled his family's shakedown operations in the corrupt corners of the globe where he wielded enormous power. And we know that former intelligence operatives were embedded across social media companies to censor the speech of American citizens who dissented from the approved narrative.

In the four years since the *New York Post* broke the story of the "Laptop from Hell," the collusion between Big Tech and the national security agencies has been exposed by Elon Musk's Twitter Files, by free speech advocates in the Supreme Court case *Murthy v. Missouri* (originally filed as *Missouri v. Biden*), and by the painstaking work of congressional investigators.

But more than anything, we owe this hard-won knowledge to a handful of brave and patriotic whistleblowers. Thanks to them, we know how the Department of Justice sabotaged the criminal investigation of Hunter in Delaware, how FBI employees hid derogatory information about the Bidens, how Joe treated Ukraine and China like piggy banks to be exploited by his son, and how inconvenient witnesses were silenced with lawfare.

This book is a tribute to those whistleblowers, named and unnamed, who sacrificed their careers, their freedom, and even their safety so we can know the truth.

THE BIG GUY

CHAPTER 1

SUGAR BROTHER

November 14, 2019
LOS ANGELES, CALIFORNIA

Joe Biden was flying into Los Angeles to shake the Hollywood money tree for his struggling campaign, and he asked Hunter to meet him at a swanky fundraiser in Pacific Palisades. There would be useful people there he wanted his son to meet.

The hostess was diehard Biden fan Lanette Phillips, a video producer whose client roster included Elton John, Rihanna, and Justin Bieber. This night, however, the biggest celebrity Phillips could muster for Joe was Alyssa Milano, best known for her role as a TV witch in *Charmed*.

Tickets were $500 but, for $2,800, guests could get a selfie with Joe.

About 100 donors would be there, gathered around the tropical-themed pool or chatting inside Phillips' living room with its gigantic curved steel staircase.

At the time, Hunter was living with his wife Melissa Cohen in a $12,000 a month rental high in the Hollywood Hills, off Mulholland Drive, a good 40-minute drive away in his Porsche Panamera.

He had married the blonde 32-year-old South African filmmaker that May, just six days after meeting her, and moved into the luxurious gated hilltop aerie the following month. Melissa had helped him get sober, his art was keeping him that way, and he was as far from Delaware as he could manage. Life should have been idyllic, but Hunter's past was catching up with him. More importantly, for Joe, it threatened to derail his last chance to become president.

Lunden Roberts, a waitress from Hunter's favorite Washington, DC, strip club Mpire, was suing him for child support for a baby girl he refused to acknowledge. Hunter claimed in his memoir that he "had no recollection of our encounter," yet documents on his abandoned laptop showed he had conducted a torrid affair with Roberts for several months after meeting her in the spring of 2017, while still in a relationship with his widowed sister-in-law, Hallie Biden. He had put Lunden on his payroll at his firm Rosemont Seneca and used to take her on business trips where they stayed in fancy hotels, according to her attorney.

He knew it was his baby, but in a few days' time, Roberts' attorney would file a motion in the Circuit Court of Independence, Arkansas, revealing to the world that a DNA test had "established with scientific certainty" that Hunter was the father of 15-month-old Navy Roberts, the sixth grandchild of aspiring presidential candidate Joe Biden.

Meanwhile, his ex-wife, Kathleen, had filed a lawsuit to enforce their marital separation agreement after the IRS placed a lien on her house over his delinquent 2015 tax debt. She hadn't been able to renew her passport as a result. When Hunter and Melissa tried to go to Mexico's Pacific Coast for their honeymoon, the outstanding tax liens caused a problem with his passport, too, so they had to go to Hawaii instead.

As if that weren't enough, Hunter was being dragged into the impeachment inquiry into Donald Trump. The hearings, meant to bring heat on Joe's rival, had drawn attention to the millions of dollars Hunter was paid by the Ukrainian energy company Burisma when his father was point man in Ukraine for the Obama administration.

In Washington, the day before the fundraiser, Deputy Assistant Secretary of State George Kent, now a star witness for the Democrats, inadvertently had made the case for why Hunter should be called to testify. Under close questioning by Republican Counsel Steve Castor, he revealed that he had raised the issue of a potential conflict of interest with the VP's office after Hunter was appointed to Burisma's board. At the time, the US was trying to help Ukraine claw back some of the billions Burisma's owner, Mykola Zlochevsky, had made after allegedly awarding himself rights to the country's natural gas assets when he was energy minister. Kent divulged that the Ukrainian government had been refusing to explain why an investigation into Burisma was shut down in 2016, after then-V.P. Joe Biden had ordered the removal of the prosecutor who had been aggressively pursuing the company.

This question was at the heart of the Democrats' case for impeaching Trump over a phone call in which he had asked Ukraine's new president Volodymyr Zelenskyy to investigate Hunter and Joe for "stopping the prosecution" of Burisma.

After a flurry of media interest, Hunter reluctantly had resigned from the Burisma board in April, the month his father announced his candidacy. It also was the month he abandoned his laptop at a computer repair store in Delaware—a ticking time bomb that was yet to explode.

As he was getting ready to drive down the hill to the Palisades, news broke of leaked bank records from the Ukrainian Prosecutor General's office showing 45 payments—$83,333 twice per month—from Burisma to Hunter between April 2014 and November 2015, totaling $3.5 million. (Ten weeks after his father left office, Hunter's director's fee from Burisma was cut to $41,500, effective April 2017.)

President Trump was calling for Hunter to be investigated by the Justice Department, and House Republicans were clamoring for him to testify, but Democrat House Intelligence Committee Chairman Adam Schiff so far was resisting the pressure.

The last thing Joe needed in the middle of the primary season was his son in the witness box opening up the Ukraine can of worms.

All Hunter's problems were coming to a head, and he could see no easy way out on his own.

Photographs of the 49-year-old at the fundraiser that night, November

14, 2019, show him looking pensive and pale in the shadows, arms folded, standing behind his father, who is the center of attention as he holds forth on some topic. Phillips is dressed in a low-cut black tuxedo-style pantsuit, her blond hair cascading over her shoulders, in her element as she totters around on sky-high platform heels, arm in arm with her "friend and legend," as she liked to call the man she fervently wanted to be president.

She has described herself as "close friends with the Biden family" since 2007, when she held three fundraisers for Joe the last time he ran for president in the nearby house she shared with her then-husband, Iggy Pop producer Scott Hackworth, and their two children. After the divorce, she moved in with Rick Lynch, owner of an entertainment marketing firm, to a better house with ocean views, where she continued to hold Democratic party fundraisers and forged a friendship with Hunter, who was about her age.

In January 2018, she asked Hunter to "sort us out for passes" to his father's *Promise Me, Dad* book tour event in Los Angeles. She later posted a photo on Facebook of herself with Joe, gushing that he was "a man of true honor and appreciation [who] reminded us all that our nation still has plenty of good people who are going to help America reclaim it's [*sic*] dignity & humanity."

Joe echoed her faith in him at this latest fundraiser, repeating the stump speech he had given at another event earlier that day, branding Trump "the most corrupt president in modern American history," and pitching himself as America's savior.

The crowd lapped it up.

Standing off to the side, quietly observing the crowd that mild evening, stood a rumpled, craggy-faced man wearing a brown cashmere Hermes sportscoat, swept back, leonine hair, and scrappy beard. Although he looked like an old surfer, Kevin Morris, then 56, was one of the most successful lawyers in Hollywood, described as a "rule breaker" and a "gunslinger" after having snared himself a couple of hundred million dollars for deals he'd cut for his most successful clients, including a $1.4 billion contract for the geniuses behind satirical cartoon South Park. Morris had met the young Trey Parker and Matt Stone at a party at the 1994 Sundance

Film Festival, when they had just one quirky short film to their names. But he loved *Cannibal! The Musical*, and introduced them to his wife, mega-agent Gaby Morgerman from WME. Morris went on to represent Parker and Stone for years without taking a dime, and then, in the messy early days of streaming, he made them a fortune and took a nice slice.

Morris had grown up the oldest of three brothers in the working-class outskirts of Philadelphia and, when he was seven, in 1971, his alcoholic father lost his job at the nearby oil refinery. He never forgot the indignity for his family of being forced onto food stamps. He would go to the grocery store and cash them in to save his mother the embarrassment. "I got in fights a couple of times," he would later tell the *Hollywood Reporter*, recalling his wild youth. "But as I get older, sometimes I regret being so violent."

Morris escaped Philly through a scholarship for financially disadvantaged students at Cornell University and his earnings as a bartender. Then it was law school at NYU, before he hopped on a plane for LA to try his luck in Hollywood. Now he owned multiple mansions, flew around in a private jet he'd bought from country singer Brad Paisley, and was regarded as a generous donor to the Democratic Party.

He always felt an affinity to Joe Biden through their shared boozy Irish Catholic roots in the hardscrabble northeast. And he was repulsed by President Trump.

Morris had grown up seven years and 15 miles apart as the crow flies from Hunter, whose privileged upbringing as the son of a senator in a mansion with ballroom in Chateau Country in Delaware could not have been more different. But he shared Hunter's struggle with addiction. He could see he was in trouble.

Morris' story of how he came to be Hunter's deep-pocketed savior is that he was introduced to Phillips through his Beverly Hills accountant and close friend Lindsay Wineberg. Phillips asked him to help the former VP's troubled son, and that, he later told Congress, was what brought him to the Joe Biden fundraiser, a couple of miles up Sunset Boulevard from his seaside spread.

There is another possibility: that the CIA was involved in Morris' sudden appearance on the scene. But those revelations are still to come.

That Saturday night at Phillips' place, Morris was a half-hearted mingler at best, but his $2,800 donation scored him a place on the selfie line with Joe. When it was his turn he said, "Hi, Joe."

Someone in the background corrected him: "Mr. Vice President."

Joe looked at him with a lopsided grin: "Call me Joe."

If there was any further conversation, no one is saying.

Toward the end of the night, Phillips found Morris and brought him over to meet Hunter.

"Hunter, Kevin," she said, and left them alone. They shook hands. Hunter seemed overcome with anxiety and mumbled something polite. The awkward encounter lasted less than a minute, according to a witness. But it was enough time for Morris to size up Hunter, with all his self-conscious unease, and decide he was worth at least meeting again to work out what he needed. Sorting out the chaos of his clients' lives was Morris' specialty.

A week later, Morris showed up at Hunter's sundrenched home high in the Hollywood Hills and met Melissa, then five months pregnant. Hunter took him down to the pool house and showed off his art, the way he blew paint through a straw onto Japanese paper to make abstract patterns. Kevin liked what he saw. At one point, he looked at Hunter and said: "How are you doing?" and for the next five hours Hunter poured out his soul.

Hunter had a way of eliciting sympathy from strangers, always beginning with the defining tragedy of his childhood, when his mother and baby sister were killed in a car accident when he was two years old. He and his brother, Beau, one year older, were injured in the crash in December 1972, which occurred a month after Joe won a longshot US Senate race in Delaware at age 29. Joe was in Washington that wintry day, setting up his new office. His beautiful young wife, Neilia Hunter Biden, had taken the children to buy a Christmas tree near their home in Wilmington, when their car was struck by a truck as she pulled out of an intersection. Hunter was hospitalized with head injuries and Beau with a broken leg.

The grieving widower got special dispensation from the Senate to be sworn in at their bedside. A podium was hauled into their hospital room and festooned with microphones as the space filled with journalists and photographers. The images of two wan, motherless boys lying in a hospital bed in the foreground as their father was sworn in as a US senator captured the nation's heart and has paid off politically for Joe in every campaign since. Nobody questioned why Joe invited the circus to his little boys' bedside rather than being sworn in outside. But the stagecraft elicited lifelong public sympathy for Joe and forged an emotional bond with millions of compassionate strangers.

His younger son never would fully recover, emotionally. In Hunter the charismatic grown man, people still could detect the lost little boy inside, forever two years old and crying for his mother.

Sitting at his kitchen table in the Hollywood Hills that afternoon, 47 years later, Hunter told Kevin everything. His first taste of alcohol at eight, when he sneaked a glass of champagne at an election-night party at home in Delaware. The binge-drinking at 14 with other private school kids in the laissez-faire atmosphere of privilege in 1980s Greenville. The cocaine arrest at 18 that was expunged from his record. The drugs and the alcohol and the infidelities he kept from Kathleen and their three daughters. The crack addiction, the countless rehab attempts. His expulsion from the Naval Reserve after a positive drug test on his first weekend of duty in 2013, aged 43, an embarrassment for his father who had pulled strings to get him accepted at such an advanced age. Spiraling out of control after the 2015 cancer death of his brother, Beau. The affair with Beau's widow, Hallie, and their mutual descent into addiction. The ugly divorce. The crushing weight of $37,000 a month alimony, the IRS bills, the millions he had squandered.

Now, with the growing focus on his dad's campaign, and Trump's impeachment pulling him into the political fray, his weaknesses had become media fodder. He knew his father's campaign didn't care about him, just about protecting Joe from his son's scandals. He was on his own.

Hunter talked and talked, past nightfall, laying out his woes and grievances, and when he finished he could see that Morris was hooked. He knew that look from all the times in his life when sympathetic strangers had come to his rescue, captivated equally by his charisma as by the power of his father. He would be excused the vilest abuse, absolved of the lowest betrayals. Not everybody forgave him, but Joe would always find someone to bail him out of trouble.

Kevin had been taking notes on a legal pad as Hunter spoke. Now, he outlined the steps Hunter would need to take to get his life on track.

First, he and Melissa had to get out of the Hollywood Hills and into a more secure house where the paparazzi couldn't get at him. Morris would find him a place down on the beach. A nice place. And he'd take care of the rent. He'd pay $160,000 immediately off the most pressing IRS bill to get the lien taken off Kathleen's house and stop the story blowing up in the media. He'd negotiate with the baby mama lawyers down in Arkansas. He'd assemble a team of lawyers, accountants, public relations experts, whatever was needed, to meet at his house for a crisis meeting after Christmas. They would speak on the phone every day.

Morris told House investigators that he was motivated by "a very tribal feeling about Hunter . . . You know, he's a guy. I have brothers . . . He was in a lot of trouble . . . like a guy getting the crap beat out of him by a gang of people. And where we come from, you don't let that happen. You get in, and you start swinging."

When Hunter's former friends heard about Morris, they shook their heads wryly. They'd seen it all before. One or two of them had been in his position, lending Hunter money, getting him out of scrapes, saving him from himself, only to get burned themselves.

They dubbed Morris the "Sugar Brother." He was Hunter's latest knight in shining armor come to solve all his problems—and more to the point, Joe's.

CHAPTER 2

ESCAPE FROM HOLLYWOOD HILLS

January 2020
VENICE BEACH, CALIFORNIA

Like everything in Hunter's life, moving house was a drama. By his telling, it was a midnight escape from the Hollywood Hills, necessitated by the appearance on his doorstep of a MAGA horde.

"Half a dozen, two dozen people, mostly men, in MAGA hats with bullhorns literally pounding at the front door," he told podcaster Moby, a 90s electronica superstar, now better known as a vegan activist, who Hunter had befriended in drug rehab. Hunter's home address had been published in court filings the previous month in his baby mama's lawsuit in Arkansas, and realtor photos of the house soon made their way into the media. Within 36 hours, Hunter claimed, MAGA had descended.

"Melissa was alone up in that house at the time, and there's a little tiny place [the pool house] where I used to paint. I came running up. So, then we moved in the middle of the night, literally left. We left at midnight the next night, packed the entire house in a van, and a friend of ours found us another place to stay. And we were able to hide out there for a period of time."

Kevin Morris had arranged a new house for them to move to on the Grand Canal in Venice Beach and would pay the rent of $25,000 a month, so Hunter could continue the luxurious lifestyle to which he had become accustomed.

Billed as a "striking architectural oasis" a block from the beach, the $5.4 million hideout was owned by Jonathan Neman, co-founder of Sweet-green, the salad restaurant chain. Morris said he chose the place because it was "entirely private [and] had specific stuff, and he wanted to be closer to me." In reality it was a three-story goldfish bowl with windows on two sides exposed to the canal. Venice Beach also is notorious as an open-air drug market, a curious choice for a recovering crack addict. But Morris had decided the first time he visited Hunter in Hollywood Hills that he and Melissa were "in danger in that house" as media interest intensified.

"So, I decided to move them [and] it had to be quickly," Morris said in a 2023 interview with the House Oversight Committee.

"Paparazzi were literally chasing him through the street, in his car. There's nobody driving him around. He's got pregnant Melissa, and it was dangerous . . . People were coming up to his door with cameras, say-ing, 'We just want to talk to him.' People were yelling from outside of the bushes, 'Hunter Biden, come out. Hunter Biden, come out.'"

To be fair, Hunter had been no shrinking violet when it came to the media.

He spent that summer pitching producers on a reality TV show star-ring himself and Melissa, ostensibly to highlight his "charity work," which he suggested would "help soften his father's image," according to a book about Joe's 2020 campaign, *Battle for the Soul* by Edward-Isaac Dovere.

In one meeting, one of the producers asked Hunter if his father had approved of the project: "He's OK with this?"

"I know where the line is," Hunter replied. "And my dad is understand-ing of what I am up to."

It's doubtful that Joe's campaign managers would have approved of spotlighting his notorious son in an election year, but, as it happened, the project never got off the ground.

That didn't stop Hunter from courting the media to refashion his image after his marriage to Melissa. He invited film crews and photographers into the Hollywood Hills house and sat for several high-profile interviews, including with the *New York Times*, the *New Yorker*, and ABC News, going on the offense in the middle of the Trump impeachment hearings to tell his side of the Ukraine story.

A series of interviews with Adam Entous at the *New Yorker*, some conducted on the phone while he was high on crack, culminated in a revelatory feature in July 2019 titled: "Will Hunter Biden Jeopardize His Father's Campaign?" Entous noted that Joe "rarely talks about Hunter" in public and that his 2017 memoir "largely glosses over" his second son, while lauding elder son Beau as "Joe Biden 2.0."

The article noted that news outlets, including the *New York Times*, "have homed in on him, reprising old controversies over Hunter's work for a bank, for a lobbying firm, and a hedge fund, and scrutinizing his business dealings in China and Ukraine." Left unsaid was the belief in Washington that Joe's Democratic Party rivals were leaking dirt to the press, even as President Trump was ramping up allegations that Joe had forced the removal of the Ukrainian prosecutor to protect Hunter. "Biden and his son are stone-cold crooked!" Trump would say at rallies. "Where's Hunter?"

Hunter boasted to Entous that he was the "provider for the Biden family; he even helped to pay off Beau's law school debts."

He also gave his side of the divorce, claiming that Kathleen kicked him out when he started using drugs and turned cold toward him after his brother, Beau, died. Kathleen's story was somewhat different, as Kathleen would reveal in her 2022 book, *If We Break: A Memoir of Marriage, Addiction, and Healing*, and as material on Hunter's abandoned laptop would confirm. Kathleen wanted Hunter back desperately, but he had embarked on a torrid affair with Beau's widow, Hallie Biden, soon after the funeral. "We were sharing a very specific grief," Hunter told the *New Yorker*. "I started to think of Hallie as the only person in my life who understood my loss."

The ABC interview aired on October 15, 2019, the day of the fourth Democratic primary debate, and it caught Joe's campaign staff unawares. But Joe knew exactly what his son was up to because he had allowed the ABC cameras to accompany him inside a fundraiser in West LA with Hunter the previous Friday night.

In the 11-minute segment, Hunter is filmed driving Melissa to the fundraiser hosted by media executive Howard Owens and his wife, Marnie, at their grand Renaissance Revival–style seven-bedroom home in the exclusive Windsor Square neighborhood.

As he steers his Porsche down Wilshire Boulevard, Hunter pointedly brags about his easy access to LA elites.

"We're going to an event to meet with a bunch of young and influential people here in the city," he says. "It's just always good to be together."

It was Hunter's first appearance on the campaign trail with Joe after he was forced to pull out of the campaign launch in Philadelphia in May over a fresh scandal involving a leaked 2016 police report from Prescott, Arizona. A crack pipe with cocaine residue had been found by Hertz employees in his rental car (after he'd wrecked the previous rental while high and speeding, according to his memoir) along with a plastic baggie containing white powder, Beau's Delaware attorney-general badge, and Hunter's driver's license. Republican prosecutors had declined to charge Hunter, but the incident had been dragged into his paternity case in Arkansas.

"I've never missed a rally for my dad [so] it's heartbreaking for me," Hunter told the *New Yorker* about skipping the campaign launch. "Dad says, 'Be here.' Mom says, 'Be here.' But at what cost?"

He showed no such reticence about the Owens' fundraiser five months later.

The ABC cameras show Hunter standing conspicuously on a step behind his father and placing his hand proprietorially on his shoulder, then pawing at him when Joe keeps jawboning to guests, before leaning down to whisper in his ear. Far from keeping a low profile, Hunter seems to want everybody to see the special liberties he is allowed with his important father.

In a short speech to about 160 people assembled on the Owens' pool patio, Joe calls for the first time for Trump's impeachment, a theme he'd been pushing the last several months but had been slower to endorse than his Democrat rivals. It is a ballsy move—urging a probe that could draw attention to his son's dealings in China and Ukraine. Now that it looks inevitable, he has no choice but to follow through.

"Nothing will happen unless we get rid of this guy in the White House," he says.

Impeaching Trump is the "right thing to do," he says. "He indicted himself. He acknowledged that he asked three different countries to dig up 'dirt' . . . The fact of the matter is, when I say he should be impeached, he should be impeached."

The rest of the ABC program features Hunter in his art studio and at his kitchen table in the Hollywood Hills being interviewed by Good Morning America anchor Amy Robach.

Tanned and healthy in a navy button-down shirt, a silver bangle on his wrist, he tells Robach that he doesn't mind having become a "household name" since his father started running for president. "The reason is because I know where I stand with my dad."

Hunter then makes the extraordinary admission that he probably would not have been asked to join the board of Burisma if his last name wasn't Biden.

"Probably not . . . I don't think that there's a lot of things that would have happened in my life if my last name wasn't Biden . . . Because my dad was vice president of the United States. There's literally nothing, as a young man or as a full grown adult that—my father in some way hasn't had influence over."

Robach asks if Hunter and his father ever discussed Ukraine—his decision to accept the Burisma board gig while Joe was VP and the Obama administration's point man in the corrupt Eastern European country. She knows he already has admitted doing so to the *New Yorker*.

"No," says Hunter, before his eyes flutter and he immediately backtracks.

"As I said, the only time was after a news account, and it wasn't a discussion in any way. There's no 'but' to this. No. We never did. [My dad] said 'I hope you know what you're doing.' And I said, 'I do' and that was literally the end of the discussion."

Hunter also claims he received "not one cent" from a Chinese business deal he made a few days after flying into China with his father on Air Force 2 in December 2013, when he received a ten percent stake in a Chinese private equity fund.

"I've traveled everywhere with my dad. I went there because my daughter [Finnegan] was on the trip too."

Robach: "But did you talk about China?"

Hunter: "No."

Robach: "Or your deal with China?"

Hunter: "No."

Robach: "A 12-hour flight over and that never came up?"

Hunter: "No, no. Of course not."

Robach: "Your father did shake hands with Mr. Li [Hunter's Chinese partner Jonathan Li], though, correct? In the lobby of that hotel?"

Hunter (eyes darting around): "I don't remember but, probably, yeah. I hope so. I hope he did. He was my friend."

Robach: "Jonathan Li?"

Hunter: "Yeah, for, for almost 13 years."

Robach: "He was your friend—and your business partner."

Hunter: "Yeah. I understand. So, look, Amy. Whether I'm in New York or whether I'm in Washington, DC, a friend and a business associate is in the hotel and my dad's sitting there, is it inappropriate for me to have coffee with them? I don't find anything wrong with that."

Robach: "So that meeting was not a mistake. It was not unethical."

Hunter: "100 percent not. No."

Robach (leaning in for the kill): "What do you say to people who believe this is exactly why people hate Washington? A vice president's son can make money in countries where your father is doing official government business."

Hunter interjects indignantly, his voice suddenly high-pitched with anxiety: "Who says this? But, but, by the way."

We never hear what he says next because there is a break in the video. In the next shot, Hunter is composed again, leaning back in the chair, hands off the table and out of sight.

During the rest of the interview, Hunter endeavors to distance his father from his foreign business dealings. His claims will be steadily undermined over the next four years as his laptop and the testimony of former friends and whistleblowers reveal Joe's possible involvement in what can be seen as a sophisticated family enterprise to sell the "Joe Biden brand" for tens of millions of dollars to unsavory characters from corrupt and adversarial countries, such as China, Russia, Ukraine, Romania, Kazakhstan, and Mexico. By 2023, when Congress begins an impeachment inquiry, evidence of Joe's involvement in the scheme has become hard to deny, showing that he made himself available dozens of times during his vice presidency to meet foreign clients of his son and his brother Jim Biden. Joe went to dinner with these business partners, invited them for breakfast at his official residence, and spoke to them on Hunter's speakerphone.

"My family's brand" was Vice President Joe Biden, and as Hunter told his business partner James Gilliar in 2017, it is "my family's only asset."

Joe's protectors in the FBI and the intelligence community would go to extraordinary lengths to suppress the ugly truth before the 2020 election. But, for now, denial is Hunter's best line of defense.

"I did nothing wrong at all," he tells Robach of his Burisma gig, "but I gave a hook to some very unethical people to act in illegal ways to try to do some harm to my father . . . Did I do anything improper? No, not in any way. Not in any way whatsoever."

At this point, Hunter opens his blue eyes wide and lifts his brow high to convey innocence. He never looks more like his dad than when he's using this Eddie Haskell–type facial expression to mask a lie.

Hunter and his father judged the interview a success. Joe publicly praised Hunter the next day for calling Trump and his lawyer Rudy Giuliani "thugs." In political terms, the interview was a "limited hangout," intelligence jargon for pretending to come clean, a favorite "gimmick of spies," as CIA whistleblower Victor Marchetti once described it: "When they can no longer rely on a phony cover story to misinform the public, they resort to admitting . . . some of the truth while still managing to withhold the key and damaging facts."

For all his insouciance, allegations of Hunter's cashing in on his father's power in Ukraine and China had caused Joe enough concern that soon after the interview aired, as he flew to Iowa, his campaign released a proposed ethics plan to use if he became president. It included measures to "rein in executive branch financial conflicts of interest," which can be seen as a tacit acknowledgment that Hunter's foreign enrichment during his father's vice presidency was a problem.

"No one in my family will . . . have any business relationship with anyone that relates to a foreign corporation or a foreign country."

The same day, Hunter issued his own ethics statement through his lawyer, saying he would be stepping down from the board of the Chinese-backed private equity firm, Bohai Harvest RST LLC (BHR), by the end of the month, and would not profit further from foreign entities if his father won the presidency.

According to Hunter's laptop, he had received his 10 percent share in BHR less than two weeks after his Air Force Two flight to Beijing in 2013 when Joe met with Jonathan Li, Hunter's partner in the firm. Robach had hit a nerve with her question because the Bidens knew how damaging it would be to admit that the son of the US vice president—and future president—was in business with the government of Communist China and would remain so—despite promises to divest himself of all foreign entanglements—until the fall of 2021, when Hunter would sign his BHR stake over to Kevin Morris.

The value of the BHR stake has been estimated at between $4 million and $20 million, based on board papers on Hunter's laptop showing the firm had $2.5 billion in funds under management in January 2019. Its best-performing investment at that time was Face++, a facial recognition firm whose technology has been linked to Beijing's mass surveillance of Uighur

Muslims. The firm also had acquired a stake in Henniges Automotive, a Michigan car parts maker of anti-vibration technologies with military applications. The potential national security implications had sparked a Senate inquiry into whether there were potential White House conflicts of interest in the sale's approval by the Committee of Foreign Investment in the US (CFIUS). That inquiry would morph into a corruption investigation into Hunter. But Republican senators Chuck Grassley and Ron Johnson complained in late 2020 that their access to documents and testimony and their ability to serve subpoenas had been obstructed by the FBI, bureaucrats, and even some in their own party, while House Democrats falsely claimed their inquiry was a "Russian disinformation campaign."

For now, Hunter blithely was promising no conflicts of interest if his dad became president. A clean slate.

"Hunter will readily comply with any and all guidelines or standards a President Biden may issue to address purported conflicts of interest, or the appearance of such conflicts, including any restrictions related to overseas business interests. In any event, Hunter will agree not to serve on boards of, or work on behalf of, foreign-owned companies," his lawyer George Mesires said in the statement.

"He will continue to keep his father personally uninvolved in his business affairs."

Joe told reporters his son's statement "represents the kind of man of integrity he is."

But Hunter's misdeeds continued to dog his father's campaign.

Joe was sinking in the polls in September 2019 when he appeared at the Polk County Steak Fry in Des Moines, Iowa. His campaign was burning through millions of dollars on private jets because he refused to take commercial flights. He had never liked Iowa.

It started raining while he was on stage, and the lackluster crowd barely applauded. Afterward, reporters started badgering him about Ukraine, and he lost his temper.

"I have never spoken to my son about his overseas business dealings," he snapped at Fox News reporter Peter Doocy, a sound bite that would come to haunt his presidency. "Here's what I know," he barked, wagging his finger at the young reporter. "I know Trump deserves to be investigated. He is violating every basic norm of a president. You should be asking him the question: why is he on the phone with a foreign leader, trying to intimidate a foreign leader. You should be looking at Trump. Trump's doing this because he knows I will beat him like a drum. Everybody who's looked at [Trump's allegations] said that there's nothing there. Ask the right question!"

Most reporters on the campaign trail didn't press Joe about Hunter. But corruption was on the minds of voters in Iowa.

At a town hall in rural New Hampton, in the northeast corner of the state, in early December, Joe lashed out at an 83-year-old retired farmer who asked if he was "selling access" in Ukraine when Hunter got the sweetheart deal at Burisma.

"You're a damn liar, man," Joe yelled. "That's not true. And no one has ever said that. . . . Get your words straight, Jack."

Then Joe called the man "fat" and challenged him to a push-up contest and an IQ test.

"Well, I'm not voting for you," said the farmer.

Needless to say, Biden bombed in the Iowa caucuses, coming in a distant fourth. The Hunter problem wasn't helping. Something had to be done.

CHAPTER 3

CRISIS TEAM

January 23, 2020
PACIFIC PALISADES, CALIFORNIA

*"Lots brewing with my dad and the shit storm that is about
to ensue . . . presidential campaigns are truly tortuous."*

—HUNTER BIDEN TO A FRIEND

Two weeks before the Iowa drubbing, Morris held the promised crisis meeting at his $10 million Spanish Colonial in Pacific Palisades, seven miles up the coast from Hunter's new home in Venice Beach. He told Hunter he was "building a team" for him.

"His morale was very low. Melissa's was very low, and I wanted to have a meeting and show them that they have a team growing and a lot of support," Kevin would tell Congress.

By the time Hunter and Melissa arrived, about ten people were gathered around the kitchen table, where Morris did most of his work, in between stepping onto his balcony to gaze over the ocean to Catalina Island

and pull on a bong. While he would tell people that he had given up booze long ago, Morris is said to consider himself "California sober," the term for only indulging in weed, which is legal in the state.

Morris' accountant friend Wineberg was there, as were his lawyer, Shep Hoffman, his real estate broker, Don Ashton, and his personal assistant. Hunter's lawyer, George Mesires, had flown in from Chicago, and his local tax guy, Troy Schmidt, was there, having been enlisted a couple of months earlier to work on his unfiled 2017 and 2018 tax returns.

Morris was used to triaging clients' problems. He described himself to Congress as a "quarterback" whose role was to manage the solutions to Hunter's messes.

"I oversee the squad. Sort of like a general counsel. But I am involved in everything."

Schmidt later would tell the IRS that, when he went to Morris' house, "he had no idea what he was walking into," according to a memorandum of his interview. He originally thought that they were going to be discussing Hunter's tax returns, but the topic never came up during the two-and-a-half-hour confab.

In Schmidt's perception, Morris was connected, not just to Hunter, but to the Biden family, as he would later tell the IRS. "He was another advisor to Hunter and [Hunter's] family. Schmidt was not surprised that a lot of attorneys were working for [Hunter]."

Morris kicked off the meeting by giving a little pep speech about Hunter and an overview of what needed to be done for him. Hunter stood up and made what Morris described as "a long thank you." Then Morris "kicked everybody that was not a lawyer out, and we had a business meeting."

A week later, Morris held another meeting at his house to deal just with Hunter's unpaid taxes. It lasted for about an hour and, this time, Hunter brought his bank statements. Another tax accountant from Schmidt's firm, Jeffrey Gelfound, was brought in and Morris was pressuring them to get the returns filed.

It wasn't easy with a client as disorganized and unreliable as Hunter, especially when his long-suffering previous Washington, DC, tax accountant, Bill Morgan, had died prematurely. Two weeks after the crisis meeting, Morris cracked the whip and declared Hunter's taxes an "emergency."

"We are under considerable risk personally and politically to get the returns in," he wrote in an email to the accountants on February 7, 2020.

It was just four days before the 2020 New Hampshire primary, so the obvious assumption was that the "political risk" Morris was talking about was Joe's perilous presidential prospects, which would be delivered a death blow by any more scandals involving his son.

That was the working hypothesis, anyway, for the IRS and FBI investigators in his home state of Delaware who, unbeknownst to Hunter, had begun following his trail. The email only added to their suspicion that the Biden campaign was behind Morris' sudden appearance as Hunter's white knight.

Already skeptical about Morris' motives for lavishing so much money on someone he had only just met, they would begin investigating whether his payment of Hunter's tax debt and efforts to keep his troubles out of the news before the 2020 election could be treated as an in-kind contribution to Joe's campaign, potentially in criminal violation of federal election laws (no charges have been brought).

When Morris was asked four years later, in a deposition to the House Oversight Committee, to explain what he meant by "political risk," he denied that it had anything to do with Joe's 2020 campaign.

Instead, he claimed, he had been referring to Trump's impeachment: "They were waving around the possibility of calling Hunter . . . I believe that was the emergen—I believe that, you know, that was the thing prompting us."

The problem was that the chronology did not fit his story. Trump had been acquitted by the Senate on February 5, 2020, two days before the email, so there was no chance that Hunter would be called to testify. In any case, Hunter was not a politician. The only "political risk" caused by his delinquent taxes would be to his father in the middle of an election campaign.

Morris' "emergency" also happened to be three weeks before the South

Carolina primary on February 29, which was Joe's last chance of surviving the campaign. He needed the endorsement of the kingmaker of South Carolina politics, Rep. James Clyburn, the highest-ranking Black lawmaker in Congress. More than one-quarter of the state's population was Black, and almost all voted Democrat, so Clyburn's endorsement was make or break. The Democrat establishment desperately wanted to stop the surging socialist Bernie Sanders, but after Biden's poor finishes in Iowa and New Hampshire, where he came an embarrassing fifth, Clyburn was sitting on the fence. "He's not going to try to rehab a corpse" was the message to Biden's people. It was hard work to persuade Clyburn that Biden would be a viable candidate, and only Joe's promise to appoint a Black woman to the Supreme Court clinched the deal.

Joe could not afford to scare off Clyburn with another Hunter scandal over delinquent taxes or baby mamas.

Hunter's tax accountants kept beavering away, now with the help of Eric Schwerin, his former factotum at his firm Rosemont Seneca. Schwerin had studied history at the University of Pennsylvania, where he met Hunter's brother, Beau, and later worked with Hunter at the Clinton Commerce Department. In my view, Hunter's friends saw Schwerin as a Uriah Heep figure, albeit harmless. He seems to have been subservient to Hunter, who treated him largely with disdain and mild annoyance while relying on him to manage his business, oversee his personal finances, pay his bills, and cover for him when he slept in or disappeared on benders. Schwerin also helped Joe with taxes and financial planning. Official visitor logs show he visited the White House and Joe's vice presidential residence at the Naval Observatory at least 36 times during the Obama years. Schwerin was rewarded for his loyalty with a plum four-year appointment to the Commission for the Preservation of America's Heritage Abroad.

During Hunter's divorce, the relationship soured after Hunter accused Schwerin of disloyalty, believing he had helped Kathleen access his phone records and had badmouthed him around town. From then on, Hunter abused Schwerin every chance he got and whined about him to his father.

"We are no longer just done as business partners you should consider

moving to somewhere in Florida I'll never go," Hunter wrote in a typical missive in 2017, when Schwerin was trying to extricate himself from
Rosemont Seneca and get Hunter to pay him what he was owed. "Naples
is perfect—you can live in perpetual timeshare with your parents and talk
about what a horrible person I am."

Despite Hunter's attacks, Schwerin was a godsend to Hunter's new accountants because he was the only person they had found alive who had a
handle on his income. But it still wasn't easy with Morris breathing down
their necks.

Hunter was such a difficult client that Gelfound would later tell IRS
investigators that the firm had had to draw up a special "representation
letter" for him to sign, vouching that he had fully disclosed all income and
that the deductions he was claiming were proper business expenses.

For IRS investigators, this would be one of many red flags, since such
letters are usually only used to protect tax accountants when they don't
feel comfortable that the information a client is providing them is truth-
ful.

Hunter allegedly tried to tell Gelfound that the millions of dollars he
had received from Burisma and from the Chinese state-linked energy
conglomerate (CEFC) were loans, not income. After doing their own due
diligence, the accountants told Hunter, no, he had to report it as income.

Among the deductions Gelfound was quizzed about by the IRS were
payments to prostitutes that allegedly were claimed as a business deduc-
tion, $10,000 for a "golf club member deposit" that the IRS alleged was
for "membership of a sex club," $30,000 for Hunter's oldest daughter
Naomi's Columbia University tuition, a hotel room for "one of his drug
dealers," and two nights for a hotel room in L.A. for Joe. (Hunter Biden
pleaded guilty to the nine federal tax charges brought against him.)

The IRS also would allege that Hunter claimed $43,693 for stays at the
Chateau Marmont, as well as looting $20,000 from his youngest daughter
Maisy's educational savings plan in 2018, at a time when he was indulging
in a long crack and hooker bender in expensive Hollywood hotels.

That year he was blacklisted from the Chateau Marmont, a rare feat for the iconic Sunset Boulevard hotel which had been the byword for Holly-wood debauchery for almost a century. IRS investigators would later testify that they had been given photographs of "the destruction that was done to the rooms" where Hunter had stayed for weeks on end.

He was shocked when told he had been banned for drug use in the summer of 2018. "WTF man. Seriously WTF," he texted a friendly bellhop who checked his file. "Drug use???? You have to be fucking kidding me. I was banned for drug use at the Chateau Marmont. You have to be fucking me . . . Well that's a fucking first in the Hotel's history I guess."

*　*　*

Hunter and Melissa were happy in Venice Beach, but the same sort of domestic disarray that had got Hunter kicked out of the Chateau seemed to follow them to the new house. Their baby, Beau, named after Hunter's late brother, was born three months after they moved in, on March 28, 2020, at the start of the COVID-19 pandemic.

"In a way, during the pandemic, we were in this beautiful moment of having Beau, and the ability just for the three of us to be cocooned for that period of time was really, really magical," Hunter told the Moby podcast. "As much suffering as there was on the outside, there was a sense of security on the inside . . . [It was] this period of amazing solitude which was a horrible time for most everyone else."

Hunter would again blame the media for hounding him out of his haven the following spring.

"There was this super right-wing filmmaker [who] rented canoes on the canal with bull horns, and for a week straight, harassed us," he told the Moby podcast. "Outside the house, the public space, and we live right next to the canal, [someone] rented like a 30 foot digital billboard on a truck bed and parked it outside my house and showed pictures on South Venice Boulevard, literally 24/7 for a week. So literally there was only one way in that house and one way out. It was impossible to do anything."

As unpleasant as such an experience would be, trashing the house and stiffing the owner allegedly on months of unpaid rent may have played a factor in Hunter's departure from Venice.

"They were totally disrespectful of Jonathan and [his wife] Leora's property," a single anonymous source alleged to the *Daily Mail*. "Melissa was rude and entitled. They destroyed the stereo equipment in the home and when someone came to fix it, they were uncooperative. They also left the place dirty."

When he moved out, leaving possibly tens of thousands of dollars in damage, Hunter told the landlord to "just call my friend Kevin Morris," according to a text message reported by CBS News. "[Morris] will work something out with you . . . [He] has been very helpful to me and has assured me he can help to resolve this ASAP."

As always, someone else cleaned up after Hunter and the house was sold.

Another mess that Morris took off the table for Hunter that winter was the baby mama case in Arkansas. Within a week of the January crisis meeting, Hunter's lawyers had told the court that he would pay Roberts the princely sum of $20,000 a month, plus her legal fees. The generous settlement, funded by Morris, saved Hunter from potentially being thrown in a jail cell in Arkansas. Independence County Circuit Judge Holly Meyer had threatened to hold him in contempt of court unless he produced the required financial records, including his un-redacted personal tax returns and all sources of income for the past five years, as well as a list of all companies he owns.

Luckily for Hunter—and, more importantly, for Joe—now he would not have to open the books on his financial affairs, which could have embroiled his entire family. The settlement also ended Roberts' appearances in the media, and ensured that her cute little blonde toddler would not become a distraction on the election campaign. Joe the family man didn't want to have to explain why he had never met his sixth grandchild.

Crisis averted, thanks to Morris' deep pockets.

Soon afterward, Hunter asked his uncle Jim Biden, Joe's younger brother, to thank Morris "on behalf of the family." The request puzzled Jim, he would claim in an interview with IRS and FBI agents in 2022. Hunter had told him that Morris "requested a thank you [from him, but

Jim] had no knowledge of what Morris had done for [Hunter] and was not sure if there was a loan between Morris and [Hunter.]" Jim was not aware if Morris asked Hunter "for anything else other than a thank you."

Jim, who was neck deep in Hunter's deals with Chinese energy company CEFC, also lived beyond his means. He regarded himself as his nephew's protector, and he seemed unimpressed by Morris when he met him at a picnic at Hunter's place. He said he didn't understand the meaning of a cryptic text Morris had sent him referring to "World Class of People," but he thought Morris "has a huge ego in being a successful entertainment attorney." He claimed Morris wanted Jim to "come work for him," but he was not interested. Morris "thought he was very knowledgeable 'politically,'" but Jim thought otherwise.

Jim said all he knew about Morris was that he was "a very wealthy guy [who] was helping [Hunter] a lot, but [he] didn't know why."

Jim wasn't wrong about the extent of the help Morris would give his nephew. In the first year of their association, Hunter would receive more than $1.5 million from his new "Sugar Brother," according to his tax return. But it wasn't until almost two years later that they formalized the arrangement as a loan so that Hunter didn't have to pay gift tax. The terms required Hunter to start repayments in 2025 and pay five percent interest. According to a letter Morris' attorney would send to the House Oversight Committee in 2024, he made five loans to Hunter, as recorded in promissory notes dated from October 2021 and December 2023.

"With respect to the loans, I am confident that Hunter will repay," Morris told Congress. "I did not and do not have any expectations of receiving anything from Hunter's father or the Biden administration in exchange from helping Hunter, nor have I asked for anything from President Biden or his administration. My only goal was and is to help my friend and client."

Morris would end up spending almost $7.5 million of his own money on Hunter by the end of 2023, paying off close to $3 million in delinquent taxes and fines, funding teams of lawyers and investigators, buying his paintings, paying his rent, his $37,000 monthly alimony, his $20,000 monthly child support and $11,000 in overdue Porsche installments, and generally funding his lavish lay-about lifestyle. Morris calculated that Hunter paying all his back taxes and fines would make it more difficult to prosecute a criminal tax case against him.

"I don't know where I would be if not for Kevin," Hunter would later tell the *Los Angeles Times*. "And I don't mean just because he has loaned me money to survive this onslaught. I mean because he has given me back my dignity. He's been a brother to me."

Morris claimed that he was motivated purely by altruism, and a fear that, if Hunter were to relapse into addiction, that would hurt his father: "I fear that he will relapse, yes, [and] I think that's the intention of the people in the world out to get him, because they know getting him to relapse is the thing that will most upset his—will do the most impact on his father," Morris told Congress.

It was a dark threat that Hunter had echoed six weeks earlier in his Moby podcast: "What they're trying to do is they're trying to kill me, knowing that it will be a pain greater than my father could be able to handle, and so therefore destroying a presidency in that way."

At a time when Hunter's various Get Out Of Jail Free cards had expired, accountability was knocking on the door, and Joe's starring role in the Biden family grift machine inexorably was being exposed, this was a transparent form of emotional blackmail.

Tax accountants have heard every excuse under the sun, human nature being what it is, and Schmidt was not convinced by Hunter's different explanations for his failure to file his taxes. In Schmidt's view, "the reasons were just excuses," he told the IRS later, listing out some of Hunter's: he "had been through a difficult divorce, his prior accountant had passed away, he had been going through difficult times . . . he had a breakup with his former business partner . . ."

Self-pitying excuses might not wash with the IRS, but Morris believed they would resonate with a public all too familiar with the ravages of drug addiction.

Ever the showman, he had plans to exploit public empathy to rehabilitate Hunter's image, and to portray Joe as a devoted family man whose only crime was loving his wayward son. To that end, Morris had a documentary film crew following Hunter around, and he helped get him a decent ghostwriter and a book contract for a memoir, *Beautiful Things*, to be published three months after inauguration day in 2021. On the cover, it featured a photograph of little Hunter, holding hands with recently bereaved widower Joe. You can't see Joe's face, but the tiny motherless tot in his white romper suit and badly tied shoelaces, looking pensively into the distance, could break the coldest heart.

Hunter had always dreamed of being an author, and Morris had just published his second novel, so this was a project they both relished. There were reports that Simon & Schuster, which secretly acquired the book in late 2019, had paid Hunter a $2 million advance, but tax returns later published by Business Insider show he made $187,500 from the book in 2020, and $374,759 in 2021, so the advance, if paid in four tranches from 2019, likely was $750,000, less than half the rumored bonanza. It was still a great deal for Hunter since the book sold fewer than 27,000 copies in hardcover, translating to a significant loss for the publisher.

From Hunter's point of view, the book would allow him to regain control of his life story, but perhaps more usefully, it was a way to launder his family's shady international business dealings. By framing the memoir as a warts-and-all tale of his triumph over crack addiction, he could divert attention from alleged influence peddling and fill the air with seemingly candid admissions about his glamorously sordid former lifestyle.

That was the plan, anyway. But Hunter didn't know about the IRS and FBI investigators who, at that very moment, were scouring every detail of his life. They saw the book as manna from heaven and would treat it as a 270-page confession, which slotted nicely into the timeline of alleged wrongdoing they were constructing. In the coming years, they would endeavor to use Hunter's own words to convict him.

CHAPTER 4

THE BIG GUY

July 30, 2017
DELAWARE

Hunter was at his father's place in Delaware one sunny Sunday morning when he sent an alleged shakedown message via WhatsApp to Raymond Zhao, the polite young man who served as the personal secretary and translator of CEFC's Executive Director Zang Jianjun.

It had been more than six months since Joe Biden had left office, and Hunter was losing patience with his partners at the Chinese energy company. He believed CEFC owed him $10 million for the work he and his business partners had done opening doors around the world using the prestige of the Biden name for over a year. Joe was "the brand" sold by the Biden family. To keep up appearances, payment had been deferred when Joe was still VP. Now that he was out of office, it was time to pay up.

Joe was in Delaware that July weekend, captured in a photograph posted by a couple of locals on social media Friday night at BBC Tavern and Grill, a nearby bar in Greenville. Joe's grandchildren, Natalie and little Hunt, Beau's kids, were there, too. Hunt was photographed fishing in the lake behind the house with a friend Sunday.

Hunter took his dad's Corvette out of the garage and tooled around with the top down, his bikini-clad niece Natalie and one of her friends beside him in the front seat. Metadata from four photographs on Hunter's laptop places the three of them in the Goodwood Green 1967 Stingray out the front of Joe's mansion that Sunday.

At 8:44 a.m., Hunter pulled out his phone and wrote a WhatsApp message to Zhao about a "highly confidential and time sensitive" matter—and claimed his father was in the room with him.

"Z—Please have the director call me . . . tonight. I am sitting here with my father and we would like to understand why the commitment made has not been fulfilled."

His tone grew more menacing.

"I am very concerned that the Chairman has either changed his mind and broken our deal without telling me or that he is unaware of the promises and assurances that have been made have not been kept. Tell the director that I would like to resolve this now before it gets out of hand.

"And now means tonight. And Z if I get a call or text from anyone involved in this other than you, Zhang [Director Zang] or the Chairman [Ye] I will make certain that between the man sitting next to me and every person he knows and my ability to forever hold a grudge that you will regret not following my direction.

"All too often people mistake kindness for weakness—and all too often I am standing over top of them saying I warned you. From this moment until whenever he reaches me.

"It's 9:45 AM here and i assume 9:45 PM there so his night is running out."

Zhao replied, "Copy. I will call you on WhatsApp."

Hunter: "Ok my friend—I am sitting here waiting for the call with my father. I sure hope whatever it is you are doing is very very very important."

Within nine days of his threats, CEFC would send $5.1 million to Hunter. That money was in addition to the $3 million CEFC already had paid in March 2017 for services rendered in 2016, while Joe was VP. That was withheld until he left office,

Hunter would receive a further $1 million in March 2018 as a legal retainer to represent CEFC executive, Dr. Patrick Ho. So much for Joe's claim in the 2020 campaign: "my son has not made money in terms of this thing about—what are you talking about—China."

The WhatsApp messages were obtained in August 2020 through a search warrant of Hunter's iCloud by IRS criminal investigators working the Hunter Biden case, codenamed "Sportsman," run out of the office of US Attorney David Weiss in Delaware.

Three years later, the lead Hunter-hunter, IRS Special Agent Joe Ziegler, would turn over the WhatsApp messages to the House Ways and Means Committee when he blew the whistle on the corruption and favoritism that had plagued the investigation.

"We couldn't believe that we saw that [WhatsApp message]," Ziegler testified. "That was more indication that the dad might have been involved."

Ziegler and his boss, IRS Supervisory Agent Gary Shapley, had wanted to obtain geolocation data to determine if Hunter and his father really were together at the time the messages were sent. This would be vital evidence to show that Joe—contrary to his denials—was involved in his son's business. But Ziegler's request was repeatedly denied in prosecution team meetings by Delaware Assistant US Attorney Lesley Wolf.

"The messages included material we clearly needed to follow up on," Shapley testified when he, too, blew the whistle in 2023. "Nevertheless, prosecutors denied investigators' requests to develop a strategy to look into the messages and denied investigators' suggestion to obtain location information to see where the texts were sent from . . .

"There were certain investigative steps we weren't allowed to take that could have led us to President Biden . . .

"We were interested in following leads that went to Joe Biden—President Biden—not because he was Vice President, but because, in any normal investigation, if you see financial transactions between son and father, and email correspondence going back and forth, text messages, and WhatsApp messages, in every investigation we have ever worked, we would follow those leads to the father. We'll never know because we weren't allowed to investigate."

The only reason Ziegler could see for the deviation from normal procedures was that someone was protecting Joe. "I went to the prosecutors with this [request for location data], and they, again, came back at me with: 'Well, how do we know that? He could just be lying and claiming that . . . his dad's there, but his dad is not there.'

"And I said: 'Well, this is what we would normally do.' And I have it on a meeting agenda where we talk about location data. And I don't know if the FBI ever did anything with it, but I would think it would be a road we would want to go down or that we could go down, and the reason being that, if President Joe Biden was getting any source of income, whether it's through someone else's entity or for his benefit at some point, that could be income. So that's why it would matter to us."

It was another lucky escape for Joe. Nobody will ever find out if he was sitting with his son, listening to his urgent conversations with the Chinese.

Six years later, when the geolocation data had long vanished from the phone company database and the WhatsApp messages were released by the House Ways and Means Committee, the president laughed in reporters' faces when they asked about them.

"President Biden, how involved were you in your son's Chinese shakedown text message?" asked the *New York Post*'s White House reporter Steven Nelson as Joe emerged from the White House and shuffled to Marine One.

At first, the president responded to him with derisive laughter, but Nelson kept pestering: "Were you sitting there? Were you involved?"

Joe: "No, I wasn't."

Nelson pressed: "Were you?"

Joe leaned in close and barked: "No!"

White House counsel's office spokesman Ian Sams would not address the WhatsApp messages but did formulate a new group of words to defend the president:

"As we have said many times before, the President was not in business with his son."

In fact, the phrase "in business with" had never been said before. The previous line from the White House, and from Joe, was that he had "never spoken" to Hunter about business and knew "nothing" about his overseas business dealings.

Hunter initially claimed the WhatsApp messages had been faked. However, in a closed-door deposition before the House impeachment inquiry into Joe Biden in February 2024, he admitted that he wrote the messages, but claimed he did so when he was "high or drunk" and had sent them to the wrong Zhao, not the one affiliated with CEFC.

Phone records released by the House Ways and Means Committee in May 2024 showed that Hunter did send the message to the correct Raymond Zhao "who not only was affiliated with CEFC but knew exactly what Hunter Biden was talking about," said Committee chairman Jason Smith.

"Hunter Biden was using his father's name to shake down a Chinese businessman—and it worked," said Smith. "And when confronted by congressional investigators about it, he lied."

Hunter also denied that Joe had been sitting next to him when he sent the messages. "My father had no awareness of the business that I was doing. My father never benefited from any of the business that I was doing."

It wasn't the first time his relatives had invoked Joe's name in a seeming shakedown. Jim Biden was notorious for dropping his brother's name at Americore Health, a cruddy business running rural hospitals that became the latest receptacle for his get-rich-quick dreams. One day, when he was pitching to a prospective client, "he said he was sitting in a car next to his brother Joe," the client claimed to *Politico*.

* * *

According to IRS whistleblower documents, Hunter continued the urgent WhatsApp messages and phone calls with his Chinese benefactors over 24 hours at his dad's place in Delaware in July 2017.

Zhao told Hunter that Director Zang "got the message you just mentioned" and gave him the number of another CEFC contact, Kevin Dong, who was based in New York.

Hunter messaged Dong: "Kevin I was told by the Director through Zhao that we were to speak tonight. If there is some extraordinary reason you can not do so please let me know. I assume that you know that this is highly confidential and time sensitive."

The "highly confidential and time-sensitive" matter was something that might give weight to the threats of his earlier messages. But he wouldn't convey it by text, not even on the encrypted WhatsApp platform.

The Chinese kept giving him the runaround.

He messaged Zhao to make sure he wasn't going behind his back to his other business partners, Tony Bobulinski, James Gilliar, and Rob Walker, who were part of the CEFC joint venture they had named "SinoHawk."

"Z—I reached out to K and he declined my call and has not returned my text. I assume he knows that our plan to speak is highly confidential. I just hope he isn't talking to Tony or J—if he is we have a real problem.

"If I can reshape this partnership to what the chairman intended then James and Rob will be well taken care of but I will not have Tony [Bobulinski] dictating to me nor the director [Zang] what we can and cannot do."

Zhao responded: "I don't think he [Kevin] is talking to Tony or the other guys, mostly with the director. I just sent an email to you and cc to Kevin. He has your phone number now." He sent Hunter a screenshotted message from Dong which read: "Raymond, many thanks for the introduction. Hunter I am based in New York and my US phone is [redacted] Let's talk tomorrow? Kevin."

A few hours later, Zhao wrote with good news for Hunter from Director Zang. CEFC had agreed to his terms but, first, they had a problem to solve.

"Hi Hunter, did you see the email from Kevin?" wrote Zhao. "The director would like to suggest you and Kevin have a meeting.

"CEFC is willing to cooperate with the family. He thinks now the priority is to solve the problem mentioned last night."

* * *

Hunter had commanded CEFC not to talk to his SinoHawk partners—Bobulinski, Gilliar, and Walker—because he was planning to cut them out of the action. He was negotiating a separate joint venture with the Chinese for himself and Uncle Jim, that would be called Hudson West III (HWIII).

The contract, titled "Amended and Restated Limited Liability Company Agreement of Hudson West III LLC," immediately struck Bobulinski as familiar when he saw it years later. It was "extensively the same document" as the one he had drawn up for the SinoHawk joint venture that Hunter and Jim had signed and then walked away from. "You'll see a serial number [in the lower left-hand corner]. It's a very long serial number. But it appears to me to be exactly the same number on both documents.

"What appears happened in July 2017 is Hunter Biden, a Yale-educated lawyer . . . took proprietary information from Oneida Holdings [the original partnership] and SinoHawk and stole that information and reproduced it," Bobulinski alleged to Congress. "And around the same time when this document was executed, Hunter Biden [sent the seeming shakedown WhatsApp that] invokes his father sitting right next to him." During his congressional testimony, Hunter Biden said, "I question the veracity of anything Tony Bobulinski has said."

Bobulinski had alienated Hunter with his insistence on proper corporate governance and refusal to allow him to use the business as his "personal piggybank." Hunter rammed home that, although Bobulinski thought he had been brought in to run the joint venture because of his business acumen and reputation, the Biden family would always call the shots.

In a series of heated WhatsApp messages between the four partners on May 19, 2017, Hunter declared: "my Chairman gave an emphatic NO" to Bobulinski's planned corporate structure.

In a private message to Bobulinksi late that night, Walker explained that when Hunter "said his chairman he was talking about his dad and I think your dismissal of it maybe offended him a bit."

Hunter kept complaining about Bobulinksi, according to messages retrieved by IRS investigators from his iCloud backup: "Bullsh-t James—all around bullsh-t," Hunter wrote to Gilliar.

"Explain to me one thing Tony brings to MY table that I so desperately need that I'm willing to sign over my family's brand and pretty much the rest of my business life? Read the f-cking documents people It's plane [*sic*] f-cking English. Why in gods name would I give this marginal bully the keys [to] my family's only asset? . . .

"If you want, we can all do a conference call with my guy and his intel. Slightly better, I'd say, than yours, James."

Sometime after these angry exchanges, Hunter and Jim decided to go it alone, or, as Bobulinski alleged in his testimony to Congress seven years on: "Hunter and Jim defrauded me at the end of July—not just me, but [Walker and Gilliar] . . . They had a fiduciary duty to not circumvent, lie, or embezzle funds. And at the end of July 2017 . . . Hunter Biden invokes his father to basically shake down and extort the Chinese to not send the money to SinoHawk Holdings and send it directly to a new entity [HWIII] that he worked overtime to form so he could put the money in his own pocket and Jim Biden's pocket."

Bobulinski was ready to sue Hunter and Jim for defrauding him but held off to allow the impeachment committee to do its work (it was never proven that Hunter & Jim defrauded Bobulinski). It wasn't about the money. "This is about getting the facts out to the American people," he told the members of Congress taking his deposition in February 2024. "If you guys do your job, I should not have to file that lawsuit."

Having jettisoned his American partners, Hunter and his family had no buffer to distance themselves from CEFC.

Hunter's fate now was tied to the billionaire wunderkind chairman Ye

Jianming, ranked second on the Forbes "40 Under 40" list of the world's most influential young people in 2016.

Ye had the blessing of President Xi and the patronage of the People's Liberation Army, where he previously had served as deputy secretary general of its propaganda arm.

No Chinese company promoted Xi's Belt and Road Initiative more ardently than CEFC.

"CEFC China's vision is very simple," Ye said in a 2017 address to his board of directors, "which is to obtain overseas resources and serve the national strategy."

Ye had built his provincial energy company into a Fortune 500 colossus virtually overnight, an achievement described wryly by Chinese investigative news agency Caixin as "another great enigma in the miraculous world of Chinese business."

Dubbed the "Belt and Road billionaire" and the "hermit-like king" by Chinese media fascinated by his rapid rise, he was described by a former American associate as a "white glove for one of the top generals."

Among China's elite, a "white glove" is the term for the person who launders your ill-gotten gains while you keep your hands clean.

"He was a quiet man full of insecurities about his young age and lack of formal education," the former associate said. "He had lots of health problems in his stomach and could only eat food made by his chef and couldn't drink alcohol. In the most lavish dinners, he would barely touch the food. Everything irritated his stomach."

Despite living in splendor and flying around the world with an entourage like a rockstar on his private jets, Ye "was a simple man in many ways," said the former associate. "He never wore fancy clothes or expensive watches or jewelry. He . . . flew too close to the sun and didn't listen to advice, only to bootlickers.

"He knew how to swim in the shark tank of China [but really] he had no idea how the world works . . . Gradually he became unmoored and out of control.

"This whole tale is about greed and hubris. The oldest sins."

The same sins afflicted Hunter and his father. But Ye would face a grimmer fate. Ye Jianming has not been seen since 2018, and so has had no way to counter the many accusations against him.

* * *

The laptop indicates Ye had courted the Biden family since October 2015, around the time Joe announced that he would not be running for president in 2016.

The first overtures came from a dad with a daughter in the same class as Hunter's middle daughter, Finnegan, at Sidwell Friends, the Quaker school serving the children of Washington's elite. Scott Oh left a message at Hunter's office about "a potential business opportunity in China that might be of interest."

They exchanged emails in which Oh sang CEFC's praises, talked up its charitable aspirations, and offered "invitations for the B's to speak in China, etc. All expenses will be covered as well as speaking engagements."

Next, Serbian diplomat Vuk Jeremic invited Hunter to a small private dinner on December 6, 2015, with Chairman Ye, "an old friend from China . . . one of the 10 wealthiest Chinese businessmen.

"He is the Chairman and majority owner of CEFC China Energy, second-largest privately owned company on Shanghai stock exchange.

"He's very young and dynamic, with the top-level connections in his country. They have recently started making big investments abroad (billions of dollars), and plan on doing much more. I am confident that many interesting projects may come out of [the dinner] in the future."

Jeremic, a former president of the UN General Assembly and former Serbian foreign minister, was on a $330,000 retainer from CEFC as a consultant and "connector" and was lobbying to become UN Secretary-General. He often pestered Hunter to get Joe, who he called "the big man," to help him.

There is no evidence Hunter attended the dinner, and Jeremic denies introducing Hunter to Ye, but the following day, December 7, 2015, he had a 10:30 a.m. meeting scheduled in his calendar with Scott Oh and Chairman Ye at Hunter's office in Georgetown. Ye never showed.

Ye was in Washington with Director Zang that week to attend a lunch at the Willard Hotel hosted by Professor Gal Luft, 51, a former Israeli Defense Force officer who was working at the time on energy issues with a CEFC offshoot—a think tank named the China Energy Fund Committee, also CEFC, that was run by Dr. Patrick Ho.

With the help of mysterious socialite Angela Chen, who allegedly also was tied up with Chinese military intelligence, Ye quickly had embedded himself in Manhattan elite circles, popping up in the social pages at glittering Lincoln Center galas with the likes of Henry Kissinger and Alan Greenspan.

Funding a non-profit that bestowed million-dollar grants to causes such as "sustainable development," "business ethics," and stopping climate change was a way for Ye to make friends in high places and "tell the China story" in international circles of influence.

Fully funded by CEFC, the think tank was registered in Virginia as a 501c3 charitable organization and filed tax returns each year with the IRS. Its 2016 tax return showed a total revenue of $1,298,778, with Dr. Ho's salary a relatively modest $110,000, and $436,677 paid in rent for offices in the suburbs of DC and in Trump World Tower in Manhattan, across the road from the United Nations.

The organization's mission, as detailed on its IRS 990 tax exempt form, was to "promote international research and dialogue on energy issue [*sic*], enhancing mutual understanding and respect through international dialogue, and develop [*sic*] strategic relationships with other organizations with similar missions."

The think tank's boss, Dr. Ho, was a gregarious eye surgeon and the former Hong Kong Home Affairs secretary married to the Taiwanese movie star Sibelle Hu.

With the grand title of Deputy Secretary General, Dr. Ho had turned CEFC's strange little offshoot into a respectable powerhouse of international conferences, workshops, and seminars. He published annual reports on energy in China and monographs on the Belt and Road Initiative. He reveled in the conviviality and pomp of the UN milieu.

Ye and Zang were delighted when the UN granted CEFC's think tank "special consultative status" for its philanthropy in 2011. But it was an honor that would lead, ultimately, to their downfall.

On that cold December morning in 2015, Ye had bigger fish to fry than the vice president's flaky son.

He stood up Hunter and sent Zang to meet him alone. Then Luft, who ran his own energy think tank, the Institute for the Analysis of Global Security (IAGS), took Ye and Ho to meet former Federal Reserve Chair Alan Greenspan, in his spacious wood-paneled office at Greenspan Associates, his private consulting business in downtown Washington, half a mile from the White House.

Zang got the ball rolling with Hunter without Ye, and over the next couple of months, Gilliar and Walker were brought in for a slice of the action. Uncle Jim would join later.

Gilliar was a bald 56-year-old former British special forces officer based in the Czech Republic whom Bobulinski nicknamed "MI6" because he believed he had ties to the British foreign intelligence service.

"He talked, he acted, he had all these relationships that would lead you to believe that [and] the sort of need-to-know kind of communication style."

Uncle Jim also told the FBI that Gilliar "was supposedly formerly MI6 in the UK [and] wore a Superman T-shirt that supposedly cost $5,000 to $7,000. Gilliar was supposedly very connected."

Walker, then 45, was a trusted Biden family friend and former Clinton administration official, originally from Arkansas, whose wife, Betsy Massey Walker, had been Jill Biden's assistant when she was Second Lady.

By February 2016, the trio were actively "pursuing business with CEFC," Walker would tell Congress. Gilliar was flying around Europe and the Middle East, using the Biden name to drum up deals for CEFC, inspecting an oil and gas project in Oman, meeting a prince in Abu Dhabi.

He planned to attend a CEFC board meeting in Beijing that month and emailed Hunter and Walker to whet their appetites.

"It has been made clear to me," he wrote on February 23, 2016, "that CEFC wish to engage in further business relations with our group and we will present a few projects to them."

CEFC executives would refer to "The B family" when communicating with Hunter and his partners. They made it clear that what they valued most about the association was the Biden brand.

Soon enough, they were ready to commit the budding relationship with CEFC to paper, writing a letter on Hunter's letterhead that appeared on his abandoned laptop as an email attachment, "H to Zang," and was inaccessible in the cloud until Walker gave a copy to the impeachment inquiry in 2024.

The letter, from Hunter to CEFC Director Zang, dated March 22, 2016, outlined the relationship they had established with CEFC and their plans for the future: "We anticipate working together on a number of opportunities in the US and abroad. I believe we have presented a collection of projects that parallel the interests of you and your team and we look forward to discussing them in detail.

"As we await your next visit to the United States, please continue to coordinate all matters with my confidant and trusted advisor, James Gilliar."

Walker later was asked by a congressional investigator why the letter was written on Hunter's letterhead, and not one of the other partners': "[It's] because he's the son of the vice president at the time, correct?"

"He is the son of a vice president at the time, yes," Walker replied.

"I can't answer for Zang, but [Hunter] had an interesting last name, probably get people in the door." The letter confirmed the business relationship between CEFC and members of the Biden family began in the last year of Joe's vice-presidency. To avoid the appearance of impropriety, Hunter, his uncle, and his partners didn't get paid until six weeks after Joe left office. That deferred payment gave Joe the cover of being a "private citizen" in early 2017, when the millions started to flow to nine Biden family members.

Despite his claim that he "did not" interact with Hunter's foreign business associates, Joe had an uncanny knack of being at the right place at the right time for the meet and greet.

Three weeks after his father left office, on Monday, February 13, 2017, Hunter flew with Hallie to Miami to meet Chairman Ye, who was there for the Miami International Boat Show, where billionaires shop for superyachts. Gilliar and Walker already had booked into the $700-a-night beachfront Nobu Hotel. They scheduled lunch for later that week with the Chinese in a private room set for ten at the Bourbon Steak restaurant in the ritzy JW Marriott Turnberry Resort & Spa up the road, where Ye was staying with his entourage.

Hunter went to a private dinner with Ye on Tuesday night, Valentine's Day, after which Ye sent a rich gift to his room—a 3.16-carat diamond worth an estimated $80,000—with a card thanking him for the conversation.

The big rock was a welcome antidote to the bills that were piling up; Hunter's office manager, Joan Peugh, had just forwarded him a tax collection notice from the District of Columbia for $47,226.78.

Photographs of the stunning diamond appear on Hunter's laptop along with a grading report that lists it as a "round brilliant" of Grade F with prime "VS2" clarity and "excellent" cut.

Hunter was in the middle of an ugly divorce from Kathleen, who caught wind of the "extremely valuable" gift within days and had her lawyer write Hunter's lawyer to demand he add it to the marital asset register and "provide proof that the diamond has been placed in a safety deposit box." (Asked by the New Yorker in 2019 if he thought the diamond was intended as a bribe, Hunter feigned naivete: "What would they be bribing me for? My dad wasn't in office.") Hunter told Kathleen's lawyer that she was mistaken, and he had no such diamond in his possession. To the New Yorker he said he "gave the diamond to his associates," and had no idea what happened to it.

On May 24, 2018, Hunter's assistant Katie Dodge sent him a crisp message: "Check arrived from jewelers."

Hunter replied: "Please deposit in WF [Wells Fargo account]."

Three years later, Agent Ziegler would email the Hunter Biden prosecution team the agenda for a meeting scheduled that day. The first interview on his list was "Alex K. / DE Jeweler," either on Tuesday or Wednesday the following week.

There's a jewelry store in Concord Mall in Wilmington, a few minutes' drive north from Joe's Greenville estate, past the DuPont Country Club. It's not known whether a jeweler ever was interviewed about the diamond, but it stands to reason that the IRS would be interested in pursuing tax on such a large gift.

A few days after the Miami meeting, in late February 2017, Hunter, Walker, and Gilliar had lunch with Chairman Ye and about nine CEFC officials in a private room at the Four Seasons hotel in Georgetown. After they were seated, a special guest showed up—Joe Biden, whose tenure as VP had finished just five weeks earlier. Joe was living a 10-minute drive away in palatial new digs in McLean, Virginia, which had once been the home of Alexander Haig and where the going rent was $20,000 a month.

Walker later would agree with the FBI that Hunter had "orchestrated" his father's attendance to "bolster the chances of making a deal work out" with CEFC.

"I think Hunter said, ah . . . 'I may be tryin' to start a company,' ah, or tried to do something with these guys and could you . . . and [I] think [Joe] was like 'if I'm around' . . . and he'd show up," Walker told FBI agent Josh Wilson in a covertly recorded interview on the porch of his Little Rock, Arkansas home on December 8, 2020.

Joe came into the lunch, "said hello to everybody" and then "literally sat down. I don't even think he drank water," said Walker.

Pressed about the meeting when he testified to the impeachment inquiry in 2024, Walker said Joe "was there maybe 10 minutes." He addressed the group and "spoke nice, you know, normal pleasantries . . . He specifically said, 'good luck in whatever you guys are doing.' I think he probably did most of the talking and then left."

A few days after the Four Seasons lunch, on March 1, 2017, CEFC affiliate State Energy HK Limited wired $3 million to Rob Walker's firm Robinson Walker LLC. Walker told the FBI the transfer represented a "thank you" payment from CEFC, "a finder's fee for some of the work in the MOU [Memorandum of Understanding] that was signed in Oman . . . drumming up projects, that we thought that they would find worthwhile."

In his congressional testimony he elaborated on the reason for that large payment: "We opened the door to some potential business that they would not normally have access to, I guess. Or 'access' may be the wrong word, but they . . . were kind of impressed."

He agreed with a congressional investigator who asked: "the $3 million payment, then, was payment for the success that you had previously shown them—do I have that right?"

"Yes," he said.

As soon as the $3 million hit his account, Walker transferred $1,065,000 to Gilliar, and then parceled out Hunter's one-third share in sums as small as $5,000 over the next two months. The money went to Hunter, his uncle Jim, and sister-in-law Hallie, according to bank documents subpoenaed by James Comer's Oversight Committee.

Hunter's law firm Owasco received $500,000 in four separate payments over three weeks.

Jim's JBBSR INC account received $360,000 in five payments over four weeks. Hallie received a single payment of $25,000 on March 20, 2017. An unknown "Biden" account received four payments totaling $70,000 over ten weeks.

Asked what work Hunter had done to earn his one-third share of the CEFC $3 million, Walker told the FBI: "Hunter was more of the door opener . . . You know, we're talking if Hunter spent five or six hours a week [working], I would consider that a win."

In a prepared statement before his congressional testimony, at which he was represented by two Wilmington attorneys, despite living in Arkansas, Walker declared that Joe was "never involved in any business activities we pursued."

Two months after CEFC's $3 million wire, with Bobulinski on board, Gilliar sent an email to the group outlining a proposed equity split of their partnership.

"The equity will be distributed as follows," wrote Gilliar on May 13, 2017, listing the shares in percentages.

20 H [Hunter]
20 RW [Walker]
20 JG [Gilliar]
20 TB [Bobulinski]
10 Jim [Biden]
10 held by H for the big guy?

In the final contract, the equity splits were changed, the "big guy" reference was removed, and Jim Biden's 10 percent share had doubled to 20 percent.

But the email remains significant because it discloses the mindset of Hunter and his partners at that time, betraying their belief that Joe not only was their rainmaker but had a right to a piece of the action.

The "big guy" was the code the partners used for Joe, as Bobulinski has testified to Congress, and as other messages on Hunter's laptop suggest.

"The big guy—100 percent—is Joe Biden," said Bobulinski. "Why was [Gilliar] using code? Why is he calling Hunter 'H'? Why is he using 'the big guy'? Well, because that's the way James Gilliar communicated because of his intel background and the things he was doing around the world.

"But when he says, '10 held by H for the big guy,' it's Joe Biden. The big guy was Joe Biden."

Bobulinski also slapped down "the other lie that's been told for the last four years, including by Hunter Biden's lawyers, [which is] that nobody responded to this email . . . Hunter Biden himself responded to this exact email at a minimum two, maybe three times.

"And what did he respond in those emails? He didn't ask, 'James, who the heck are you talking about? Who is the big guy?' What did Hunter

Biden scream about? Because if you read the emails . . . he is demanding getting paid more money, talking about his divorce and alimony payments, and that $850,000 isn't anywhere near enough. That he's going to
have to . . . make at least $2 million.

"Hunter responded to it numerous times. He was aware of the contents. He was arguing over the contents of the email, and not once did
anybody else that was on the email chain go, 'Guys, who is the "big guy"
that we're talking about?' . . . You can't find any document or email exchange that says that.

"So, the '10 held by H for the big guy' was Hunter Biden, and the big
guy was Joe Biden."

It was all moot by August, anyway, once Hunter and Jim decided to
keep all the Chinese money for themselves.

CHAPTER 5

PAYDAY

August 2017
NEW YORK CITY

The week after Hunter's WhatsApp shakedown, the money started to flow from CEFC to the Bidens.

But first, as was typical with Hunter, there were fights and drama. He became increasingly impatient with Dong, a man he described condescendingly as Chairman Ye's "emissary" and treated with disdain, particularly when he had the temerity to question Hunter's expenses.

Gongwen "Kevin" Dong, 48, was more than a mere emissary. He was entrusted with managing his billionaire boss's fortune in the US. A Chinese national and graduate of Columbia Business School, who congressional investigators said had worked for the Chinese government, Dong lived with his wife and children in a $6 million six-bedroom mock chateau in the Long Island enclave of Great Neck, Great Gatsby territory. He traveled back to China on business every month.

Ye would transfer more than $130 million to US entities controlled by Dong from June through August 2017, according to bank records obtained by congressional investigators, and embark on a spending spree. Dong signed the deeds in March 2017 for Ye's $50 million penthouse at 15 Central Park West, the exclusive new condo dubbed the "Limestone Jesus," and for a $33 million apartment at 432 Park Avenue.

Dong worked with another CEFC employee, Mervyn Yan, to facilitate the payment of millions of dollars from CEFC to Hunter, his uncle Jim, and other Biden family members over the next 15 months.

They also set Hunter up with a Manhattan office two blocks from theirs, at 40 West 57th Street, "Billionaire's Row," above Robert De Niro's once fashionable Japanese fusion restaurant Nobu Fifty Seven.

Still, Hunter was never satisfied. When Dong appeared confused about Hunter's extravagant demands for payment and expenses before the joint venture had earned a single dollar, Hunter erupted in a series of grandiose emails.

"I am tired of this Kevin. I can make $5M in salary at any law firm in America."

He informed Dong that Chairman Ye originally had offered to pay him $10 million a year "for introductions alone," but that the joint venture they now were putting in place with Hudson West III was "much more interesting to me and my family."

"The chairman changed that deal after we met in Miami TO A MUCH MORE LASTING AND LUCRATIVE ARRANGEMENT to create a holding company 50% percent owned by ME and 50% owned by him . . .

"The reason this proposal by the chairman was so much more interesting to me and my family is that we would also be partners in the equity and profits of the JV's [joint venture's] investments."

Hunter's invocation of his "family" was a hallmark of his relationship with CEFC. In emails and WhatsApp messages made public by Hunter's partner-turned-foe Bobulinski, Hunter asserts that CEFC is "coming to be MY partner to be partners with the Bidens," and says that he deserves to be paid more than the other partners because "I'm the only one putting an entire family legacy on the line."

When Bobulinski balked at Jim Biden getting a 20 percent stake for contributing nothing, Gilliar assured him that Jim "strengthens our USP [unique selling proposition] to the Chinese as it looks like a truly family business." In other words, a Biden family business.

Dong never appeared to treat Hunter with the reverence he felt his family name demanded. Over the course of their business relationship, the pair would lock horns over Hunter's insatiable demand for money. At one point, when Dong queried his exorbitant expenses, Hunter launched into a tirade: "I will personally sue you Kevin . . . if you forward my expense report to [CEFC headquarters]. I am the managing director of CEFC [US] . . . If you refuse to sign the wire Kevin I will seek to have you removed from the board . . .

"I will bring suit in the Chancery Court in Delaware [where] I am privileged to have worked with and know every judge on the chancery court."

The ease with which Hunter threatened to assert his special status in Delaware as a Biden alarmed Senators Grassley and Johnson when the emails became public. They raised concerns with Delaware US Attorney Weiss in 2022 about "the Bidens' possible undue influence over judicial officers in the Delaware Court of Chancery and . . . concerns that [Hunter's] asserted influence extends beyond the Court of Chancery." It was a worthwhile point to make, considering Hunter would have to face a judge in Delaware if and when Weiss' investigation finally concluded.

In any case, Dong was unruffled by Hunter's threat. "You cannot sue us for not paying incorrect expenses," he responded coolly.

Dong was simply following orders from Chairman Ye, and so on August 2, 2017, he finally ironed out the details of the deal. Hunter would be paid $100,000 a month and a "one time retainer fee" of $500,000. Uncle Jim would get $65,000 a month. Hunter and Dong signed an LLC Agreement that day with 50 percent equal ownership of HWIII.

"The Bidens are the best I know at doing exactly what the Chairman wants from this partnership," Hunter told him.

* * *

On August 3, 2017, Hunter opened a bank account for HWIII at the Fifth Avenue branch of the Chinese-American Cathay Bank. That night, Dong forwarded him a message from Director Zang's translator: "Hi, Hunter.

Sorry to ping you at late hours. I'm texting to convey some information—or info from Director Zang . . . his best regards to you, Jim, and VP."

On August 4, 2017, HWIII transferred $100,000 to Hunter's law firm, Owasco, according to bank records obtained by the Johnson-Grassley inquiry, and later confirmed by Delaware tax investigators. That was the first portion of Hunter's $500,000 retainer.

On August 8, 2017, CEFC affiliate Northern International Capital Holdings (HK) Ltd. wired $5 million to HWIII, and Hunter immediately transferred $400,000, the remainder of his retainer, to himself at Owasco.

Thereafter, HWIII transferred $165,000 every month to Hunter for a total of about $4.8 million, after office costs.

On August 14, 2017, Hunter wired $150,000 to Lion Hall Group, a company owned by Jim Biden and his wife, Sara.

A week later, Sara did something peculiar. She withdrew $50,000 in cash from Lion Hall's account. Later that day, she deposited the same amount into her and Jim's personal joint checking account.

Six days later, on September 3, 2017, Sara cut a check for $40,000 to Joe Biden and marked it as "loan repayment" in the memo field.

James Comer, the Republican chairman of the House Oversight committee, had served as a director of the South Central Bank in his hometown of Tompkinsville, Kentucky for 12 years. He knew his way around a spreadsheet, and he had spent countless hours poring over thousands of bank documents subpoenaed from the Biden family and associated accounts.

This complicated financial transaction, just weeks after Hunter had threatened his Chinese partners with his father's wrath, fit the description of money laundering, said Comer.

"Remember when Joe Biden told the American people that his son didn't make money in China? Well, not only did he lie about his son Hunter making money in China, but it also turns out that $40,000 in laundered China money landed in Joe Biden's bank account in the form of a personal check."

White House spokesman Ian Sams accused Comer of peddling "lies and conspiracy theories" and said the transaction was perfectly innocent. "The President, when he was a private citizen, loaned his brother money, and his brother promptly paid him back."

It wasn't the only check to Joe from his brother labeled as a "loan repayment." Comer found a check for $200,000 written by James Biden to Joe Biden, dated March 1, 2018. This was the same day that $200,000 landed in Jim Biden's personal account from an insolvent company named Americore Health, with which Jim was doing business while liberally dropping his brother's name. Americore then went bankrupt and has been accused by the federal government of massive Medicare fraud.

Keep in mind, these two "loans" from Joe Biden to Jim Biden were made by a brother who made a politician's salary for over 40 years to his brother who had been in the private sector just as long.

"Even if this was a personal loan repayment, it's still troubling that Joe Biden's ability to be paid back by his brother depended on the success of his family's shady financial dealings," Comer said.

Over 2017 and 2018, Hunter transferred $1.4 million from Owasco to Jim's firm Lion Hall in multiple smaller installments.

He once complained to his eldest daughter about allegedly sharing his money with his father. "I hope you all can do what I did and pay for everything for this entire family for 30 years," he wrote to Naomi in a text message found on his laptop. "It's really hard. But don't worry, unlike pop, I won't make you give me half your salary."

Once the Chinese money started sloshing into his bank account, Hunter settled into a pleasant routine of spending it as fast as he could. He'd nailed the deal with CEFC, putting the squeeze on Chairman Ye to get him to pay up, and now he was enjoying the spoils. He splashed out $29,460 on Brunello Cucinelli apparel at his favorite luxury menswear store, Riflessi, next door to his new office. He spent $69,977 getting his teeth fixed at Smile Design Manhattan across the road after years of drug abuse had made them rot. He had to travel a little further afield to 12th Avenue to drop $12,000 dollars that month on strip shows at Larry Flint's Hustler Club.

Hunter also had his eyes on bigger prizes, emailing a real estate agent to ask about buying a $4 million house in Annapolis, Maryland, not far from where he was renting with his sister-in-law, Hallie Biden, and her children, ten-year-old Natalie and nine-year-old Hunter.

His volatile affair with Hallie began soon after Beau's death in 2015. He left Kathleen and their three daughters, then aged fifteen, seventeen, and twenty-two, and moved into his brother's house.

Hallie and Beau's marital home soon became party central, where people would sit all night on the porch smoking crack.

The couple were in and out of rehab and fought incessantly. He accused her of cheating and would search through her phone looking for evidence of infidelity.

While Hunter partied, the lives of his Chinese partners were already unraveling.

A few hours after Hunter sent Director Zang's translator his shake-down message via WhatsApp, at a hotel in midtown Manhattan, Dr. Patrick Ho received an urgent call from Shanghai.

It was CEFC president Chan Chauto telling his trusted think tank president that he was in grave danger and needed to "drop everything, get out of the US and come back [to China] immediately."

That "highly confidential and time sensitive" information Hunter had just delivered seemed to have sent CEFC head office into a spin.

Dr. Ho caught the first flight to Shanghai and, 19 hours later, hopped a cab straight to CEFC's palatial marble headquarters in the upscale French Concession District, worrying all the way. Uniformed young women wearing earpieces ushered him silently into Chairman Ye's office.

Sitting on a golden chair, Ye told Dr. Ho that he had received a tip about a sealed indictment in the Southern District of New York containing four names of CEFC officials. One of those names was Ho's. He should go directly home to Hong Kong, and stay there until they figured out what to do next.

Neither man knew it yet, but it was the beginning of the end.

CHAPTER 6

THE COAST IS CLEAR

August 2017
HONG KONG

Patrick Ho was back home in his spacious apartment in Central Hong Kong, trying to keep up a cheery front for his wife of 20 years, Sibelle, and their 17-year-old daughter, Audrey. But questions swirled through his mind. Why was he in trouble? How long did he have to remain in limbo? Who else was on the indictments? Who leaked the names? Had Chinese intelligence infiltrated the FBI?

Chairman Ye had not been forthcoming when he saw him in Shanghai, and Ho didn't altogether trust him.

Although Hunter (who once used the racial slur "no yellow" to reject Asian women as potential dates) treated Ho like just another Chinaman, the ophthalmologist was a proud native Hongkonger with excellent English and a superb American education. He also was a bon vivant whose love for long lunches had made him hugely fat. Slender Ye, twenty years Ho's junior at 48, grew up in a provincial town in Fujian in southern China. He was poorly educated, spoke no English, ate meagrely, and never drank.

The two men didn't have much in common and had become increasingly estranged.

Born in Hong Kong in 1949, at the end of the Chinese Civil War, the son of a civil engineer dad and a Catholic schoolteacher mom, Patrick Ho Chi-ping attended the prestigious Anglican Diocesan Boys' School, where he was known for his talent as a classical violinist.

He won a music scholarship to attend the private Stetson College in Florida, where friends say he developed a lifelong affection for America. Another scholarship took him to medical school at Vanderbilt University in Nashville, Tennessee, where he worked nights as a session musician playing fiddle in country music bands. He specialized in ophthalmology and became a fellow at Harvard Medical School, remaining in the US for 16 years.

After his first marriage broke up, he returned to Hong Kong in 1984 to become professor of surgery at the Chinese University. He later went into private practice and remarried in 1997, the year of the handover of Hong Kong from Britain to China. Many Hong Kongers fled the city when the communists took control, especially those who'd managed to lay down roots in Western countries. Ho chose to take his chances with the new regime.

He was persuaded to enter politics after performing eye surgery for the high-ranking Chinese Communist official Ji Pengfei, known as "China's man in Hong Kong," according to the *South China Morning Post*. Ho joined the Chinese People's Political Consultative Conference, a body that helps coordinate influence operations for the Chinese Communist Party (CCP), according to a report by the Heritage Foundation.

In 2002, Ho joined the government of Tung Chee-hwa, the first Chief Executive of Hong Kong. As Secretary for Home Affairs, the following year he attended a Lunar New Year ceremony at the famous Che Kung Temple and performed the official ritual of drawing from a stack of Kau Chim fortune sticks, which purport to tell the future for the city-state.

Local media reports noted with horror that Ho picked the number 83. The temple's fortune-teller interpreted it as a boat struggling in turbulent waters, portending hard times ahead.

Within months, the mysterious SARS virus hit Hong Kong. A coronavirus related to Covid-19, SARS killed hundreds of people and sparked a panic—made worse by the new regime's secrecy—that brought the economy to a halt. Ho's personal fortunes struggled on turbulent waters that year when he made the ill-fated decision to join CEFC.

The company founded by Ye in 2002 was to grow from an obscure private fuel trader to a global finance and energy conglomerate and one of China's richest companies.

Ho was hired to make VIP contacts in the US through CEFC's think tank for the benefit of the parent company, but Ye had been making his own high-level contacts, including with the Bidens, and he jealously guarded them.

Ho frowned on Ye's prodigious spending and wondered how he got away with it in the face of CCP restrictions on overseas investment. Ye had been buying expensive Manhattan real estate—and paying cash for it: $83 million in total for the Central Park West penthouse and the Park Avenue spread. That's a lot of $100 bills to stash inside his corporate jet. Ho warned Ye he was playing with fire. "You cannot make these deals without drawing the attention of Chinese government officials, who will view them unfavorably," he told him. Ye ignored the warning.

When Ye told Ho about the leaked indictment, he turned for advice to his old friend, the Israeli professor Gal Luft, with whom he had been collaborating on energy conferences since 2015. Luft's own think tank, IAGS, a 501c3 charitable organization registered in Maryland, received $350,000 grants in 2015 and 2016 from CEFC.

Luft always seemed to know things other people didn't, so Ho sent him some "cryptic messages about serious problems" and two weeks later Luft flew to Hong Kong to help Ho confront Chairman Ye and find out what the hell was going on.

Ye flew into Hong Kong a few days later on the larger of his two private jets, a $60 million A319 Airbus that had a bed and a shower and plenty of room for an entourage of 20. In sunnier times, Ye used to laugh with Luft and Ho about the tail number: VP-CIA. His idea of frugality was to use the smaller $35 million Gulfstream G550 for shorter trips.

The three men met on August 14, 2017, at Ye's palatial $40 million townhouse in a gated estate at Residence Bel-air, overlooking the glittering Waterfall Bay.

News of the indictment, Ye told them, had come via an FBI mole connected to Hunter.

As Luft tells the story, the informant, who Ye called "One Eye," was a current or former employee of the FBI, "extremely well placed," who had been paid a lot of money to leak the indictments.

"One-Eye" had told Ye that two Asians, an African, and "a Jewish guy" also were named on the sealed indictment with the SDNY.

Mediated through a translator, Luft assumed Ye thought he was the "Jewish guy," but he knew that was not the language used to describe people in an indictment, he told me in an interview. Luft discovered much later that Ye had his wires crossed.

As far as the other people on the list, Ye would not say who they were, only that Ho was among them. He claimed, falsely, as it turned out, that the indictments were not related to work they had done for CEFC.

They asked if the leak had come from Chinese intelligence and Ye said "categorically no," Luft recalls. They asked how trustworthy the mole was, but Ye refused to be drawn, other than to say he had "many connections undercover."

Finally, Ye reassured Ho that if he sat tight for a couple of months, his "powerful friend," Hunter, will "make the problem go away."

In China, the term "make the problem go away" means bribing someone, says Luft. Ye believed money solved everything.

Luft and Ho caught each other's eye as they stood to leave. They were skeptical. None of it made sense.

They drove across Hong Kong Island to Ho's office in Convention Plaza Tower overlooking Victoria Harbor and spent the next few hours mulling over Ye's tidbits. They couldn't figure out what potential legal trouble could be brewing for Ho in the US. Ho ruled out Africa, where he had been traveling for several years, because Ye had been so adamant that the indictment didn't involve CEFC business. He couldn't think of anything else, other than treachery.

He confided to Luft that he thought Ye was "jealous of him and had fabricated this information as a scheme to keep Ho out of the United States," Luft later would tell the FBI.

The leak of the indictment to CEFC executives had come at a crucial stage in their negotiations to buy a $9.1 billion stake in Russian state-owned energy company Rosneft, which they were about to announce to the world, despite not having shored up financing.

The leak also came just 10 days before a curious meeting in Albania that may hold a clue to the identity of Hunter's FBI mole.

On September 9, 2017, CEFC adviser Dorian Ducka met dirty G-man Charles McGonigal, then counterintelligence boss at the FBI's New York Field Office, which had been surveilling Ho and his associates.

McGonigal, a 22-year veteran of the FBI, and once one of the most powerful spy-hunters in the US, would be jailed in 2023 on twin indictments, first for conspiring to violate US sanctions by providing information to Russian oligarch Oleg Deripaska, and then for taking bribes from Albanians. While he was supposed to be supervising the investigation of Deripaska, McGonigal was getting secret payments from the Kremlin-backed oligarch, who was described by prosecutors as a "Russian tycoon who acts as Vladimir Putin's agent."

Among the services McGonigal performed for Deripaska was trying to get him removed from a classified list of Russians being considered for sanctions and finding dirt on his rivals. Deripaska was a personal friend of Putin, and at one time the wealthiest man in Russia, having emerged triumphant from the bloody 1990's "Aluminum Wars" when gangsters battled for control of privatized state assets in the aftermath of the collapse of the Soviet Union.

When Deripaska was sanctioned in 2018 over the 2014 annexation of Crimea, the Treasury Department accused him of money laundering, bribing and illegally wiretapping government officials, ordering the murder of a businessman, and "taking part in extortion and racketeering."

McGonigal's second indictment related to Albania. He received three cash payments totaling $225,000 in October and November 2017 from Agron Neza, a former Albanian intelligence officer living in New Jersey. Neza introduced McGonigal to his "friend and business associate" Ducka, a former Albanian energy minister who worked for CEFC while also serving as an adviser to Albanian Prime Minister Edi Rama.

According to prosecutors, Rama also was at the meeting between McGonigal and Ducka in September 2017. At Ducka's request, McGonigal urged Rama to be careful about awarding oil field drilling licenses in Albania to Russian front companies.

A photograph published in Albanian media, sourced from the *China Daily* in May 2017, showed Ducka standing with Chairman Ye.

McGonigal's ties with Deripaska also intersected with CEFC—and with Hunter.

CEFC's Director Zang was Deripaska's biggest investor, via a CEFC entity in Singapore, Anan International, that Zang controlled as Chairman. In October 2017, Anan committed $500 million to an initial public offering for Deripaska's company EN+ Group PLC, which owned power and aluminum assets in Russia. The investment was part of a strategic alliance with Russia and came just a month after CEFC agreed to buy the stake in Rosneft, part of efforts to feed China's insatiable appetite for energy and metals.

Luft recalls having dinner at Ye's townhouse in Hong Kong with Ye, Zang, Ho, and former CIA director James Woolsey and his wife Nancye, on February 21, 2017, when Ye and Zang had to cut the meal short to fly to Russia immediately and meet Deripaska.

Hunter once tried to exploit his connection to Deripaska to sell intelligence on the oligarch to Alcoa, a giant US aluminum firm, for $80,000, documents on his abandoned laptop show.

In an email to Daniel Cruise, Alcoa's then–Vice President of Government and Public Affairs, on June 3, 2011, Hunter offered to "provide Alcoa with statistical analysis of political and corporate risks, elite networks associated with Oleg Deripaska (OD), Russian CEO of Basic Element company and United company RUSAL."

Alcoa had just signed a two-year metal supply agreement with RUSAL, Deripaska's Russian aluminum company.

Included in Hunter's proposal to Alcoa was a "list of elites of similar rank in Russia, map of OD's [Deripaska's] networks based on frequency of interaction with selected elites and countries."

He wanted to charge Alcoa fees of "$25,000 for phase one of the project [and] $55,000 for refined analysis."

It is a mystery where Hunter obtained the valuable details on the Kremlin oligarch, but it is possible he knew McGonigal in 2011, when the G-man was working on Russian counterintelligence at the FBI's Washington field office, and Hunter's dad was VP. At the time, both men lived in the Washington suburbs with young families, six miles apart.

Hunter was also involved with other Moscow oligarchs in Putin's inner sanctum, including Ara Abramyan, who was awarded one of Russia's highest civilian honors by Putin, the Order of Merit to the Fatherland. According to the diary on his laptop, Hunter flew to Russia in 2012 to meet Abramyan at his home in the upscale Odintsovsky district of West Moscow.

Another possible personal link with McGonigal shows up on Hunter's laptop. Both had daughters who played lacrosse in the Washington area. Hunter and McGonigal's wife, Pamela, each received the same 29 lacrosse-match emails in 2014 and 2015 referring to their then-teenage girls.

There is no direct evidence that Hunter and McGonigal knew each other, but the lacrosse games are recorded unusually meticulously in Hunter's calendar. It would have been easy for the two dads to meet discreetly on the sidelines if they needed to exchange information.

Another intersection between Hunter and McGonigal comes through Ducka, CEFC's man in Albania. Someone with the same unusual first name as Ducka appears in Hunter's laptop in an email discussion about CEFC between Hunter and associates James Gilliar and Rob Walker.

"Dorian was a real help early on so we should consider how we include him," Gilliar wrote in the May 13, 2017, email.

"No way we don't do it," replies Hunter, "and if majority says no I'll take it out of my salary."

This was uncharacteristic generosity from Hunter, who at the time was crying poor to his business partners and demanding a larger cut of the profits.

Why were the Albanians paying McGonigal? According to Belind Kellici, an opposition Democratic Party politician in Albania, McGonigal was operating a racket in which he opened FBI investigations into political opponents of Prime Minister Rama's Albanian Socialist Party, and declared them "personae non gratae," unable to do business or open a bank account in the US. About a dozen opposition politicians or businesspeople who supported the opposition party were supposedly added to the McGonigal "blacklist."

That included former conservative prime minister Sali Berisha, who was slapped with persona non grata status and forbidden to travel to America by US Secretary of State Antony Blinken.

Berisha told me that Ducka paid for five trips by McGonigal to the Albanian capital Tirana. "McGonigal was engaged in a very Mafia process," he said. "Like in a movie they invented a big scheme of bribing [extorting] businesspeople. They spread the news that there is a list of 152 people to be blacklisted by the [US] State Department and [told people], 'You are on the list, but we can save your skin if you can pay 5 million, 2 million, etcetera.'"

Berisha is one of several prominent people who made allegations about McGonigal that did not appear on either of his indictments. The most remarkable thing about his arrest was the lack of public interest in the wider espionage implications. The FBI worked hard to bury the story, which was not merely embarrassing for the agency but also had the potential to compromise McGonigal's counter-espionage investigations of the previous 22 years.

McGonigal's downfall was treated simply as a public corruption case, not as an espionage case. The curious incuriosity of DOJ prosecutors is a hallmark of every case that touches on Hunter and his Chinese partners.

McGonigal had been involved in some of the bureau's biggest espionage investigations over the years, including leading a secret task force of CIA officers and FBI agents investigating the CIA's biggest intelligence disaster since World War Two. Between 2010 and 2012, in the early days of the Obama-Biden administration, the CIA lost as many as 30 of its spies in China due to at least one suspected mole.

The *New York Times* reported that the investigation led by McGonigal was code-named "Honey Badger" and operated out of a secret office in Northern Virginia.

In January 2018, former CIA officer Jerry Chun Shing Lee was arrested and pleaded guilty to helping dismantle America's Chinese spy network, but the devastating losses never were completely explained. A decade later, the CIA still was trying to rebuild its spying operation in China.

Curiously, Hunter would allude to the CIA's losses in China in a self-pitying text message to his lover Hallie Biden in 2018. He wrote that he was "dealing with the aftermath of the abduction and likely assassination" of Chairman Ye and the conviction of Patrick Ho, as well as the "ouster and arrest of US suspected CIA operatives inside China."

McGonigal left the FBI in September 2018 after a former mistress spilled the beans to his boss about bags of cash lying around his Brooklyn apartment.

Ironically, he was one of the well-connected experts tapped by the Atlantic Council before the 2020 election to warn about the threat of Russian election interference. At the time, McGonigal was taking money from sanctioned Russian aluminum tycoon Deripaska.

A protégé of former FBI chief James Comey, McGonigal was also involved in the FBI investigation into false claims that the Trump campaign had colluded with Moscow to steal the 2016 election. As section chief of the Cyber-Counterintelligence Coordination Section at the FBI's Washington field office, he reportedly was instrumental in opening the original Crossfire Hurricane probe which launched "Russiagate."

After he moved to New York, one month before the 2016 election, McGonigal was involved in fraudulent surveillance warrants on Trump campaign aide Carter Page.

How McGonigal fit into the Biden-CEFC picture is still unclear, but he was in charge of FBI counterintelligence in New York at the time when the SDNY was surveilling Ho and his CEFC associates, so he must have been aware of Hunter's connection—and his meetings with CEFC operative Ducka coincided with key dates in the investigation.

"The existence of a potential mole within the FBI who conveyed to Chinese individuals information about sealed indictments has, apparently, to this day never been solved," says Luft.

* * *

Back in New York, two weeks after his meeting in Hong Kong with Ho and Luft, Ye invited Hunter and Uncle Jim for lunch at his new penthouse with its panoramic views over Central Park and the Hudson River. Ye's family and personal chef had not yet arrived from Shanghai, so he cooked for them, and they ate together in the kitchen.

"I was the first guest in his new apartment," Hunter later would boast to Bobulinski. "He cooked me lunch himself and we ate in the kitchen together. He has me helping him on a number of his personal [issues] (staff visas and some more sensitive things) . . . Anyway, he and I are solid. . . . We have a standing once a week call as I am also his personal counsel (we signed an attorney client engagement letter) in the US."

A secret plan for Ye to defect to the US with Biden assistance was on the agenda. Dong asked Hunter ahead of the lunch: "Are you familiar with L1 visa [a pathway to permanent residency for executives of multinational companies] and green card application? Chairman is going to ask that."

Hunter replied: "Yes and no will study up on it."

Hunter told Dong he was bringing his father to the lunch, using capitals to impress the seemingly blasé CEFC emissary.

"Where is luncheon Kevin?" he messaged Dong on August 27, 2017.

"My uncle will be there with his BROTHER who would like to say hello to the Chairman. He is here to visit my daughter."

A little while later, having not received a reply, Hunter followed up: "So please give me location and time. Jim's BROTHER if he is coming just wants to say hello. [H]e will not be stopping for lunch."

It is not known if Joe did show up to Ye's penthouse, but Jim deemed the lunch a triumph, writing an email to Hunter the next day: "Great day yesterday!! We are on our way."

It was likely at that lunch that Ye offered Hunter $1 million to "represent" Ho in his upcoming legal issues because, within four days, Dong had sent Ho a draft of an attorney agreement to retain Hunter as his attorney. Hunter told the *New Yorker* that Ye was worried US law-enforcement were investigating CEFC.

Hunter signed the agreement on September 18, 2017. CEFC paid the million dollars on Ho's behalf. It was sent from CEFC in China to CEFC's Hong Kong HSBC bank account on October 10, 2017, and from there it was wired to Dong at the Hudson West III account at Cathay Bank. Dong wired the money to Hunter's Owasco LLC account at Wells Fargo the following March, as confirmed by bank documents subpoenaed by the House Oversight Committee. Nine days after the money hit his account, Hunter took off for an epic bender in Los Angeles.

The five-month delay for the wire to reach Hunter was likely due to the backlog of Suspicious Activity Reports involving Hunter and CEFC. Ho also told Luft there had been some sort of mix-up with the original wire, which had to be re-sent.

The day after Ye cooked lunch for the Bidens, Director Zang was photographed clinking champagne glasses with Russian President Vladimir Putin at the opening ceremony of the 2017 World Judo Championship in Budapest, Hungary.

Within weeks, Reuters would report that CEFC was set to acquire a 14 percent stake Rosneft. The deal was destined to cement the Sino-Russia alliance—to the detriment of America's national interest.

Hunter and his partners knew about the deal ahead of time. Hunter told Bobulinski that at lunch with Chairman Ye, "He and I discussed the Rosneft deal and he is pissed off but only by the exception [execution] which I guess was Zang's deal."

Gilliar earlier had told Bobulinski that Ye would be meeting with Putin to progress the deal, but he was waiting for the green light from President Xi—whom he called "No. 1."

Meanwhile, Jim had cooked up another get-rich-quick scheme in Louisiana, in which CEFC was supposed to invest in "a $4 billion deal to build the fucking largest fucking LNG port in the world" to ship liquefied natural gas to China. Jim told Hunter this is the deal that finally will make them rich.

Trouble loomed on the horizon, however. Director Zang and his family were having problems with their visas. Hunter and Jim's fixit guy for visas, John Sandweg, a former acting director of Immigration and Customs Enforcement in the Obama administration, seemed unable to perform his usual magic.

On September 11, 2017, Uncle Jim emailed Hunter urgently: "Director Visa. Call."

Bobulinski raised the issue with Hunter: "Director had his visa denied 3x [three times] and his kids and wife's visas denied 3x."

"I know," replied Hunter. "We are out of it per the instructions of the Chairman last time I saw him."

The Spence School on the Upper East Side, where Zang's daughter Rouqi was enrolled, emailed Uncle Jim to ask what had happened to the Zangs.

"They paid their tuition for the year," wrote Susan Parker, director of admissions. "They kept in touch for a while telling us about Rouqi's visa problems etc. In the past few weeks, though, they have stopped responding to our emails—we have lost contact."

According to Luft, Ye had been counting on the Biden connection to protect him when he defected to the US but hedged his bets after Joe left office, amid Zang's visa problems and the Trump administration's heightened scrutiny of Chinese interests in the US.

"He was preparing a Plan B in case his Biden buddies fail to organize him a new life in NY," says Luft. "He asked me to arrange Portuguese passports for him and went on a shopping spree there." Starting in October 2017, CEFC bought controlling stakes in Portuguese insurance businesses and a $500 million stake in Portugal's Partex Oil and Gas Corporation.

"It all happened very fast. He never had an interest in Portugal until I told him about the golden passport program."

The golden passport, or "golden visa," scheme was introduced by the Portuguese government in 2012 to salvage an economy shattered by the 2008 global financial crisis by giving rich foreigners access to the European Union's borderless Schengen zone in exchange for investment. It offered five-year residence permits to non-EU nationals who invested at least 500,000 Euros (US$540,000) in real estate or transferred one million euros to a Portugese bank account.

Ye, meantime, was busy installing his wife, Wu Liqiong; daughter Yiken Ye; mother, Rongyu Qiu; and nanny, Lizhen Yao, in his Central Park West penthouse, on B1/B2 visitor visas.

His son, Junkun Ye, already was in New York on an F1 student visa, attending the exclusive Columbia Prep, on the Upper West Side, where Barron Trump, the then-ten-year-old son of Donald and Melania Trump, was a student.

With Hunter's contacts, Ye would apply for more visas in September 2017 for the rest of his household in preparation for defecting to America, where he planned to go into partnership with Hunter and his father in the US subsidiary of CEFC.

To reflect the new partnership, Hunter ordered a new nameplate for his Georgetown office in the House of Sweden, with its panoramic views of the Potomac River and the Watergate complex, just half a mile from a favorite Biden family haunt, Cafe Milano.

"Please have keys made available for new office mates Joe Biden, Jill Biden, Jim Biden, Gongwen Dong, Chairman Ye CEFC emissary," Hunter wrote to House of Sweden General Manager Cecilia Browning on September 21, 2017.

"I would like the office sign to reflect the following:

"The Biden Foundation [Joe's nonprofit]

"Hudson West (CEFC US)."

But more storm clouds were gathering, unbeknownst to Hunter at the time.

Many of his transactions with CEFC were being flagged in bank suspicious activity reports (SARs) as "potential financial criminal activity," a designation used by the Financial Crimes Enforcement Network (FinCEN) at the Treasury Department to identify money laundering, political corruption, or other crimes. Hunter is described in various SARs as a "PEP" for Politically Exposed Person, someone flagged as potentially a high risk for bribery and corruption.

The House Oversight Committee found that banks such as Wells Fargo had raised so many red flags about the CEFC payments to Hunter and Jim Biden, many of which were labeled "consulting fees," that more than 150 Suspicious Activity Reports had been filed with the Treasury Department.

"The sheer number of flagged transactions in this case is highly unusual and may be indicative of serious criminal activity or a national security threat," Oversight chairman James Comer declared.

In one internal email from June 2018, obtained by the Oversight committee, an unnamed bank investigator who had been monitoring Hunter due to his PEP designation as "the son of former US Vice President Joe Biden" warned of "unusual" activity on his account "with no current business purpose" which indicated he was a "high risk" customer.

The bank investigator noted that the $5 million transfer to HWIII the previous August was listed a "business loan," yet there "was no loan agreement document submitted."

Further, the money mainly funded 16 wires totaling $2,915,375.25 to Hunter's firm Owasco, which were listed as "management fees and reimbursements."

"We find it unusual that approximately 58% of the funds were transferred to the law firm in a few months and the frequency of payments appear erratic [and] HUDSON WEST III LLC does not currently have any investment projects at this time."

The email questioned why "millions in fees are being paid [when it] does not appear to have any services rendered by Owasco."

The bank investigator went on to raise allegations aired from Hunter's ex-wife, Kathleen, during their divorce of "financial concerns about his extravagant spending on his own interests (drugs, strip clubs, prostitutes, etc.) which put his family in a deep financial hole."

He also was troubled by recent reports of "China targeting children of politicians and [the] purchase of political influence through 'sweetheart deals'" and referred to Hunter's previous "$1.5 billion deal with the Chinese-State to establish a private equity firm [BHR] in which they manage the funds over time and make huge fees. The management company's purpose is to invest in companies that benefit Chinese government."

Finally, the bank investigator recommended "re-evaluation of [the bank's] relationship with [Hunter]."

But by the time the bank was raising red flags, CEFC had imploded.

Years later, the House Oversight Committee would subpoena those Suspicious Activity Reports and discover a maze of Biden enrichment schemes.

Chairman James Comer, who had served as a director of the South Central Bank in his hometown of Tompkinsville, Kentucky for 12 years, spent countless hours poring over thousands of bank documents from the Biden family. His hair turned three shades grayer in the first year after Republicans seized power in the House. It wasn't just the late nights and the avalanche of bank records.

The more he revealed about Biden family corruption, and the closer he got to Joe, the more vicious and personal were the attacks from opposition research groups funded by deep-pocketed Democrat dark money groups that were supporting Joe and Hunter.

The media started camping out in Tompkinsville, population 2,500, trying to find dirt to augment oppo research handouts.

There were nasty billboards placed above a highway smearing Comer and other attempts to damage him electorally.

But Comer was the seventh generation of his family in the town. He was related to half the people in the county. They knew who James Comer was before he was even born. He won 90 percent of the vote in the county.

So, there were a lot of doors politely closed on out-of-town muckrakers in Tompkinsville.

Comer's committee produced five detailed "Bank Memorandums" in 2023 tracing some of the millions of dollars in foreign money that had flowed through the accounts and laying out the opaque corporate structure of shell companies associated with the Bidens, most of which were formed in Delaware during the eight years of Joe's vice presidency.

The memos recorded a pattern suggestive of money laundering, in which "Biden associates would receive significant deposits from foreign sources into their bank accounts and then transfer smaller, incremental payments to Biden bank accounts. These complicated and seemingly unnecessary financial transactions appear to be a concerted effort to conceal the source and total amount received from the foreign companies."

Money laundering is defined by FinCEN as "the disguising of funds derived from illicit activity so that the funds may be used without detection of the illegal activity that produced them."

It is "a well-thought out process" accomplished in three stages: placement, layering, and integration.

First, the money has to be placed in a financial institution, often in structured amounts of cash deposits, or "physically moved," for instance, by smuggling currency across international borders. Once the illicit funds have entered the financial system, "multiple and sometimes complex financial transactions are conducted to further conceal their illegal nature, and to make it difficult to identify the source of the funds or eliminate an audit trail. "Transferring funds between accounts and using wire transfers facilitate layering." Buying luxury goods or virtual assets, such as cryptocurrencies and non-fungible tokens (NFTs), are other ways of concealing the proceeds of crime.

Finally, the illicit funds "re-enter the economy disguised as legitimate business earnings (securities, businesses, real estate). Unnecessary loans may be obtained to disguise illicit funds as the proceeds of business loans."

IRS Special Agent Joe Ziegler, the lead investigator on the Sportsman investigation into Hunter in Delaware, also searched for foreign bank accounts in the Cayman Islands and Hong Kong, using what is known as an "Egmont" request, according to documents he released under whistleblower protections to the House Ways and Means Committee.

An "Egmont" request refers to an international network of over 100 member countries, known as the Egmont Group of Financial Intelligence Units, that will conduct searches of suspicious transaction reports (SARs) for names submitted by the FBI in terrorism financing or significant money laundering investigations.

Ziegler later was questioned during a Ways and Means hearing about the elaborate matrix of shell companies and convoluted money transfers that he had uncovered. To his trained eye, was the complexity designed to hide income and avoid paying taxes?

"It is not normal," he replied. "In our investigations, we work complex international money laundering. It is very common for people to set up different entities to obfuscate the normal reporting requirements. That is typical of what we see."

His boss, Gary Shapley, added: "There could be some legitimate business reasons. But that is the whole point here in this investigation. There were no legitimate business reasons for all these entities to be set up. There really weren't many services being provided by some of them, and some of them were just flow-through entities that were high on the list of red flags for potential tax evasion or tax noncompliance."

But the IRS investigators were prevented by Delaware US Attorney David Weiss, and the rest of the DOJ's gatekeepers, from doing their jobs and pursuing those red flags to uncover potential money laundering. It was a pattern of obstruction and obfuscation, slow-walking and favoritism to the Biden family, that Shapley and Ziegler eventually would find intolerable.

* * *

In Hong Kong, Patrick Ho received some surprise visitors on November 1, 2017. Hunter and Uncle Jim unexpectedly showed up at the Grand Hyatt next door to CEFC's offices in Wan Chai and told Ho they wanted to meet him. When Ho went to their hotel, Hunter asked him to buy them two burner phones, which he led Ho to believe were needed to communicate covertly with his law enforcement contacts in the U.S. Hunter specified iPhones which Ho went out and bought immediately. It was his first time meeting Hunter, and he was not impressed.

Two days later, still in Hong Kong, Jim announced to Ho that they had received word from their sources that he was in the clear. His name was no longer on an indictment. There was no warrant for his arrest. He could go back to America.

Ho was a bit dubious, and asked Jim to doublecheck with his sources. Two days later, Jim called Ho back, and insisted that the coast was clear. Ho welcomed the news because he had a big energy conference in Washington later that month to host with Luft, and he didn't want to miss it.

The Bidens updated Ye on the news, and left Hong Kong the next day, hitting Ho with a massive bill from the Grand Hyatt for room service, massages, and other "entertainment" he was too polite to specify when he complained to Luft about the impost. Hunter later tried to expense the trip to CEFC, only for Dong to refuse to pay: "You need to take out expenses related to HK trip . . . Your expenses will be reimbursed today. The amount is $157,494.19 after deducting those already paid and HK expenses."

Jim and Hunter had another unpleasant gift in store for Ho when they left Hong Kong. Jim hired a private investigator from Lowery & Associates to spy on Ho for ten days, at a cost of $2,500.

"Due diligence investigation, world watch, and social media investigation on the following: Patrick Chi Ping Ho," read the invoice on Hunter's laptop. "Consultation and oral briefing on findings."

Why were they keeping tabs on Ho? Were they afraid he would contact the US authorities? That he wouldn't leave Hong Kong? Or did they just want to know when he left?

When Jim was questioned in the impeachment inquiry seven years later, he was evasive about the private eye. He said that he and Hunter had met with Ye before flying to Hong Kong, and Ho's name came up, "so I was just being cautious, because I don't like to be put in a position where I am meeting someone, especially in China, that, at least for myself, that I wasn't comfortable with."

Asked if he had a reason to feel uncomfortable about Ho, Jim said it was just his "sixth sense."

His explanation made no sense because the private eye didn't start following Ho until after Jim and Hunter left Hong Kong.

On November 18, 2017, Ho flew into New York and was arrested at JFK Airport as soon as he got off the plane. His first call was to Jim Biden.

CHAPTER 7

BUSTED

November 19, 2017
MANHATTAN CORRECTIONAL CENTER

Hunter arrived half an hour late to visit Patrick Ho at the notorious Metropolitan Correctional Center in lower Manhattan, dubbed the "Guantanamo of New York" for its brutal conditions. Inmates have included mob boss John Gotti, Mexican drug lord "El Chapo" and, until his untimely death, Jeffrey Epstein.

The CEFC executive was still in shock after being arrested the previous day on bribery and money laundering charges by two FBI agents as he got off his flight at JFK Airport.

Ho was read his Miranda rights at 2 p.m., according to police records obtained by the *New York Times*. Nine minutes later, he made his first phone call—to Jim Biden.

Chairman Ye had told Ho that Jim was the person he should contact if he ever had trouble in the US. But Jim told the *New York Times* it was a case of mistaken identity and that Ho meant to call his nephew Hunter. Jim claimed to be surprised by the call, even though he'd hired a private eye to follow Ho in Hong Kong for the previous nine days.

"There is nothing else I have to say," Jim told the *Times*. "I don't want to be dragged into this anymore."

Later that afternoon, Hunter emailed lawyer Edward Kim, a former prosecutor with the Southern District of New York (SDNY) whose boutique Fifth Avenue law firm, Krieger Kim & Lewin, specialized in cross-border criminal cases.

"Per our discussion I would like to engage your firm on behalf of Dr. Patrick Ho of Hong Kong in the matter we discussed. I am authorized by Dr. Ho as his attorney to do so," Hunter wrote Kim at 4:46 p.m.

According to Kim, Hunter had already contacted the FBI on Ho's behalf: "If you're able to find the names of the FBI agents you spoke with that would be helpful."

Hunter replied: "Working on it."

He was unresponsive the rest of the evening as Kim and colleagues worked on Ho's case until after midnight, trying to contact Hunter by phone and email.

He finally responded at 3:03 a.m.: "Guys sorry.—I came back to thmy [*sic*] room and fell asleep—the hotel was ringing my uncles room which is next door to mine. Just woke up if anyone is still awake. If I not I iwill [*sic*] call first thing in the morning."

Hunter was staying at the five-star Peninsula Hotel on Fifth Avenue and would keep busy racking up thousands of dollars on his American Express card on strip clubs and luxuries over the next couple of days: $3,500.00 at the Vivid Cabaret Adult entertainment club, for instance, and $1,405.57 at Davidoff of Geneva cigar store on Madison Avenue.

He was supposed to meet Kim outside the jail at 8:15 a.m. the day after Ho's arrest, but he didn't make it on time. Showing up late to jail that morning was the last thing Hunter did for Ho in return for the million dollars he was paid by CEFC for legal representation, according to Ho, who burned with resentment for years.

Unusually for a bribery case, Ho was denied bail.

During his trial, prosecutor Dan Richenthal alleged that Ho, the head of

CEFC's think tank, the China Energy Fund Committee, had bribed leaders in Chad and Uganda with $2.9 million, in exchange for oil permits for parent company CEFC. He also was accused of money laundering.

The Bidens' relationship with CEFC was never mentioned in the trial. In fact, Richenthal successfully convinced the judge to redact Hunter's name from an email between Ho and a witness, Vuk Jeremic.

A court transcript shows a dispute between Richenthal and Ho's lawyer Kim over redactions to Exhibit 2739, an email, in which Ho asked Jeremic to invite "prominent and powerful friends" to a dinner in Washington, DC, on December 6, 2015.

"The name of that individual is not relevant and could introduce a political dimension to this case that we don't think is worth dealing with," Richenthal told District Court Judge Loretta Preska, who agreed to the redaction.

Jeremic crops up a lot in emails on Hunter's laptop discussing business opportunities in China and lobbying Hunter for help in his campaign to become UN Secretary General.

In one email, in June 2016, he asks Hunter to set up a meeting with his father's national security adviser, Colin Kahl, but later complains that the meeting "did not last very long" and that the vice president's office appeared to be "outside the decision-making loop."

Jeremic ultimately failed in his bid to become Secretary General, but not before he introduced Hunter to the Serbian royal family, who asked if he could get Joe to help with the expensive refurbishment of their Belgrade palaces.

"We were having problems with the state budget for the Royal Compound consisting of two palaces [and] were hoping that Hunter might be able to help with his father to solve the problem," Crown Prince Alexander Karađorđević told the *New York Post*'s Jon Levine.

The Serbian government ended up footing the bill, but Joe remained unpopular in Serbia because of his enthusiastic advocacy of the 1999 NATO bombings. As the ranking member on the Senate Foreign Relations Committee at the time, he urged President Bill Clinton to wage war on the former Yugoslavia. "At stake is our entire policy in Europe since the end of WWII to promote stability and democracy," he said.

Once the bombing began, Joe declared that US ground troops should follow: "We should announce there's going to be American casualties," he told NBC. "We should go to Belgrade, and we should have a Japanese-German-style occupation of that country."

He would retain a belligerent foreign policy outlook into his presidency.

* * *

It was not just Hunter whose name was erased from the Ho trial.

When the indictment was unsealed on November 17, 2017, it listed only one co-defendant, Cheikh Gadio, the former Senegalese Foreign Minister.

But Ye had told Ho and Gal Luft at his house in Hong Kong in August that there were two Chinese names, along with Ho, on the indictment, as well as an African and "a Jewish guy." Gadio probably was the African mentioned, but there was no sign of the other three names.

Chairman Ye and Director Zang were not indicted, or even listed as "co-conspirators," even though prosecutors made clear throughout Ho's trial that they orchestrated the bribery scheme, while Ho just followed their orders.

Ye appeared in the indictment 66 times, under the codename "Chairman," authorizing the operation and getting regular updates from Ho.

Zang was listed as "Executive-1" and appeared 15 times, overseeing the scheme and leading a CEFC delegation to Chad to personally hand gift-wrapped boxes full of cash to President Idriss Déby, whose rejection of the bribe would lead to CEFC's downfall.

Prosecutors cited an email from May 2015, in which Ho's secretary told Gadio that Zang would be taking the lead role in the Chad relationship: "As Dr. Ho has currently moved into other projects and this project is in the hand of [Zang], the decision and related issues of this project are made by [Zang]."

From then on, Zang and another CEFC official "became the main points of contact for the Chad-related discussions with Gadio, and Ho became less involved."

In October 2018, prosecutors filed an explosive pretrial motion accusing Ho of exploring arms deals to Chad, Qatar, and Libya, and of looking for ways for CEFC to act as a "middleman" to help Iran avoid American sanctions and gain access to funds frozen in the Bank of China so it could buy precious metal through a Hong Kong bank.

Ho was not charged with any additional offenses, but the new filing offered an insight into CEFC's shadowy global activities that had led to Chairman Ye's final and most spectacular deal, the $9 billion stake in Rosneft, the state-controlled Russian oil giant. It would also echo charges against Luft brought by the same prosecutors years later, under the Biden administration.

It also raises further questions about why Ho was the only person involved with CEFC who was indicted over such a vast global conspiracy.

Richenthal even told the court that Ho was operating entirely at the direction of Chairman Ye, who sought to corrupt foreign officials with cash and a promise that they—and their families—would share in CEFC's future profits.

On the day of Ho's arrest at JFK, Hunter had been at Ye's Central Park West penthouse. Ho was instructed to come straight from the airport and join them for lunch. But he never made it.

Ho's deputy Andrew Lo, who had prepared the "gift boxes" containing the cash bribes, also was questioned by the FBI that day, and allowed to return to Hong Kong, says Luft.

A few days later, Lo phoned Luft, sounding "deeply distressed," and asked him to come to Hong Kong to discuss a "very important matter."

"He was terrified," recalls Luft. "He wanted to say something face to face but I couldn't travel until weeks later and by then it was too late."

Before they could meet, Lo, a healthy 66-year-old, had died in mysterious circumstances.

Sing Tao Daily reported that Lo was "suffering from flu and experiencing pain and diarrhea" when he was admitted to Queen Mary Hospital. He died two days later, on February 14, 2018. The newspaper said Lo had a "healthy lifestyle and regularly hiked and walked dogs."

Luft thought his death suspicious enough to bring it up with the FBI in Brussels.

Ye, meanwhile, had been a target for surveillance by the FBI in 2016 and 2017, according to an associate who claimed the CEFC chairman was "constantly followed by the FBI" when he was in New York, "even when he took walks in Central Park."

However, somehow, by November 2017, Ye escaped being indicted, or even named as a co-conspirator.

It made no sense. Why was Ye not arrested in New York along with Ho, the junior member of their bribery scheme?

Was Ye let off the hook to protect the Bidens? Hunter and Jim's names inevitably would have come up in any court case and would not have been as easy to redact as had been the case with Ho, who hardly knew them.

Or was it because Ye was perceived as being too close to China's President Xi? After all, Jim Biden called him Xi's "protégé." Did the Trump administration decide the diplomatic fallout was not worth the scalp, and it would be best to allow the Chinese to take care of their own, albeit in more brutal fashion?

Director Zang's visa was blocked mysteriously in September, for what reason nobody knew, but it meant he conveniently was stuck in China when Ho was arrested, so there was no dilemma about what to do about him.

Ho was a Hong Konger, so he could be sacrificed. In fact, in an email to a friend during his trial, Ho described himself as the "first of the sacrificial lambs" of America's new "hostility" to China.

In Luft's view, Ho was a "naïve . . . patsy" who was lured to New York to give Ye a "get out of jail free" card, not that the chairman's good fortune would last long.

And what of Hunter? While his primary CEFC partners, Ye and Zang, remained at large, his role with the Chinese could remain hidden.

It was the second time in 18 months that Hunter had come onto the SDNY radar and emerged unscathed. The first time was in May 2016, when his best friend and business partner Devon Archer was arrested and charged over a $60 million securities fraud. Hunter was questioned about his role as vice-chairman of the collapsed Burnham Asset Management, but nothing came of it. Hunter received a subpoena from the Securities and Exchange Commission in March 2016 asking for information in its investigation of the Burnham bonds scheme.

In response, Hunter's lawyer Michael MacPhail played the "dad card," as the Oversight Committee put it when releasing his email.

"We request that you treat this matter with the highest degree of confidentiality," wrote MacPhail, George Mesires' partner at law firm Faegre Drinker Biddle & Reath (then known as Faegre Baker Daniels) on April 20, 2016.

"The confidential nature of this investigation is very important to our client and it would be unfair, not just to our client, but also to his father, the Vice President of the United States, if his involvement in an SEC investigation and parallel criminal probe were to become the subject of any media attention."

On May 11, 2016, the SEC issued a press release announcing it had charged seven people over the scheme, without charging Hunter.

Once again, Joe Biden's reckless son escaped scot-free while those around him wound up in jail, broke, missing, or worse.

* * *

According to court documents, the FBI had been surveilling Ho's electronic communications under the Foreign Intelligence Surveillance Act (FISA) since June 2016. FISA allows the federal government to spy on suspected foreign agents on domestic soil, and often inadvertently scoops up American citizens in its surveillance net.

The FBI executed search warrants to seize Ho's cell phones, an iPad, six USB drives, and computers when it scoured his offices in Manhattan and Arlington, Virginia. They collected more than 100,000 emails from five email accounts, according to DOJ records obtained by Paul Sperry at RealClearPolitics. The prosecution produced over 30,000 documents at Ho's trial.

Ho's indictment shows that Chairman Ye and Director Zang's communications were also captured. The surveillance occurred during a time when the Biden family and their partners were in regular communication with CEFC. It's likely Hunter's and even Uncle Jim's communications were captured, exposing the full extent of their entanglement with the Chinese state-backed company.

Senators Johnson and Grassley asked the DOJ in 2021 for more information about the FISA warrants to assist their investigation into Hunter but were ignored.

At the time of Ho's arrest, Charles McGonigal was head of counterintelligence at the FBI's New York Field Office and oversaw the initial espionage probe into CEFC, including the FISA surveillance, even though the corrupt G-man was engaged in clandestine liaisons with CEFC figures associated with Director Zang, which posed a clear conflict of interest.

On November 19, 2017, one day after Ho's arrest, McGonigal had an undisclosed meeting with CEFC adviser Dorian Ducka in Albania over dinner and drinks, according to his later indictment. The FBI was told about the leak from the CEFC investigation, but it's not known if they ever investigated McGonigal as the potential source.

McGonigal would not be the first agent to go rogue in New York, the hub for FBI counterintelligence operations, because the presence of the United Nations headquarters makes the city a hotbed of international spies. Robert Hanssen spied for the Russians undetected for more than two decades after being assigned to the New York counterintelligence unit in 1976.

The FBI's investigation into McGonigal began sometime in 2018, reportedly after they were tipped off by British intelligence that he was in London meeting a Russian contact who was under surveillance. McGonigal's indictment says he went to London to meet Oleg Deripaska, at the Kremlin oligarch's $52 million mansion in Belgrave Square, but it is not known whether the meeting was before or after McGonigal abruptly retired from the FBI in September 2018, aged 50.

After suspicions fell on McGonigal, FBI Director Chris Wray ordered a comprehensive damage assessment to determine if any of his past counterintelligence operations had been compromised.

The assessment cannot have been very thorough because nobody questioned Ho about the leak to CEFC officials of the SDNY's sealed indictment, which Ye told him had come from Hunter's FBI mole. Ho spent nearly three years in the MCC prison, right next door to the office of the SDNY prosecutors and was never asked a single question.

* * *

Ho was prosecuted with "particular zeal," the *Wall Street Journal* reported, and Richenthal took the opportunity to shine a spotlight on China's use of foreign bribery to win contracts for President Xi's Belt and Road Initiative.

Ho's defense during the jury trial was that his payments to African officials were charitable corporate donations by a man on a patriotic mission to generate goodwill for China.

"Dr. Ho and his colleagues asked for nothing in return," his lawyer told the jury.

However, Richenthal accused Ho of seeking to exploit poor countries to secure unfair business advantages for CEFC.

The jury agreed and on March 25, 2019, Ho was sentenced to three years in prison, 16 months of which he already had served before trial. He was released a few months early, in June 2020, in the middle of the COVID-19 pandemic, and was deported to Hong Kong, aged 70 and much slimmer.

He always wondered if his early release was to get him out of the way before the presidential election in November, for fear he might let slip Biden secrets.

After Ho was sentenced, Geoffrey Berman, the US Attorney for the Southern District of New York, exploded: "The defendant does not deserve such a shockingly low sentence."

It was a paltry payoff for a resource-heavy case his office had run for three years.

"It is difficult to quantify the damage the defendant did . . . But the damage caused by corruption is real and lasting."

What a rich irony considering Berman had allowed the corruption mastermind, Chairman Ye, to slip through his fingers, and apparently had turned a blind eye to Hunter and Jim Biden's involvement with CEFC.

Ye remained in New York for several weeks after Ho's arrest. In December 2017, he left his wife, daughter, son, mother, and nanny in his Central Park West penthouse and flew to Shanghai where he would be arrested for "economic crimes" within weeks, on the direct orders of President Xi, according to Chinese news agency Caixin.

News of Ye's detention broke in February 2018, and he never was heard from again. Hunter told people that Ye was "a prisoner on death row in China." Rumors spread in Hong Kong that he had been thrown into the Yangtze River.

CEFC collapsed with $15 billion in debt. The Rosneft deal, announced just two months before Ho was arrested, was kaput, and China had to pay Russia $250 million compensation. The deal had brought too much heat on the Chinese government, who must have known that Ye was planning to defect.

Director Zang stayed out of jail but Luft alleges he was instructed to forfeit all his own assets and liquidate Ye's empire to pay back the debt to the state.

"It's a riches-to-rags story," said Luft. "He is free but cannot leave China for the rest of his life . . . He was on the world's billionaire list. Now he has nothing."

Hunter, on the other hand, merrily collected the $1 million legal retainer that CEFC had paid him to represent Ho, and left New York in April 2018 for an extended crack bender in Los Angeles.

A couple of months later he would reflect on the fate of his Chinese partners in a voice memo on his laptop titled "Most Genius Shit Ever Made."

At the time, he was holed up at the legendary Chateau Marmont, on Sunset Strip in Hollywood, frittering away the Chinese money on escorts with Eastern European names, and whiling away his time learning to cook crack, at age 48, in a baby food jar on a four-burner stove in the tiny kitchen of his cottage by the pool.

"I get calls from my father to tell me the *New York Times* is calling," he tells a female friend on the recording.

"I have another *New York Times* reporter calling about my representation of Patrick Ho, literally the fucking spy chief of China who started the company that my partner [Chairman Ye], who is worth $323 billion, founded and is now missing. The richest man in the world is missing, who was my partner.

"He was missing since I last saw him in his $58 million apartment inside a $4 billion deal to build the fucking largest fucking LNG port in the world, and I am receiving calls from the Southern District of New York, from the US attorney himself.

"My best friend in business Devon has named me as a witness, without telling me, in a criminal case. . . . I'm talking about a fucking criminal case in which Devon has named me as a witness."

Nobody but Hunter believes that Ho was the "spy chief of China," but it is an assertion he repeatedly makes.

And if Hunter really had been getting calls from Berman, "the U.S. Attorney himself," it may have been because Archer's fraud trial was about to start, and prosecutors wanted to interview him as he was listed as a witness for the defense.

Berman, now in private practice in New York, would not say whether or not he phoned Hunter.

"I am not commenting on or off the record on that," he said in an email.

In the end, Hunter was not called to testify, but Archer's lawyer described him to the jury as "part of this deal." Archer was chairman, and Hunter was vice-chairman of Burnham Group. Hunter drew $200,000 from the business, while Archer argued that he lost money when the $60 million scheme collapsed.

"It is not clear whether Justice Department prosecutors did much to investigate [Hunter] Biden's involvement—just as DOJ seems to have been remarkably uninterested in . . . his complicity in the family business of cashing in on his father's political influence," Andy McCarthy, a former Assistant US Attorney for the SDNY, wrote in the *National Review*.

Mervyn Yan signed a document on November 2, 2018, to dissolve Hudson West III, the last link between the Bidens and CEFC.

That might have been the end of it, if it hadn't been for IRS Special Agent Joe Ziegler, who opened a file on Hunter a few days later.

The IRS investigation wasn't the only chicken coming home to roost for Hunter in his year of living dangerously.

On November 16, 2018, Hunter told his personal assistant Katie Dodge to remove Lunden Roberts off the payroll of his company Owasco PC, just three months after she gave birth to the baby girl he refused to acknowledge.

"Is Lunden still on payroll???" he asked Dodge, in a message retrieved by the IRS with a search warrant of his iCloud.

Dodge: "Yes Lunden is still on payroll . . . Do I remove Lunden from payroll & health insurance? They go hand in hand."

Hunter: "Take Lunden off payroll. I thought you said she decidedly dint [sic] want to work and didn't need health insurance anyway. Remember that conversation?"

Dodge: "No. I do not remember that conversation . . . Maybe she told you that but I wasn't involved."

Hunter: "Regardless Katie . . . I haven't talked to Lunden in 7 months???????" He then proceeded to pay himself $10,000.

In hindsight, the $750 a week plus $260 in health care that Roberts received from Owasco PC since Hunter put her on the payroll that May was a bargain. His miserliness had awakened a sleeping giant, and Roberts would get herself the best attorney in Independence, Arkansas, to sue him for paternity.

Gal Luft, too, was about to drop a bucketload on Hunter and Jim. The day his friend Ho was sentenced was the day Luft received a letter from US Attorney Berman telling him that prosecutors Richenthal and Catherine Ghosh would meet him in Brussels, as he had asked, and hear what he had to say about the Bidens.

As for Ho, it would take him six years to strike back.

In March 2024, Ho sent a legal letter to Hunter requesting that their attorney-client agreement be terminated and threatening legal action unless he received a detailed list of services provided by Hunter and reimbursement for the unused funds, as laid out in the 2017 contract.

"Patrick says he paid him, and that Hunter never did anything for him," a friend of Ho's said, "and that according to the contract, the money should be reimbursed."

Hunter's name does not appear as an attorney of record for the Patrick Ho case in the Southern District of New York.

Under oath, Hunter told US District Judge Maryellen Noreika in Delaware in 2023 that he received the $1 million as "payment for legal fees for Patrick Ho [through] my own law firm."

Noreika wanted more detail: "Who is that payment received from, was that the law firm?"

Hunter: "Received from Patrick Ho, Your Honor."

Noreika: "Mr. Ho himself?"

Hunter: "Yes."

Noreika: "Were you doing legal work for him and apart from the law firm?"

Hunter: "Yes, Your Honor. Well—"

Sensing danger, Hunter's lawyer Chris Clark stepped in at this point: "That wasn't through Boise Schiller, Your Honor, Mr. Biden was engaged as an attorney."

Noreika: "Right. So that's why I asked. You were doing work for him—"

Hunter: "My own law firm, not as counsel."

Noreika: "So you had your own law firm as well?"

Hunter: "I think Owasco PC acted as a—acted as a law firm entity, yeah."

Noreika: "Okay."

Hunter: "I believe that's the case, but I don't know that for a fact."

Ho, who had been keeping a close eye on Hunter's travails from Hong Kong, was "baffled" by Hunter's responses to Noreika. He was stuck with a massive legal bill for Kim's representation, which he had to pay out of his own pocket.

If he could claw back even part of the million dollars Hunter had been paid for not representing him in court, then revenge definitely was a dish best-served cold.

CHAPTER 8

THE PROFFER

March 28–March 29, 2019
BRUSSELS, BELGIUM

In March 2019, before Joe Biden announced he would run for president, before his wayward son Hunter abandoned his laptop at a computer store in Delaware, before separate IRS and FBI investigations into Hunter were transferred into the Bidens' incestuous home state of Delaware, and before Senator Chuck Grassley initiated his own investigation into Biden family corruption, Dr. Gal Luft tipped off the DOJ about the whole shady business with China.

Luft, a former Israel Defense Forces lieutenant colonel with deep intelligence ties in Washington and Beijing, describes himself as "patient zero of the Hunter Biden investigation [and] a key witness to a national security breach."

For his efforts, he would be arrested, skip bail, and become a fugitive living in the shadows of an unknown country. But that was all four years in the future.

For now, he had arrived at the US Embassy in the historic center of Brussels on that misty spring morning to meet four FBI agents and two prosecutors who had flown in from the Southern District of New York

(SDNY) for what lawyers call a "proffer" session. A prelude to possible cooperation with law enforcement, a proffer is a voluntary interview in which a target or witness in an investigation offers information in return for some benefit, preferably no charges.

Luft, then 52, who had been in a business relationship with the non-profit think tank arm of CEFC, was concerned about a leak from an FBI mole to his Chinese associates who had told him that his name was on a sealed indictment at the SDNY.

He wanted to know why, and in return he had information that Chinese state-controlled energy company CEFC had paid $100,000 a month to Hunter Biden and $65,000 to his uncle Jim for their FBI connections and use of the Biden name to promote China's Belt and Road Initiative around the world.

He said he believed Joe Biden had attended a meeting with Hunter and CEFC chairman Ye Jianming at a Four Seasons hotel in Washington DC at around the time that Hunter Biden received a multimillion dollar payment from CEFC.

Luft also delivered another bombshell to the SDNY team. He told them they had a mole in their ranks who had tipped off Hunter's CEFC partners that they were under investigation. He said he believed the mole was either a current or former FBI employee who the Chinese called "One Eye" and who was paid a lot of money to leak the contents of four sealed indictments to CEFC executives in 2017. He considered the leak to be a national security concern.

Only days before the Brussels meeting, Luft's friend Patrick Ho had been sentenced to three years in prison for his part of a CEFC scheme to bribe leaders of poor African countries in return for oil and gas permits. The two Assistant US Attorneys who had prosecuted Ho, Daniel Richenthal and Catherine Ghosh, had come to Brussels to meet Luft. They knew as well as anyone in the DOJ about China's use of foreign bribery to win contracts for its Belt and Road Initiative, because it was the basis for their case against Ho.

Luft, an Israeli-American energy expert, was well connected in intelligence circles in Washington DC, where he ran a think tank, the Institute for Analysis of Global Security, with former CIA Director James Woolsey and former national security adviser Robert McFarlane as advisers. From 2015 to 2018, he organized international energy conferences in partnership with Ho's think tank, the nonprofit China Energy Fund Committee (CEFC-USA), a front organization for CEFC.

Luft served in the IDF for 15 years and left active duty as an artillery battalion commander to move to Washington, DC, in the early 2000s to complete a doctorate in international security at Johns Hopkins University. He focused on renewable energy as a way to reduce dependence on Middle Eastern oil producers.

In Brussels, Luft and his two lawyers sat on one side of a long table in the embassy's ground floor conference room, and the six New Yorkers sat on the other side, taking notes with pen and paper. The DOJ had ruled out meeting in Israel, where Luft was living, and had chosen Brussels as neutral territory for the proffer session. Geoffrey Berman, the US attorney for the SDNY, whose agents had arrested Ho the previous year, signed a letter promising Luft temporary immunity from arrest.

"The US Attorney's Office for the SDNY will not arrest or cause to be arrested your client, Gal Luft, during the time that he is in Belgium between approximately Tuesday, March 26, 2019, and Monday, April 1, 2019, in connection with his attendance at meetings with this office on March 28 and 29, 2019," Berman wrote to Luft's attorneys.

Also present in Brussels were two FBI agents from the National Security Branch at FBI headquarters, as well as Thomas McNulty, a veteran FBI Special Agent on the Ho case who recently had retired and was working for the FBI as a contractor, and Josh Wilson, from the FBI's Baltimore field office, who would become one of the lead agents in the Hunter Biden investigation run by US Attorney David Weiss out of Delaware.

Luft told them about the millions of dollars CEFC had paid Hunter and Jim Biden, and that Biden family associate Rob Walker was involved in distributing the payments, a fact later corroborated by bank records subpoenaed by the House Oversight Committee.

For 18 hours, over two days, he told them everything he knew. Occasionally, they would break for a coffee or meal in the embassy's basement cafeteria. The first day "was all about the Bidens and the Chinese," recalled Luft. "The FBI agents looked like out of central casting . . . They seemed to know quite a lot. Knew all the main characters." The next day, there were "all kinds of follow up questions about the Bidens, but then everything changed." The rest of the day was taken up with questions about Luft's relationship with CEFC and allegations that he had been working as an arms dealer. The details would become clearer in the years to come.

The information that Luft delivered in Brussels to the DOJ about the Biden family's influence-peddling scheme was accurate and disturbing, and would be backed up nine months later when the FBI subpoenaed Hunter's laptop from the Mac Shop in Wilmington, Delaware. But his story would be buried for more than three years, until he went public, and two IRS investigators blew the whistle on the cover-up.

Two weeks later, on April 12, 2019, an inebriated Hunter dropped off a laptop for repair at the Mac Shop in Wilmington Delaware and did not come back.

Two weeks after that, on April 25, 2019, Joe Biden would announce his long-shot candidacy for President of the United States.

Luft heard nothing more from the DOJ for four years.

Then, on February 16, 2023, he was arrested in Cyprus as he prepared to board a flight to Tel Aviv, on an Interpol warrant requested by the FBI. The charges were arms trafficking to China and Libya, violations of the Foreign Agents Registration Act—and lying to the FBI. If convicted, he faced up to 96 years in prison.

Luft was jailed in Cyprus pending extradition to the United States but managed to get a message posted on social media, claiming he was innocent of the charges and had been arrested to stop him revealing what he knew about the Biden family and FBI corruption.

"I've been arrested in Cyprus on a politically motivated extradition request by the US," Luft tweeted on Feb. 18. "The US, claiming I'm an arms dealer. It would be funny if it weren't tragic. I've never been an arms dealer.

"DOJ is trying to bury me to protect Joe, Jim, and Hunter Biden. Shall I name names?"

The tweet caught the eye of Republican James Comer, the newly appointed chairman of the House Oversight Committee, who was leading the investigation into Biden family influence peddling. He resolved to interview Luft, in jail if need be. Two weeks after Luft's arrest Comer described him as a "missing witness" and "the straw that broke the camel's back."

"We've had three people that were involved in the Hunter Biden shady business schemes that have communicated with my committee staff," he told Fox News. "I think that people see the heavy-handedness of the Bidens. Either you're getting picked up by the DOJ or you're getting a letter from Hunter Biden's personal attorney trying to intimidate you."

Congressional investigators had begun speaking with Luft in Cyprus. His lawyer, Robert Henoch, a former Assistant US Attorney in the Eastern District of New York, told reporters: "Dr. Luft gave information about corruption at the highest levels of the US government in 2019. Nothing happened. Instead, four years later, the government issued a warrant for Dr. Luft's arrest. It is clear Dr. Luft is being punished for the information that he gave to the DOJ as opposed to the DOJ investigating the information Dr. Luft provided. Dr. Luft is a whistleblower, and he is being punished for it."

But Luft disappeared before Comer could call on him as a witness. After weeks in jail, he had been released on bail while he tried to fight extradition and then, one day, he failed to report to Cyprus police.

His car was found abandoned in a village near Larnaca International Airport on March 29, 2023. Police said he may have fled the country, and his Greek Cypriot lawyer filed a missing person's report, expressing concerns for Luft's life.

Weeks later, via an intermediary, I made contact with Luft in an undisclosed location through an encrypted messaging service. He would not say how he escaped Cyprus because "I don't want to get people in trouble." But he said he had been forced to skip bail and become a fugitive "because I did not believe I will receive a fair trial in a New York court."

The DOJ had not communicated Luft's arrest warrant to Israel, with whom it has an extradition treaty, leading Luft to claim that they waited until he left Israel to arrest him and had chosen Cyprus because it was a small country they could "push around."

He claimed that after his arrest, US Ambassador to Cyprus Julie Fischer met twice with Cyprus's defense minister, foreign minister, and president in order to pressure the Cypriot government not to release him on bail.

He also saw sinister intent in the date of the extradition order, November 1, 2022, seven days before the midterm elections when the Republicans were expected to win control of the House and start investigating allegations of Biden family foreign influence peddling.

"When it was clear the Republicans are going to win the House or the Senate, all of a sudden comes Comer and [House Judiciary Committee Chairman Jim] Jordan and the game is changing. There will be questions and subpoenas and investigations [so] they [the Biden administration] have to discredit me. I never thought of coming forward. Through 2020 I sat quiet like a fish . . .

"I didn't want to get caught up in this game, but when they arrested me, I had no choice but to blow it up."

Richenthal and Ghosh, the two assistant US attorneys who interviewed him in Brussels, had signed his Cyprus extradition order.

Luft was facing serious charges, so why did it take four years? And why had Ho never been questioned about an alleged FBI mole who leaked a sealed SDNY indictment in the almost three years he was jailed next door to the SDNY offices?

On July 6, 2023, Luft released a video to the *New York Post* laying out his allegations against the president's family and the FBI mole who shared classified information with CEFC.

"I, who volunteered to inform the US government about a potential security breach and about compromising information about a man vying to be the next president, am now being hunted by the very same people who I informed—and may have to live on the run for the rest of my life . . .

"I'm not a Republican. I'm not a Democrat. I have no political motive or agenda . . . I did it out of deep concern that if the Bidens were to come to power, the country would be facing the same traumatic Russia collusion scandal—only this time with China. Sadly, because of the DOJ's cover-up, this is exactly what happened . . .

"I warned the government about potential risk to the integrity of the 2020 elections . . . Ask yourself, who is the real criminal in this story? . . .

"Why did the government dispatch to Europe so many people? . . .

"They knew very well I'm a credible witness and I have insider knowledge about the group and individuals that enriched the Biden family.

"Over an intensive two-day meeting, I shared my information about the Biden family's financial transactions with CEFC, including specific dollar figures. I also provided the name of Rob Walker, who later became known as Hunter Biden's bagman."

Four days after his video, the SDNY unsealed its indictment.

"Gal Luft, a Dual U.S.-Israeli Citizen, Allegedly Evaded FARA Registration While Working to Advance the Interests of China in the United States and Sought to Broker the Illicit Sales of Chinese-Manufactured Weapons and Iranian Oil to China," announced Damian Williams, who had replaced Berman as US Attorney; Matthew Olsen, Assistant Attorney General for National Security; and Christie Curtis, Acting Assistant Director of the FBI's New York Field Office, McGonigal's old patch.

The gun-running allegations in the indictment mirrored those made belatedly against Ho in his trial, but for which he was not charged. Luft described the charges as "a thought crime . . . I was asked by a bona fide arms dealer, an Israeli friend, to inquire with a company I knew if they had an item and what would be the price of an item. This is where the conspiracy ended. No follow-up, no money, no brokering activity . . . Ask yourself why would the US government spend so much resources going after someone who never traded a bullet?"

Luft also denied the charge that he attempted to broker deals for Iranian oil in violation of US sanctions.

"What they don't want to tell you is that at the time I was leading CEFC's effort to buy a controlling stake in Paz Oil, Israel's top energy company," and Israel had told CEFC that the sale would be blocked if they had dealings with Iran. Luft claimed that Ye was being pressured "to explore business in Iran which would have killed my deal [so] I had to make all types of maneuvers to derail competing agendas. It was absolutely against my interest that they deal with Iran."

In any case, he said that his patrons in Israel understood the situation and continued to support him.

He also scoffed at FARA charges against him for acting as an unregistered foreign agent of CEFC because his relationship was not with a foreign entity but with the think tank arm of CEFC, a 501c3 charitable organization registered by the IRS in Virginia.

"The DOJ says I caused a payment of $6,000 a month to former CIA Director James Woolsey in order to put his name on an article I had ghost-written for the China Daily newspaper . . . Woolsey had been an adviser to my think tank since 2002 and nothing in the article represented Chinese interests . . .

"Why am I being indicted . . . for ghostwriting an innocuous article for which I received no payment, let alone from a foreign government, when the mother of all FARA cases, the Bidens' systemic influence-peddling on behalf of foreign governments, for which they raked [in] millions, goes unpunished?"

Whatever the merits of the indictment, the effect was to discredit Luft as a potential witness for the Oversight Committee investigation into Biden corruption and for the upcoming impeachment inquiry of Joe Biden.

However, Luft's credibility would receive a boost after IRS investigators working on the Hunter probe finally decided to blow the whistle on the extraordinary misconduct in June 2023.

In fact, the SDNY had not sat on Luft's allegations in Brussels. They had provided the portion of his interview that related to the Bidens to US Attorney Weiss, who was conducting the Hunter Biden investigation in Delaware. But obstruction of Weiss' investigators by prosecutors and the DOJ would ensure that no leads that might incriminate Joe Biden would be followed, and slow-walking and other hanky panky nearly let Hunter off the hook.

Luft's account of his disclosures to the FBI was corroborated by IRS whistleblower Joe Ziegler in August 2023 when he provided the House Ways and Means Committee with a redacted copy of the FBI report, called an FD-302, of Luft's Brussels interview.

"The interview of Gal Luft took place prior to the IRS and FBI investigations combining in the District of Delaware," Ziegler testified.

"I have been able to corroborate information provided in this interview to include the meeting between [Hunter] and the Chairman [Ye] in Miami and the reference to $10 million, the amounts of the wires from CEFC China Energy paid to [Hunter] . . . and the amounts of the monthly payments [Hunter] and [Jim] Biden would receive from CEFC China, through Hudson West III."

Luft's fugitive status had ruled him out as witness, anyway, but he would not have been the first witness in the Biden investigation who was a convicted felon, in jail or under indictment. As Chairman Comer said when he was criticized for seeking to interview shady characters: "That's a reflection about Biden, not our inquiry."

When Luft was branded a "Chinese spy" by Democrats and allied media because of his association with CEFC, Comer had a devastating comeback: "All I know is that he was getting money from the same company the Bidens were getting money from . . . Is the president's son a Chinese spy? They took money from the same company."

Rep. Dan Goldman (D-NY) interjected: "Who cares if they had money from the same company?"

His comment was an apt summation of the double standards that operated around the Bidens.

CHAPTER 9

LAPTOP FROM HELL

April 12, 2019
WILMINGTON, DELAWARE

The door of John Paul Mac Isaac's computer repair store swung open just before closing time on a wet Friday evening, and Hunter Biden walked in, wobbly on his feet, stinking of booze and cigar smoke.

"I'm glad you're still open," Mac Isaac recalls Hunter telling him. "I just came from the cigar bar, and they told me about your shop, but I had to hurry because you close at seven."

The FBI later would use financial records to show that Hunter was at the Sikar Cigar lounge on Delaware Ave, that night, April 12, 2019, just a two-minute stagger from the Mac Shop in the nondescript Trolley Square strip mall in Wilmington.

IRS supervisor Gary Shapley cited "other intelligence" which showed Hunter was "in the vicinity of" Mac Isaac's store at the time.

The FBI also accessed phone records which showed calls back and forth between Hunter and the store over the next few days.

The information on the laptop was "largely duplicative" of data investigators already had obtained in a search warrant from Apple for Hunter's iCloud account, said the DOJ.

Hunter's distinctive loopy signature was on the work order at the computer repair shop, and matched the signature on his driver's license and other official documents. His phone number and email address were on the order.

His lawyer even phoned The Mac Shop 18 months later, asking about the laptop Hunter had left there.

Yet Hunter, assisted by his team of 18 lawyers, would continue to insist for years, even under oath, that he didn't know if the laptop was his, and could not recall if he had ever been to Mac Isaac's store, while his various court filings offered contradictory versions of the tale.

"There could be a laptop out there that was stolen from me. It could be that I was hacked. It could be that it was Russian intelligence," Biden told CBS in 2021.

Asked during his deposition for the impeachment inquiry in February 2024, Hunter claimed he couldn't remember dropping his laptop off at the repair shop.

Q: "Did you have a laptop in 2019?"

Hunter: "I've had many laptops . . ."

Q: "Did you ever drop a laptop off at a repair shop?"

Hunter: "I dropped a laptop off at the Apple repair shop that was literally three blocks from my office in Washington, DC. If I was ever going to repair one, I would have walked up the street and dropped it there."

Q: "Did you ever drop off a laptop in Delaware?"

Hunter: "The Apple store in Georgetown."

Q: "Yeah. My question is about Delaware. Did you ever drop off a laptop in Delaware?"

Hunter: "The largest Apple store in America is . . . at the Christiana Mall [in Newark, Delaware]. If I was going to drop off a laptop, I don't ever remember doing that, but if I was going to drop off a laptop, I would have gone to the Apple store, which was seven minutes from my parents' home there."

Q: "Do you recall ever leaving a laptop at a repair shop?"

Hunter: "I do not."

Mac Isaac, on the other hand, was certain it was Hunter who visited the Mac Shop that night. "I am 100 percent sure that the person in those photos, videos and other data I was hired to recover is the same person that came into my shop and dropped off that machine." He noted Hunter had a "surprisingly high-pitched voice [and] an air of entitlement."

Mac Isaac, 44, is legally blind, a fact that would later be used to try to discredit his story. He has the pale skin, white-blonde hair, and vision-impairment typical of albinism.

He had loved Apple products since he was 12 years old and saw his first Macintosh. At 28, he was "lead genius" at the Apple store in Christiana Mall.

Opening his own Mac repair business was a dream come true. He had built up The Mac Shop over nine years, decking out his little store with an eight-foot palm tree and framed posters of old Apple advertisements. Customers could park right out front. He was good at his job, and patient with the technologically challenged. All his Google reviews were five-star.

But his life was about to be torn apart.

He has told his story repeatedly in the years since, in interviews with me, in YouTube videos, in courtroom depositions, and in his 2022 book, *American Injustice: My Battle to Expose the Truth*. The facts have never changed.

Hunter dumped three liquid-damaged MacBooks on his counter to get fixed that night. One of the MacBooks was beyond repair. Another had a fried keyboard, so Mac Isaac lent Hunter a spare keyboard to take home.

But first he had to ask for the password to log on. It was "analfuck69."

Hunter laughed when he told him: "Don't be offended!" Mac Isaac didn't find it funny, just puerile, and gross, like so much else he would discover about his new client.

The third laptop, a thirteen-inch 2016 MacBook Pro, had power problems and kept shutting down. It would take at least 24 hours for Mac Isaac to recover the data.

He made out a work order, number 7469, which Hunter signed in front of him before leaving the store.

After closing up for the night, Mac Isaac pulled the damaged laptop apart and managed to power it up to begin data recovery. He decided to "clone" the laptop onto his store server, which means uploading an exact replica of all the data. He set the process to run overnight and went home.

The next day, he found the laptop had lost power in the middle of the data transfer, forcing him to manually drag files across, an all-weekend process in between serving customers. He had to keep a close watch, as the laptop kept powering down. The desktop was a haphazard mess of hundreds of disorganized files and photos, including Hunter's homemade pornography.

He saw Hunter posing in a tight jock strap with a red scarf around his neck, smoking crack, and starring in assorted sex videos.

There were endless selfies of Hunter's erect penis, photos of naked hookers and chaotic hotel rooms strewn with bottles of booze and drug paraphernalia.

"Gross," thought Mac Isaac, hoping he could keep a straight face when Hunter returned.

At one point Mac Isaac noticed a document titled "income.pdf" listing dollar amounts for the years 2013 ($833,000), 2014 ($1,247,000), and 2015 ($2,478,000) and the name "Burisma." Underneath was a note from Hunter's partner Eric Schwerin: "Since you couldn't have lived on $550,000 a year, you 'borrowed' some money from RSB [one of his shared firms] in advance of payments."

It was a glimpse into Hunter's life of excess, but it was none of his business, so he moved on.

On Monday, he called Hunter and asked him to bring in an external drive so that Mac Isaac could transfer his data off the store server. On Tuesday evening, Hunter returned with the hard drive in a Best Buy bag and Mac Isaac told him he would call when it was ready.

But Hunter never set foot in the store again. Two weeks later his father announced he was running for president.

Mac Isaac says he called Hunter three or four times over the next couple of months and sent repeated email reminders to pay his $85 bill and return the borrowed keyboard. But there never was a response.

After ninety days, as per the fine print on the work order signed by Hunter, the laptop and its contents were deemed "abandoned" and became Mac Isaac's legal property.

Three years and eight months after the *New York Post* first broke the news of its existence, Hunter's laptop was brought into evidence on the second day of his gun felony trial in Delaware.

At 2:10 p.m., Tuesday, June 4, 2024, in courtroom 4A of the Wilmington District Court, prosecutor Derek Hines held aloft the silver MacBook Pro13, covered in a clear plastic wrapper, and carried it across the courtroom, past the jury and showed it to his first witness, FBI Special Agent Erika Jensen. She confirmed it was Hunter's laptop from the serial number on the back.

Sitting at the bar table, Hunter was inscrutable behind salmon pink reading glasses as the laptop that would sink him in court coasted serenely past him.

Jensen said that the FBI obtained the laptop in December 2019 with a subpoena from The Mac Shop in Wilmington where it had been "abandoned" by Hunter.

She said investigators then corroborated content on the laptop with content from Hunter's iCloud that they had obtained with a covert search warrant from Apple Inc. on April 16, 2019, coincidentally just four days after Hunter abandoned his laptop at Mac Isaac's repair store.

* * *

At the time he entered the Mac Shop, Hunter's life was at rock bottom. His crack addiction was out of control, and he'd been bouncing between cheap motels filming himself having threesomes with hookers.

He was in a rage with his family. His relationship with his widowed sister-in-law, Hallie, had grown toxic. He accused her of cheating, and she had banned him from seeing her children until he sought rehab. He accused his father of siding with her and was on the outs even with Uncle Jim.

A few weeks earlier he had ranted at his father about a Maureen Dowd piece in the *New York Times*, headlined "Uncle Joe's Family Ties," which claimed "the troubled Hunter" was Joe's biggest impediment to running for president.

"Maureen Dowd points to me as the reason you'll most likely lose it?" he texted Joe on February 24, 2019.

Then he accused Joe's staff of throwing him under the bus. "Don't you not see what just happened? Your team just made me the uncontrollable troubled tax cheat philanderer sex and drug addict that you tried so hard to fix but couldn't. They just totally wrote my life away.

"And if you try and say otherwise, I'll have a hard time understanding how you rationalize this shit . . . Well, dad, the truth is, as you and Hallie point out, I am a fucked-up addict that can't be trusted relied upon, nor defended."

He raged at Hallie, too: "You seem to have made it out of this relationship clean. The Maureen Dowds of the world and Vanity Fair and all the gossip that you allow about me to be repeated over and over . . . I cannot forgive you for saying that you didn't know what other bullshit business deals and other shit that [I was doing] . . . I've never done a dishonest business transaction in my life. I'm the most ethical man you will ever know. You say 'shady business deals'?"

Hallie: "Ok then there won't be any articles like that."

Hunter: "Yes that's how it works Hallie. If it's not true they won't write it. You stupid fucking cunt. Everything they've written about me is true. Otherwise, they would never have written it. Hmmmm."

Hallie: "Stop."

Hunter: "So you believe I've had children burned alive in Donetsk."

Hallie: "Your text not making sense."

Hunter: "Or that I had people murdered in Beijing."

Hallie: "I don't know what u are talking about."

Hunter: "They write about it all the time . . . about how I run a criminal empire."

Hallie: "Just stay sober."

Hunter: "That I'm worth billions of dollars. That I fund the entire democratic elite machine . . . That I'm the head of the largest criminal enterprise in the world, that I'm a traitor."

Hallie: "Just focus on staying sober."

Hunter: "You think that I need to apologize to them for the damage I've done through my 'shady' business deals? Thank you again for the support. On this day that Maureen Dowd just fucking skewered me and made me the person that he wins or loses."

Hallie: "You have things all wrong still."

Hunter: "Fuck you fuck you forever fuck you."

(These texts are from a backup of his phone on the laptop Hunter has disavowed.)

In October 2018, Hunter had left Los Angeles, where he had been living for six months, gone home to Delaware and bought a gun.

On the Firearms Transaction Record he signed, he responded "No" to a question that asked, "Are you an unlawful user of, or addicted to, marijuana or any depressant, stimulant, narcotic drug, or any other controlled substance?"

A photo of him asleep with a glass "crack pipe" in his mouth was taken in Malibu just eight days earlier. He admitted in his memoir to being a crack addict during this period.

Lying on that federal background check form is illegal, and in June 2024, after a failed sweetheart plea deal, Hunter stood trial in his hometown of Wilmington and was convicted by a jury of three felony gun charges.

Testifying for the prosecution were his ex-wife Kathleen, and ex-lovers Hallie and Zoe Kestan, a young stripper he cavorted with in New York and LA throughout 2018.

Hallie found the gun in Hunter's pickup less than two weeks after he bought it and threw it in an open trash can outside Janssen's gourmet grocery market in their local Greenville Center shopping mall, across the road from a high school. The gun was discovered by an elderly Navy veteran, Ed Banner, who was searching the trash for recyclables to sell. Police later recovered it from his home after identifying him from a surveillance video. No charges were laid against the star-crossed couple at the time, and it didn't make the news, but the incident was another example of an invisible hand protecting Hunter.

The Delaware State Police were first on the scene. When they interviewed Hunter outside Janssen's he told them he used the gun for "target practice." Asked if he had called his father yet, Hunter replied, "I have never called my dad for anything." The FBI and Secret Service also showed up, even though Joe and Hunter were not under Secret Service protection at the time.

Two men claiming to be Secret Service agents went to StarQuest Shooters in Wilmington, where Hunter had bought the gun, flashed their badges and identification cards to Ron Palmieri, the store's owner, and asked to take possession of Hunter's Firearms Transaction Record, according to *Politico*.

Palmieri refused to hand over the document and the Secret Service would later deny any involvement.

The gun incident would haunt Hunter in years to come, when he thought it had been safely forgotten. It also deepened the fractures in his relationship with Hallie.

"The fucking FBI Hallie," he texted her on October 23, 2018. "It's hard to believe anyone is that stupid // so what's my fault here Hallie that you speak of. Owning a gun that's in a locked car hidden on another property? I'm proven unstable when you put a gun in the trash can at Jansens [*sic*] out of FEAR."

Hallie replied: "I'm sorry, I just want you safe. That was not safe, And it was open unlocked and windows down and the kids search your car."

Two weeks later, Hunter texted Hallie a photo of what looked like a big rock of crack cocaine on the lid of an orange Hermès box, with a broken crack pipe and assorted paraphernalia inside the box.

"From beneath your mattress and behind picture of me, momom [his late grandmother] and beau," Hunter wrote, in text messages extracted by the conservative Marco Polo group from an encrypted iPhone XS backup on his laptop.

"Should I put them back and bring Natalie to see first hallie. You're cruel but you're also insanely myopic.

"Don't tell me I put this between your mattress and [put] this on the shelf.

"I will ruin you if you do."

Hallie accused him of planting the drugs: "Are you trying to set me up? Fuck you, I'm sober. Get the fuck out of my house forever hunter."

Almost six years later, Hallie would testify in the Wilmington District Court as a witness for the prosecution in Hunter's felony gun trial.

Her appearance in courtroom 4A on June 6, 2024, the fourth day of the trial, represented a very Delawarean tragedy. The daughter of a local dry-cleaner who married the Biden prince, Hallie had been destined to become the first lady of Delaware, maybe first lady of the United States.

But Joseph Robinette "Beau" Biden III died in 2015 of brain cancer, aged 46, leaving Hallie bereft and dashing Joe Biden's dream that his first-born golden child's political career as Delaware attorney general would soar to the heights that he, himself, would reach five years later.

Instead, Hallie, 50, was in the witness box, having to tell strangers about the torrid affair and crack use she shared with her late husband's black-sheep brother in the ensuing three years.

"It was a terrible experience I went through, and I'm embarrassed and I'm ashamed," the president's widowed daughter-in-law told the jury.

"I regret that time of my life."

She testified that Hunter had "introduced" her to crack cocaine in late 2015 or early 2016, soon after they began a "romantic relationship," as prosecutor Leo Wise delicately put it.

She had been clean for two months on Oct. 23, 2018, when he turned up at her house in Wilmington early in the morning looking disheveled.

"He was tired, exhausted, looked like he hadn't slept," she told the jury. Suspecting him of using drugs, she searched his unlocked truck and found "some remnants of crack cocaine and [drug] paraphernalia."

When she also found the handgun and a box of hollow-point bullets in the center console of the truck she "panicked." She told the jury that she drove to the family's neighborhood gourmet grocery store, Janssen's Market, and threw the gun in an outdoor open trash can. A short time after she drove away, the gun was scooped up by a man scavenging for recyclables, and went missing for six days, triggering a police operation to retrieve it.

Prosecutors showed Hallie a series of damning text messages from Hunter's laptop that were crucial to their case that Hunter lied on a federal background form when he stated that he was not a drug addict when he bought the gun.

"Why won't you answer my calls," she texted him on October 13, 2018, the day after the gun purchase.

He replied that he was behind a baseball stadium in Wilmington "waiting on a dealer named Mookie."

The next day, she texted him to say she had tried calling him "500 times in the past 24 hours." He responded: "I was sleeping on a car smoking crack on 4th Street and Rodney."

Like her one-time nemesis Kathleen Buhle, Hunter's ex-wife who had testified in similarly pinched fashion the previous day, Hallie cut a sympathetic figure with the jury. Both women testified to Hunter's extreme drug abuse and their valiant but ultimately doomed efforts to get him sober.

Kathleen, who reverted to her maiden name after their 2017 divorce, told the jury in world-weary tones that she first realized her husband was using crack cocaine when "I found a crack pipe in an ashtray on the side porch of our home" in Washington, DC, on July 3, 2015.

She tried to help Hunter get sober but realized their 22-year marriage was over when she discovered "the adultery" with her sister-in-law Hallie, with whom she had always had a frosty relationship.

A working-class Catholic girl from Chicago when she met Hunter fresh out of school, Kathleen wrote in her memoir that she was blown away by the grandeur of the Du Pont mansion where Hunter grew up.

"A kid from a middle-class family does not have a ballroom," she once told him. His family always made her feel unworthy to be a Biden. Joe made sure everyone knew that Hunter had once dated a Du Pont heir.

Kathleen took to searching his car before their daughters drove it and testified to regularly finding crack fragments and drug paraphernalia.

For Hallie, at least, there was a happy ending. The weekend before the trial she married wealthy Ohio financial broker John Hopkins Anning II and had a large diamond on her ring finger to prove it.

She broke into smiles when she spotted Anning in the courtroom, sitting on the opposite side from the Bidens.

Hunter stared at Hallie through her testimony with a neutral expression, but his attorney Lowell slammed her in closing arguments.

"Hallie did something incredibly stupid," Lowell said. "She may have done it for love," or perhaps out of jealousy because she suspected Hunter had been with another woman.

Hallie's suspicions were correct, as former stripper Zoe Kestan told the jury when she testified to her chaotic year of living on and off with Hunter.

A graduate of the Rhode Island School of Design, the busty brunette was 24 and Hunter 48 when he asked her for a "private dance" at the "gentleman's club" in Manhattan where she worked in December 2017.

He lit up a crack pipe within minutes, she testified. She found him "charming," gave him her number, and spent most of 2018 bouncing around luxury hotel rooms with him in New York and LA, including five weeks in a bungalow at the Chateau Marmont where he taught himself to cook crack from powdered cocaine.

She testified that he was smoking crack "every 20 minutes" in the fall of 2018, including a month before he bought the gun.

He gave her thousands of dollars in cash and in return she was content to be at his beck and call whenever he texted to say he was lonely. But he lied continually and let her down when he grew tired of her, promising that he would join her for her birthday before ghosting her, she said.

Photographs from her cellphone were shown to the jury which charted Hunter's chaotic crack-fueled years, the luxury hotel rooms he turned into pigsties, with clothes and detritus on the floor and bottles of booze and crack paraphernalia strewn over every surface.

Lowell had chosen the jury carefully to be sympathetic to Hunter's drug addiction. Of the final 12, seven had a family member or close friend suffering from addiction to drugs or alcohol.

But it was hard to tell what these 12 ordinary Delawareans—a bartender, a construction worker, an aspiring lab technician, a retiree—made of Hunter's lifestyle, his $3.4 million bank balance flashing up on the courtroom video screen, his $50,000 a month in ATM withdrawals, his frenetic crack purchases, the plush hotels, the expensive rehab, the yoga retreats, the glittering résumé studded with privilege—Archmere Academy, Georgetown, Yale, MBNA (but not a mention of Burisma).

Hunter had hit rock bottom a few times, but there was always a soft landing. His privilege was on display throughout the trial, with the First Lady center stage in the public gallery, wearing vivid power suits, and flanked by Secret Service agents. Hunter's wife, Melissa, sat alongside her, also dressed to the nines, as was the president's sister, Val Owens, and daughter Ashley Biden who sat together in the front row with Kevin Morris. Joe's old Delaware cronies sat behind them with the First Lady's powerful senior adviser, Anthony Bernal, known as her "work husband."

Some days there were 25 Biden family members and hangers-on crammed into the first three or four rows of the public gallery. The appearance in the third row of a local Black pastor, Baptist Reverend Christopher Bullock, and half a dozen Black men and women appeared designed to impress the majority Black jury. On the morning of the third day of the trial, when Black gun store employee Gordon Cleveland was scheduled to appear for the prosecution, Bullock and friends stood in the center of the public gallery in full view of the seated media, put their heads together and huddled in prayer for Hunter before the jury was brought in.

Bullock, who describes himself as the Catholic Biden family's "spiritual advisor," told reporters, "Biden family is Delaware . . . There is a lot of support here for them."

But Cleveland, the sales assistant at StarQuest Shooters in Wilmington who sold Hunter the Colt Cobra .38 Special in October 2018, was a devastating witness, testifying in a straightforward fashion that he watched Hunter fill out the gun form, check the box saying he was not a drug addict and sign it.

A father-of-three with diabetes who drives a trash truck for the city, Cleveland had a second job at the gun shop to make ends meet when the fresh prince of Delaware strolled in late one Friday evening.

Hunter told Cleveland to keep the $13.19 change from the $900 cash he paid for his purchases.

But the salesman was so honest he thought it would be wrong to keep the money so he put it in an envelope and left it by the cash register.

"I don't keep tips," he told the Wilmington jury. "It's not what you do in sales."

Lowell tried to portray Cleveland as a pushy salesman who coerced Hunter into buying the gun, along with ammunition, a speed loader, a BB gun, and a utility tool gadget. His colleagues dubbed him "the whale-hunter" for his impressive sales.

But Cleveland told the jury that he received the same salary whether he sold anything or not. He was just good at his job and loved guns. Hunter kept grabbing accessories off the shelves to add to his haul with no input from Cleveland before driving off in his father's Cadillac.

Cleveland's boss, Ron Palimere, the owner of StarQuest Shooters, had told the FBI that he and his employees were "all scared to death" when Hunter's gun purchase blew up into a "big scandal" after the revolver went missing. Palimere "felt they were going to get in trouble just for going up against Biden."

Only one member of Hunter's family testified in his defense, Naomi, 30, a Washington DC lawyer. She did her best to paint a rosy picture of her father's sobriety when she visited him in LA in August 2018, after one of his many stints in drug rehab. "He seemed like the clearest that I had seen him since my uncle died, and he just seemed really great."

But the prosecution undercut her testimony in cross-examination, showing her text messages from Hunter's laptop from October 2018, when she visited him in New York a few days before he bought the gun and found him incommunicado and erratic, indicating that he was using drugs at the time.

Naomi and her boyfriend (now husband) Peter Neal had borrowed Hunter's truck to move house and were in New York to swap it back for Joe's luxury black Cadillac CTS.

But Hunter was unreachable for most of the three days she tried to meet him.

"I'm really sad, dad," she wrote after he failed to show up at a planned rendezvous. When Hunter finally responded on October 18, 2018, he bizarrely asked her to deliver the truck to his hotel at 2 a.m.

"I'm sorry daddy, I can't take this, I don't know what to say," Naomi wrote, adding a sad-face emoji.

"I just miss you and want to hang out with you."

At the time, Hunter was buying crack and partying with Kestan, according to earlier testimony.

Jurors interviewed after the verdict said Naomi's testimony backfired on the defense.

"I think that was a bad mistake for them to put her on the stand," one 68-year-old white male juror told reporters.

"I don't think any daughter should have to be up there testifying on her father's behalf . . . That was heart-wrenching and I think all the jurors felt the same thing."

"It just seemed so sad for her to see her father in such a state," said another juror, a 51-year-old Black woman.

In the end, the jury did not believe Lowell's claim that Hunter was not using drugs at the time he bought the gun. Text messages from Hunter's laptop suggested he bought drugs the night before the gun purchase. The October 11, 2018, messages were produced by the prosecution for a brief rebuttal appearance by FBI agent Erika Jensen on the last day of the trial and showed Hunter arranging to meet up with a since-convicted drug dealer at a Delaware 7/11 store. An email on his laptop showed he withdrew $800 at 6:30 p.m. from an ATM nearby.

"The day before he bought the gun, he was at 7-Eleven," said the male juror. "What was he doing there? The defense wanted us to believe he was just there to buy a cup of coffee, but I didn't buy that. He wasn't there to buy a cup of coffee . . .

"We all knew Hunter Biden was a drug addict, and he was addicted, and he was making [drug] deals like 12 days prior to buying the gun, so in his mind, how could he write 'No,' he was not an addict?"

The female juror felt much the same, pointing to Hunter's text messages with Hallie. "He was trying to get drugs," she said. "He looks kind of helpless to me. I think he just needs to get away somewhere and get some real rehab, if he hasn't. Hopefully he's still not using."

* * *

In the six months after Hallie threw his gun in the trash, Hunter's life continued to spiral downwards.

He borrowed $75,000 from his father which he claimed he needed for rehab and alimony. His accountant was hassling him about overdue tax returns. Kathleen was hassling him about a tax lien on her house. He told his shrink that Hallie had accused him of being "a bad influence [on the kids] that I endanger their health that I've been sexually inappropriate [and] I would be 'walking around naked watching porn masturbating and doing drugs in front of [a child].'"

When he went home to his parents' place in late 2018 he told his stepmother Jill Biden she was "a fucking moron. A vindictive moron," according to texts he sent his uncle Jim describing an argument over his drug use.

Hunter claimed he told Jill: "I suooorted [supported] my . . . family including some of the costs you should have used your salary to lay [pay] for—for the last 24 years. And you do know the drunkest I've ever been is still smarter than you could ever even comprehend and you're a shut [shit] grammar teacher that wouldn't survive one class in a [sic] ivy graduate program.

"So go fuck yourself Jill let's all agree I don't like you any more than you like me."

He also complained to his uncle that he had been to drug rehab seven times, but his father "litteraly [*sic*] has never come to one never actually called me while in rehab."

Hunter also was fighting with his business partner Eric Schwerin. His former "best friend in business" Devon Archer was being prosecuted for fraud. His Chinese associate Patrick Ho had been convicted of bribing African officials to help Iran evade oil sanctions. The *New York Times* was calling his lawyer for comment on a story they were writing about his involvement with Ho's controller, CEFC Chairman Ye. His family tried to stage an intervention when he went home for Christmas. And his father was about to run for president.

It was a lot of stress.

"I get calls from my father to tell me the *New York Times* is calling," he told a stripper friend in a recording found on his laptop.

"I have another *New York Times* reporter calling about my representation of Patrick Ho."

When the *Times* story was published online on December 12, 2018, the Bidens were in the headline: "Chinese Tycoon Sought Power and Influence . . . Ye Jianming courted the Biden family and networked with former US security officials. Today, his empire is crashing down in court." But Hunter's involvement boiled down to an astonishing nothing in the piece: "It is unclear whether Hunter Biden struck any business deals with CEFC or Mr. Ye."

That was a relief.

"You did an incredible job of keeping this basically to a big fat nothing," Hunter told his lawyer George Mesires in a text message.

"At the end of the day, I think people jadedly say 'this is how the world works,'" Mesires replied.

Joe called Hunter as soon as the story went online: "Hey pal, it's Dad. It's 8:15 on Wednesday night," Joe is heard saying in a voicemail stored in the iPhone XS backup.

"If you get a chance, give me a call. Nothing urgent. I just wanted to talk to you. I thought the article released online, it's going to be printed tomorrow in the *Times*, was good.

"I think you're clear."

It was a far cry from Joe's frequent campaign refrain: "I have never spoken to my son about his overseas business dealings."

By February 2019, Hunter's resentment was boiling over. In a text to his daughter Naomi, he railed against news articles that attributed Joe's delay in announcing his campaign to his concern about the toll on his family of running against Trump.

"I told Pop [Joe] the first time he said it to never say it again—'I'm worried about how it will impact the family' . . . There is literally not a single brain cell he has used considering what the impact would be on me or you or anyone. His factoring in the family had been simply to gauge whether any of us have screwed up so bad it would diminish his chances . . . how the Skeleton's [*sic*] of his family may make it hard for him to put us thorough the ringer in his pursuit of the office . . .

"How he can't see how angry and frustrated it makes you guys to have the world think Pop may be prohibitively barred from the presidency because your Dad is such a fuck up . . . We obviously can't imply that he is using the family excuse To buy time because that would make him look pretty Machiavellian. Ruthless even."

In this frame of mind about his father's ruthless ambition, Hunter bought an audiobook copy of Joe's new memoir *Promise Me, Dad*, which had a photo of his brother, Beau, on the cover, hugging Joe.

The book's premise is that it was a last wish of Beau, who Joe lauds as "Joe Biden 2.0," that his father run for president.

"Beau believed, as I did, that I was prepared to take on the presidency," Joe writes. "That there was nobody better prepared."

As Adam Entous had noted in his July 2019 *New Yorker* interview with Hunter, Joe rarely talked about Hunter in public and his memoir "largely glosses over" his second son.

Hunter appears in the book mainly as an addendum to the brother he adored and felt inferior to all his life. But there are a couple of passages in which Hunter briefly takes center stage, if only to tell his father that he must run for president because Beau is dying and won't get a chance to run himself.

"It has to be you, Dad," Hunter is quoted saying.

Five weeks after he bought the audiobook, Hunter abandoned his laptop, lighting the fuse that eventually would threaten Joe Biden's campaign, damage his carefully cultivated reputation as an honest politician, and expose a deep state coverup worse than Watergate.

* * *

Over the summer of 2019, Mac Isaac began to notice news reports about Hunter's Ukrainian connections. In July, President Trump asked Ukraine's President Zelenskyy to investigate Hunter and Joe's involvement with Burisma, a phone call which would trigger his first impeachment.

The name "Burisma" rang a bell. Mac Isaac did a word search and began to read the emails and documents that popped up.

What he found frightened him. Hunter and Archer had taken in millions of dollars from the corrupt Ukrainian energy company, and there were similar entanglements in China, Kazakhstan, Romania and elsewhere.

The more Mac Isaac looked at the laptop, the more convinced he was that there were national security implications.

He enlisted the help of his father, retired Air Force Col. Steve Mac Isaac, sending him a copy of the laptop that he had transferred onto an external hard drive about the size of a cigarette packet with instructions to get it to the FBI. On October 9, 2019, Steve took the hard drive, along with a copy of the work order with Hunter's signature, to the FBI's field office in his hometown of Albuquerque, New Mexico. He was treated with disdain, according to Mac Isaac.

"You better lawyer up and don't talk to anyone about this," an FBI agent told Steve. But the agent at least made a copy of the work order.

Three weeks later, Steve received a call from FBI Agent Josh Wilson, of the Baltimore Field Office, expressing interest in the laptop. Wilson was the case agent on the Hunter Biden investigation, codenamed "Sportsman," run out of the US Attorney's office in Delaware, where a slightly garbled message had filtered through from Albuquerque.

IRS supervisory agent Gary Shapley recorded the information in a memo: "Richard Steven McKissack [*sic*] reported to the FBI office in Albequerque [*sic*] 'his son is in possession of a [Hunter Biden] computer that had not been retrieved and was not paid for . . . said it contains evidence of white collar crime . . . he did not view this data personally.'"

Wilson then phoned Mac Isaac and asked for the device number of the laptop and quickly verified its authenticity "by matching the device number against Hunter Biden's Apple iCloud ID," Shapley would tell Congress.

On December 9, 2019, Agents Wilson and Mike Dzielak arrived at Mac Isaac's store with a subpoena and took away the laptop and hard-drive, along with the original work order.

A few days later, IRS case agent Joe Ziegler signed a search warrant to access the content of the laptop.

Over the next few weeks, FBI forensic computer experts assessed that the laptop "was not manipulated in any way" and could be used as evidence in court, according to Shapley. They also had been able to determine precisely when each file was created, to verify that Mac Isaac had not tampered with the contents. (While federal prosecutors have now used the laptop's contents as evidence against Hunter in a trial, he continues to maintain it could have been tampered with.)

Despite the fact that it was Ziegler's search warrant, the investigators were not given a "forensic report of actual hard drive or laptop," Shapley would testify. He was told by Assistant US Attorney Wolf that "for a variety of reasons [the prosecution team] thought they needed to keep it from the agents . . .

"We don't even think we got a full, even a redacted version. We only got piecemeal items," Shapley said. "It was an example of pertinent, relevant evidence that a prosecutor kept from an agent."

Just before Christmas 2019, according to Mac Isaac, Agent Dzielak phoned him to ask if Hunter had come in asking for the laptop.

Mac Isaac told him no, but the agent "seemed genuinely surprised, and that worried me."

After Trump's impeachment trial, Mac Isaac was convinced the FBI had buried the laptop. A Trump supporter, he believed the Burisma material would have helped the former president during his trial. He and his father tried to contact various Republican members of Congress, to no avail.

Finally, he found an email address for Rudy Giuliani, then Trump's attorney, and wrote to him on Aug. 26, 2020.

"For almost a year I have been trying to get the contents of Hunter Biden's laptop to the proper authorities. I first reached out to the FBI and they came and collected it, but I have reason to believe they have destroyed it or buried it in a filing cabinet. After months of waiting for something to come of this, I can only assume that members of the FBI, who are against the President [Trump], have it and it will never be seen again. Luckily, for my protection, I made several copies and I have been trying quietly to bring it to people's attention . . ."

Mac Isaac's email was forwarded to attorney Bob Costello by Rudy's personal assistant, who usually threw out unsolicited emails. But Costello was looking for correspondence that might help Giuliani in his defense against foreign agent allegations, so two days earlier he had told her to send the "crazy" emails to him for a final look because, he told her, "You never know when you are going to find a pearl in an oyster." Costello found Mac Isaac's email credible enough to pursue.

He had been Giuliani's student assistant in 1971 at the Southern District of New York, and then returned as an assistant US Attorney, rising to deputy chief of the Criminal Division, before going into private practice. He has the air of a hard-boiled prosecutor who has seen a lot of human frailty and can gauge the credibility of a witness.

After grilling Mac Isaac and getting him to send various emails from the laptop, Costello wrote Giuliani an email letting him know what he'd found.

"I believe that we are on the verge of a game changing production of indisputable evidence of the corruption we have long suspected involving the Bidens and Ukraine . . .

"You really need to advise the President of this amazing discovery and strategize how you want to use the information contained. This is really big."

Six weeks later, out of the blue I received a text message on a Friday night from Costello.

"I have been asked to send you a small taste of evidence that I have quite legally, that you might have an interest in. I have approximately 40,000 emails, at least a thousand text messages and hundreds of photographs and videos involving the subject. I have no desire to offend you or bore you, so I will simply send you a few of the photos to see if you are interested in this story. The story is more about the emails but the photos set the tone."

The photos were arresting, and unmistakably Hunter. In one, he was in bed, lighting some sort of crack pipe. In another he was asleep with a pipe in his mouth. Another photo showed him in a bathroom mirror, sporting a fresh tattoo across his back which appeared to be a map of the Finger Lakes in upstate New York, where his late mother, Neilia, was from. Hunter had named his various ill-fated companies, Owasco, Seneca, and Skaneateles, after the lakes.

I didn't know Costello back then. But only days before, Giuliani had delivered me a scoop for the *New York Post*: the first public words from President Trump after he'd been airlifted to hospital with COVID-19. "I'm going to beat this," he told Giuliani. "Then I will be able to show people we can deal with this disease responsibly, but we shouldn't be afraid of it."

Trump loved the column, and tweeted it, accidentally including my email address for his 87 million followers to spam with messages like "You suck." The upshot was that, when Giuliani was looking for one last journalist to get the story into the president's favorite newspaper, I came to mind.

"Call Miranda," he told Costello.

Giuliani and Bannon had been shopping the story all over town. They already had tried at least four journalists at different news organizations but were reluctant to hand over the hard drive without a commitment to publish and, without the hard drive, journalists would find it hard to convince editors and lawyers to run the story. There also was limited appeal in a sordid sex scandal about a candidate's tragic druggie son.

The October Surprise four years earlier—Comey's decision to reopen the Hillary Clinton email investigation on the eve of the election—was blamed for her loss to Trump, an outcome viewed as catastrophic by much of the press. No one wanted to be responsible for that happening again.

This close to an election, the pitch had to be strong—hard news with indisputable public interest.

That was Costello's pitch. He told me in precise detail about Mac Isaac, the work order with Hunter's signature, the FBI subpoena, the emails suggesting Hunter had made millions cashing in on his father's name, and the six weeks of due diligence that had convinced him and Giuliani that this was the real deal.

In one of the emails Costello identified, Hunter's Ukrainian associate, Vadym Pozharskyi, thanked him for meeting with his VP father, putting the lie to Joe's claim that he knew nothing about his son's "overseas business dealings." This was where the news value lay.

"Dear Hunter, thank you for inviting me to DC and giving an opportunity to meet your father and spent [sic] some time together," Pozharskyi wrote on April 17, 2015.

"It's realty [sic] an honor and pleasure."

The Biden campaign would deny that any such meeting took place. It wasn't until after the election, when I discovered the meeting was actually a dinner at Cafe Milano, that the White House eventually admitted Joe had attended.

Costello had another astonishing email from Pozharskyi to Hunter, dated May 12, 2014, complaining about "pretrial proceedings . . . initiated by the [Ukrainian] Ministry of Internal Affairs with regard to Burisma

Holdings companies. . . . We urgently need your advice on how you could use your influence to convey a message/signal, etc to stop what we consider to be politically motivated actions."

Next, Costello pointed to documents relating to China: an attorney agreement for Hunter to receive $1 million from CEFC; an image of a handwritten organizational chart outlining a 50:50 deal between Hunter and CEFC Chairman Ye; an email from Hunter claiming an agreement with CEFC gave him "consulting fees based on introductions alone a rate of $10M per year for a three year guarantee total of $30M. The chairman changed that deal after we met in MIAMI TO A MUCH MORE LASTING AND LUCRATIVE ARRANGEMENT [that] was so much more interesting to me and my family."

There were also messages in which Hunter complained about having to "pay for everything for this entire family for 30 years" and giving "half" his salary to his father.

The value in the photographs, very few of which we would publish, was the fact they showed Hunter was a degenerate addict with no real earning capacity at the time he was making all this money.

The story was a potential bombshell—but the decision to publish was above my paygrade.

I texted my boss, Col Allan, the *Post*'s Australian-born senior editorial advisor and former editor-in-chief who had brought me to the paper the previous year.

I sent him three images of Hunter: "Huge. Hard drive. 20k emails and pix."

"Call you shortly," he replied.

Allan was Rupert Murdoch's longest-serving editor. He was fearless, and nobody had better news judgement. He could sense a "ball tearer" (Australian newspaper slang for an exceptional story) a mile off, and immediately dispatched news teams to the Mac Shop in Delaware to interview Mac Isaac, and to Giuliani's apartment on Manhattan's Upper East Side to pick up a hard drive copy of the laptop.

As the formidable *Post* news machine sprang into action, it had a secret weapon at the lead. Emma Jo Morris, the enterprising deputy political editor, had been working on the story for two weeks, after being tipped off by Bannon.

The paper was ready with its first laptop scoop for Page One on Wednesday, October 14: "BIDEN'S SECRET E-MAILS."

But first, the *Post* needed a comment from Hunter Biden, and a reporter put in a call to his lawyer.

* * *

The night before the *Post*'s story ran, the phone at Mac Isaac's shop rang just before closing time.

"Hello, my name is George Mesires. I'm a lawyer for Hunter Biden," said the man on the line.

"My client dropped off some equipment, maybe a laptop, in 2017, and we're checking to see if you're still in possession of it."

Mac Isaac was quick witted enough to get Mesires to send an email from his law office address to verify his bona fides.

Before he hung up, Mesires asked: "So are you still located on the back side of Trolley Square?"

The email from Chicago law firm Faegre Drinker Biddle & Reath came through at 6:59 p.m.

"John Paul: Thank you for speaking with me tonight. As I indicated, I am a lawyer for Hunter Biden and I appreciate you reviewing your records on this matter. Thank you. George."

The cat was out of the bag.

Two hours after Mesires' email, on the other side of the country, FBI Supervisory Special Agent Elvis Chan, head of the bureau's San Francisco cyber branch, fired up the Teleporter, a secure one-way communications channel from the FBI to Twitter, that reportedly deleted all content every two weeks.

He sent 10 documents to Twitter's chief censor Yoel Roth, the Head of Site Integrity.

At 9:24 p.m. ET (6:22 PT), Roth replied, "Received and downloaded—thanks!"

Roth could not recall the contents of the documents when he testified before Congress three years later.

But the curious interaction between the FBI and Twitter, just hours after the *New York Post* alerted Hunter Biden that it had his laptop, seemed to fit into a coordinated censorship operation, set in train months earlier, to kill the story.

The next day Twitter would join Facebook in throttling the nation's oldest newspaper—the fourth largest by circulation—benefiting one of the two candidates for president.

CHAPTER 10

FBI COVERUP?

October 14, 2020
TWITTER HEADQUARTERS, SAN FRANCISCO

The morning the Hunter Biden laptop story dropped, Twitter was abuzz with emails and phone calls as executives frantically debated what to do. These internal communications were released two years later in what came to be known as the "Twitter Files" when self-described "free speech absolutist" Elon Musk bought the social media company for $44 billion.

"It isn't clearly violative of our hacked materials policy," wrote Yoel Roth, Twitter's chief censor, defending the story in an email to colleagues at 8:51 a.m., on October 14, 2020.

"Nor is it clearly in violation of anything else. That said . . . this feels a lot like a somewhat subtle leak operation."

Roth hardened his stance once Twitter's deputy general counsel, Jim Baker, weighed in on the side of censorship.

Baker, formerly the top lawyer at the FBI, where he was involved in every one of the bureau's Russiagate plots against Trump, had been parachuted into Twitter five months before the 2020 election as second fiddle to general counsel Vijaya Gadde. He played an instrumental role over the next two days ensuring the *New York Post* was censored.

At 9:26 a.m., Baker wrote to Roth and others: "I've seen some reliable cybersecurity folks question the authenticity of the [Hunter] emails in another way (ie, that there is no metadata pertaining to them that has been released and the formatting looks like they could be complete fabrications."

Baker repeatedly pushed the notion to colleagues that the Hunter Biden story was "faked" or "hacked," or somehow violated Twitter policy. Not everyone was convinced.

"I'm struggling to understand the policy basis for marking this as unsafe," wrote Trenton Kennedy, Twitter's US policy communications manager, in an internal Google Doc conversation revealed in the Twitter Files.

Roth replied: "The policy basis is hacked materials—though, as discussed, this is an emerging situation where the facts remain unclear."

Another Twitter executive asked: "Can we truthfully claim that this is part of the policy?"

Baker then intervened with a message tagged "PRIVILEGED AND CONFIDENTIAL."

"I support the conclusion that we need more facts to assess whether the materials were hacked. At this stage, however, it is reasonable for us to assume that they may have been and that caution is warranted. There are some facts that indicate that the materials may have been hacked, while there are others indicating that the computer was either abandoned and/or the owner consented to allow the repair shop to access it for at least some purposes."

Baker's reply ignored the fact that there was zero evidence of hacking, and that the *Post* had published photographs both of the work order from the Mac Shop signed by Hunter, and the FBI subpoena for the physical laptop and hard drive, both of which contradicted the hacking theory.

At 10:12 a.m., Roth notified colleagues by email that Twitter would censor the *Post*'s story, for supposedly violating the rules against "distribution of hacked material." The "key factor informing our approach is consensus from experts monitoring election security and disinformation that this looks a lot like a hack-and-leak," he wrote.

Then he cited what could be a baseless, made-up theory: "The suggestion from experts—which rings true—is there was a hack that happened separately, and they loaded the hacked materials on the laptop that magically appeared at a repair shop in Delaware . . . Given the severe risks we saw in this space in 2016, we're recommending a warning + deamplification pending further information."

"Deamplification" is a euphemism for censorship. It means the same as "shadowban," as Musk has acknowledged, which means the user is tweeting into thin air, without an audience.

Even that wasn't enough punishment for the *Post*, whose Twitter account would be locked at 2:20 p.m. for more than two weeks, imposing a significant financial cost on the newspaper.

Twitter also blocked users from sharing links to the article, labelling it "potentially harmful." Anybody who tried to share it by private direct message, including White House Press Secretary Kayleigh McEnany, had their accounts locked.

At 7:55 p.m. Twitter CEO Jack Dorsey weighed in on the controversy at the company he had founded, calling its actions "unacceptable."

"Our communication around our actions on the @nypost article was not great," he tweeted.

But behind his back, Dorsey's executives continued to censor the *Post*. Baker was active into the wee hours of October 15, making sure the next instalment of the laptop series was throttled.

At 3.44 a.m., he emailed Roth and Gadde a link to the *Post*'s Thursday story that was about Hunter's deals with CEFC and included the "10 [percent] for the big guy" email.

"Folks," wrote Baker. "I'm guessing that we are going to restrict access to this article as a violation of our Hacked Materials policy but after yesterday I don't want to assume anything."

Twitter had been groomed for weeks by the FBI and other shadowy operatives to recognize the *Post*'s story as somehow malign the minute it appeared. The warnings became more overtly political as the election drew closer.

During one of its weekly meetings with the FBI in the run up to the federal election, Twitter was told to look out for "hack-and-leak operations" involving Hunter Biden, and "likely" in October, according to a sworn declaration by Roth.

"I was told in these meetings that the intelligence community expected that individuals associated with political campaigns would be subject to hacking attacks and that material obtained through those hacking attacks would likely be disseminated over social media platforms, including Twitter," said Roth in a Dec. 21, 2020, declaration to the Federal Election Commission.

"I also learned in these meetings that there were rumors that a hack-and-leak operation would involve Hunter Biden . . . likely in October."

Roth's signed declaration formed part of Twitter's defense against a complaint by the Tea Party Patriots Foundation that its censorship of the *Post* ahead of the 2020 election was an "in kind" campaign contribution to Joe Biden's campaign. The FEC dismissed the Tea Part Patriots Foundation's complaint.

But how did the FBI know to pre-bunk the *Post*'s story before it was published?

For one thing, the FBI had had the laptop in its possession for ten months so knew it contained information that was damaging to Joe.

For another, the FBI was spying on Rudy Giuliani's iCloud for at least two years, under the pretext of an investigation into alleged foreign agent registration violations, according to Costello. A year after raiding Giuliani's Upper East Side apartment in 2021, the FBI returned all his devices, without charging him, and told the *New York Times* he was no longer under investigation.

But the covert surveillance warrant of Giuliani's iCloud likely would have given the FBI access to the detailed email in August 2020 from John Paul Mac Isaac disclosing what he had found on the laptop Hunter had abandoned at his store 16 months earlier. The FBI also would have had access to my messages with Giuliani in October 2020 discussing the *Post*'s plans for the story.

In the week before the election, the FBI's Baltimore field office, whose agents were assigned to the Delaware tax investigation of Hunter, was sending Twitter multiple censorship requests. Twitter legal executive Stacia Cardille thought the situation unusual enough that she reported it in an email to her boss, Baker, on November 3, 2020.

"They have some folks in the Baltimore field office and at HQ that are just doing keyword searches for violations. This is probably the 10th request I have dealt with in the last 5 days."

The FBI also was conducting pre-bunking meetings with Facebook before the election, warning them to be on "high alert" for a "dump" of "Russian propaganda," CEO Mark Zuckerberg told podcast host Joe Rogan in 2022.

"Basically, the background here is the FBI basically came to us, some folks on our team, and was like, 'Hey, just so you know you should be on high alert,'" said Zuckerberg. "'We thought there was a lot of Russian propaganda in the 2016 election, we have it on notice that basically there's about to be some kind of dump that's similar to that so just be vigilant.'"

When Rogan asked if the FBI had told Facebook to be on guard specifically for the *Post*'s story about Hunter Biden's laptop, Zuckerberg claimed, rather unconvincingly, that he did "not remember . . . specifically" but "it basically fit the pattern."

Unlike Elon Musk, Zuckerberg chose not to be transparent. Facebook refused to give the date of the FBI private briefing or details of the "pattern" the FBI told it to look out for.

But when I asked if the FBI had mentioned Joe Biden, Hunter Biden, Ukraine or a laptop, Facebook's answer was curiously limited: "nothing specific about Hunter Biden."

Whatever was said, the briefing must have been specific enough for Facebook to recognize the *Post* story as the "dump" the FBI had been warning about and to move at record speed to throttle it, ahead of Twitter, which was still debating the issue.

At 11:10 a.m. the morning the story went live, Andy Stone, Facebook's communications manager, announced on Twitter, "we are reducing its distribution on our platform [while] the story is fact checked by Facebook's third-party fact checking partners."

The "fact-check" doesn't appear to have happened. Nobody ever reached out to Tony Bobulinski or Devon Archer, two recipients of emails published by the *Post* who should have been the first point of contact for anyone wanting to fact-check the stories.

Stone was hardly an impartial actor. He had joined Facebook from a Democratic super PAC and previously had worked for Democratic senator Barbara Boxer and the Democratic Congressional Campaign Committee. He also spent 16 months on the failed presidential campaign of John Kerry, the former secretary of state who was tied to the Biden family through his stepson Chris Heinz, a one-time business partner of Hunter.

The FBI agent who organized the weekly "election security" meetings with Twitter and Facebook was Elvis Chan, the same agent who had sent the mysterious documents over the Teleporter to Twitter the night before the laptop story broke.

He also organized meetings with Google, Microsoft, Yahoo!, and Reddit, he would divulge in sworn testimony in 2022 in the landmark free speech lawsuit against the Biden administration by the Republican attorneys general of Missouri and Louisiana, *Missouri v. Biden*.

The FBI used the meetings to lobby the social media platforms to change their terms of service to be able to quickly take down "hacked material," said Chan, whose postgraduate thesis claimed that Russia interfered with the 2016 election to help Donald Trump.

Agent Chan testified that the FBI had no actual intelligence to suggest the Russians were planning in 2020 what he described as a "2016-style DNC hack-and-dump operation." Twitter executives also told the FBI over and over in the months before the 2020 election that they had seen very little activity from Russia-linked entities. But that didn't stop Chan from repeatedly going to the social media companies to warn them of the "potential" of Russian mischief and asking them to follow up far-fetched news stories.

"Through our investigations, we did not see any similar competing intrusions to what had happened in 2016," Chan testified. "So, although from our standpoint we had not seen anything, we specifically, in an abundance of caution, warned the companies in case they saw something that we did not . . .

"I warned the companies about a potential for hack-and-dump operations from the Russians and the Iranians on more than one occasion, although I cannot recollect how many times."

In one of many demands that Twitter respond to dubious claims in news stories, the FBI asked Roth to look into a *Washington Post* story which alleged foreign influence behind a pro-Trump tweet.

Roth replied that "the account in question is domestic in origin. The article makes a lot of insinuations about foreign interference but we saw no evidence that that was the case here (and in fact, a lot of strong evidence pointing in the opposite direction)."

The pressure from the FBI on Twitter to look for something that wasn't there escalated all the way to the election, the Twitter Files show.

Hunter Biden's name was raised in an FBI meeting with Facebook in October 2020, a few days after the *New York Post* was censored, Chan testified. A Facebook analyst asked Laura Dehmlow of the FBI Foreign Influence Task Force for "any information they could share about the Hunter Biden investigation."

Her response was "something to the effect that the FBI has no comment on this," Chan recalled.

Dehmlow, who would become the task force's section chief, testified to the House Select Committee on the Weaponization of the Federal Government in 2023 that on the day the *Post* story broke, she was in a scheduled meeting with Twitter when one of their employees asked about the authenticity of laptop.

An analyst in the FBI's Criminal Investigative Division began to respond that the laptop was real, when an FBI lawyer interrupted to say that the FBI had "no further comment" about the laptop's provenance.

After the meeting, FBI personnel decided that, if they were asked about the laptop in future meetings, they would say "no comment," Dehmlow testified, despite the bureau having had possession of Hunter's MacBook Pro for almost a year.

"The FBI's failure to alert social-media companies that the Hunter Biden laptop story was real, and not mere Russian disinformation, is particularly troubling," wrote Judge Terry Doughty in *Missouri v. Biden* on July 4, 2023, when he issued an injunction preventing the government from working with social media platforms or outside groups to censor social media content.

"The FBI had the laptop in their possession since December 2019 and had warned social-media companies to look out for a 'hack and dump' operation by the Russians prior to the 2020 election. Even after Facebook specifically asked whether the Hunter Biden laptop story was Russian disinformation, Dehmlow of the FBI refused to comment, resulting in the social-media companies' suppression of the story. As a result, millions of U.S. citizens did not hear the story prior to the November 3, 2020, election.

"Additionally, the FBI was included in industry meetings and bilateral meetings, received and forwarded alleged misinformation to social-media companies, and actually misled social-media companies in regard to the Hunter Biden laptop story."

It wasn't just the laptop. The lawsuit alleged that White House officials and federal agencies were coercing social-media platforms to censor "disfavored speakers, viewpoints and content," in contravention of the First Amendment, by threatening retaliatory action.

Whether it was the origins of COVID-19, the efficacy of COVID vaccines, the botched withdrawal from Afghanistan, the war in Ukraine, or climate change skepticism, anything that dissented from the government-approved narrative was targeted for suppression.

The Biden administration appealed Doughty's ruling, and *Missouri v.*

Biden, renamed *Murthy v. Missouri*, headed to the US Supreme Court in 2024.

The new media, the robber barons of the digital age, increasingly were acting in concert with—even in obeisance to—a government that wielded the anti-trust stick, and threatened to break up their monopolies, just as it did to their Gilded Age antecedents.

During the Trump administration, support had grown among both Republicans and Democrats to repeal Section 230 of the Telecommunications Act that gave Big Tech immunity from civil liability, a blessing not granted to other publishers, whose advertising dollars they plundered.

In oral arguments on March 18, 2024, Supreme Court Justice Samuel Alito zeroed in on the extraordinary aggression by the White House and federal government toward the social media platforms to force them to control dissident views.

"When they're unhappy, they curse them out," said Alito while questioning the DOJ's Principal Deputy Solicitor General Brian Fletcher.

"There is constant pestering of Facebook and some of the other platforms and they want to have regular meetings and they suggest rules that should be applied and [say], 'Why don't you tell us everything that you're going to do so we can help you and we can look it over?' And I thought, 'Wow. I cannot imagine federal officials taking that approach to the print media . . .'

"The only reason why this is taking place is because the federal government has got Section 230 and antitrust in its pocket. And so, it's treating Facebook and these other platforms like they're subordinates.

"Would you do that to the *New York Times* or the *Wall Street Journal* or the Associated Press or any other big newspaper or wire service? . . . There's all the rest, constant meetings, constant emails: 'We want answers. We're partners. We are on the same team.' Do you think that the print media regards themselves as being on the same team as the federal government, partners with the federal government?

"So, whenever they write something that [you] don't like, [you] can call them up and curse them out and say, 'Why don't we be partners? We're on the same team. Why don't you show us what you're going to write before-hand? We'll edit it for you, make sure it's accurate.'"

The threats go some way to explaining why Big Tech, founded on the idea that the world would only gain from its unimaginable free-flow of information, caved so easily to government pressure to censor its opponents and became, instead, an instrument of oppression, and a haven for spooks.

It didn't hurt that the FBI was also paying Twitter millions of dollars.

"For the time spent processing requests from the FBI . . . I am happy to report we have collected $3,415,323 since October 2019!" a Twitter executive wrote to Baker in February 2021.

Dozens of former US government intelligence agents from the FBI, CIA, NSC, and State Department were embedded in senior roles across the social media platforms.

At Twitter, at least half a dozen executives with previous FBI ties, and one from the CIA, had joined the company after Trump was elected.

"As of 2020, there were so many former FBI employees . . . working at Twitter that they had created their own private Slack channel and a crib sheet to onboard new FBI arrivals," wrote Michael Shellenberger, one of the independent journalists Musk invited to access the Twitter Files.

Baker was the most senior operative. Even though he had left the FBI under a cloud after being investigated twice, in 2017 and 2019, by the DOJ for allegedly leaking classified information to the press and was accused by House Republicans of being instrumental in Russiagate, he still held his FBI security clearances. On Sept. 15, 2020, Dehmlow and Chan requested to give Baker a classified briefing, without any other Twitter staff present.

Baker also was a member of the National Task Force on Election Crises, a left-wing group ostensibly set up to ensure a "free and fair" 2020 election.

Between leaving the FBI in 2018 and joining Twitter, Baker worked for the Brookings Institution, and wrote for the Lawfare Blog, published by David Priess, an ex-CIA agent who signed the "Dirty 51" letter. Six more signatories of the letter were linked to the Lawfare Blog.

It's hard not to see Baker's role as a gatekeeper planted at Twitter to ensure information detrimental to the election of Joe Biden never saw the light of day.

Musk fired Baker on December 6, 2022, four days after the first "Twitter Files" dump, accusing him of suppressing information he had ordered released about the censorship of the *Post*.

The "most important data was hidden [and] may have been deleted," Musk said.

Musk had deputized independent journalist Matt Taibbi to release the information, and he would later detail much of the government interference, but initially he found nothing to support the FBI cover up of the Hunter Biden story. "There's no evidence—that I've seen—of any government involvement in the laptop story," he tweeted in the first installment of the Twitter Files.

Musk realized that Taibbi wasn't being provided complete information and hauled Baker in to ask what he was up to. "His explanation was . . . unconvincing," Musk said, drily.

During a live Q&A session on Twitter at the time, Musk said: "If Twitter is doing one team's bidding before an election, shutting down dissenting voices on a pivotal election, that is the very definition of election interference. . . . Frankly Twitter was acting like an arm of the Democratic National Committee. It was absurd."

Around the time Baker joined Twitter, Facebook also parachuted in an anti-Trump activist to assist with content moderation: Stanford University law professor Pamela Karlan, best known for cracking a joke at the expense of Trump's 13-year-old son Barron while testifying at the president's first impeachment.

Karlan was a member of Facebook's content-moderation oversight board from April 2020 to January 2021—the duration of the election campaign, placing her in the hot seat at the precise time that the *Post* was censored.

Once Biden was safely in office, Karlan scored a federal job as Principal Deputy Assistant AG in the DOJ Civil Rights Division while still drawing a $1 million salary from Stanford University. She left the DOJ 17 months later, shortly before the American Accountability Foundation revealed the unusual pay deal through the Freedom of Information Act.

A couple of months after she left, the civil rights division went after Musk on the curious pretext that he had not employed foreigners and border crossers at Space X, even though it was against the law to hire foreigners at Space X on national security grounds.

It was just one of a raft of lawsuits and investigations into Musk's various businesses by the Biden administration, as the eccentric South African–born billionaire continued to defy government censorship on Twitter.

Despite having voted for Biden in 2020, Musk understood that the censorship of the Hunter laptop story in 2020 was election interference which prevented the American people from doing the necessary due diligence on one of the two candidates for president.

* * *

On the morning the *Post* story broke, Roth received an email from Garrett Graff, Director of Cyber Initiatives at the Aspen Institute, which had organized a curiously prescient event for social media executives and journalists a few weeks earlier, that Roth attended.

The Aspen Institute was a non-profit known as "the mountain retreat for the liberal elite" and in September 2020 it held a "tabletop exercise" that predicted a theoretical "hack and leak" dump of Hunter Biden material weeks before the election. The exercise would take on a sinister import when details were revealed in the Twitter Files.

It's not hard to guess what Graff told Roth because his tweets that morning were stridently critical of the *Post* story, calling it "this fake Hunter Biden scandal."

"Re: this Biden-Burisma crap this morning," he tweeted at 8:23 a.m. "I literally wrote and ran a tabletop exercise at @AspenDigital this summer about this very type of incident—and then wrote about how the media should react better."

Vivian Schiller, executive director of Aspen Digital, who had designed the Hunter Biden tabletop exercise, also weighed in, tweeting: "Garrett invented almost this identical scenario over the summer to test readiness of some MSM [mainstream media] to fall for such nonsense in the week before the election. And here we are."

The exercise effectively had acted as a "pre-bunking" operation to ensure that Aspen's invited audience of social media executives, national security reporters, journalists and executives from the *New York Times*, the *Washington Post*, CNN, NPR, NBC, the *New Yorker*, and the *Daily Beast* would treat the *Post*'s Hunter Biden laptop story the following month with suspicion, and easily succumb to the lie that it was a Russian disinformation operation.

Marked "Confidential" and titled "Aspen Digital Hack-and-Dump Working Group—September 2020 EXERCISE: The Burisma Leak," one four-page document outlines an elaborate mythical scenario in which an anonymous website, BIDENCRIMES.info, and a Twitter account, @HUNTERLOLZ, post documents "tied to Hunter Biden . . . that purport to be from Burisma."

It's worth quoting the document at length because of its Nostradamus-like prediction of the *Post*'s upcoming scoop. The tabletop exercise prepared its influential media participants "to suppress and delegitimize information contained in Hunter Biden's laptop about the Biden's family business schemes," the committee would find. In other words, it was prepping newsrooms not to cover the story if it were to occur in real life.

"Day One: Monday, October 5th. Splashed across the top of the site, in English, is 'Joe Biden betrayed America before for $$$. He'll do it again.' Initially the documents, mostly in Ukrainian appear to be minutes of various Burisma board meetings, internal emails, and financial records. There is initially no sign of a smoking gun . . .

"Day Two: Tuesday, October 6th. The Drudge Report links to the anonymous website, BIDENCRIMES.info . . .

"Day Three: Wednesday, October 7th. Fox & Friends discusses the story in its 7 am block. @RealDonaldTrump tweets six minutes later, 'Is Joe Biden biggest criminal of all time? Check out @HUNTERLOLZ.'

"Day Four: Thursday, October 8th. The Biden campaign . . . says they will not confirm the veracity of any documents.

"CrowdStrike announces, without further detail, it has reason to believe that BIDENCRIMES.info is the work of [Russian hackers] Fancy Bear (APT 28).

"Cesar Conde, the chairman of NBC News, announces that because of the suspicion that the BIDENCRIMES.info leaks are coming from a foreign power with a goal of undermining America's free and fair elections, no aspect of NBC News or MSNBC will report on the allegations or use the materials as the basis for reporting . . . The Guardian quickly announces it will follow the same principle, as does The Huffington Post.

"At Ohio Trump rally that night, crowd starts chanting 'LOCK HIM UP.' President Trump, at podium, pumps his fists as the crowd chants.

"Day Five: Friday, October 9th. In a statement released at 9 am and signed only by him, Director of National Intelligence John Ratcliffe says he has no reason to believe the documents posted by BIDENCRIMES.info are forgeries, nor does the IC have reason to believe the website is a Russian operation.

"At 11 am, on the House floor, House Intelligence Chair Adam Schiff says that . . . the IC is not being forthright with the American people about the source and veracity of the leaks . . .

"At 2 pm, @HUNTERLOLZ tweets a link out to a zip file that appears to contain a new tranche of 20,000 documents, mostly in Ukrainian, stolen from Burisma and posted on BIDENCRIMES.info . . .

"That afternoon, Facebook's sources inside the IC tell Facebook to be wary about the DNI's statement.

"Day Six: Saturday, October 10th. Overnight, progressive blogger Josh Marshall . . . tweets out one document in the new tranche of zip files that appears to be a confirmation of a wire transfer for $1 million from Deutsche Bank to an off-shore account in the name of Hunter Biden, dated two days after the firing of the chief prosecutor, Shokin. Overnight, independent security researchers and news organizations find the majority of the zip files are authentic, but some are manipulated . . .

"At 10 am, the New York Times posts a story saying that two anonymous 'senior Justice Department officials' in Washington say that the acting US attorney in DC has empaneled a grand jury to investigate Joe Biden.

"Day Seven: Sunday, October 11th. On the Sunday shows, Biden campaign staff dismiss the entire hack-and-leak as dirty tricks by Vladimir Putin . . .

"The Daily Beast quotes two 'former senior intelligence officials' that the directors of the CIA and NSA refused to sign onto Ratcliffe's Friday statement, although sources differ why they did not sign it . . .

"Alex Berenson announces on Twitter that he's conducted an interview, via DM, with the person behind @HUNTERLOLZ and that he believes the person is an American.

"Day Eight: Monday, October 12th. At 7:15 am, President Trump calls into Fox & Friends and says he hopes the FBI will investigate Joe Biden.

"At 9 am, Attorney General Bill Barr holds a press conference to say the American people deserve the truth and that he has instructed the FBI to verify the allegations of Joe Biden and Hunter Biden's alleged corruption. He announces that the Justice Department is investigating wrongdoing by Hunter Biden and Joe Biden for alleged money laundering, tax fraud, theft of honest services, and acting as an unregistered foreign agent . . .

"At 7:30 p.m., Rudy Giuliani says on Fox News that he was right all along re: 2019 Ukraine pressure campaign.

"Day Nine: Tuesday, October 13th: @RealDonaldTrump tweets at 6:15 am: 'See, Ukraine phone call was perfect—I knew Sleepy Joe was actually Crooked Joe! Tell FBI: LOCK HIM UP!'"

The fake timeline continues on in this vein until Day Eleven.

A few weeks after this imaginary exercise, Graff, the Aspen facilitator, will write an article in *Wired* on October 7, 2020, titled "The Right Way to Cover Hacks and Leaks before the Election," which outlines the behavior modification expected of the participants. For one thing, he wanted to trigger an unusual desire in reporters to "check with other news organizations [and] intelligence agencies and law enforcement" before publishing stories based on Hunter Biden's emails.

Remember, this was a week before the *Post*'s story was published. Yet somehow the Aspen Institute's crystal ball predicted the future appearance of something eerily similar to Hunter's laptop, and Joe's future false characterization of it as a Russian "plant."

Early that morning of October 14, 2020, Aspen tabletop alumni took to Twitter to instruct their colleagues to ignore the *Post*'s story. It was a most peculiar way for journalists to behave.

The *Daily Beast*, whose editor-in-chief, Noah Shachtman, participated in the Aspen exercise, questioned the laptop's legitimacy and claimed it was "stolen."

Natasha Bertrand from *Politico*, who would publish the Dirty 51 letter days later, tweeted a "reminder" that an alleged Russian agent had been "releasing/teasing misleading or edited Biden material for nearly a year."

Washington Post fact-checker Glenn Kessler tweeted the paper's policy "regarding hacked or leaked material during the final weeks of an election season. Be carefull [*sic*] what is in your social media feeds."

Mother Jones' DC bureau chief David Corn tweeted: "The whole story is predicated on this false Fox/Giuliani talking point that has been repeatedly challenged. The NY Post's presenting it as fact signals its bad faith & advances disinformation. Anyone who promotes this story w/o noting this is doing a disservice."

Corn was one to talk. He was the journalist who broke the news of the Steele dossier, compiled by discredited British ex-spy Christopher Steele, with its lurid lies about Trump, such as the so-called "pee tape," in which the notoriously germaphobic president supposedly paid Russian prostitutes to urinate on his hotel bed in Moscow. Talk about fake news.

Corn, incidentally, was linked to Baker, who allegedly communicated with him before Corn reported on the existence of the Steele dossier a week before the 2016 election.

CNN, whose vice president for news standards attended the Aspen event, trashed the *Post*'s story as a "dubious" product of the "right-wing media machine."

CNN's National Security Analyst Juliette Kayyem tweeted: "Why are you all amplifying a New York Post story with no context, a bizarre factual basis for receipt of the computer, nor acknowledgement that the amplification is the key to the disinformation campaign. We knew this desperation was coming. They are the same. Why are you?"

In CNN's daily 9 a.m. news conference in the cable channel's glamorous new Hudson Yards headquarters in Manhattan, CNN president Jeff Zucker instructed his staff to ignore the *New York Post* bombshell, according to audio recordings released by a whistleblower to undercover news outfit Project Veritas.

"On the *Breitbart, New York Post, Fox News* rabbit hole of Hunter Biden," said Zucker, "the *Wall Street Journal* reported that their review of all corporate records showed no role for Joe Biden on the Chinese deal. And yes, I do put more credibility in the *Wall Street Journal* than I do in the *New York Post*."

"Hey, Jeff, it's just David on the Burisma story," David Vigilante, general counsel for CNN, is heard telling Zucker. "We should be awfully careful about that obviously, but I do think there's a media story in what in the world are [*New York Times'*] Maggie Haberman and [*Politico*'s] Jake Sherman doing retweeting that story?"

CNN political director David Chalian piped up: "Obviously, we're not going with the *New York Post* story right now on Hunter Biden. We'll just continue to report out this is the very stuff that the president was impeached over . . . that Senate committees looked at and found nothing wrong in Joe Biden's interactions with Ukrainians."

And that was how the story was killed.

As Shellenberger noted, the Aspen participants "broadly followed the guidance in the wake of the *New York Post* bombshell."

There was a whole constellation of government and private organizations that came together to pre-bunk and then crush the story of alleged Biden corruption on October 14, 2020.

Shellenberger described it in testimony to Congress as the "Censorship Industrial Complex." It included Stanford University's Cyber Policy Center, which published a report eight months before the election urging editors and journalists to "Break the Pentagon Papers Principle." In other words, do not report leaked information, even if it's true.

The Biden campaign boasted after the election that the pre-bunking of the *Post*'s story was no accident but the product of meticulous planning.

"We were able to put it in a box and have the media treat it like it deserved to be treated—which was like a conspiracy theory, and not like it was Clinton's emails or the crazy parade of accusers at the St. Louis debate. We had been preparing the whole ecosystem to respond to some crazy Trump October surprise. And it responded responsibly.

"That doesn't happen by accident. This all stems from the way we responded on Ukraine."

Biden's campaign had relied on a year's worth of preparation and groundwork, wrote Edward-Isaac Dovere in *Battle for the Soul*: "of discrediting Giuliani, of reporters' learning the lessons of how their 2016 coverage had failed (or at least being shamed enough to pretend they had learned the lessons), of greater literacy about Russian and other disinformation, of building Americans' trust in Biden's relationship with his son through that moment talking about his addiction onstage [in the presidential debate]."

There was one magic ingredient still to come. The CIA was preparing a disinformation operation of its own to help Joe Biden.

CHAPTER 11

DIRTY 51

October 14, 2020
WASHINGTON, DC

With his floppy hair, European reserve, and bilingual fluency, Antony Blinken's foreign affairs pedigree could not have been designed better to impress Joe Biden. He'd grown up a world away from Scranton, Pennsylvania—in Paris, in East Hampton, and in the tony River House co-op on New York's Upper East Side, which his father, Donald Blinken, an investment banker-turned-ambassador to Hungary, once described as "a special island in the midst of Manhattan" inhabited by "people who are not as exposed to the vicissitudes."

At the École Jeannine Manuel in Paris, where the lonely nine-year-old moved in 1971, after his parents' divorce, to live with his mother, Judith, and her new husband, Samuel Pisar, a Holocaust survivor who served as an adviser to John F. Kennedy, he found a kindred spirit in Robert Malley, the son of an Egyptian journalist. He would later recruit his childhood friend to be the Obama administration's lead negotiator on the ill-starred Iran nuclear deal, only to suffer the embarrassment of Malley being suspended without pay in 2023 during Biden's presidency, the target of a mysterious

FBI espionage investigation. (As of this writing, the Malley investigation is still ongoing.)

Blinken's career trajectory was rather more tranquil. After Harvard, and Columbia Law School, he transformed himself into the consummate Washington staffer, with a sideline as a guitarist in a rock band named Cash Bar Wedding.

Joe Biden, the top Democrat on the Senate Foreign Relations Committee, identified the urbane young staffer early on as a "superstar" and a useful source of the erudition he lacked. Working for Joe, Blinken learned the crude ways of Tammany Hall and soon became embedded in the senator's private life.

He was an older brother figure to Joe's adult sons, Beau and Hunter, and a frequent weekend visitor to his Delaware compound where he would join the family and assorted staffers at the kitchen table as they plotted the disastrous 2008 presidential campaign. His wife, Evan Ryan, a comely former Hillary Clinton staffer, worked on that campaign as deputy manager and went on to become White House cabinet secretary in the Biden administration.

As different as they were, Blinken's career became firmly entwined with Joe's over the decades. When Joe was tapped by Barack Obama as his running mate, Blinken became National Security Advisor to the Vice President and rose to deputy Secretary of State. He waited out the Trump years in a series of lucrative consultancies and ran Joe's University of Pennsylvania think tank, the Penn Biden Center.

He would reach the summit of his profession under President Biden as Secretary of State at age 59.

But first Blinken had to find a way to put out the fire that threatened to destroy Joe's candidacy.

On October 14, 2020, three weeks out from the election, with Joe and President Donald Trump neck and neck in the polls, the *New York Post*'s first story about Hunter Biden's abandoned laptop exploded like a bomb. The front page featured an email from Hunter's Burisma paymaster, Vadym Pozharskyi, thanking him for "the opportunity to meet your father." It was hard to square with Joe's assertions throughout the campaign that he knew nothing about Hunter's seeming international influence-peddling operation.

Candidate Biden had been lying low since the story broke, self-isolating in his basement under cover of the COVID pandemic, but behind-the-scenes his campaign struggled to find a coherent response to explain the email away.

In a carefully worded statement to the *Post* the campaign said there were no meetings on Joe's "official schedules" in 2015 with Pozharskyi. But to other media outlets they issued more emphatic denials.

The Biden campaign categorically denied a meeting ever happened. 'They never had a meeting," Andrew Bates, a campaign spokesman, told *USA TODAY*.

Amos Hochstein, described as a former Biden staffer, told *Politico*: "I've literally never heard of this guy in my life." That wasn't the question.

But, then, Hochstein wasn't just any Biden staffer. He was a Ukraine energy expert. Only two days earlier he had abruptly resigned from the board of Ukrainian state-owned energy company Naftogaz, on Oct. 12, 2020, according to the *Kyiv Post*. As the Obama administration's energy envoy, Hochstein traveled with the vice president to Ukraine, including in December 2015 when Biden demanded the removal of Prosecutor General Viktor Shokin, who was investigating Burisma at the time.

The *Post*'s reporters were combing through thousands of documents, everything from bank statements and emails to homemade porn, and would continue to publish fresh, damning revelations every day. Even as Twitter and Facebook, in apparent collusion with the FBI, censored the stories, and the mainstream media collectively looked the other way, the Biden campaign knew that the sheer weight of the evidence would eventually be impossible to ignore.

Blinken's solution was to set in motion one of the most brazen dirty tricks in US electoral history. Using the intelligence community to sound the false alarm of "Russian disinformation," ground already prepared by corrupt elements inside the FBI, he set out to discredit the whole laptop story.

First, he phoned CIA veteran Mike Morell for advice on combating the *Post*'s reporting. Morell was thrilled the campaign was asking him for help. After more than 30 years of loyal service to the CIA, he'd never made it to the top. He'd come close—serving as acting director twice. The second time, after the Petraeus scandal, he thought he would at last become director, but Obama chose the less qualified John Brennan instead.

Morell, 62, the boyish, bespectacled, Ohio-born son of an autoworker and a homemaker, had been working toward the top job his whole life. He had the expertise. He had the respect of his colleagues, having served both Republican and Democrat administrations, and had been one of the first to slime Trump during the 2016 campaign as an "unwitting agent" of Russia. Surely that was worth something.

But he was an anachronism in a post-post 9/11 world that was backing away from the overreach of the War on Terror. He'd defended the drones that Obama used to blow up foreigners in places like Yemen and Afghanistan. And he'd stood up for "enhanced interrogation techniques." He would forever be branded a torture apologist.

He quit the CIA in 2013 after being passed over for Brennan. Since then, he had been filling his time as a CBS News contributor and had taken a position at the Washington DC–based strategic advisory firm Beacon Global Strategies, which had a half dozen other CIA veterans on its roster.

But he hadn't given up hope of fulfilling his life's ambition. When he got a call from Blinken, he saw his chance, at last, to be CIA director in a Biden administration. The campaign would even leak to the *New York Times* that he was a strong contender. Morell couldn't have been more eager to please. He would later testify to Congress that Blinken's phone call prompted him to organize 50 intelligence colleagues to sign a letter falsely insinuating that the damning material from Hunter's laptop published by the *Post* was Russian disinformation.

The Dirty 51 letter, as it came to be known, was timed to appear on the eve of the final presidential debate, to maximize its benefit to Joe, by giving him a "talking point to push back on [President] Trump on this issue," as Morell put it.

Blinken followed up his call a few hours later, emailing Morell a new, anonymously sourced, thinly reported—but conveniently timed—*USA Today* article claiming that the FBI was examining whether Hunter's laptop was part of a "smoke bomb of disinformation pushed by Russia" to damage Biden.

At the bottom of Blinken's email was the signature block of Andrew Bates, the Biden campaign's director of rapid response. The Biden campaign was orchestrating the Dirty 51 letter. This was the real disinformation operation—51 of the most powerful people in the intelligence world were arguably uniting to deceive the American people and help Joe win the 2020 election. When his alleged role in the Dirty 51 letter was revealed some three years later, Blinken denied all: "Didn't ask for it, didn't solicit it," he said.

But, until Blinken called and implanted the idea, Morell had not considered floating the idea of Russian interference.

"Prior to [Blinken's] call, you did not have any intent to write this statement?" Morell was asked as part of a deposition for Congress.

"I did not," he replied.

Q: "Okay. So, his call triggered—"

Morell, interrupting: "It did, yes."

Q: "—that intent in you."

Blinken had "triggered . . . that intent" in him. A purported hoax was born. Morell knew what he needed to do. He agreed to mobilize the intelligence community to "help Vice President Biden . . . because I wanted him to win the election."

To draft the letter, he enlisted the help of Marc Polymeropoulos, 51, a squat former CIA senior operations officer. Polymeropoulos had retired early from the CIA, stating he was a victim of the mysterious "Havana syndrome."

The syndrome, a collection of symptoms including listlessness, buzzing ears, and headaches that afflicted dozens of US diplomats stationed abroad, was said to be caused by a secret Russian electro-magnetic energy weapon. A CIA report would later rule out the involvement of a new weapon or foreign adversary. The more likely culprits were judged to be an undiagnosed medical condition, stress, the mating calls of insects, or a psychological phenomenon commonly known as mass hysteria.

But at the time that Morell called him, Polymeropoulos did not take much convincing that the Russians were behind this latest plot.

He would later boast that he "basically wrote" the letter which claimed that material from Hunter's laptop published by the *Post* "has all the classic earmarks of a Russian information operation," and "the Russians are involved in the Hunter Biden email issue."

Russia was "trying to influence how Americans vote in this election . . . Moscow [will] pull out the stops to do anything possible to help Trump win and/or to weaken Biden should he win.

"A 'laptop op' fits the bill, as the publication of the emails are [*sic*] clearly designed to discredit Biden . . . It is high time that Russia stops interfering in our democracy."

Morell let Polymeropoulos know from the start that the Biden campaign had instigated the letter to discredit the *Post*'s reporting on the laptop.

"Morell said that to me, that someone from kind of the Biden world had asked for" it, Polymeropoulos would later testify to Congress.

Morell sent the draft letter to his network of intelligence contacts, explaining in an email that he and Polymeropoulos had "drafted the attached because we believe the Russians were involved in some way in the Hunter Biden email issue and because we think Trump will attack Biden on the issue at this week's debate and we want to give the VP a talking point to use in response."

Morell told former CIA officer Kristin Wood, who was helping garner signatures: "The more former intelligence officers the better. Campaign will be thrilled."

Over the next two days, Morell gathered signatures from 51 former intelligence officials. Five former CIA directors signed: Mike Hayden, Leon Panetta, John Brennan, John McLaughlin (acting) and Morell (acting) would sign—as well as former Director of National Intelligence, James

Clapper, eight CIA intelligence officers, seven analysts, and four chiefs of staff; 41 of the 51 signatories were former CIA.

He asked them to "highlight your Russia work" in their affiliations when they signed the letter and assured them that he would "clear the statement with the Publication Review Board at CIA" in record time.

On October 19, 2020, Morell told the CIA's Prepublication Classification Review Board (PCRB) that he needed the letter approved as an unusual "rush job, as it needs to get out as soon as possible." Sure enough, the PCRB fast-tracked approval in 5.5 hours, but added a disclaimer that its clearance was not proof of CIA verification of the claims. The disclaimer was not included in Morell's letter when it was published.

Extraordinarily, the letter appeared to have been approved at the very highest levels of the CIA, although that unsavory matter was kept hidden for more than three years, until it was prised out of the CIA's email archives by congressional investigators.

Andrew Makridis, the CIA's Chief Operating Officer at the time the letter was published, testified to the House Judiciary Committee that he was sent a draft version of the letter by the PCRB on October 19, 2020, and recognized it as an inherently political document.

Because of its political sensitivity, Makridis walked across the hall from his office to inform then–CIA Director Gina Haspel about the letter. He testified that he felt at the time that the letter "rises to the level where I felt that I wanted to make sure the director and the deputy director were aware. [But] we had no discussion other than the notification that this was coming. . . .

"I mean, it's talking about President Trump, Vice President Biden. I mean, you can't read that and say there isn't politics involved of some nature," he testified in April 2024.

After notifying Haspel, Makridis had his executive assistant send an email to the PCRB stating that they "may notify Former DDCIA [Deputy Director of the CIA] Morell." An hour later, the PCRB notified Mr. Morell that the letter could be published.

Internal CIA staff emails confirmed that at least some of the letter signatories were on active contract with the CIA at the time of its publication, the committee found.

The PCRB also raised the letter to the attention of the chief operating officer of the Office of the Director of National Intelligence, who deferred to the CIA's judgement on whether or not it should be approved. Makridis could not confirm that this was a standard interaction between the two intelligence organizations or if it was due to the political nature of the letter.

After the letter was published, Polymeropoulos sent media talking points to the PCRB for approval. Internal CIA emails show some agency employees were concerned that the talking points were "pro-Biden campaign and may be disclosing classified information."

One employee wrote that the letter "frustrates me. I don't think it is helpful to the Agency in the long run. Sigh."

In another email chain, a CIA employee wrote that it was "interesting to see what was submitted and approved by the PCRB."

Makridis speculated that "these individuals could have been frustrated by the politicized nature of the statement," the committee found.

It wasn't the first time the CIA had intervened to protect the Bidens. A congressional whistleblower claimed that the CIA had interfered with the IRS investigation into Hunter, his business partners had been asked to become CIA informants, and Burisma had the whiff of a CIA operation.

Careerists at the CIA realized the value of hitching their wagons to Morell, as he nailed the disinformation operation for the Biden campaign.

At least one serving CIA employee actively recruited people to sign Morell's letter. Former CIA analyst David Cariens said that, when he received a call from the CIA's prepublication review section to discuss the approval of his manuscript, the CIA staffer on the phone asked him to sign the letter.

"When the person in charge of reviewing my book called to say it was approved with no changes, I was told about the draft letter," Cariens said in a statement to Congress. "The person asked me if I would be willing to sign . . . I agreed to sign." His wife, Janice Cariens, a former CIA officer, also agreed to sign.

Polymeropoulos congratulated Morell for securing the lightning-fast pre-publication approval, according to text messages obtained by the House Judiciary Committee.

"You have some juice," he texted.

"With the PRB [Prepublication Classification Review Board]?" asks Morell.

"Yes, ha," replies Polymeropoulos.

"Ha is right," texted Morell. "They are probably scared I am coming back."

Like Morell, the Dirty 51 were part of Washington's cozy, bipartisan consensus of the spook, military, and foreign policy elite that Obama officials dubbed the "Blob." These are the people responsible for the weapons-of-mass-destruction intelligence hoax that justified the Iraq war, and the warrantless spying on American citizens that followed 9/11. They are devotees of color revolutions and regime change to preserve US global dominance. They work together in cozy gigs in the same think tanks and lucrative consultancy firms. They speak at the same events and liberal TV shows, write for the same publications, pal around with the same journalists, and some even pretend to be journalists. They retweet each other's anti-Trump memes and share hawkish views about Russia. The Dirty 51 were the Blob, and Biden was their guy.

Seven signatories were connected to George Mason University, through the Schar School of Policy and Government and the Michael V. Hayden Center for Intelligence, Policy, and International Security. Many also wrote for the Cipher Brief, a national security publication that has a strategic partnership with the Hayden Center and an ultra-hawkish view on Russia.

Several were paid contributors on television networks. Clapper appeared on CNN, Brennan on MSNBC. Six were connected to Beacon Global Strategies, the DC firm where Morell worked. Three were with The Center for Strategic and International Studies. Two were with the SpyEx consultancy.

According to one old Russia hand who refused to sign the Dirty 51 letter and knew of other refuseniks, it was instructive to look at "who didn't sign it." Names of the top Russia experts in the country were conspicuously absent, which made the letter seem all the more phony.

On the morning of October 19, 2020, while Morell still was gathering signatures, and while the CIA was vetting the letter, Director of National Intelligence John Ratcliffe made a public declaration that the *Post*'s story was not Russian disinformation. Everyone played their role, just as predicted in the Aspen Institute's "tabletop exercise" the previous month.

Ratcliffe rebuked Adam Schiff, then-chair of the House Intelligence Committee, who had been all over the media claiming: "this whole smear on Joe Biden comes from the Kremlin."

"Let me be clear," Ratcliffe said. "The intelligence community doesn't believe that, because there's no intelligence that supports that. The laptop is not part of some Russian disinformation campaign." Within 24 hours, the Department of Justice and the FBI had issued statements backing Ratcliffe's declaration.

But it was too late. Morell had already emailed Nick Shapiro, John Brennan's former CIA aide, to coordinate the press release, passing on detailed instructions from the Biden team on how to handle it: "[b]etween us, the campaign would like" a specific reporter with the *Washington Post* to publish the letter first.

Shapiro, an Obama campaign alum, crafted a release for the *Washington Post*, the Associated Press, and *Politico*, titled "Public Statement on the Hunter Biden Emails," and sent a copy to Bates at the Biden campaign, saying, "This is what I gave them."

Only *Politico* published the story that evening, under the headline: "Hunter Biden story is Russian disinfo, dozens of former intel officials say."

Five dramatic paragraphs down, the Dirty 51 admitted they had no evidence for their assertions: "We want to emphasize that we do not know if the emails . . . are genuine or not and that we do not have evidence of Russian involvement—just that our experience makes us deeply suspicious that the Russian government played a significant role in this case."

The next day, October 20, Clapper appeared on CNN and said that the laptop and emails were "classic textbook Russian tradecraft at work."

Signatory Jeremy Bash, Panetta's former chief of staff, told MSNBC: "This looks like Russian intelligence, this walks like Russian intelligence, this talks like Russian intelligence. This effort by Rudy Giuliani and the *New York Post* and Steve Bannon to cook up supposed dirt on Joe Biden looks like a classic Russian playbook disinformation campaign."

En masse, media outlets fell for the Russian disinformation lie being pumped out by the intelligence grandees. It was a convenient excuse to keep ignoring evidence published by the *New York Post* that Joe Biden had met with his son's foreign clients while he was VP.

NPR's Managing Editor Terence Samuel tweeted: "Why haven't you seen any stories from NPR about the NY Post's Hunter Biden story?

"We don't want to waste our time on stories that are not really stories, and we don't want to waste the listeners' and readers' time on stories that are just pure distractions."

Morell was cockahoop, writing an email to his co-signatories to congratulate them. "I just want to thank everyone for signing the letter on the Hunter Biden emails," he wrote. "I think this is the most important election since 1860 and 1864 when the very existence of the country was on the ballot. Now, it is our democracy and the Constitution that are on the ballot. We all, of course, took an oath to 'preserve, protect, and defend' the Constitution. I think all of you did that yesterday by signing this letter."

Two days later, candidate Biden used the letter in the final debate against Trump to deflect accusations about his involvement in his family's alleged international influence-peddling operation.

"Look, there are 50 former national intelligence folks who said that what he's accusing me of is a Russian plant," Joe told the audience. "Four, five former heads of the CIA, both parties, say what he's saying is a bunch of garbage. Nobody believes it except him and his good friend Rudy Giuliani . . .

"You know his character. You know my character. You know my reputation is for honor and telling the truth . . . The character of the country is on the ballot."

Joe had dismissed as a Kremlin smear all the evidence of illicit or unreported payments from China, Ukraine, Russia, Romania and Kazakhstan that was on his son's laptop. The Dirty 51 letter, like the Steele dossier and Russia collusion hoax peddled by many of the same people, had helped exacerbate a moral panic about Russia that would soon heighten the risk of nuclear war.

In the years since, not one of the signatories has expressed regret for potentially misleading the public, even when the DOJ confirmed in a court filing that the laptop belonged to Hunter, that he had abandoned it in a Delaware computer repair shop, and that the material it contained crossmatched with his iCloud.

"It's not my fault if people don't look up definitions," former CIA officer David Priess told Fox News two years later. "Those words are still true. It has all the classic earmarks."

Clapper blamed the media, which he said "deliberately distorted" the letter.

Douglas Wise, a former CIA deputy director, eventually would admit that he and others among the "Dirty 51" knew at the time they signed the letter that the emails on the laptop "had to be real."

Still, they collectively seem to have decided that Trump was an existential threat, and the American people could not be trusted to choose the right president.

Using the institutional weight of their esteemed former roles, they had succeeded in potentially misleading voters 15 days before the election. If not for their intervention and the censorship of the *New York Post*, the outcome of a very close contest could have been different.

Former AG Barr later said he believes the suppression of the Hunter Biden laptop story "probably affected the outcome" of the 2020 election, "given how close the election was."

After the debate, Morell received a call from Steve Ricchetti, chairman of the Biden campaign, to thank him. The call with Ricchetti was organized by Bash, "who I work with at Beacon and who is active politically," Morell said.

Bash would later be rewarded with a prestigious role on the President's Intelligence Advisory Board.

Morell, on the other hand, never did become CIA director. But his actions protected Joe Biden from revelations that might have derailed his candidacy. The Dirty 51 had killed the story stone dead.

However, what they did not know was that Hunter Biden's business activities were under investigation in Wilmington, Delaware.

Far from the tight-knit world of Washington's intelligence community, the criminal investigators attached to the Sportsman case, Joe Ziegler and his supervisor Gary Shapley, had information from covert search warrants of Hunter's iCloud and subpoenaed bank records that corresponded with what the *New York Post* had been reporting from the laptop.

Ziegler had signed the search warrant for Hunter's laptop after the FBI picked it up from the Delaware computer repair store where Hunter had abandoned it in April 2019, a few weeks before his father announced he would run for president.

The IRS investigators felt the laptop was real—and it wasn't Russian disinformation.

However, the American people were in the dark, and polls after the election suggested that the full story of the Bidens' alleged international influence-peddling scheme may have changed sufficient votes in crucial marginal seats to flip the result.

Blinken's gambit paid off. The letter can be seen as a domestic disinformation operation to deceive the American people and help Joe Biden win the 2020 election.

CHAPTER 12

INNOCENT BABY

October 23, 2020
FBI WASHINGTON FIELD OFFICE

It was eleven days before the 2020 election. The FBI had instructed Tony Bobulinski not to walk in the front door when he came for a "proffer" interview to warn them about his former business partner Hunter Biden's lucrative deals with China, and the potential compromise of his father, who might soon be president.

They told him to drive into an underground parking garage at the back of the Washington Field Office, a nondescript eight-story building in the northwest of the city, one mile from FBI headquarters. The agents didn't want anyone to see him arrive.

Twenty-four hours earlier, Bobulinski, 48, had appeared in Nashville at a press conference before the final presidential debate, as a "special guest" of the Trump campaign to corroborate the *New York Post*'s reporting from Hunter's laptop about Joe's alleged involvement in his son's seeming foreign influence peddling operation.

The successful Californian businessman had been caught up in the Biden family's last tumultuous Chinese deal that had its genesis in the tail end of Joe's vice-presidency and ended in tears in 2017. Along the way, Hunter had taken in more than $7 million from CEFC.

A former naval officer and nuclear submarine instructor at the elite Naval Nuclear Power Training Command in South Carolina, Bobulinski was from a family of Navy, Army, and Air Force veterans going back three generations on both sides. Born in the Portsmouth Hospital while his father was stationed on the Norfolk Naval base in Virginia, he attended Penn State, studied mechanical engineering, was captain of the wrestling team, and worked his way into a wrestling scholarship. In his junior year, he was recruited by the "Navy Nukes" before graduating with distinction, having made the Dean's List nine out of ten semesters. In 1995, his final year at Penn, he was named Big Ten Male Academic Athlete of the Year.

His job in the Navy was to train the officers and enlisted personnel who operate nuclear reactors on submarines and surface ships. Needless to say, he was a perfectionist. "When you are a mile underwater sleeping 10 feet from a nuclear reactor, your margin of error is zero," he says.

Lieutenant Bobulinski's final assessment before he left the Navy in 1999 was exemplary. His commanding officer described him as "truly an exceptional naval officer: a great leader, unusually productive and always inspired."

He was commended for: "Sustained extraordinary performance [with the] strongest possible recommendation for . . . early promotion to lieutenant commander."

On military bearing and character, he was judged an "exemplary representative of the Navy . . . a leader in physical readiness. [He] exemplifies Navy core values: Honor. Courage. Commitment."

Hunter Biden also had something of a naval career, but it was brief and ignominious. He obtained a rare and hard to get age waiver to join the reserves in 2013 and an exemption for a youthful cocaine arrest. He didn't last a month. On the first day of his first weekend of reserve duty, a random urine test detected cocaine in his system. Hunter told the Navy it wasn't his fault, that he had accidentally smoked cocaine-laced cigarettes that random strangers outside a bar had given him the night before he reported for duty. Somehow, the Navy bought it, and he received an administrative rather than a dishonorable discharge.

Bobulinski and Hunter were only two years apart in age, but they could not have been more different. Little wonder they ended up on the collision path which had brought Bobulinski to this bleak, windowless room that the Trump campaign had reserved for his press conference at the Marriott Hotel in Nashville on October 22, 2020.

Wearing a well-tailored black Canali suit over his wrestler's frame, he was tense as he stood in front of the few reporters and TV cameras that had shown up. The campaign had not bothered to set up a podium for him, or a microphone, or even a glass of water. He had to ask for a chair so he could put down his phones. It was just him standing against a wall.

He did not relish throwing himself into the center of the biggest political scandal of his lifetime. But he drew on his military training, and the memory of his forebears, and did his duty.

With a steady voice, he began to read from the sheaf of papers in his hand: "I'm making this statement to set the record straight about the involvement of the Biden family, Vice President Biden, his brother Jim Biden, and his son, Hunter Biden, in dealings with the Chinese.

"I have heard Joe Biden say that he's never discussed business with Hunter. That is false. I have first-hand knowledge about this because I directly dealt with the Biden family, including Joe Biden.

"I've never been political. The few contributions I have made have been to Democrats. But what I am is a patriot and a veteran. To protect my family name and my business reputation, I need to ensure that the true facts are out there.

"In late 2015, I was approached by James Gilliar, whom I had known for many years, about joining him in a deal which he said would involve the Chinese state-owned enterprise CEFC China Energy and what he called one of the most prominent families in the United States. I was informed, first by Gilliar, and then by Hunter Biden and by Rob Walker, who was working with the Bidens, that the Bidens wanted to form a new entity with CEFC, which was to invest in infrastructure real estate and technology in the US and around the world, and the entity would initially be capitalized with $10 million and then grow to billions of dollars of investment capital.

"After months of discussion, I agreed to Gilliar and Hunter Biden's request to become CEO of the entity, to be called SinoHawk, 'Sino' representing the Chinese side, 'Hawk' representing Hunter Biden's brother Beau's favorite animal.

"Between February and May 2017, we exchanged numerous emails, documents, and WhatsApp messages concerning SinoHawk and its potential business. On May 2, 2017, the night before Joe Biden was to appear at the Milken conference, I was introduced to Joe Biden by Jim Biden and Hunter Biden.

"At my approximately hour long meeting with Joe that night, we discussed the Bidens' history, the Bidens' family business plans with the Chinese, with which he was plainly familiar, at least at a high level.

"After that meeting, I had numerous communications with Hunter, Walker, Gilliar, and Jim Biden regarding the allocation of the equity ownership of SinoHawk. On May 13, 2017, I received an email concerning allocation of equity, which says '10 [percent] held by H for the big guy.' In that email, there is no question that 'H' stands for Hunter, 'big guy' for his father, Joe Biden, and 'Jim' for Jim Biden.

"In fact, Hunter often referred to his father as 'the big guy' or 'my chairman.' On numerous occasions, it was made clear to me that Joe Biden's involvement was not to be mentioned in writing, but only face to face. In fact, I was advised by Gilliar and Walker that Hunter and Jim Biden were 'paranoid' about keeping Joe Biden's involvement secret.

"I also had a disagreement with Hunter about the funds CEFC was contributing to SinoHawk. Hunter wanted $5 million of those funds to go to himself and his family, so he wanted the funds wired directly to an entity affiliated with him. I objected because that was contrary to our written agreements concerning SinoHawk. He said, referring to the 'chairman,' his father, that CEFC was really investing in the Biden family, that he held the trump card, and that he was the one putting his 'family legacy' on the line.

"He also said to me on May 17, 2017, that CEFC wanted to be 'my partner,' to be partner with the Bidens. During these negotiations, I repeated to Hunter and others that SinoHawk could not be Hunter's personal piggy bank, and I demanded the proper corporate governance procedures be implemented for capital distributions. Hunter became very upset with me. CEFC, through July 2017, was assuring me the funds would be transferred to SinoHawk, but they were never sent to our company. Instead, I found out from Senator Johnson's September report that the $5 million was sent in August 2017 to entities affiliated with Hunter.

"Tomorrow I will be meeting with the Senate committee members concerning this matter, and I will be providing to the FBI the devices which contained the evidence corroborating what I have said."

Not one television network carried Bobulinski's press conference live. As he walked out the door, a journalist called out to him: "Did Rudy Giuliani have anything to do with your appearance here?"

No, Giuliani had nothing to do with Bobulinski, who had spent his own money for a private jet to fly from California to team up with the Trump campaign because he thought it was the best way to warn America that "Honest Joe" was not what he claimed to be.

But hitching his wagon to the campaign just gave the media the excuse they wanted to ignore him or dismiss what he said as a partisan stunt.

Even among outlets that did cover Bobulinski's accusations, many, like *Politico*, sneered at him as a "fringe" character who "stood awkwardly in a tight-fitting suit [and was] peddling dubious stories into the center ring of our political circus."

Bobulinski put his black COVID mask back on and headed to the auditorium with the rest of the socially distanced audience to watch the debate. Trump was nearly ten points behind in the polls and was champing at the bit to deliver a fatal blow to his opponent's credibility.

"Don't give me this stuff about how you're this innocent baby," he barked at Joe. "They are calling you a corrupt politician."

The president raised Hunter's "Laptop From Hell" repeatedly during the 90-minute debate and mentioned Bobulinski's accusations, although he got some of the details wrong.

"You're the big man, I think," Trump told Joe.

"I don't know, maybe you're not. But you're the big man, I think. Your son said we have to give 10% to the big man. Joe, what's that all about? It's terrible . . .

"The emails are horrible. The emails of the kind of money you were raking in, you and your family. And Joe, you were vice president when some of this was happening. And it should have never happened. And I think you owe an explanation to the American people . . . You do live very well. You have houses all over the place. You live very well."

Joe coolly replied: "I have not taken a penny from any foreign source ever in my life . . . Nothing was unethical . . .

"With regard to Ukraine, we had this whole question about whether or not, because [Hunter] was on the board, I later learned, of Burisma, a company, that somehow I had done something wrong.

"Yet every single solitary person, when [Trump] was going through his impeachment . . . said I did my job impeccably. I carried out US policy. Not one, single, solitary thing was out of line. Not a single thing . . .

"My son has not made money in terms of this thing about—what are you talking about—China."

Almost everything Joe said seemed to be a lie. He not only knew of Hunter's job, but he'd met at least a dozen of his partners, from China, Ukraine, Russia, Kazakhstan, and Mexico, during his vice presidency and in the weeks and months after he left office.

He'd had dinners with them, invited them to his place for breakfast, talked to them on speaker phone. He'd written recommendations for their children to go to swanky schools.

A senior US diplomat testified at Trump's first impeachment that he'd raised concerns with VP Biden's office about Hunter's Ukraine connection, to no avail. Joe didn't want to hear.

Hunter had taken millions from China. But the facts would take more than two years to begin to break through to the American public. The protective shield around the Bidens was strong, and the coverup was orchestrated by some of the most devious operators in the security state, including many of the same shadowy cabal who had set up Trump with the Russia collusion hoax.

Thanks to his Deep State guardian angels, Joe had a secret weapon that night, a letter from 51 former intelligence officials claiming, without evidence, that Hunter's laptop was Russian disinformation.

The Dirty 51 letter did what it had been designed to do. It got Joe off the hook and provided the figleaf needed by Biden-friendly media not to follow up on the *New York Post*'s story.

The next day, Bobulinski flew to Washington for his appointment with the FBI. He was met by James Dawson, Special Agent in Charge of the Criminal and Cyber Division, and FBI Supervisory Special agent Giulio Arseni.

After brief pleasantries, they turned him over to two younger agents, William Novak and Garrett Churchill, who conducted the interview and provided a receipt for a flash drive of emails and messages that Bobulinski had provided from three phones he had used from 2015 to 2018. They contained the WhatsApp messages he had exchanged with Hunter, Jim, and their partners in the SinoHawk joint venture.

For more than five hours, he told the agents about the Biden connection to CEFC in the last year and a half of Joe's vice presidency, and how he saw the Biden name was used to help the company expand into Oman, Romania, Georgia, Kazakhstan and beyond, the FBI record of interview shows.

He told them the involvement of the VP's son and brother lent legitimacy to CEFC's mission, as part of the Belt and Road initiative, to extend the communist party's empire. The Biden name would soothe misgivings about China's acquisition of strategic energy assets and the superpower's reputation for exploiting weak states and ensnaring them in debt traps.

He laid out in forensic detail the times that Joe met with Hunter's business partners, both during and after his vice presidency. He showed the agents documents in which the Chinese talked of their delight about doing business with the "B family," and the encrypted WhatsApp messages and emails in which Joe was referred to in code as "the big guy" or by Hunter as "my chairman."

Novak and Churchill were silent, interrupting Bobulinski only to leave the room and consult with their superiors. Arseni came into the room occasionally, and an FBI forensic team visited to look at his phones, although he did not want to relinquish them.

He told the FBI agents that, after leaving the Navy he had worked as a technology equity analyst at Citibank before joining a private investment firm in Los Angeles. He had acquired enough wealth to retire in his early 40s and spent the next eight years as an independent investor traveling the world negotiating business deals.

It was during his travels that Bobulinski met Gilliar, whose globe-trotting existence was something of a mystery. Gilliar had divorced his first wife and left rural England in the mid-2000s to settle in Prague with a glamorous new Czech wife, with whom he bred racehorses. He ran a political consultancy with clients as varied as the South Korean government, a United Arab Emirates royal family, and the US Department of Homeland Security.

Bobulinski's experience of doing business in China was of particular interest to him.

According to Bobulinski, Gilliar's most promising project was advising an enigmatic young Chinese client, Ye Jianming, the forty-year-old chairman of CEFC, who would embark on an extraordinary spending spree in the Czech Republic in 2015, laying out billions of dollars to buy everything from football teams and a brewery to an airline and a bank, with the aim of establishing the Central European country as China's "Gateway to the European Union," a priority of China's President Xi Jinping. Uncle Jim would later tell the FBI that Hunter had "portrayed [Chairman Ye] as a protégé of President Xi."

Bobulinski remembers Gilliar repeatedly trying to recruit him for a big investment partnership he was cooking up between CEFC and "one of America's most prominent families."

In April 2016, Gilliar brought together Bobulinski and Rob Walker in Las Vegas. Walker told Bobulinski that he acted as a "proxy" for the Biden family on business deals and investments.

Also with them in Vegas at the time, to celebrate the 50th birthday of a friend, was Gabriel Popoviciu, a Romanian real estate tycoon who had just started paying Hunter, Gilliar, and Walker $180,000 a month to use their influence to get him off corruption charges. (There's no evidence that Hunter or his father acted improperly or violated any laws. But the arrangement, government ethics experts say, raises concerns that Hunter Biden was used as a prop in Popoviciu's effort to dodge criminal prosecution.)

Once Bobulinski started telling his tale to the young FBI agents, he could not stop.

He told them the astonishing role that Hunter played as CEFC Chairman Ye's confidant and visitor to his $50 million Manhattan penthouse at the time the company was brokering China's $9 billion acquisition of the Russian state oil giant Rosneft—and how the deal fell apart after Ye was arrested in China in 2018. He told the agents that CEFC did not pay Hunter and Jim for their assistance while Joe was VP because they were concerned that it would appear "improper" due to the company's "close affiliation with the Chinese government."

Bobulinski told the agents about the first time he met Joe at the Beverly Hills Hilton Hotel bar to discuss his alleged involvement in the family's Chinese joint venture SinoHawk.

It was back on May 2, 2017, and Bobulinksi had arrived an hour early to meet Hunter and his uncle Jim, who bore an uncanny resemblance to his famous brother, despite being seven years younger and slightly heavier. Jim had spent his entire life in loyal service to Joe, raising money for his political campaigns, moving in to help the newly widowed Joe bring up his sons, and dragging Hunter periodically to drug rehab. Biden matriarch Jean, nee Finnegan, had put her eldest son on a pedestal, and his two brothers and sister Val were expected to act accordingly. Occasionally Jim had bristled at his inferior status, but with his nephew, he was 100 percent loyal.

When Bobulinski arrived at the bar, Jim explained immediately that the meeting with Joe was strictly "high level."

"We will not go into any detail about the business," added Hunter. "I just want my dad to be comfortable with you."

When Joe arrived, Bobulinski stood up to shake his hand. "This is Tony, Dad," said Hunter, "the individual I told you about that's helping us with the business that we're working on with the Chinese."

Joe spent most of the time talking about his family tragedies and telling tall tales of his derring-do. Bobulinski briefly described his military service, and Joe thanked him for "helping my son."

Hunter told Joe that Bobulinski had been "working hard" on the Chinese deal, and Joe said: "My son and my brother trust you emphatically, so I trust you."

The meeting was over in 45 minutes, but Joe invited Bobulinski to meet him again at 8:30 a.m. the following day in the hotel ballroom to hear his speech to the prestigious Milken Institute Global Conference.

Bobulinski messaged Jim Biden on WhatsApp at 11:40 p.m.: "Great to meet u and spend some time together, please thank Joe for his time was great to talk thx."

The next morning, Bobulinski went back to the Beverly Hilton for Joe's speech. Afterward, they walked outside together to his waiting car and shook hands.

"Keep an eye on my son and brother and look out for my family," Joe said.

Bobulinski then, according to his statement to the FBI, went to the nearby Peninsula Hotel to meet Jim, who was sitting alone in a blue and white striped cabana by the rooftop pool.

"How are you guys getting away with this?" Bobulinski asked Jim of the risk of Joe being involved in deals with companies owned or affiliated with foreign governments, such as China and Russia, "without being accused of impropriety."

"Aren't you afraid for Joe's political campaign?"

Jim looked knowingly at him. "Plausible deniability," he said.

According to the FBI record of the interview, Bobulinski told the agents that he understood Jim's reply to mean that "financial transactions that ultimately benefitted Joseph Biden and his family were brokered through and managed by Joseph Biden's family members such as Hunter Biden and [Jim] Biden—to protect Joseph Biden's direct involvement.

"The structure gave Joseph Biden the ability to plausibly deny his involvement and knowledge of the transactions, while still benefiting indirectly."

Two weeks after the meetings, Gilliar sent Bobulinski an urgent WhatsApp message service, warning him not to tell anyone about Joe's alleged involvement in the CEFC deal.

"Don't mention Joe being involved, it's only when u are face to face, I know u know that but they are paranoid," Gilliar told Bobulinski.

"OK they should be paranoid about things," Bobulinski replied.

He told the agents that, when Joe became the Democratic nominee for president in August 2020, Bobulinski decided that, as a former naval officer, he "had a duty to tell someone what he knew" about the Biden family's ties to China.

His resolve to blow the whistle only hardened after he heard Joe claim during the campaign that he "never talked business" with Hunter, a statement Bobulinski "knew to be false." He also learned in September 2020, from a Senate report into Hunter Biden by Republicans Chuck Grassley and Ron Johnson, that Hunter had "gone behind his back" and received almost $5 million from a CEFC-linked entity, money that he believed was supposed to have funded SinoHawk. Before the Oversight committee, Hunter testified, "So there was constant friction between Mr. Bobulinski and myself and my uncle, who—like the three-sevenths when everybody else got one-seventh or—it just didn't make sense to us. And we were at a constant impasse together and constantly fighting."

He remembered thinking how absurd Trump's impeachment trial was when he watched it in 2019: "the lies and ridiculousness, because I knew how the Bidens operated in business . . . All the claims around Hunter Biden was on Burisma's board because he's a highly qualified lawyer—I just knew all of that was ridiculous . . . claiming that it was purely innocent that [he] was on the board . . . making a million dollars a year.

"I had all this knowledge of how the Biden family operated, and I started thinking through, this is insane to me. I was willing to die for this country for six years of my life, and I know all these facts. How do I put them together and get somebody to understand them or look at them?"

Eventually, he contacted a friend in the orbit of Trump's eldest son, Don Jr., who set up a clandestine meeting on October 9, 2020, in a private house in McLean, Virginia, between Bobulinski's lawyer and *Wall Street Journal* White House reporter Michael Bender, who would write about the encounter in a book the following year. In *Frankly, We Did Win This Election: The Inside Story of How Trump Lost* Bender admits that he wasn't particularly interested in Bobulinski's story. He showed up late for the interview and, even before he heard what Bobulinski had to say, he was "skeptical" because Joe had "long said he wasn't involved in any of his son's foreign deals." It didn't seem to occur to him that Joe may have lied. He claimed that he had been lured to the meeting with the promise that Bobulinski had documents that detailed specific payouts for Joe. But Bobulinski never made such claims.

On October 14, 2020, the *New York Post* published its first scoop from Hunter's laptop, a 2015 email from Burisma executive Vadym Pozharskyi thanking Hunter for introducing him to his father.

In his book, Bender blames the *New York Post*'s "mishandling" of the story for the failure of the "mainstream media" to pick up the story. He does not explain what that "mishandling" could be. In the months after the election, the *New York Times* and the *Washington Post* would belatedly start reporting on the Hunter Biden scandal, although always with a paragraph absolving Joe of any involvement.

Their faith in his honesty would be sorely challenged over the next three years. Even as evidence about Joe's possible involvement in the family business piled up there was never any introspection or expression of regret from the establishment media about missing the biggest political story of their lives. Instead, with each new admission from the Bidens, journalists adjusted the framing a little at a time, until their readers believed the narrative had always been that the laptop was real and, while Joe might have met his son's business partners to talk about the weather, he never was "in business" with Hunter and never took money directly.

The morning the *Post*'s story broke, Gilliar organized a conference call with Bobulinski and Walker. They were in a panic about Hunter's recklessness, worried that his father's campaign would try to offload blame onto them.

"Will Hunter and/or Joe or Joe's campaign try to make it 'Oh, we were never involved' . . . and try to basically make us collateral damage?" one of the men asked.

"I don't see how that would work for them," Gilliar responded, trying to reassure the others that revelations about Joe's involvement in his son's foreign deals would not damage them—regardless of the outcome of the election.

"I think in the scenario that he wins they would just leave sleeping dogs lie."

"If they lose, honestly, I don't think that the Big Guy really cares about that because he'll be too busy focusing on all the other shit he is doing," said Gilliar, using Joe's code name.

The following day, October 15, 2020, in another conference call, at 8:35 a.m. EST, Gilliar told his associates not to be worried that the Biden campaign would throw them under the bus.

"I've circled round and made sure that's not the case," Gilliar can be heard saying in an audio recording. "It's not like us and them, or like we're thrown out in the garbage. We just need to do things the right way. Do the right thing and not rise to this."

Bobulinski was angry about the lies Democrat Rep Adam Schiff told every day on television. Then the chairman of the powerful House Intelligence Committee, Schiff attacked the *Post*'s reporting on Hunter's laptop as "Russian disinformation."

"We know that this whole smear on Joe Biden comes from the Kremlin," he told CNN.

Bobulinski was irate. He knew the emails published by the *Post* were authentic because he had been cc'd on a lot of them. He felt personally affronted by Schiff's comments, which he believed falsely associated his name with a Russian plot. He demanded that Walker use his relationship with the Bidens to get Schiff to retract his claims, or he would go to the media himself to set the record straight.

"Ah, Tony, you're just going to bury all of us, man," Walker responded.

* * *

Bobulinski was still waiting for the *Wall Street Journal* to publish his story, as was a certain person in the White House.

The story promised to be huge. Bobulinski was a credible, independent source of demonstrable probity whose account verified much of the material on the laptop, disproving the Russian disinformation lie. He also offered a first-hand perspective on how Hunter and his uncle had seemingly leveraged Joe's power for millions in China. Plus, he had encrypted messages with Hunter and their Chinese partners, some of which referenced Joe, which he would hand over to congressional investigators.

As he would tell Congress in 2024, "From my direct personal experience . . . it is clear to me that Joe Biden was 'the Brand' being sold by the Biden family. Joe Biden was more than a participant in and beneficiary of his family's business; he was an enabler, despite being buffered by a complex scheme to maintain plausible deniability. The only reason any of these international business transactions took place—with tens of millions of dollars flowing directly to the Biden family—was because Joe Biden was in high office. The Biden family business was Joe Biden, period."

Bobulinski's account of his personal interactions with Joe and Hunter would be a lot harder for the Biden campaign to dismiss as "Russian disinformation."

Then Trump put his foot in it. On October 19, 2020, in a conference call with staff to which reporters had been invited, the president let slip that "the *Wall Street Journal* is working on a very, very important piece, which should be very good, actually."

It was just an offhand mention, but it put the *Journal* in a dilemma.

"We were screwed" was the reaction from Bender, one of the reporters listening in on the call. "An already tricky story about the son of the Democratic presidential nominee just days before the election had suddenly become even more challenging. We'd be accused of carrying Trump's water if we wrote it. We'd be accused of burying a kill shot on Biden if we spiked it. And neither accusation would be correct."

Bobulinski was sick of waiting. On Wednesday, October 21, he turned over all his evidence to Senators Johnson and Grassley. They had contacted him and Hunter's other partners after their names appeared in the *Post*'s reporting on the laptop.

That night, he issued a 684-word statement to the media confirming that he was one of the recipients of the "10 [percent] for the big guy" email.

"I could no longer allow my family's name to be associated or tied to Russian disinformation or implied lies and false narratives dominating the media right now," he wrote.

The next day, just as the debate in Nashville was ending, the *Wall Street Journal* published a brief 760-word item online. It was not the story Bobulinski had been expecting. Instead, it refuted his claims.

"Hunter Biden's Ex-Business Partner Alleges Father Knew About Venture" read the headline. "Former vice president says he had no involvement; corporate records reviewed by the *Wall Street Journal* show no role for Joe Biden."

To stick the boot in, there was a disingenuous quote from Gilliar, the very author of the "big guy" email: "I would like to clear up any speculation that former Vice President Biden was involved with the 2017 discussions about our potential business structure. I am unaware of any involvement at any time of the former Vice President. The activity in question never delivered any project revenue."

Bobulinski couldn't believe, in his opinion, that Gilliar would lie so blatantly. "He doesn't say Joe Biden was never involved. He says, 'I am unaware.' It's a lie. He was aware that I met with Joe Biden. He was aware that Joe Biden came into that conference room and shook Chairman Ye's hand. He was aware that they were invoking the Biden name, and that's all the Chinese cared about . . . What an absolute lie that altered history, in my opinion."

Gilliar "didn't want the facts to impact Joe Biden being elected," Bobulinski told Congress. "I had numerous discussions with him, and they were of the impression that Joe Biden was going to win the election. And they were concerned that, if the truth came out about this, that it could alter the election. And I believe it did."

The *Journal*'s downplaying of Bobulinski's story gave extra legitimacy to the rest of the media ignoring it.

Bobulinski was disappointed, but he still had his appointment with the FBI.

About an hour into his interview at the Washington Field Office the next day, his Blackberry rang.

Bobulinski looked down at the screen and registered with disbelief the name of the caller: Jim Biden dialing in on WhatsApp.

Bobulinski wordlessly raised the still ringing Blackberry to show his lawyer and the FBI agents who was calling.

The agents got up out of their chairs like scalded cats and quickly left the room.

"You can take that call if you want," they said.

When Bobulinski answered the phone, there was nobody on the line.

He doesn't know if Jim was trying to send him a warning. But that was the last time he heard from the Bidens.

* * *

Two weeks later, Hunter felt a great weight off his shoulders as he stood on stage in front of a sea of honking cars in the Wilmington convention center parking lot after his father's victory speech.

Wearing a black pandemic mask, with little Beau on his hip, he gave his father a proprietorial hug in front of the world. It had taken a few days for the results of the agonizingly close election to come through.

But, now, on November 7, 2020, it was official. He was to be the First

Son, protected from the consequences of his actions by his father's pardon power.

"A Trump victory was not only a threat to democracy [but] it also seemed a threat to my personal freedom," he wrote in his memoir.

"If Dad hadn't won, I'm certain Trump would have continued to pursue me."

He was "100 percent certain" that the Delaware investigation into his finances would clear him of wrongdoing.

But the IRS and FBI investigators in Delaware were operating under a very different assumption. As soon as the election was over, so, too, were DOJ demands to suspend all overt actions on the Sportsman case.

The shackles were off, and they would be able to pursue the usual investigative steps, recommend charges, and finally be done with this cursed case. Or so they thought.

CHAPTER 13

DAY OF ACTION

December 8, 2020
VENICE BEACH, CALIFORNIA

The "Day of Action" finally was scheduled for December 9, 2020, more than five weeks after the election. It was to be the grand finale of the Sportsman investigation that IRS Supervisory Agent Gary Shapley and his FBI counterpart Joe Gordon had been working toward for months, the day when they could go "overt."

But, still, there were obstacles. Because the 2020 election had been contested, the original plan to go overt on November 17 was delayed. Their search warrant for Hunter's LA house was denied. Then the DOJ said they didn't want to ruin the Biden family Thanksgiving holiday by approaching Hunter while he was visiting Delaware.

Delaware US Attorney David Weiss came up with excuse after excuse to delay. Because there had been no leaks—yay team!—he decided that his priority was to continue "to protect the integrity of the investigation," which was a euphemism for keeping it "concealed from the public," Shapley recalled in congressional testimony three years later.

In a marathon Sportsman meeting at Weiss's office in downtown Wilmington lasting about 12 hours on December 3, the usually buttoned-down

US Attorney began by "jubilantly" congratulating the investigative team for keeping the probe quiet or, as Weiss called it, "secret."

Weiss was in and out of the room for the rest of the meeting, "but it went downhill from there," said Shapley. "We shared with prosecutors our outline to interview Hunter Biden's associate, Rob Walker. Among other things, we wanted to question Walker about an email that said: 'Ten held by H for the big guy.' We had obvious questions like who was H, who the big guy was, and why this percentage was to be held separately with the association hidden."

But Assistant US Attorney Wolf, "interjected and said she did not want to ask about the big guy and stated she did not want to ask questions about 'dad.'

"When multiple people in the room spoke up and objected that we had to ask [about Joe], she responded, there's no specific criminality to that line of questioning. This upset the FBI too. And . . . the IRS and FBI agents conducting this interview tried to skirt AUSA Wolf's direction."

But, when the "Day of Action" finally arrived, agents across the country were in place, ready to knock on doors simultaneously and interview a dozen Biden family members and associates, such as Jim Biden and wife Sara in Pennsylvania, and Rob Walker in Arkansas.

Shapley and Gordon would take care of Hunter themselves. They had flown to California the previous night and now they were sitting in a car in Venice Beach about a block from Hunter's place, just after dawn on December 8, waiting for the all-clear from the FBI's LA field office.

A complication of the delay was that Hunter had been assigned Secret Service protection on December 3, and they were concerned about a potential "blue-on-blue" event if they arrived unannounced.

"I personally was not going to go to armed Secret Service agents and demand that I interview their protectee," Gordon would later testify to Congress.

"As somebody who has to provide protection, having an IRS supervisor and an FBI supervisor, also armed, coming to a scene would cause confusion. And as the worst case . . . it could be a blue-on-blue matter. They don't know who we are. They don't know if our credentials are faked."

So, they decided to "deconflict" any potential problems and get the FBI's LA boss to call the Secret Service LA boss at 8 a.m. and alert them that Shapley and Gordon were about to knock on the door and interview Hunter as part of an official investigation.

But someone at FBI headquarters in Washington sabotaged their plan the previous night, informing Secret Service headquarters as well as Joe Biden's transition team.

"This essentially tipped off a group of people very close to President Biden and Hunter Biden and gave this group an opportunity to obstruct the approach on the witnesses," recalled Shapley, who said that when he met up with Gordon early the next morning he was "clearly dejected about how our plan had been interfered with."

They were told to sit tight and wait for Hunter to call them. "SSA Gordon and I waited in the car outside of Hunter Biden's California residence waiting for a phone call. It was no surprise that . . . we received a telephone call later that morning from Hunter Biden's attorneys, who said . . . we couldn't talk to his client. The public news of our investigation hit the press the next day."

They drove over to Kevin Morris' place in the Pacific Palisades and tried to interview him, but Morris had already lawyered up and clammed up.

"I can't know for certain whether FBI's advance notice played a role or not, but of the 12 interviews we hoped to conduct on our day of action, we only got one substantive interview," said Shapley.

"It was with Rob Walker in Arkansas, and it was exactly the sort of interview we expected to have if the FBI hadn't tipped off Secret Service and the transition team. In the interview, the FBI agent tried to get Rob Walker to talk about the 'ten held by H' email while not directly contradicting AUSA Wolf's direction not to ask about the, quote, 'big guy.'"

It was FBI Special agent Josh Wilson from Delaware who showed up with IRS agent Adam Soline at Walker's Little Rock house at 10:03 a.m. with a hidden microphone and asked about the "big guy" email. This was the 2017 email in which Hunter's partner James Gilliar had suggested Hunter would hold 10 percent of the equity in their deal with CEFC on behalf of his father.

Walker answered: "I think that maybe James was wishful thinking or maybe he was just projecting that, you know, if this was a good relationship and this was something that was going to happen, the VP was never going to run, just projecting that, you know, maybe at some point he would be a piece of it, but he was more just, you know. It looks terrible, but it's not. And fuck Tony [Bobulinski] for taking little pieces of emails, you know, and not showing the structure of an LLC or taking pieces of conversation that he recorded of me . . . I don't know what's in it for Tony but that email looks bad and it's probably hard to explain for James. Do I remember it? No. Does it look real? Yeah. And, you know, I certainly never was thinking at any time that the VP was a part of anything we were doing."

But then Walker was asked if Joe had ever met with CEFC executives, he admitted that he had—including during his vice presidency.

He told the agents all about the time the former Vice President "stopped by" a lunch he, Gilliar and Hunter were at with CEFC officials at the Four Seasons hotel in Georgetown.

Wilson asked: "Any times when he was in office, or did you hear Hunter say that he was setting up a meeting with his dad with them while dad was still in office?"

"Yeah," said Walker.

Inexplicably, Wilson changed the subject. Maybe he was worried that he'd already overstepped Wolf's edict not to ask about Joe. But he had left a crucial question unanswered about Joe's involvement in his son's alleged influence peddling operation.

December 8 had become their disappointing Day of Inaction. But one thing the investigators did learn that day was that Hunter had vacated his office at the House of Sweden and his documents were in a storage unit in northern Virginia.

Ziegler prepared an affidavit in support of a search warrant for the unit, and emailed Wolf: "I would like to possibly execute this sometime next week. I think that is reasonable, given the upcoming holiday."

Her response was characteristically negative: "We are getting to work on this, but I want to manage expectations with you regarding timing. It has to go through us, DOJ Tax, possibly OEO [DOJ Office of Enforcement

Operations], and definitely [Eastern District of Virginia], who has never seen the case before, layer in the filter requirements in the Fourth Circuit, and it's just not clear it's going to happen next week, even with everyone making it a priority."

Ziegler smelled a rat straight away. "So that tells me two things right there," he later testified. "That David Weiss wasn't really in charge. And it also tells me that I have never had a case to where, if we needed to get records and preserve them, that we didn't do everything in our power to get a search warrant approved and get moving on that expeditiously.

"So, I guess with the storage unit—we asked them to keep an eye on it and tell us if anyone went to it. But it was highly unusual that I'm being told that we couldn't even do it the following week . . . It was ultimately decided by AUSA Lesley Wolf to not do the storage unit search warrant . . . I told her that I completely disagreed with her and that we weren't following the appropriate investigative steps to get the stuff in the storage locker and that I thought that she might be acting inappropriately."

Ziegler was so upset about Wolf's reaction that he took detailed notes of that December 11 phone call, referring to himself in the third person.

He told Wolf that he had worked very hard on the case, "going above and beyond what is required, and he doesn't believe that his prosecutors are supporting him in the decisions he is making. Ziegler also pointed out that he was afraid moving forward that the AUSAs were going to be afraid of pending litigation and issues with the case . . .

"Wolf became verbally offended and said that . . . Ziegler was afforded a big seat at the table and that she is often going ahead with his suggestions even when she doesn't agree with them. Wolf said that she has concern with the relationship moving forward and that if Ziegler has this concern regarding the case that maybe they need to address that with upper management . . . because Ziegler had questioned her integrity.

"Ziegler apologized for offending Wolf and said that he was expressing how he felt and was providing various evidence of why he felt that way. Wolf stated that she has always been going along with what we [investigators] want [and] she didn't think that Ziegler understood how much effort it took on their office's part just to get the overt action accomplished this past week. Ziegler said that he doesn't want to have a bad relationship but . . . that he has the support of his [bosses] with how he is feeling."

After fretting over this latest obstacle, Ziegler went back to Wolf a few days later with an idea: "What if we didn't tell Hunter Biden's counsel about the storage unit? He's been given a request for records. What if at the time that he's given those requests for records he doesn't access the unit? And if he doesn't access the unit, we know he's not complying with that request. So, if at the end of that time he doesn't access it, let's do a search warrant on it then. She told me she would think about it. So, I pushed this up to my leadership. I pushed it through [Shapley]. They all agreed with it. They thought it was a great idea."

Shapley got his boss to join a call to help pressure Weiss to take action for once. Weiss, 64, was the inscrutable saboteur of the investigation, always giving the impression of genial cooperation. But, in my opinion, he was subtly undermining investigators behind their backs, and passively allowing his underling, Wolf, and the faceless men and women of Main Justice in DC to call the shots. To Shapley, Weiss seemed to be a slippery customer, and so Shapley started keeping detailed notes of their interactions which he passed up the line to his superiors.

"Look, we got to do this," Shapley told Weiss during the call. "We need unfettered access to this evidence."

Weiss eventually made the concession that, if Hunter had not accessed the storage unit within 30 days, they could execute a search warrant on it.

But Wolf sabotaged the plan immediately, said Shapley.

"No sooner had we gotten off the call [with Weiss] than we heard AUSA Wolf had simply reached out to Hunter Biden's defense counsel and told him about the storage unit, once again ruining our chance to get to evidence before being destroyed, manipulated, or concealed."

Ziegler was frustrated, too. "They literally went around my back, my idea, around what we already talked about, and did something completely different. And I guess it was at this point—there were a lot of things that happened before this. But it was at this point for me that I started to believe that the attorneys with the Delaware US Attorney's Office and DOJ Tax were not acting appropriately, they were not following the appropriate investigative steps, and that we were not a part of the trajectory and the planning of the investigation as we normally are."

Ziegler would later sum up in his whistle-blower testimony what he saw as the real issues at stake: "This case at the end of the day was about access and introductions to high-level government and political officials for wealthy foreign individuals . . . in Ukraine, Romania and China, in exchange for money to enrich a well-known political family—of which, Hunter Biden had failed to file and pay his taxes [in a] timely [fashion] as is required by law on millions of dollars of income and had allegedly wilfully filed false tax returns to the IRS. And at the end of the day, it appears that the Department of Justice attempted to sweep everything under the rug."

After successfully dodging the IRS and FBI, Hunter would issue a statement, not in his own right, but on the official letterhead of his father's "Biden-Harris transition" operation, confirming that he was under federal investigation for tax fraud.

By using Joe's letterhead he was sending the signal, without having to state it plainly, that the investigation was a political stitch-up, aimed at damaging his father, an idea that would find traction in the paranoid post-election climate.

"I learned yesterday for the first time that the US Attorney's Office in Delaware advised my legal counsel, also yesterday, that they are investigating my tax affairs . . . I am confident that a professional and objective review of these matters will demonstrate that I handled my affairs legally and appropriately, including with the benefit of professional tax advisors."

The statement had an addendum from his father: "President-elect Biden is deeply proud of his son, who has fought through difficult challenges, including the vicious personal attacks of recent months, only to emerge stronger."

Shapley and Gordon never did get to interview Hunter. It wasn't the first time investigators had been stymied as they got close to evidence potentially incriminating Hunter and his father—and it would not be the last.

CHAPTER 14

HUNTING HUNTER

November 2018
WILMINGTON, DELAWARE

S pecial Agent Joe Ziegler was regarded as the most talented criminal investigator in the crack IRS team dubbed the "Seal Team 6" of tax fraud investigations: the International Financial Tax Crimes group.

In November 2018, he was examining bank reports as part of an investigation into a foreign-based amateur online pornography platform when Hunter Biden's name popped up. Under US anti-money laundering laws, banks are required to report to Treasury any suspicious transactions that might suggest criminal activity, even if they may not necessarily prove wrongdoing.

Some of the Suspicious Activity Reports leaked to research non-profit Marco Polo identified Hunter as paying tens of thousands of dollars to escorts in a potential Eastern European prostitution ring. Hunter was described as a "Politically Exposed Person" and some of the transactions were flagged as being "consistent with possible human trafficking."

Hunter was an enthusiastic user of escort services, as his abandoned laptop would attest. He also was an avid user of Pornhub, a Canadian amateur porn-sharing site where he uploaded hundreds of videos of himself having sex with various women, encounters he gave such titles as "Lonely Widow."

There was evidence in the reports that Hunter was spending lavishly from his corporate bank account. "This is a typical thing that we look for in tax cases—criminal tax cases," Ziegler, 38, would tell Congress five years later.

When he opened the case into the former VP's 50-year-old son, Ziegler had no idea of the political buzzsaw he was walking into. After he reluctantly turned whistleblower, he would point out to critics who tried to pigeonhole him as a Republican partisan that he is a gay registered Democrat and is married to a man. For him, politics was irrelevant to his job. He was just conducting the investigation into Hunter, the way he did with anyone else, and diligently following an investigative trail wherever it led.

It didn't take long before the trail led to Hunter's acrimonious divorce the previous year, which raised a red flag over his taxes. Ziegler found media reports in which Kathleen Biden's lawyer had told the court that Hunter "has created financial concerns for the family by spending extravagantly on his own interests, including drugs, alcohol, prostitutes, strip clubs, gifts for women with whom he had sexual relationships, while leaving the family with no funds to pay legitimate bills.

"The parties' outstanding debts are shocking and overwhelming. The parties have maxed-out credit card debt, double mortgages on both real properties they own, and a tax debt of at least $300,000."

When Ziegler pulled Hunter's file he found he wasn't exactly the model taxpayer. He had stopped paying his overdue federal taxes for 2015, failed to pay his 2016 taxes, and hadn't even filed his 2017 tax return, while living an extravagant lifestyle. It looked as if Ziegler had enough to open an investigation, but colleagues warned him to be careful. "Big cases, big problems, was the thing I was constantly hearing. I responded to say it shouldn't matter the name of the person on whether we work a tax case or not. It should be the merit of the evidence, the allegation, and the clear understanding of why we are opening that investigation. So doing the right thing for the right reason."

Ziegler spent the next four months following leads that suggested Hunter was dodging his taxes before requesting permission from the DOJ to take the case to the US Attorney in Washington, DC, where Hunter had been living.

His manager at the time told him, "'No, you cannot do that. That's a tax disclosure [confidentiality] issue.' I didn't agree with him because there's been multiple instances where we do that. That's a normal part of our job. But he was my manager, and I wasn't going to fight him on it."

Ziegler found another way to get the case approved, via the DOJ's Tax Division, but it took him three tries. Each time, his supervisor, Supervisory Special Agent Matt Kutz, set the bar for evidence higher. It was almost as if he didn't want him to try.

According to Ziegler, Kutz told him: "a political family like this, you have to have more than just an allegation and evidence related to that allegation. In order for this case to move forward, you basically have to show a significant amount of evidence and similar wrongdoing that would basically illustrate a prosecution report."

Ziegler replied, "We have to treat each taxpayer the same. It shouldn't matter on their name."

He didn't agree with Kutz, "but he was my manager, and I had to do what he said."

What Ziegler didn't know was that the FBI also had opened an investigation into Hunter in early 2019, based on bank reports of suspected illicit activity, including money laundering. Dozens of Suspicious Activity Reports had been generated by banks such as Wells Fargo that Hunter was using to allegedly funnel cash from shady benefactors in China, Ukraine, Russia, Kazakhstan, and Romania, through to dozens of shell companies in Delaware.

In April 2019, after Joe Biden announced he was running for president, Ziegler was told that the DOJ, under Trump Attorney General Bill Barr, had decided to merge his tax inquiry with the wider active investigation into Hunter's activities that was being conducted by the Delaware FBI and US Attorney David Weiss. Codenamed Sportsman, they wanted the probe run out of Delaware.

Ziegler thought that was a crackpot idea. For one thing, Hunter lived in Washington, DC, so that is where charges would have to be brought. For another, Wilmington was a small office, ill-equipped to run a case of this complexity.

Most importantly, the subject's father was the most powerful person in the state with tentacles of influence developed over five decades.

Ziegler was concerned about the risk that any investigation would be compromised in the state where Joe had ruled the roost for so long as senator and then VP.

The second smallest state in the nation, Delaware's strict corporate secrecy rules and lenient taxation mean that almost two-thirds of Fortune 500 companies are incorporated there, including Google's parent company Alphabet, Amazon, CVS Health, and CNBC parent company Comcast. Delaware also is home to thousands of anonymous shell companies and is renowned as a haven for transnational crime.

The Financial Secrecy Index dubbed Delaware "America's Liechtenstein," judging it the world's most opaque financial jurisdiction, where legislation beneficial to financial services interests is worked out with lawmakers behind closed doors.

Delaware even has its own special court, the Court of Chancery, to rule on corporate law disputes without juries, a cozy arrangement with which Hunter professed familiarity. When one of his Chinese business partners questioned his profligate expenses, Hunter threatened to "bring suit in the Chancery Court in Delaware—which as you know is my home state and I am privileged to have worked with and know every judge on the Chancery Court."

Joe's style of quid pro quo cronyism and favor trading for political influence has come to be known as the "Delaware Way."

His network of corporate donors and political allies kept him and his family in a lavish lifestyle out of reach of the usual senator's salary, including private schools and the Du Pont mansion where Hunter and his brother, Beau, grew up.

Ziegler was aware of the power of the Biden name in Delaware. From

2007 to 2015, Beau Biden served as the Attorney General for the state, based in Wilmington. Members of the investigative team lived in Wilmington, where the FBI field office and US Attorney's office were located a few blocks from each other, all just five miles west of Joe Biden's grand lakeside estate in the exclusive enclave of Greenville. (Joe had always referred to the man-made reservoir next to his custom built mansion as a "lake," but during his presidency, as questions mounted about his wealth, he started calling it a "pond.")

An early indication of how the oppressively nepotistic atmosphere in Delaware would affect the investigation came in September 2020 when FBI case agent Josh Wilson, who had just moved back to his hometown of Wilmington, expressed concern about "the consequences for him and his family" if they conducted sensitive interviews and executed a search warrant on a guest house at Joe's property where Hunter was living. Another time, Joe dropped by the FBI office in Wilmington, apparently on an unrelated matter, an awkward moment for the agents on the Hunter investigation at the time. Ziegler said they all cracked jokes about his presence later, but it nonetheless brought home the special challenges of investigating a Biden in the state the family dominated.

More of an irritation throughout 2019 was his IRS supervisor whom he alleges needlessly interfered in ways Ziegler thought could potentially sabotage the case, though there has been no official finding it was sabotaged.

His supervisor also kept talking about Donald Trump's tweets in alarmist tones, and bombarded him and the prosecution team with articles in the media that, however tangentially, might relate to the case.

"I recall that at one point I had to go around my supervisor and ask his boss . . . to tell him to stop sending me and the Hunter Biden prosecution team these emails and that I was searching media articles on a weekly basis and was aware of everything being written," Ziegler recalled.

Nevertheless, he plugged along, telling himself: "There is nothing we can change. We just have to deal with every challenge and roadblocks that were put in front of us and continue to do what is right, for the right reasons." As hard as it would be over the next three years, his perseverance paid off, against all odds.

At college, Ziegler had thought he would follow in his brother's footsteps and become a doctor, but pre-med wasn't for him. He switched to accounting, where he found he had a gift for analyzing and organizing complicated information. His photographic memory would later make him a formidable expert witness in court—or when delivering whistleblower testimony to Congress.

Growing up in Cleveland, Ohio, in a conservative Baptist family, Ziegler struggled with his sexuality early on and tried to conform to his father's expectations. But, after his first marriage to a woman failed, he eventually came out as gay at age 30, and moved to Atlanta, Georgia, where he lives with his husband, a personal trainer.

After a stint at the big accounting firm Ernst & Young, he joined the IRS in 2010. He worked his way up from healthcare fraud cases into the elite international criminal investigation unit, where he helped recover hundreds of millions of dollars from fraudsters and tax cheats.

His salary of $150,000 was a fraction of what he might have earned if he'd stayed in the corporate world, and chump change to the likes of Hunter Biden. With two dogs, a mortgage, and student loans to pay off, he lived paycheck to paycheck. But he loved his job and was suited to it. Nobody was more dedicated.

In January 2020, things started looking up. He got a new boss, criminal supervisory special agent Gary Shapley, who he later would tell Congress is the "best supervisor I've ever worked with in my life. He was someone I could come to whenever I needed to vent, was someone who always fought with his heart and soul to do what was right, even if we didn't agree on the path, and would try to make sure that we always were heard. He is someone I look up to as a leader in our organization."

Shapley, 45, the father of four daughters and a decorated 14-year veteran of the IRS, led the team of 12 elite agents, including Ziegler, who worked on complex high-dollar international tax investigations. He also was head of the Joint Chiefs of Global Tax Enforcement (J5) group that investigated international tax and financial crimes with Australia, Canada, the Netherlands, and the United Kingdom. He reported directly to the chief of IRS Criminal investigation Jim Lee.

He had investigated some of the largest and most complex cases in IRS history, recovering more than $3.5 billion for the US taxpayer.

The three and a half years he worked on the Hunter Biden case would prove to be the most difficult time of his life. Shapley says that at every stage, DOJ officials in Washington and prosecutors in Weiss' office obstructed and slow-walked and hampered the investigation. He also says he and his team were misled and kept in the dark, and Weiss was unwilling to intervene unless pushed. Every "deviation from the normal process" had the effect of benefiting Hunter and making it more difficult to bring charges. Gradually, the scope of the investigation shrank, and delays grew longer. Shapley did his best to protect the case and go to bat for his investigators. He wrote detailed memos to his IRS bosses, recording each perceived infraction as it happened, but he felt they failed to do their jobs, leaving him in the unusual position of dealing directly with Weiss, who he felt acted at times as if he were a passive bystander.

Ultimately, Shapley would blow the whistle, making protected disclosures to the IRS and DOJ inspector generals and then testifying to Congress with Ziegler.

It was a testament to the tenacity and integrity of both men that the investigation into Hunter got as far as it did.

As frustrated as Shapley was, from Ziegler's point of view, things had started to improve on the team once he had him as his boss.

His initial tax probe had expanded to include potential bribery, money laundering, illegal foreign lobbying, human trafficking, and gun violations.

When the FBI picked up Hunter's laptop from John Paul Mac Isaac's computer repair shop in December 2019, they notified the IRS that it likely contained evidence of tax crimes. Ziegler signed a search warrant for the data and requested access, but the prosecutors kept fobbing him off.

In any case, an electronic search warrant of Hunter's iCloud backup in

August 2020 would soon yield a treasure trove of evidence that matched what was in the laptop.

Bubbling along behind closed doors was a grand jury. On May 15, 2019, it authorized a subpoena for Hunter's transactions involving the Bank of China, according to bank documents obtained by anti-corruption non-profit Marco Polo, raising concerns that compromising material about then-candidate Joe had been hidden from voters. The subpoena was issued by US Attorney Weiss to JP Morgan Chase. It asked for the records of any international financial transactions in the past five years involving Hunter, his uncle Jim Biden, and former business partners Devon Archer and Eric Schwerin. Joe had just announced he was running for president the previous month.

Just when Ziegler thought they were getting somewhere in the Hunter investigation came what he called a "devastating blow" in the summer of 2020. The lead Delaware prosecutor on the case, Assistant US Attorney Jamie McCall, abruptly left for a high-paid job as a partner with Pennsylvania law firm Kessler Topaz Meltzer & Check. A Judge Advocate in the Marine Corps, McCall was "hard-working, no-nonsense" recalled Ziegler.

"He wanted to do the right thing for the right reason. He would constantly push the envelope, and it was apparent that he was following the evidence and not working to create roadblocks."

In McCall's place was Assistant US Attorney Lesley Wolf, 38, a Democratic donor and Yale graduate. She lived 40 minutes from the Wilmington office in an upscale Philadelphia suburb with her husband, Daniel, a psychiatry professor, and had been working in the Delaware office since 2007, serving under three US Attorneys. Over 13 years she had observed the power Joe Biden wielded over legal processes in the state, and she did not appear to be a person to rock the boat.

When McCall left, everything became a grind, said Ziegler, who liked Wolf and counted her as a friend. However, he felt the prosecution team "did not follow the ordinary process, slow-walked the investigation, and put in place unnecessary approvals and roadblocks."

He felt that every avenue that would lead to Joe was blocked by Wolf, with the implicit authority of Weiss, who would rarely appear at meetings. For instance, on August 7, 2020, the FBI shared a draft of an email search warrant related to a Foreign Agents Registration Act (FARA) investigation into Burisma. The search warrant identified "Political Figure 1" as "Former Vice President Joseph Biden."

Wolf demanded that Joe's name be removed. "As a priority, someone needs to redraft attachment B," she emailed the team. "There should be nothing about Political Figure 1 in here."

Later that month, the IRS received the results from an electronic search warrant of Hunter's iCloud, including a WhatsApp message in which Hunter tells a Chinese associate: "I am sitting here with my father." Ziegler wanted to check geolocation data to find out if Joe really had been sitting with his son, but prosecutors denied his request.

In a prosecution team meeting on September 3, 2020, Ziegler again asked for permission to access the location data and again was denied. He kept trying, but eventually the request fell off the list of agenda items.

In the same meeting, Wolf agreed that there was "more than enough probable cause" to support a search warrant for a guest house on Joe's Greenville estate where Hunter frequently stayed. But she questioned "whether the juice was worth the squeeze," according to contemporaneous notes taken by Shapley.

She claimed that "optics were a driving factor in the decision on whether to execute a search warrant," and the optics were bad. At a later meeting, Wolf told the prosecution team that US Attorney Weiss also had agreed that there was probable cause to search the guest house, but there would be no search warrant.

It's worth noting that the unusual obstacles placed in Ziegler's way by the DOJ and the prosecutors in Delaware at this time occurred during the Trump administration, when Attorney General Bill Barr was in charge. The kid gloves treatment of candidate Biden by the FBI may be less a case of direct political manipulation than of institutional aversion to being seen to intervene in an election, as then–FBI Director James Comey claimed when he announced he was reopening an investigation into Hillary Clinton's improperly stored emails days before the 2016 election. Clinton blamed Comey for her subsequent defeat, and the FBI was roiled by the political fallout.

Recriminations in powerful Democratic circles about Trump's shock victory would echo through the FBI for years to come. Similarly, CNN boss Jeff Zucker, awash in accusations that he personally was responsible for Trump's ascendancy, set about trying to salvage his reputation. At NBC, he had given Trump his start on smash hit reality show *The Apprentice* and then enthusiastically showcased him on CNN in the 2016 campaign to boost ratings. Perhaps to make amends with the liberal New Yorkers who had stopped inviting him to dinner, Zucker would dedicate the next four years to a CNN program schedule heavy on Trump Derangement Syndrome.

In any case, it was DOJ policy—the so-called 60-day rule—to delay public actions during the final stages of an election that might influence perceptions of a candidate and improperly affect the vote. So, on September 4, 2020, Deputy Attorney General Richard Donoghue issued an instruction that all politically sensitive cases must refrain from overt activity until after the election.

Wolf immediately convened a prosecution team call to communicate the stand-down instructions and declared that the DOJ was "under fire and that it was self-inflicted," as Shapley recorded her comments in a memo of the meeting. She also claimed that the DOJ "needs to repair their reputation [and] has a zero tolerance for risk that any of these requests [for search warrants] somehow tip off someone that would leak them to the media."

Weiss seemed content to allow Wolf to arguably hobble the investigators and give Hunter Biden preferential treatment, with the effect that the statute of limitations would run out in November 2022 on the most serious tax and foreign lobbying charges from the years 2014 and 2015—years when Joe was VP.

Worse obstruction was to come as the investigation limped along.

But in the fractious days before the 2020 election, there was one more damning piece of evidence that Weiss and Wolf were accused of hiding from their investigators.

Pittsburgh US Attorney Scott Brady had been asking to brief Delaware about an FBI FD-1023 report he had uncovered. FD-1023 forms are used by special agents to record unverified reporting from confidential human sources. The report from a trusted, long-term, paid FBI informant sensationally alleged that Hunter and possibly Joe each had been paid a $5 million bribe by an executive of Burisma. (The debate over the informant's reliability would break into the open much later.) But Wolf kept refusing to meet Brady to hear what he had to say.

Finally, after Brady complained to the Justice Department, Weiss's office was ordered to take the Pittsburg briefing, but neither Shapley, nor Ziegler, nor anyone on the IRS criminal investigation team ever saw the FD-1023, nor were told that it existed, despite the fact it was directly relevant to their case.

The invisible hands that were protecting the Bidens had been working overtime. But people of integrity were starting to stand up, and it would be impossible to silence them all.

CHAPTER 15

THE HUMAN BLAST SHIELD

January 29, 2020
PITTSBURGH, PENNSYLVANIA

Rudy Giuliani and his attorney Bob Costello flew to Pittsburgh in January 2020, to meet with Scott Brady, the US Attorney for the Western District of Pennsylvania, armed with a thick file of allegations from Ukrainians alleging Biden family corruption.

It was the middle of President Trump's impeachment trial over a phone call in which he asked Ukrainian president Volodymyr Zelenskyy to investigate Joe Biden and son Hunter, and Giuliani had been to Ukraine gathering information he hoped would exonerate Trump, or at least justify his request of Zelenskyy.

Giuliani had been the tough-on-crime mayor of New York who led the city through the trauma of 9/11. Before that he had been a crusading DA for the Southern District of New York (SDNY) who took down the Five Families in the 1980s and rose to the prestigious role of US Attorney.

"America's Mayor" would forever be a legend to the loyal cops and firefighters who gather downtown at Cipriani Wall Street every September 11 to fete Giuliani and remember their brothers in arms who were lost in the Al Qaeda terrorist attacks of 2001.

But his latest chapter, as the scotch-swilling consigliere to the president, had damaged his hard-won reputation. He got offside with nearly everyone in the administration and became the media's favorite punching bag as he loyally defended Trump through multiple controversies, culminating in the last disastrous scramble to prove the 2020 election was stolen. After his efforts on Trump's behalf, he was sued by everyone, including one of his three ex-wives, and was forced into bankruptcy at the age of 79. He lost his beloved Upper East Side apartment, with its oak paneled library, carved ceilings, and working fireplaces, his proof that the working-class Italian kid from Flatbush was a prince of the city.

Yet he remained irrepressible, lashing Democrats daily on his WABC radio show in New York, until WABC owner John Catsimatidis canceled his show in May 2024 because he refused to stop talking about "fallacies of the November 2020 election," in violation of company policy. Giuliani simply moved his show to X, where he has 1.7 million followers. But, when it came to the Biden saga, his old prosecutorial instincts would be vindicated.

Tired of the delicate approach of his former attorneys, Trump had enlisted Giuliani as his new "Roy Cohn" in March 2019 in the aftermath of the Mueller investigation, which ultimately had cleared the president of colluding with Russia. Giuliani began looking into the origin of the "Russia hoax," as Trump called it, and believed that it was a dirty trick hatched by Hillary Clinton's campaign using Ukrainian operatives to frame Trump with the assistance of corrupt FBI agents. He believed that the real collusion was between Clinton's campaign and Ukrainians who wanted her to win in 2016.

He discovered Biden bribery allegations in the process, traveling to Ukraine and assembling a file of evidence from former Burisma employees and past and present prosecutors, including Viktor Shokin. Giuliani was convinced that his client was being impeached for Joe Biden's sins.

"[Trump] was my friend for 30 years. This was an innocent man being framed by a group of scoundrels," he said.

Giuliani tried to interest Secretary of State Mike Pompeo and Attorney General Bill Barr with his Ukraine file, to no avail. He regularly went on TV expounding his theories until the Biden campaign publicly demanded the networks stop booking him. His combative style and persistent demands irritated Barr, an establishment Republican with a distinguished legal career who had served as AG once before, under President George H.W. Bush, and had a deep affinity for the CIA.

When he was a high school junior, Barr's ambition was to become CIA director, according to his memoir *One Damn Thing After Another*. He worked for the CIA in the 1970s, protecting its secrets as the agency's liaison to Congress, and remained a staunch defender through every CIA scandal of the post-Watergate era.

If Hunter was being protected by the CIA, as suggested by his Burisma links, the Dirty 51 letter, Joe's career trajectory, Hunter's laptop blurtings, Langley's meddling in the IRS investigation of Hunter, and assorted other data points, then AG Barr was not the man to rock the boat. The mystery of why Barr funneled all Biden-related allegations to Joe's nepotistic home state of Delaware, to be "investigated" by a weak and potentially biased US Attorney, may be explained by his CIA roots.

In any case, Barr thought Giuliani was a loose cannon. Giuliani thought Barr was weak, and he didn't keep that opinion to himself.

"I would say, 'Hey fatso, you took your oath to the United States, not to your career,'" Giuliani recalled of their interactions.

Barr felt that the FBI investigation of Trump for so-called Russia collusion was "one of the greatest travesties in American history" and an effort by the FBI to "sabotage" his presidency. He saw his role as Trump's second AG as restoring the reputation of the DOJ after its Obama-era scandals, including the ruinous Comey intervention in the 2016 campaign. Barr's resolve to eliminate political interference was sorely tested in his 22 months serving President Trump, when he was attacked from left and right, eventually getting slammed in presidential tweets.

He quit a month before the end of his term after incurring Trump's wrath for saying the DOJ had found no evidence of voter fraud in the

2020 election. Trump was also angry with Barr for having kept the Hunter Biden investigation under wraps before the election.

"Why didn't Bill Barr reveal the truth to the public, before the Election, about Hunter Biden," Trump exploded on Twitter. "Joe was lying on the debate stage that nothing was wrong . . . Big disadvantage for Republicans at the polls!"

* * *

Giuliani wasn't the only source of derogatory information about alleged Biden family influence-peddling in Ukraine and China that was flooding into the FBI and US Attorney's Offices around the country between 2016 and 2020.

Republican Senator Chuck Grassley would later allege in a letter to FBI Director Wray and Attorney General Merrick Garland that more than 40 confidential human sources had provided alleged "criminal information" about the Biden family to the FBI—which the DOJ then tried to discredit as "foreign disinformation."

The informants, managed by various FBI field offices, had given the bureau details of alleged crimes by Hunter, Jim, and Joe Biden, claimed Grassley, who had developed a reputation as a champion of whistleblowers.

"Based on the information provided to my office over a period of years by multiple credible whistleblowers, there appears to be an effort within the Justice Department and FBI to shut down investigative activity relating to the Biden family," Grassley wrote.

Grassley and colleague Ron Johnson had been investigating the Biden family's foreign financial dealings since August 2019. As they zeroed in on Joe's alleged role in foreign payments to Hunter, they faced escalating interference with their inquiry, including a bogus FBI defensive briefing that was leaked to the press.

When Johnson issued a subpoena asking for records from Blue Star Strategies, the Democratic party lobbying firm Hunter had enlisted to represent Burisma, Democrats accused him of "potentially inadvertently" spreading Russian misinformation.

Andrew Bates, a spokesman for the Biden campaign, told reporters that Johnson was "running a political errand for Donald Trump [and trying to] resurrect a craven, previously debunked smear against Vice President Biden."

The intense pressure soon intimidated two of the more delicate Republican senators on the committee, Mitt Romney and Rob Portman. The pair withheld crucial votes so that Johnson was no longer able to issue subpoenas, and the inquiry was hobbled.

Back in 2018, one of the people reporting bribery allegations involving Joe and foreign nationals was Bud Cummins, the former US Attorney for Arkansas.

In an October 8 email to SDNY US Attorney Geoff Berman, Cummins claimed he had evidence that Joe had allegedly "exercised influence to protect" his son's Ukrainian employer "in exchange for payments to Hunter Biden, Devon Archer, and Joe Biden."

Cummins said that Ukraine's then–Prosecutor General Yuriy Lutsenko wanted to travel to the United States to meet Berman and could produce two "John Doe" witnesses to corroborate his claims about the Bidens.

Berman never responded to the email. Instead, in a move Cummins later told me felt like "retaliation," federal prosecutors secretly obtained data from his iPhone with a grand jury subpoena to Apple, on December 9, 2019, in the middle of impeachment proceedings against President Donald Trump.

"It doesn't make much sense to investigate the guy who brings you the allegation," said the former Arkansas chief federal prosecutor.

When Cummins received the notice from Apple telling him that his data had been accessed three years earlier, he said he found it "perverse that you report an allegation of a pretty serious crime, and they don't investigate [it] but they were investigating you. I can't really imagine a legitimate reason for the DOJ not to follow up on an offer like that. I felt like it was stonewalled."

Then there was Israeli professor-turned-fugitive Gal Luft who, in 2019, provided the SDNY with information about payments to Hunter and Jim

Biden from Chinese company CEFC. But the only result was that Luft was arrested four years later.

All the allegations against the Bidens seemed to fall into the same black hole as the evidence about the CEFC joint venture that Tony Bobulinski gave to the FBI before the 2020 election.

Bobulinski's material corroborated some of Luft's claims and bolstered evidence the FBI had secretly authenticated almost a year earlier from Hunter's laptop. Further corroboration came from evidence subpoenaed by IRS whistleblowers Shapley and Ziegler in the Delaware investigation into Hunter that was being conducted by US Attorney David Weiss.

But in every case, the evidence was suppressed and ignored in the way Grassley had mapped out.

As attorney general, Barr knew that Giuliani was under investigation by the SDNY for possible foreign agent violations. The probe would lead to an FBI raid in April 2021 on the former mayor's home and office in New York. Giuliani tried to get agents searching his Upper East Side apartment to take several hard drive hard drive copies of Hunter's laptop from his desk, but they refused, despite the warrant specifying that all electronic devices should be seized.

The investigation into Giuliani was closed in November 2022 without charges being laid, but it had given the FBI the opportunity to spy on his iCloud.

Barr also knew that there was an investigation into Hunter that had quietly been percolating in Delaware, and he didn't want to jeopardize it.

So, he set up what he called an "intake process" in January 2020 to vet Rudy's material as well as other non-Giuliani allegations from Ukraine in an attempt to prevent misinformation from that corrupt nation tainting investigations in Delaware and in the Southern and Eastern Districts of New York. He tasked US Attorney Scott Brady from the Western District of Pennsylvania to lead the independent "taint team" of prosecutors and FBI agents to filter material and ensure it was credible, before passing it on to—or in some cases withholding it from—the relevant investigators.

Brady described his role to a friend as "basically a human blast shield around Mayor Giuliani."

* * *

Giuliani and Costello were treated courteously when they arrived in Pittsburgh. They were picked up at the airport by two FBI agents and driven to Brady's office, Costello recalled, where they spent almost four hours going through Giuliani's Ukraine file.

Giuliani handed over bank account details and other evidence of alleged bribery of the Biden family that he said came from former Burisma bookkeeper Zhanna Lisin. She was the widow of Mykola Lisin, the former co-owner of Burisma, who died in a car crash in 2011, after which his stake in the company was taken over by Mykola Zlochevsky, who kept Zhanna on the payroll. Giuliani claimed to have bank records of wire transfers suspected of going to the Bidens, including $10 million in February 2014, that took a circuitous route through banks in Latvia and Cyprus and wound up in a Citibank New York account.

It is not known if that bank account was subpoenaed, but no concrete link to the Bidens ever emerged.

Costello says Zhanna went into hiding in 2023 as the Ukraine war raged and fake reports of her death circulated in the US but that she was still in touch with a Ukrainian-American named Michael.

Costello says that two assistant US attorneys from the SDNY interviewed Michael in Florida in September 2020 in relation to Giuliani's alleged foreign lobbying violations. However, when he "volunteered that he had spoken to [Lisin. They] said 'we don't want to talk about her.'"

It was a tangled web, to say the least, and it was Brady's job to sort it out.

But he kept hitting obstruction from the FBI and from prosecutors in Delaware. For instance, the FBI required 17 higher-ups to sign off on his requests, "mostly at the headquarters level" where there was always a "choke point" that caused delays, Brady would testify later to Congress.

The FBI didn't even open the so-called assessment—the lowest level of FBI investigation—Brady had requested until March 2020, and it had to be renewed every 30 days via this unprecedented 17-person signoff.

FBI agents "had to go pens down sometimes for two or three weeks at a time before they could re-engage and take additional steps because they were still waiting on, again, someone within the 17-chain signoff to approve," Brady said. He was forced to go to the deputy attorney general's office repeatedly to clear logjams—at least five or six times in nine months.

Brady also testified that line agents had been told to withhold information from his office. "We were told that someone at FBI Headquarters, unknown to me, said: 'Don't share that with the US Attorney's office,' to which I said: 'I'm a presidentially appointed United States Attorney. We're on the same team.'"

The FBI did not tell Brady that it had Hunter's laptop, either. When the *New York Post* broke the story in October 2020, Brady said he was "surprised" that he had been kept in the dark. FBI HQ also refused Brady's request for a copy of their Domestic Investigations and Operations Guide, so he could pinpoint the deviations from procedure he was encountering, and he was forced to scrounge a redacted copy from a public website.

It was a frustrating waste of time. Five months would go by before he struck gold.

* * *

In late May 2020, Brady's request for keyword searches of the FBI database hit paydirt. Buried in the files of the Washington Field Office since 2017 was a brief reference to Hunter's Ukraine connections. It was a throwaway line in a so-called FD-1023 report, information provided by a trusted, long-term, highly paid FBI confidential human source (CHS) to his FBI handler.

Brady met resistance when he asked the FBI to reinterview the informant in early June. Finally, on June 30, 2020, the CHS was reinterviewed and delivered the bombshell allegation that Burisma's owner Zlochevsky had paid $10 million in bribes to two people named Biden to get Shokin fired. Zlochevsky referred to one of the two Bidens as the "Big Guy," which was the codename that Hunter's American partners used for Joe.

"Don't worry, Hunter will take care of all those issues through his dad,"

Zlochevksy allegedly told the CHS when asked about Shokin's investigation during a meeting at a coffee shop in Vienna, Austria in 2016.

"It costs 5 (million) to pay one Biden and 5 (million) to another Biden."

While it has been widely speculated that the two Bidens who were bribed were then-VP Joe and Hunter, that's not explicit in the FD-1023.

The informant's FBI handler wrote in the FD-1023: "Zlochevsky made some comment that, although Hunter Biden 'was stupid, and his (Zlochevsky's) dog was smarter,' Zlochevsky needed to keep Hunter Biden (on the [Burisma] board) 'so everything will be okay.'

"CHS inquired whether Hunter Biden or Joe Biden told Zlochevsky he should retain Hunter Biden; Zlochevsky replied, 'They both did.' CHS reiterated CHS's opinion that Zlochevsky was making a mistake and he should fire Hunter Biden and deal with Shokin's investigation directly so that the matter will remain an issue in Ukraine, and not turn into some international matter. Zlochevsky responded something to the effect of, 'Don't worry, this thing will go away anyway.'"

In a subsequent phone call in 2016 or 2017, the "CHS inquired whether Zlochevsky was happy with the US election results," wrote the FBI handler. "Zlochevsky replied that he was not happy Trump won the election. CHS asked Zlochevsky whether he was concerned about Burisma's involvement with the Bidens. Zlochevsky stated he didn't want to pay the Bidens and he was 'pushed to pay' them . . . CHS then stated, 'I hope you have some back-up (proof) for your words (namely, that Zlochevsky was 'forced' to pay the Bidens). Zlochevsky replied he has many text messages and 'recordings' that show that he was coerced to make such payments."

In a 2019 phone call with Zlochevsky and another Ukrainian, Alexander Ostapenko, the CHS told Zlochevsky he "might have difficulty explaining suspicious wire transfers that may evidence any (illicit) payments to the Bidens," wrote the FBI handler.

"Zlochevsky responded he did not send any funds directly to the 'Big Guy' (which CHS understood was a reference to Joe Biden). CHS asked Zlochevsky how many companies/bank accounts Zlochevsky controls; Zlochevsky responded it would take them (investigators) 10 years to find the records (i.e., [allegedly] illicit payments to Joe Biden). CHS told Zlochevsky if he ever needed help in the future and wanted to speak to somebody in the US government about that matter, that CHS could introduce him to someone."

The informant then added a note of caution, suggesting to his FBI handler that the Ukrainians might have been full of hot air and that he could not verify Zlochevsky's allegations.

"Regarding the seemingly open and unsolicited admissions by Pozharskyi and Zlochevsky about the purpose for their retention of Hunter Biden, and the 'forced payments' Zlochevsky made to the Bidens, CHS explained it is very common for businessmen in post-Soviet countries to brag or show-off," wrote the FBI handler.

"Additionally, it is extremely common for businesses in Russia and Ukraine to make 'bribe' payments to various government officials. [So] CHS did not perceive Pozharskyi's or Zlochevsky's statements to be unusual, self-serving, or pretextual.

"Additionally, regarding important business meetings, it is also common in Ukraine and Russia for persons to make covert recordings. However, CHS has only met Zlochevsky in person on one occasion and has spoken to him only twice on the telephone; as such, CHS is not able to provide any further opinion as to the veracity of Zlochevsky's aforementioned statements."

The FD-1023 records a separate meeting in which Burisma executive Vadym Pozharskyi allegedly told the CHS that Burisma had hired Hunter to "protect us, through his dad, from all kinds of problems."

After Brady's team received the FD-1023, they asked the FBI handler to go back to his confidential informant and get more information about the "covert recordings" Zlochevsky supposedly had made.

So on June 29, 2020 the FBI handler updated the FD-1023 with the following information: "ZIochevsky said he had a total of '17 recordings' involving the Bidens; two of the recordings included Joe Biden, and the remaining 15 recordings only included Hunter Biden. CHS reiterated that, per Zlochevsky, these recordings allege [that] Zlochevsky was somehow coerced into paying the Bidens to ensure Ukraine Prosecutor General Viktor Shokin was fired. Zlochevsky stated he has two documents (which CHS understood to be wire transfer statements, bank records, etc.), that evidence some payment(s) to the Bidens were made, presumably in exchange for Shokin's firing.

"Regarding aforementioned Oleksandr Ostapenko (alternate spelling, Alexander Ostapenko), who originally introduced CHS into this matter, Ostapenko currently 'works in some office for the administration of President Zelensky,' and also works for Valery Vavilov, who is the founder/CEO of cryptocurrency and blockchain technology business BitFury."

The allegations were astonishing, although uncorroborated.

Brady's team made inquiries, within the limit of their remit, to assess their credibility. Without a grand jury, they had to rely on information provided by the informant's FBI handler and the intelligence services, as well as whatever they could find in the FBI files.

Brady verified with the Eastern District of New York, the lead district investigating Russian disinformation, that none of the material in the FD-1023 accorded with known sources of disinformation. Through open-source information, Brady confirmed other aspects of the FD-1023, such as the fact that Burisma had bought a US gas company for $30 million.

None of it was proof that Zlochevsky's allegations were true, but Brady had seen enough to recommend that the FD-1023 deserved further investigation by Weiss' team in Delaware.

Instead of gratitude for his team's diligence, he hit a brick wall in Delaware. Assistant US Attorney Lesley Wolf resisted all cooperation. Multiple times, she refused the Brady team's requests to brief her on what they had found.

This had been the pattern from the beginning. Brady had to keep phoning his Delaware counterpart to get him to intervene, but Weiss doesn't appear to have been much help. One time Brady called Weiss and said in "colorful language . . . can you please talk to your team, this is important."

Eventually, Principal Associate Deputy Attorney General Richard

Donoghue had to intervene to order Weiss to accept Brady's briefing on October 23, 2020.

Weiss did not bother attending, but Brady's team briefed Wolf on their preliminary assessment of the FD-1023, told her they found the bribery allegations credible and stressed that they had nothing to do with Giuliani.

According to congressional testimony by IRS supervisory agent Shapley, Wolf declared in a meeting that she was refusing to cooperate with Brady's office because "no information from that office could be credible [because] it all came from Rudy Giuliani," which was untrue, as Brady's team told her. Wolf's criticism ignored the fact that Brady had been assigned to vet Ukraine information precisely to ensure that it was credible before it was passed on.

Brady told Weiss directly that "the [FD-]1023 was from a credible CHS that had a history with the FBI, and that it was not derived from any of the information from Mr. Giuliani."

Nevertheless, the FD-1023 was concealed from the very people who should have investigated it—the IRS and FBI criminal investigators working the Hunter probe.

For three years, the allegations remained unexplored, until a whistleblower alerted Grassley to the existence of the FD-1023. Grassley then told Oversight Chairman James Comer, since the bribery allegations were directly relevant to the Biden corruption inquiry, and Comer subpoenaed the document.

Initially, Director Wray claimed the FD-1023 didn't exist. Then, after the two Republicans told him that they had already seen the document, he admitted its existence, but still refused to release it, citing concerns that the valuable informant's life would be put at risk.

A month later, it took a threat by Comer to hold Wray in contempt of Congress before the FBI provided the document in redacted form for limited viewing by select House Oversight Committee members in July 2023.

Before Comer and his Democratic counterpart, ranking member Jamie Raskin, were allowed to view the document, four senior FBI officials delivered a 30-minute briefing to provide "context and narrative."

In a press conference after the viewing, Raskin divulged what they said: "The FBI explained at length during today's briefing [that] releasing this form publicly could place the Confidential Human Source in grave danger and undermine the integrity of FBI programs and investigations going forward . . . The source, who has been described as highly credible by the FBI, told the FBI he could not provide any opinion on the underlying veracity of the information provided [about the Bidens by] Ukrainian individuals."

Raskin then disparaged the allegations in the FD-1023 as "stale and debunked Burisma conspiracy theories long peddled by Rudy Giuliani."

Comer, unsurprisingly, contradicted his Democratic counterpart. "The claims made in the document are consistent with what we found and disclosed to you all [from] Romania," Comer told reporters, referring to bank records his committee had released the previous month showing more than $1 million allegedly flowing from an allegedly corrupt Romanian businessman to Hunter Biden.

"It suggests a pattern of bribery where payments would be made through shell accounts and multiple banks . . . Given the severity and complexity of the allegations contained within this record, Congress must investigate further."

Fed up with what he regarded as obstruction from the FBI, Grassley would later release a redacted version of the FBI-1023 to the public, asking, "What, if anything, has the Justice Department and FBI done to investigate? They no longer deserve the benefit of the doubt."

At least one element of the FBI briefing to Oversight Committee members the day they first viewed the FD-1023 was misleading. The FBI briefers said that the document had been "closed out" in August 2020, a point which Raskin used in his press conference to falsely claim that AG Barr and Brady had looked into the allegations against the Bidens, found them groundless, and closed the assessment.

But, as the FBI well knew, the allegations in the FD-1023 had been found by Brady's team of FBI agents and prosecutors to be credible and worth further exploration.

The FBI's "closing out" of its assessment was mere bureaucratic procedure, not a conclusion that the Biden bribery allegations "did not merit continued investigation," as the *New York Times* would falsely assert.

Barr rejects the claims by Raskin and the *Times*, and declares that the FD-1023 inquiry was never closed, but instead was referred to Delaware for further investigation.

"Mr. Raskin seems confused about the limited scope of Mr. Brady's review," Barr told the *New York Post*. "The Pittsburgh office was simply adding evidence to ensure that it was not disinformation before passing it on to one of the already existing investigations underway in the department.

"He [Brady] was not authorized to open his own investigation. In other words, he was assessing the credibility of the evidence, not investigating its ultimate merits," said Barr.

"That's why the evidence was passed on to Delaware. Nothing was closed."

But, as with every allegation implicating Joe, the FD-1023 went into a black hole.

The FBI continued to rely on its "highly credible" informant for another three years. But three years later would come a twist in the tale that would upend everything.

CHAPTER 16

TOO BAD YOUR COVER'S BLOWN

September 27, 2023
LAS VEGAS, NEVADA

Alexander Smirnov had been an FBI informant for 13 years and had become so familiar with his handler, an agent in a white-collar crime squad in Seattle, Washington, that he often used his personal phone instead of the secure bureau device for their daily conversations. It felt almost like a friendship.

A dual Israeli American citizen, fluent in Russian, Hebrew, and English, and willing to take great risks, Smirnov, 43, was one of the highest-paid, most valuable informants on the FBI's books.

So, when new FBI investigators turned up at his doorstep in Las Vegas on September 27, 2023, he was unconcerned, and did his best to tell them what they wanted to know. He didn't realize that his whole world would soon come crashing down.

What little is known about Smirnov is pieced together from court documents. Born in Soviet-controlled Ukraine in 1981, in the late phase of the Cold War, Smirnov grew up speaking Russian before moving to Israel with his family at age 11 and learning fluent Hebrew. He moved to the United States in 2006, aged 25, and at some point fell in love with Diana Lavrenyuk, the mother of his best friend, Nikolay. That friend would go on to be a Marine and an economist for the US government.

According to the *Wall Street Journal*, Smirnov initially went into the "import-export" business in Wisconsin with Diana and her Ukrainian husband Boris Nayflish, and moved in with her after the couple divorced in 2010.

Smirnov became a "confidential human source" or CHS, as FBI calls its informants, at about that time, two decades after the collapse of the Soviet Union and Ukraine's subsequent independence. At some point, he also began assisting the Defense Department.

In Russia, former KGB man Vladimir Putin was in power, and the Obama-Biden administration's attempted Russia "reset" under Secretary of State Hillary Clinton had failed to cool tensions. Putin resented NATO expansion and US meddling in Ukraine and Georgia. He saw increasing US funding of "civil society" and democracy programs in the region as an attempt to subvert Russia's sovereignty.

It was a time when Russian speakers with Ukrainian ties were invaluable informants as the FBI expanded its international reach, part of its post-9/11 transformation into a powerful counterintelligence agency.

Smirnov's information from high-level contacts in multiple foreign intelligence agencies, including in Russia, came to be so valuable that he was authorized by the FBI to commit crimes, which put him in an elite category of informant only used in national security or serious organized crime cases. There also are indications he was working for the Israeli government.

He traveled often to multiple countries and reported back to his handler on his meetings with Russian spies and assassins, and with Mykola Zlochevsky, owner of the corrupt Ukrainian energy company Burisma, which had appointed Hunter to its board in 2014.

On at least one occasion Smirnov gave his handler the name of a Russian spy operating abroad. He kept nine guns, including automatic weapons, at his luxury condo in Las Vegas where he had moved with Diana in 2022 from Los Angeles.

In February 2022, a month before Russia invaded Ukraine, Smirnov told his handler that he had asked for a favor from one of his Russian contacts: that his associate, a Ukrainian official, would not be harmed during any Russian incursion.

About twice a year, between October 2010 and September 2023, he would provide evidence to his handler that was used to convict criminals, and he would testify in court.

But on September 29, 2023, two days after the FBI investigators came calling, Smirnov's career as an informant was over, although he didn't know it yet. His handler would string him along for a few more months, but the requests to testify dried up. He had health issues to distract him that year, having undergone seven eye surgeries to treat worsening glaucoma, a buildup of pressure inside the eye that damages the optic nerve. He thought he was going blind.

Smirnov was arrested on Valentine's Day, 2024, after flying into Harry Reid International Airport from overseas. The indictment was unsealed, and his cover was blown. His life in the shadows was at an end.

He was described in the press as an "alleged Russian double agent," and courtroom artists produced sketches of him without his face covered, showing a man of average build with close-cropped salt and pepper hair and a thick, trimmed beard.

Prosecutors for Delaware US Attorney David Weiss accused him in the indictment of lying to the FBI, including in June 2020, when he made the bombshell allegation to his handler that Zlochevsky had paid a $10 million bribe to the Bidens to protect Burisma from a corruption investigation by Ukrainian prosecutor Viktor Shokin. Shokin then was fired on the orders of Vice President Biden.

Further, Smirnov allegedly was involved in a Russian disinformation plot to interfere with the 2024 presidential election, said Weiss' top prosecutor Leo Wise. Smirnov "actively peddl[ed] new lies that could impact US elections after meeting with Russian intelligence officials in November," and the fallout from his previous false bribery accusations about the Bidens "continue[s] to be felt to this day."

Smirnov also was accused of making up a new story in which Hunter had been recorded making phone calls in a grand old hotel in Kyiv, named the Premier Palace, that he claimed was "wired" by Russian spies who intercept cell phone calls made by "prominent US persons," so the Russian government could find "kompromat" (blackmail material) in order to influence the 2024 election. Smirnov would plead not guilty.

The prosecutors alleged that Smirnov had told them that Hunter had been to the Premier Palace Hotel, a story that was provably false because Hunter had "never travelled to Ukraine."

Smirnov rejects the prosecution claims and has pleaded not guilty.

Weiss's office had been asked by the FBI to help investigate Smirnov's initial allegations in July 2023, soon after Senator Chuck Grassley released the three-year-old FD-1023. Smirnov's identity had been secret at the time, and he was simply named "CHS" in the document.

The first time Smirnov mentioned Hunter Biden to his handler was in March 2017, in the context of a "kleptocracy" investigation the FBI was conducting into Zlochevsky, who had awarded Burisma lucrative gas production licenses when he was energy minister for the corrupt former Yanukovych government.

The Zlochevsky kleptocracy case was opened in January 2016 by a Foreign Corrupt Practices Act—aka bribery—squad in the FBI's Washington Field Office and then was quietly closed in December 2019, the month that Donald Trump was impeached over his phone call asking Ukraine's new president Volodymyr Zelenskyy to investigate the Bidens—and the same month that the FBI took possession of Hunter's laptop.

In March 2017, Smirnov was briefing his handler about a conversation with Zlochevsky as part of the kleptocracy probe when he made his fateful throwaway remark about Hunter's appointment to the Burisma board. The handler dismissed the remark as unimportant: "Zlochevsky briefly discussed Hunter Biden, but the topic was not relevant to Burisma's interest in acquiring a US-based petroleum business for $50–$100 million." The FBI handler duly recorded the snippet of conversation on an FD-1023 form.

Smirnov said nothing more about it until Scott Brady's vetting operation in Pittsburgh in June 2020 caught the keywords "Burisma" and "Hunter Biden" in a search of the FBI database. They had found the FD-1023, and now they wanted more information.

Brady would tell the House Judiciary Committee that the FBI initially obstructed his attempts to search their database and then have Smirnov (whose identity he never was told) re-interviewed because they were "trying to protect him as a source so that they could continue to use him."

In fact, the FBI did continue to use Smirnov as an informant for three more years, right up until two days after Weiss sent investigators to interrogate him in Las Vegas in September 2023.

Smirnov gave his handler what Brady had asked for, more detail on Hunter from his 2017 meetings with Burisma. His recollections were then recorded, in the FBI's old-fashioned and notoriously imprecise way, onto a new FD-1023, dated June 2020. It was the handler's rendition of what Smirnov had said, rather than a verbatim transcript.

Brady's team's preliminary due diligence on the new FD-1023 found it to be credible, but they heard nothing more after transmitting their findings to Weiss' office in Delaware.

For more than three years, these grave—albeit uncorroborated—allegations against Joe and Hunter Biden were locked in a drawer in Delaware and never examined.

If Smirnov really was compromised, then it was extraordinarily negligent of Weiss to hide the FD-1023 and allow the FBI to continue to run him as an informant.

IRS investigators Shapley and Ziegler felt so aggrieved that the FD-1023 had been hidden from them that they would return to Congress to supplement their testimony after Grassley's explosive revelation. Shapley stated that the document would have "likely been material to the ongoing criminal investigation of Hunter Biden . . .

"Prosecutors never provided such information to IRS-CI [Criminal Investigation]," said Shapley. "As such, neither IRS-CI nor the FBI agents working with them were provided the opportunity to conduct a proper investigation into the allegations presented by this CHS. I, along with other IRS-CI investigators, requested to be a part of briefings that the Delaware USAO and DOJ were having with the Pittsburgh USAO during the investigation, but our requests were denied.

"If IRS-CI investigators had participated in those briefings, we would have ensured that proper investigative steps were conducted to determine the veracity of the information provided by the CHS as it would have likely been material to the ongoing criminal investigation of Hunter Biden.

"During a criminal investigation, it is pivotal that all investigative leads are shared with investigators so the appropriate investigative steps can be executed. This appears to be another example of prosecutors obstructing the investigative process . . .

"As a result of the [FD-1023] information being concealed by prosecutors from the IRS-CI [Criminal Investigation unit] and FBI investigators assigned to this investigation, we were unable to follow alleged criminal activity as would normally be completed."

Leo Wise—the prosecutor brought in to replace Wolf in the uproar over Shapley and Ziegler's revelations—would try to airbrush over this seeming failure by his boss, David Weiss, to investigate Smirnov's allegations.

"Fast-forward to July of 2023," he said, breezily. "That's when the FBI asked the US Attorney's Office in the District of Delaware to assist in evaluating the claims in the 2020 1023."

But something was terribly wrong in the US Attorney's office in Delaware that no amount of fast-forwarding could hide.

* * *

Smirnov was locked up in the Pahrump jail in the middle of the Mojave Desert in protective custody so stringent the entire facility had to be "frozen" to allow him to take a brief phone call from his lawyers.

His Las Vegas attorneys, David Chesnoff and Richard Schonfeld, argued in the Nevada District Court for Smirnov's release on bail, saying "he has strong ties to the community and has the strong support of family and friends." With him in court were Smirnov's de facto wife, Diana, her son Nikolay, Smirnov's cousin from Florida, Linor Shefer, 38, a one-time winner of Moscow beauty pageant "Miss Jewish Star," and Smirnov's business partner Nadav Rozenberg, 42, also an Israeli-American.

Prosecutor Wise countered that Smirnov had failed to disclose that he had $6 million in "liquid funds," had no discernible job in Las Vegas, and that the only activity in a "security business" he had registered in California was "large wire transfers from what appear to be venture capital firms and individuals."

So determined was the federal government to keep Smirnov in jail that, after he was released by one judge in Nevada, prosecutors convinced another judge from California that he was a flight risk and had him arrested the next day at his lawyers' office. In the process of convincing the judge that the once trusted FBI informant had transformed over a few months into a threat to democracy, Wise vomited up into open court a long list of contacts with high-level Russian intelligence officials that Smirnov had reported back to his FBI handler over the years.

He gave detailed descriptions of Smirnov's contacts with Russian intelligence bosses, company executives, and assassination squads, and dates and locations of where some of those meetings took place, right up until a few months earlier.

Wise had put a target on Smirnov's back.

Some of Smirnov's overseas exploits sounded like a plot for a Bond movie. For example: "Smirnov was invited to and planned to attend the birthday party of an identified individual in the Middle East . . . on a mega yacht owned by a high-ranking member of Russia's largest steel and mining company."

Wise, who was running the gun and tax crimes prosecution against Hunter, indicated that Smirnov had been working for Israeli intelligence in 2002 and had cultivated a Russian consular official in Israel who he would pump for high-level intelligence over the next 20 years.

He concluded with a dire warning: "Smirnov's contacts with Russian officials who are affiliated with Russian intelligence services are not benign."

But, as defense attorney Chesnoff told the court, Smirnov's Russian contacts were "at the direction of the government . . . to accomplish his role" as an FBI informant.

"They've thrown him to the wolves."

Blowing Smirnov's cover seemed to serve little purpose other than to ensure he was permanently incapacitated as an informant—not just for the FBI but for Israel—and could be targeted by Russian intelligence for arrest or assassination.

The list of Russian contacts Wise placed on the public record had been declassified only recently and was certain to create a chilling effect on existing informants relying on confidentiality to keep them safe from the unsavory characters on whom they were asked to spy. It also potentially blew apart past convictions that had been secured with Smirnov's testimony.

The damage to the FBI's already controversial confidential human source program by David Weiss and his top attack dog Wise and his men was incalculable.

In court, Wise maintained that he needed to blow Smirnov's cover because, "these contacts make this defendant different from other defendants who merely have foreign ties, and they heighten the risk of flight dramatically. And that is because he can use these contacts with foreign intelligence services to flee and to resettle overseas."

If Smirnov were to resettle in Russia, "we couldn't extradite him. Russia won't extradite under these circumstances."

Nevada Magistrate Judge Daniel Albregts was skeptical that Smirnov would jump bail and try to settle in Russia: "My guess is at this stage he probably thinks that's not the most attractive place to go," he noted drily.

The judge also said that Wise's recitation of Smirnov's Russian contacts was gratuitous and irrelevant to the question of bail. "I understand the concern about foreign intelligence agencies potentially resettling Mr. Smirnov outside of the United States, his connections to them, but I think on some level that's speculative."

The view was very different from the Central District of California, led by US Attorney Martin Estrada, a Biden nominee. In his district, Judge Otis Wright ordered Smirnov be rearrested and transported to a California jail.

At a hearing in downtown Los Angeles, where a woman in a dinosaur suit stood outside the courthouse waving a placard, "I'll take my Smirnov on ice," and someone else held a "Go Putin Lies" sign, Judge Wright declared: "There is nothing garden variety about this case . . . The defendant will be remanded pending trial."

Smirnov had gone from being a high-value informant the FBI had relied on for 13 years to a fearsome national security threat due to his troubling "extensive foreign ties" to Russian intelligence for which the FBI once had paid him handsomely, and which he had reported back dutifully to his handler.

The elaborate measures Smirnov took to disguise himself when arriving at court were an indication of his fear of being identified. He wore dark sunglasses on top of spectacles with a black beanie and scarf covering his face.

The decks were stacked against him, except in one crucial way. He could not have chosen a better attorney. Chesnoff was renowned as a well-connected fixer, the first person celebrities, organized crime figures, poker stars, and assorted other heavyweights call when they find themselves in legal trouble in Sin City.

A protégé of former Las Vegas mayor and mob attorney Oscar Goodman, he had represented Britney Spears, Mike Tyson, Lindsay Lohan, Leo DiCaprio, Shaquille O'Neal, and Martha Stewart.

Chesnoff told Judge Wright that his client was pleading not guilty and that the prosecutors' claims that he lied to the FBI "will be a highly contested part of this trial . . . This is going to be an interesting and complicated case" with Smirnov "contacting people around the world . . . who can refute allegations against him."

Chesnoff had a wealth of material in the indictment to pull apart on behalf of his client.

The indictment also didn't square with the initial due diligence done in 2020 by the Pittsburgh US Attorney Scott Brady, who had confirmed aspects of Smirnov's story that prosecutors now called into question, such as his travel records.

There also were key discrepancies between the indictment and what Smirnov told his FBI handler in 2020, as recorded in the infamous FD-1023 form that Senator Grassley released.

For instance, in that FD-1023, Burisma owner Zlochevsky is quoted by Smirnov saying: "it cost 5 (million) to pay one Biden, and 5 (million) to another Biden."

The indictment assumed that one of the Bidens was Joe, and the other was Hunter.

Although the media had always claimed Joe was the other Biden, Devon Archer speculates that it could be him, since he was also on the Burisma board and resembled Hunter, who had once told him: "you are a Biden . . . You are part of a great family."

Hunter was paid $4.1 million by Burisma from March 2014 to April 2019, and Archer $2.3 million. Hunter's final take would have been more than $5 million but his $83,333 monthly payments were slashed in half a few weeks after his father left office. Archer's Burisma takings didn't hit $5 million because he had to step down from the board prematurely in 2016 before he was indicted in the Burnham case.

One element of Smirnov's story ignored in the indictment was more difficult to refute. He referred to Joe Biden as the "Big Guy." This was in June 2020, four months before the *New York Post* published emails from Hunter's laptop that revealed the codename which Hunter's partners used for his father. Quite some coincidence.

The indictment's central claim was that Smirnov lied about meeting Zlochevsky and other Burisma executives because his dates didn't match travel records and the statements of two witnesses.

From this discrepancy, prosecutors made the leap to rejecting the Biden bribery allegations as false. But there was no evidence offered in the indictment that proved such a thing, one way or the other. The indictment did not indicate that any effort was made to investigate those bribery allegations, only to prove Smirnov a liar.

Discrepancies in dates of Burisma meetings cited by Smirnov compared with the recollections of two witnesses are portrayed by prosecutors as a deliberate lie by Smirnov. One of the witnesses was an American dubbed "Associate 2" who owned a cryptocurrency firm and was a former business partner of Smirnov's. The other was a Ukrainian, Alexander Ostapenko, who Smirnov said worked "for the administration of President Zelenskyy," and for cryptocurrency firm Bitfury.

But the discrepancies in dates may stem from an incorrect assumption by the FBI of what Smirnov meant when he said the meeting with Zlochevsky at a coffee shop in Vienna, Austria, happened "around the time" that Joe Biden "made a statement about [Shokin] being corrupt and that he should be fired/removed from office."

The FBI assumed Smirnov was talking about a speech Joe gave to the Ukrainian Rada on December 9, 2015, and framed its entire timeline around that putative date. But Joe never mentioned Shokin in that speech, and said nothing about firing or removing anyone.

Perhaps Smirnov meant, instead, the infamous speech in which Joe told the Council on Foreign Relations in Washington on January 23, 2018 that he had threatened to withhold $1 billion in US loan guarantees for Ukraine unless the corrupt prosecutor was fired. "Well, son of a bitch. He got fired."

If that speech is what Smirnov meant when he dated the Vienna meeting, then the other dates calculated by the FBI fall apart, and so does the prosecution case. Perhaps Smirnov did not lie, the FBI screwed up, and Weiss's prosecutors never checked the most basic facts in their indictment.

Smirnov had placed the date of an earlier meeting in Kyiv with Burisma executives and Associate 2 as coming "one or two months" before the Vienna meeting, so his FBI handler worked backwards to calculate the date as "late 2015 or 2016."

But if Smirnov's Vienna date actually was January 2018, then the Kyiv meeting was in late 2017, and that accords with Associate 2's travel records, which show he traveled to Ukraine in September 2017.

Prosecutors accused Smirnov of lying about attending the Kyiv meeting because they were operating on the FBI's assumed—and potentially incorrect—timeline.

Perhaps Smirnov's real sin was sending his handler a series of text messages in May 2020 "expressing bias against [Joe Biden] who was then a candidate for President of the United States of America."

These text messages feature prominently in the indictment, and allude to recordings that had been released that day in Ukraine purporting to be of phone calls between Joe and Ukrainian president Petro Poroshenko discussing the firing of Shokin.

"I'll get those other recordings of [Joe's] son telling to Boriama [Burisma] that his dad will take care of [Shokin]," Smirnov texted his FBI handler. "Bribe to [Joe] and his son."

His handler replied: "That would be a game changer."

On May 21, 2020, Smirnov messaged his handler: "Ukraine opening investigation $" and sent him a photograph of Joe, Hunter, and Archer on the exclusive Sebonack Golf course in Southampton with Ralph Pascucci, son of car leasing magnate Michael Pascucci, who owns the club, where the $650,000 membership fee is an invitation-only privilege.

Smirnov captioned the August 2014 photo incorrectly as being Joe and Hunter with the "CEO of Burisma," an error that prosecutors presented as evidence of his dishonesty. But the same photo had already received widespread coverage in conservative media, with the same incorrect caption.

The indictment stated that "one month later [after he sent his handler the photo], and three years after first reporting on Burisma, [Smirnov] reported bribery allegations against [Joe] and [Hunter]."

This was misleading. Smirnov did report Zlochevsky's allegations to his handler in June 2020, but only because he was expressly asked, as a result of the Brady request, to provide more detail of his conversations with Zlochevsky.

He had done exactly what was asked of him. He kept the information to himself when his handler told him it was irrelevant, and he reported the information when his handler specifically requested it.

In the indictment, Ostapenko is the most damaging witness against Smirnov. According to prosecutors "Ostapenko has never met or spoken with Zlochevsky."

That denial directly refuted a claim made by Smirnov in 2020, that he had had a conference call with Ostapenko and Zlochevsky. Smirnov told his handler that during that conference call on February 27, 2017, he was told that Burisma executive Vadym Pozharskyi was planning to travel to Washington later that month.

Smirnov was correct. Pozharskyi traveled to Washington that month, and had a meeting scheduled with Hunter at 11 a.m. on Thursday March 9, 2017, per emails on Hunter's laptop from his partner Eric Schwerin and office manager Joan Peugh. It appears Hunter did not show up to the meeting and told Pozharskyi that he was unwell.

Ten days later, Pozharskyi informed Hunter that his monthly $83,333 director's fee had been cut in half. In an email to Hunter and Schwerin on March 19, 2017, just eight weeks after Joe ceased to be vice president, Pozharskyi wrote: "The only thing that was amended is the compensation rate. Unfortunately, Hunter and I didn't get to meet in Washington during my recent visit. However . . . the remuneration is still the highest in the company and higher than the standard director's monthly fees. I am sure you will find it both fair and reasonable." From then on, the amount listed on Hunter's monthly Burisma invoices was $41,500, paid in euros.

The visit of Pozharskyi to Washington, just as Smirnov had predicted, seemed to give credence to his account. Yet the federal government preferred the word of Ostapenko, who had worked for the Zelenskyy government, and might have a vested interest in protecting the US president at a time that Ukraine was dependent on the US government for military assistance to defend itself against Russia.

Ostapenko and his boss, Vavilov, had been helping the Ukrainian government build digital markets using blockchain technology to process billions of dollars of assets. Everything accelerated in February 2022, after the Russian invasion began, when Ukraine asked for donations on social media in digital currency and posted addresses to its Bitcoin, Ethereum, and Tether wallets.

The following month, Zelenskyy signed legislation to legalize cryptocurrency and establish a market for virtual assets, one of the first countries in the world to do so. The move was explained as a way to provide additional stable funding for the military. The partnership between Ukraine's government and Bitfury Group was heralded as a way to stamp out corruption.

But the fact that one of the most corrupt countries in the world was such an early adopter of cryptocurrency raised eyebrows, given the new market's prevalence in money laundering and corruption.

It is curious that Ostapenko was presented by prosecutors as an unimpeachable truthteller, and the FBI's own trusted informant of 13 years as a dangerous liar.

If Smirnov was a liar, the FBI didn't care until he crossed the Bidens.

His trial initially was set for April 23, 2024. But Judge Wright agreed to the prosecution request to delay it until December 3, 2024, thus ensuring that no embarrassing facts would be aired before the presidential election.

The judge ordered Smirnov to remain in pre-trial detention for the additional eight months, despite his worsening vision problems due to glaucoma.

Weiss opposed all requests by Smirnov's lawyers to allow him out for urgent eye surgery to save his eyesight. Smirnov was originally scheduled for surgery in March 2024 and was complaining of blurred vision and crippling headaches.

At one point, his lawyers alleged that the Santa Ana City jail had confiscated his vision-preserving eye drops.

His eye specialist, Dr. George Tanaka, wrote a letter to the court in May 2024: "These eye drops are not 'Pain-Reducing' medications meant to provide comfort. They are necessary to prevent blindness from glaucoma. Glaucoma patients are required to take daily eye drop medications to control their intraocular pressure around the clock [and] prevent irreversible blindness. . . .

"Withholding Mr. Smirnov's eye drops is tantamount to allowing [him] to go blind. [He] will lose a vital bodily function (vision) as a direct result of the negligence committed by the jail officials."

Smirnov was subsequently scheduled for surgery with a government-approved doctor some two weeks after Tanaka's letter and provided with two of the three eye medications Tanaka had prescribed. He was moved into solitary confinement in the Metropolitan Detention Center, the federal prison in downtown Los Angeles, where his lawyers complained of limited access to their client.

Smirnov's arrest and incarceration was manna from heaven for Democrats in despair over the growing pile of evidence of Joe's alleged corruption that the impeachment inquiry had amassed.

President Biden seized on the Smirnov indictment as vindication, making a rare live statement at the White House to assert that the impeachment inquiry against him had been destroyed, and demanding that House Republicans drop their investigation, saying it was "an outrageous effort from the beginning."

Democratic congressmen Jamie Raskin and Dan Goldman took to the airwaves to spin the Smirnov charges into a new Russia hoax, and Hunter's attorney Abbe Lowell declared in a new court filing that Smirnov had fatally tainted the case against his client, who he claimed was being unjustly prosecuted because of his last name.

Biden-allied media followed suit. In unison, CNN, the *New York Times*, *Politico*, and others declared the impeachment inquiry was kaput.

"The campaign to impeach Biden has crashed and burned," thundered progressive magazine the *New Republic*.

"The Biden impeachment inquiry has utterly collapsed," opined the *Washington Post* editorial board.

They created a straw man out of Smirnov, pretending he was the "lead informant" of the impeachment inquiry, but that simply was not true.

Until the DOJ deigned to investigate, Smirnov's claims remained un-corroborated.

House Oversight Committee Chairman James Comer, leading the im-peachment inquiry, could do nothing with the allegation, other than pub-licize it and read it into the Congressional Record, because the FBI had kept the informant's identity secret, as well as the existence or otherwise of any "ongoing investigation."

Despite the spin, the Smirnov indictment did not mean that Joe and Hunter were in the clear. Quite the contrary.

CHAPTER 17

NO ONE FUCKS WITH A BIDEN

October 5, 2022
FORT MYERS, FLORIDA

For all his bonhomie as he toured hurricane-struck Florida that sunny Wednesday afternoon, the noose that had been tightening around his family must have been top of mind for Joe Biden.

Both his son Hunter and brother Jim were under federal investigation, the scandal of his classified documents stash was bubbling away, and polls showed Republicans were poised to take back the House in the November midterms amid an avalanche of damning whistleblower allegations about a yearslong coverup in the FBI and DOJ. However, the president knew something that few people outside his son's high-powered legal team knew. The family's secrets would remain safe in Delaware, where IRS and FBI investigators had been poring over Hunter's finances for almost four years.

Joe was smiling in every minute of footage during the visit as the presidential motorcade drove by wind-shorn trees, upended buildings, and downed power lines.

Their destination was Fishermans Wharf, Fort Myers, deep red country, where Joe was scheduled to hold a joint press conference with Republican Florida governor Ron DeSantis. He wasn't expecting to find many allies. But then he spied Ray Murphy, the "nonpartisan" mayor of that conservative city, a jolly, portly fellow who was decked out for the occasion in a wide-brimmed safari hat. The two men had never met before, but Joe made a beeline for him on the way to the podium where DeSantis was waiting.

He knew at once that Murphy was a kindred spirit. He had a sixth sense like that about people and felt a special tribal bond with Irish Catholics. They quickly bonded as Murphy recited a list of people they knew in common from Joe's hometown of Scranton, Pennsylvania.

Unbeknownst to either man, their words were being captured on a hot mic, and nearby TV cameras waiting for the press conference filmed the interchange.

"Thanks for everything. Thanks for coming down. We appreciate it," says Murphy, vigorously shaking the president's hand and squeezing his shoulder.

"Keep the faith," says Joe, under his breath.

"I keep the faith," says the mayor, before the conversation takes a turn for the weird.

Joe is bursting to boast about his secret triumph. He can't hold it in any longer.

"And by the way," he says, drawing Murphy in close. "You were raised the same way I was."

Murphy takes off his sunglasses and studies Biden's face: "I was. I was."

"No one f*cks with a Biden," says the president, giving him a knowing look.

Murphy pauses and then laughs uproariously.

"Yeah, you're goddamn right," he says, although he doesn't have a clue what Joe is talking about.

Joe keeps pumping Murphy's hand: "You can't argue with your brothers outside the house."

"That's exactly right. That's exactly right," says Murphy, finally managing to break his hand free.

At the time, Joe's boastful outburst seemed puzzling. But the next day, the potential reason for his cockiness was revealed. A story appeared in the *Washington Post* that hinted at the internal struggle that had been raging in the Delaware US Attorney's office, a struggle Joe knew he had won.

Joe walked across to the podium, a slight smirk on his face. He knew things were going his way.

"Federal agents investigating President Biden's son Hunter have gathered what they believe is sufficient evidence to charge him with tax crimes and a false statement related to a gun purchase, according to people familiar with the case," trumpeted the *Washington Post*. "The next step is for the US Attorney in Delaware, David Weiss, to decide on whether to file such charges."

What was missing in the story was any mention of previous potential charges of alleged money laundering and alleged foreign lobbying violations, both of which would have led investigators to the president's possible role in the alleged international influence-peddling scheme allegedly run by his son and brother during his time as vice president (but no such role was ever found and no scheme was ever proven). Joe was off the hook. The offenses that were perilous to him were off the table. Now it was just a matter of minimizing the damage to Hunter. And, if all else failed, he could always pardon his son.

The story had been leaked by "people familiar with the situation, who spoke on the condition of anonymity to discuss an ongoing case," and it emphasized that the final decision whether to bring charges rested with the DOJ—and ultimately with Biden's political appointees.

As *Washington Post* reporters Devlin Barrett and Perry Stein wrote, "Agents determined months ago they had assembled a viable criminal case against the younger Biden. But it is ultimately up to prosecutors at the Justice Department, not agents, to decide whether to file charges in cases where prosecutors believe the evidence is strong enough to lead to a likely conviction at trial . . . Justice Department policy would require any criminal tax charges to be approved by the department's tax division."

It was the first time the gun case had become public, but investigators in Delaware had been gathering evidence, including from his self-incriminating memoir, to charge Hunter with lying about his drug use on a federal background check form when he bought a Colt Cobra .38 special revolver in October 2018 from a gun store in Wilmington.

Lower down in the story, Hunter's pugnacious lawyer, Chris Clark, a former prosecutor for the Southern District of New York, was quoted in high dudgeon, accusing investigators of leaking these details to the newspaper, while praising the prosecutors.

"It is a federal felony for a federal agent to leak information about a Grand Jury investigation such as this one," Clark told the *Washington Post*. "Any agent you cite as a source in your article apparently has committed such a felony. We expect the Department of Justice will diligently investigate and prosecute such bad actors. As is proper and legally required, we believe the prosecutors in this case are diligently and thoroughly weighing not just evidence provided by agents, but also all the other witnesses in this case, including witnesses for the defense. That is the job of the prosecutors. They should not be pressured, rushed, or criticized for doing their job."

Clark stepped up his attacks in a statement, saying: "It is regrettable that law enforcement agents appear to be violating the law to prejudice a case against a person who is a target simply because of his family name."

It was a curious spin on a leak that benefited only Hunter by escalating his lawyers' apparent pressure campaign on Weiss and the DOJ to convince them to shut down the probe (which they have denied).

The Weiss investigation had been remarkably leak-free in the four years since it began, despite escalating internal friction and enormous publicity about the target. After the election, a delighted Weiss even had congratulated the team for keeping everything under wraps.

To a journalist's eye, the story could just as easily have been leaked by Hunter's team, and Clark's bluster only added to the impression.

A source close to Hunter was even bolder when asked about the *Washington Post* story that day, telling me they guessed the story had been leaked by "rogue investigators" worried that Weiss was not going to indict Hunter. He called them "Trump prosecutors."

"They want the scalp [and] they're putting Weiss in a box. He's in a horrible, horrible spot. The case has been going for four years and nothing has happened with it . . . They've investigated [Hunter] thoroughly . . . These people have tried to find everything."

Amusingly, he also theorized the delays in the case were due to vindictive investigators refusing to admit Hunter was innocent.

"If it was going well, they would have indicted Hunter. You can indict a ham sandwich . . . They are trying to back Weiss into a corner by leaking [to] set the table for if [Hunter] does get exonerated—they get this s–t out there. So, when Weiss looks at the decision and decides not to prosecute, they've gotten out in front of it with all this smoke."

Joe had kept entirely out of the case, the source claimed: "I know his father doesn't get involved at all. Neither does [Attorney General Merrick] Garland. It's all done from Baltimore and Delaware and is a co-thing between the IRS and the US Attorney's Office."

The source also claimed that Hunter had paid off his tax debt and that had hurt the IRS case. The investigators "went nuts the day the tax payment came in because it f–ked their case up," he said.

Thanks to the generosity of his "Sugar Brother," Hunter indeed had paid off more than $3 million of delinquent state and federal taxes in 2020 and 2021. The leak went to the *New York Times*, which ran an anonymously sourced piece on March 16, 2022, with the headline, "Hunter Biden Paid Tax Bill, but Broad Federal Investigation Continues."

The whole point of the story came in the *Times*'s conclusion that "the payment could make it harder for prosecutors to win a conviction or a long sentence for tax-related offenses, according to tax law experts, since juries and judges tend to be more sympathetic to defendants who have paid their bills."

Wish-casting from Pacific Palisades held that Hunter's payment of his overdue taxes should conclude the investigation.

That had been the message from Hunter's attorneys to Wolf and her prosecution team in a taxpayer conference on March 14, 2022, two days before the *Times*' leak. It was at that meeting that Hunter's team saw the IRS Special Agent Report, now awaiting approval with the DOJ's Tax Division, that had recommended six felony charges ("False Return" and "Evasion of Assessment") for 2014, 2018, and 2019 and five misdemeanor charges ("Failure to Timely File and Pay") for 2015–2019.

A couple of weeks later, in a second taxpayer conference, Hunter's lawyers tried to talk the prosecutors out of charging their client. Clark had brought a 100-slide PowerPoint presentation to make his case.

The first slide referred to Trump's first impeachment over Ukraine and his "constant" claims that Hunter was a criminal, according to *Politico*. Clark told the prosecutors it would be "devastating to the reputation" of the Justice Department if they caved in to Trump's political pressure campaign and charged Hunter.

Slide after slide showed Trump assailing Hunter, including at a speech the night before the January 6, 2021, Capitol riot: "Where's Hunter? Where's Hunter?"

He was making as much a political argument as a legal one.

There also was an emotional element, as Hunter's attorneys repeatedly raised his drug addiction and the death of his brother, Beau, as mitigating factors that would weigh heavily on a jury.

Clark's PowerPoint barrage was just the beginning of a relentless campaign by Hunter's growing army of high-priced lawyers, a year of badgering prosecutors to ensure that Hunter would never be charged with a felony.

It would all end badly the following July but, until then, the president's son was smugly complacent about his fate.

An early indication of the optimism Hunter felt about the investigation came on September 21, 2021, in an email sent to Jim Lee, the chief of IRS Criminal Investigations, from IRS communications director Justin Cole.

Titled "Sensitive Case Heads Up," it detailed a call from a CNN producer, claiming that Hunter had sent him an email saying he "expected all this 'stuff' to go away when his dad becomes President."

"Producer said he is aware that a plea deal has been offered to Hunter but Hunter is not willing to accept it."

This jaw-dropper set off a flurry of emails down the chain to Special Agent Joe Ziegler, asking if there really had been a plea deal.

Ziegler checked with Assistant US Attorney Lesley Wolf and reported back to his bosses that she "made it clear that we haven't offered a plea and if one was going to be offered, that we would obviously be in the loop. She doesn't even think that we are at the point that we could engage in that since no charges have been authorized. So I think we are a ways off from plea negotiations."

Perhaps Hunter had been heartened by his father's appointment of Biden ally Matthew Graves as the new US Attorney for the District of Columbia, where the 2014 and 2015 tax charges relating to his Burisma money would have to be brought, as that was where he had been living at the time.

Graves, a 47-year-old registered Democrat, Democratic donor, and Pennsylvania native, had worked for the Biden presidential campaign as a volunteer member of the domestic policy committee from May 2020 through to the election. He was handpicked by Joe to lead his pet project, the cavalcade of prosecutions against Trump supporters charged over the January 6, 2021, riot at the US Capitol. Graves' wife, left-liberal activist Fatima Gross Graves, was a favorite at the Biden White House, reported to have visited at least 28 times.

Sure enough, in March 2022, after the DOJ's tax division had signed off on a 2014 felony tax charge and 2015 misdemeanor charges against Hunter in DC, and an indictment was in the process of being written, Graves dropped the bombshell that he was refusing to bring the charges in his jurisdiction. He declined to partner with Weiss or offer his office any assistance. Graves' refusal, Weiss' passive response, and DOJ inaction led to the statute of limitations expiring on these most serious tax charges against Hunter, charges which would have shone the spotlight on his activity in Ukraine and potentially on his father's role in facilitating it.

"The statute of limitations [had previously] been extended through a tolling agreement with Hunter Biden's defense counsel, and they were willing to extend it past November 2022," Shapley testified to congress. "Weiss allowed those to expire."

Graves effectively had killed the 2014–2015 case. Hundreds of thousands of dollars of unpaid taxes on Hunter's $2 million Burisma income from 2014 and 2015 never would be paid. For 2014, alone, Hunter owed the IRS $145,000 on income he had not declared, investigators alleged.

In a later deposition to the House Judiciary committee, Graves was unrepentant, telling Republican lawmakers that there had been no conflict of interest, and no need for him to recuse himself. "I'm not aware of any ethical canon that says that US attorneys have an obligation to recuse whenever a family member of the President is implicated."

Soon after Graves shot down the case, key figures at the White House began proclaiming the president's utmost confidence in his son's innocence, an extraordinary and improper intercession in an active investigation.

White House Communications Director Kate Bedingfield declared at a press briefing on March 31, 2022, that the White House stood by the president's position that his son had done nothing "unethical" in his business dealings with Ukraine and China.

"Of course, the president's confident that his son didn't break the law," White House chief of staff Ron Klain told ABC News' George Stephanopoulos on April 3, 2022. "The president is confident that his family did the right thing . . . That's a matter that's going to be decided by the Justice Department, by the legal process. It's something that no one at the White House has involvement in."

No involvement other than sending out your chief of staff on Sunday morning television to telegraph to the Attorney General—and everyone who reports to him—that his boss has prejudged the case and you're wasting your time.

When Garland was quizzed about the matter in the Senate the following month by Republican Senator Bill Hagerty, from Tennessee, he stuck to his mantra. "There will not be interference of any political or improper kind."

Hagerty brought up the Klain and Bedingfield comments. "This is on national television. The President's already told his subordinates, clearly—these are people that he can fire at will—that he and his family did nothing wrong . . . There's an obvious conflict of interest here because, if those who are investigating the Biden family and their enterprise can be fired by the head of the family who's being investigated—that is, Joe Biden can fire [Weiss]—he can have an impact on all of your staffing . . .

"How can the American people be confident that his Administration is conducting a serious investigation?"

Garland responded with another favorite talking point: "Because we put the investigation in the hands of a Trump appointee [Weiss]."

Hagerty didn't buy it, not least because, regardless which president nominated him, the only way Weiss could be selected was with the sign-off of the two Delaware senators, Chris Coons and Tom Carper, both Democrats, and both staunch Biden allies. Weiss had spent most of his career working in the US attorney's office in Delaware, not rocking the boat in a state where the Biden family had ruled the roost for half a century.

He had proved himself unwilling to challenge the Bidens in a 2012 case involving corrupt donations to Joe's campaign by wealthy Delaware liquor distributor Chris Tigani. Weiss threw the book at Tigani, tacking on two felony tax charges to his election bundling offense, ruining his business, and sending him to jail for two years.

But he never came near the Bidens. Tigani pleaded guilty and cooperated with the FBI by wearing a wire for four months to try to entrap local businesspeople and state politicians. But he says he was warned off approaching anyone in the Biden family, despite the fact that it was Joe and his sons, Hunter and Beau, who had solicited $100,000 from him at a 2007 campaign event, and Joe's campaign finance director, Dennis Toner, who allegedly taught him how to "bundle" the donation through his employees, to get around contribution limits.

The FBI even slapped down Tigani's suggestion that he go to Washington, DC, and try to get the then–vice president on tape.

"They were not terribly interested in that part of the investigation,"

Tigani recalls. "They wanted to get other people . . . The FBI were political when they were investigating me." (Joe, Hunter, and Toner were not charged with wrongdoing in Tigani's case.)

He also suspects someone tipped off the Biden campaign that he was wearing a wire, because when he tried to get Toner to repeat what he had told him about bundling, he hit a dead end: "I don't know what you're talking about," said Toner on the phone, "and I don't know who's listening to this call."

After that, the FBI took back the wire, ended the probe, and unsealed his indictment.

The Bidens "were made to look like victims," says Tigani. "The newspapers made it sound like, 'Oh, Chris was playing them.' It was just crazy."

Once again, Joe had proved himself untouchable.

There were skeletons in David Weiss' own family's closet that might explain his wary relationship with IRS investigators and reluctance to stick his neck out.

When he was in his final year of law school, his father, Meyer Weiss, an IRS agent in Philadelphia, was caught in a big bribery scandal and sentenced to four years in prison for accepting cash from businessmen to help them break federal tax laws.

"In the early 1950s, Mr. Weiss began a pattern of receiving bribes in return for compromising portions of tax liabilities under audit," found Federal Tax Judge Carolyn Parr. "This pattern continued until 1983 [when he was caught]. Mr. Weiss received bribes totaling $210,500."

At the time his father was arrested, David Weiss, the middle of three children, was studying at the Widener University School of Law in Wilmington, Delaware, where Senator Joe Biden would become an adjunct professor. Meyer spent almost $71,020 on David's tuition.

Like the Bidens, the Weiss family liked to live beyond their means. Meyer and his wife, Betty, were members of the stylish Melrose Country Club in Cheltenham, Pennsylvania, where Betty played tennis three times a week.

In its judgement, the court found that Betty Weiss knew they belonged to a country club, where they lunched, played tennis, and golfed frequently, and that there were costs associated therewith. Surely, in her conversations with other women at the club with whom she lunched, or from other sources, she was made aware that it was expensive. In fact, the country club cost approximately $5,000 per year, which during the years in issue represented from 20 to 25 percent of Mr. Weiss' annual take-home pay.

"She knew that she was not required to go to work to help pay for her children's educations, which included medical school and law school. . . . Her way of life was uninterrupted by their schooling, a statement that most middle- and even upper-middle-class parents cannot make."

Unless their name is Biden.

* * *

Whatever was the cause for Hunter's sunny outlook in the spring of 2022, behind closed doors in Wilmington, a grand jury had been hard at work for the Sportsman investigation. Hunter's former business partners, including Devon Archer and Eric Schwerin, had testified, as well as his baby mama Lunden Roberts and various prostitutes.

One witness had been asked: "Who is the Big Guy?" suggesting that threads were being pulled that might lead to the president.

But, in reality, prosecutors were quick to block any inquiry that could implicate Joe and had prohibited investigators from asking about him in witness interviews.

Ziegler, his boss Gary Shapley, and their FBI colleagues kept trying to follow the investigative trail wherever it led. But the constant deviations from usual practice, unusual delays, and meddling by the prosecutors in Delaware and the DOJ in Washington frustrated them.

After Joe took office, and Garland was confirmed as the new Attorney General, things went from bad to worse. For instance, the FBI had been investigating whether millions of dollars in loans to Hunter from his "Sugar Brother," Democrat donor Kevin Morris, had benefited Joe's 2020 presidential campaign in the form of a campaign finance violation.

Morris told Congress that he provided $6.5 million in loans to Hunter, formalized in five promissory notes drafted by lawyers.

Hunter used the loans to fund his lifestyle and to pay off delinquent state and federal taxes in several stages over 2020 and 2021, including $112,805 to the IRS in March 2020, and $453,890 in July 2020 to the District of Columbia. He paid a further $2.6 million to the IRS in 2021.

While the promissory notes were dated over two years from October 2021, Morris testified to the House Oversight Committee that the loans began in 2020: "The loans happened before we papered it, as we say."

When asked if these were "illusory loans" to spare Hunter gift tax, Morris replied: "Well, that's a legal concept that somebody can try to enforce. To me, it's not."

Morris' testimony was corroborated by what Delaware investigators had found, which was that, in 2020 alone, Morris paid more than $1.2 million for Hunter's benefit.

The FBI was exploring the idea that, if Morris' money had prevented damaging scandals from breaking out around the candidate's son, perhaps it should be treated as an undeclared benefit to the campaign.

But every time FBI Supervisory Special Agent Joe Gordon brought up the topic in one of the prosecution meetings in Delaware, Wolf shot it down.

"This investigation has been hampered and slowed by claims of potential election meddling," Shapley wrote in a "Sensitive Case Report" to his bosses on May 3, 2021, four months after Biden's inauguration.

"Through interviews and review of evidence obtained, it appears there may be campaign finance criminal violations. AUSA Wolf stated on the last prosecution team meeting that she did not want any of the agents to look into the allegation. She cited a need to focus on the 2014 tax year, that we could not yet prove an allegation beyond a reasonable doubt, and that she does not want to include their [DOJ] Public Integrity Unit because they would take authority away from her. We do not agree with her obstruction on this matter." Wolf came before Congress to testify, but only to point 79 times to a DOJ stating she was not authorized to comment on ongoing investigations. She has never been charged with any obstruction.

Ziegler also complained about interference with the campaign finance investigation into the 2020 Biden presidential campaign. "Things related to the campaign were kind of, at least during the investigative stages, were off limits," Ziegler testified to Congress.

Gordon's FBI agents continued their inquiries, nonetheless. But eight months later came another clash with Wolf on the topic.

According to handwritten notes taken by Shapley at a prosecution team meeting on January 12, 2022, Gordon "brought up campaign finance case and evidence so far. Leslie [Wolf] said she is not 'personally' interested in pursuing it [and] said law is not clear—so doesn't support investigating it."

Gordon responded by saying, "They were talking to PIU [Public Integrity Unit]," Shapley noted. "But Leslie doesn't want PIU involved [as it would mean] 'more levels of approval.'"

The campaign finance investigation died after that.

The CIA's intervention likely played a hand in killing the campaign finance probe, as well as obstructing the IRS tax investigation.

In an affidavit provided to the House Ways and Means Committee in May 2024, Shapley said that the CIA had blocked investigators from interviewing Morris in August 2021. That's when Wolf and DOJ Tax Attorney Jack Morgan were summoned to CIA headquarters in Langley, Virginia, and were told that Morris "could not be a witness" for their investigation into Hunter.

"Wolf stated that they were provided a classified briefing in relation to Mr. Morris and as a result we could no longer pursue him as a witness. [She] reiterated more than once that they were summoned to the CIA in Langley concerning Mr. Morris, and that because of the information provided there, he could not be a witness for the investigation."

Shapley recalled that Wolf "proudly referenced a CIA mug and stated that she purchased some CIA 'swag' at the gift shop while she was there. . . .

"It is unclear how the CIA became aware that Mr. Morris was a potential witness in the Hunter Biden investigation and why agents were not told about the meeting in advance or invited to participate," Shapley said.

"It is a deviation of normal investigative processes for prosecutors to exclude investigators from substantive meetings such as this."

The CIA denied that it stonewalled any interview with Morris, saying that it "does not obstruct investigations."

"Without confirming or denying the existence of any associations or communications, CIA did not prevent or seek to prevent IRS or DOJ from conducting any such interview," James Catella, the CIA's director of the Office of Congressional Affairs, wrote in a letter to chairmen Jordan and Comer. "The allegation is false."

But the CIA did not deny that it told two DOJ officials something in August 2021 that convinced them not to interview Morris.

It was around that time, August 18, 2021, when IRS investigators shared with Wolf various interviews they had planned for the following month. She told them they would require approval from the Tax Division, unusually. "I do not think you are going to be able to do these interviews as planned," she emailed.

The FBI was still investigating Hunter for potential violations of the Foreign Agents Registration Act (FARA), which requires anyone advocating for foreign entities to US government officials to register with the DOJ.

Top of the list was $3 million paid by Romanian real estate tycoon Gabriel Popoviciu to Hunter and his associates as part of an alleged influence campaign to persuade Romanian prosecutors to drop a corruption case against him.

Popoviciu was introduced to Hunter by Walker through his friend Chris Larson, a staffer-turned-employee of former New York Republican Governor George Pataki. Larson also introduced Walker to Gilliar.

The money from Popoviciu began flowing into the bank account of Hunter's partner Rob Walker five weeks after then–Vice President Joe welcomed Romanian President Klaus Iohannis to the White House on September 28, 2015, according to bank records released by congressional investigators.

Between November 2015 and May 2017, Popoviciu wired 17 payments of $180,000 to Walker's account. Walker transferred one-third to Hunter and his widowed sister-in-law-turned-lover Hallie, for a total of $1,038,000.

Sixteen of the 17 payments from Popoviciu (or "Gabs" as Hunter and his partners called him) were made during the Obama-Biden administration. The final payment was extracted by Bobulinski when he came on board. "But, when I met with [Popoviciu] he was very vocal about the fact that he had stopped paying [Rob Walker's LLC] Robinson Walker when Joe Biden left the White House, and the reason why he had stopped paying them," Bobulinski told Congress, "and the reason was because he viewed that he no longer had the power or the leverage of the Biden family to—for what he was dealing with in Romania." Hunter was "livid" when the money stopped.

"While Vice President Biden was lecturing Romania on anti-corruption policies, in reality he was a walking billboard for his son and family to collect money," House Oversight Chairman James Comer would allege in 2023.

Hunter worked with lawyers from the law firm Boies Schiller Flexner, where he held an "of counsel" role, to allegedly lobby the US embassy in Bucharest to intervene in Popoviciu's case.

He also met with Hans Klemm, then ambassador to Romania, on behalf of Popoviciu: in Romania in November 2015, and again on March 29, 2016, in Washington, DC, at Afghan restaurant Lapis, according to calendar entries on Hunter's laptop and Walker's testimony to Congress. Walker said that Klemm did not do anything "on behalf of Mr. Popoviciu."

The laptop also shows Hunter sought advice on helping Popoviciu from the man his father has described as his "best personal friend," former US ambassador in Romania Mark Gitenstein, who Joe later would appoint as EU ambassador. The IRS investigators found a calendar entry in Hunter's iCloud showing a January 7, 2015, lunch with "Gitenstein, former Romanian Ambassador." Gitenstein did not know who would be the next Ambassador to Romania, according to an email nine days later from Hunter to Walker and DC lobbyist Mike Smith. Klemm was nominated to the post in March 2015. Walker also testified to Congress that he met Gitenstein at his DC law office to ask about Popoviciu.

Popoviciu would be convicted of bribery in Romania in 2016, after which he fled to London. In 2023, Romania's High Court suspended his seven-year prison sentence and ordered the case be re-judged.

FARA came up in a Sportsman meeting on July 29, 2022, when Wolf told FBI Forensic Accountant Michelle Hoffman that she wanted to "separate the FARA Romania piece from the tax side," so that it was no longer discussed at their meetings.

Meanwhile, Ziegler kept plugging away on the tax case. Because the prosecution team had grown "skittish" after Clark's forceful PowerPoint presentation, he reinvestigated the evidence for the 2014 and 2015 tax years and found emails from Hunter allegedly outlining a plan to evade paying taxes on the $83,333 a month he was receiving from Burisma.

But it still wasn't enough to convince DOJ Tax.

The pressure from Hunter's attorneys kept ratcheting up through the summer. In August, at a prosecution team meeting in Wilmington, Shapley learned that Clark had warned the prosecutors, saying they would be committing "career suicide" if they charged Hunter.

Ziegler later testified: "It was relayed to us that [Hunter's] counsel said something like 'if you charge this case, good luck with finding a job outside of here . . . it's career suicide,' I think is what he said."

Wolf had continued being unhelpful, for instance denying a request to interview Joe's adult grandchildren, because she said it would get them into "hot water."

Weiss was making positive noises about charging the 2014 and 2015 tax years within six weeks, but then he would talk to DOJ Tax, "and they convince him otherwise," Shapley complained to his bosses in an email.

"This has happened a couple times. As a result, we will continue to communicate our position to ensure this moves forward consistent with how other tax cases would be treated with similar fact patterns.

"I explained that if 2014 is not charged how it would severely diminish the picture of the overall conduct and would essentially sanitize some major issues to include the Burisma/Ukraine unreported income. I also explained that if 2014 is not charged and/or included in a statement of facts in a guilty plea, that the unreported income from Burisma that year would go untaxed."

Weiss told Shapley in a meeting on August 16, 2022, that he would weigh his arguments against the concerns of DOJ Tax "that the death of Beau Biden and Hunter Biden's subsequent drug use will undermine the case before a jury."

Two days after that meeting, Mark Daly, Senior Litigation Counsel at DOJ tax, emailed the Sportsman team to approve three interviews Ziegler had requested for mid-September: with Hunter's former lawyer George Mesires in DC, his uncle Jim Biden, and their CEFC associate Mervyn Yan in New York.

Daley also announced that they would be heading to Los Angeles in the week of September 19 to present the case for the 2017, 2018 and 2019 tax charges to the US Attorney's Office in the Central District of California, where Hunter had lived at the time.

This was news to Shapley, who was frustrated that the charges had been "in limbo" for six months, and believed this sudden announcement was typical of what he described as DOJ Tax's "lack of transparency."

The reason for the secrecy and delay became clear the week that they were due to present their case in Los Angeles.

On September 19, 2022, Biden nominee and Democrat donor Martin Estrada was sworn in as US Attorney for the Central District of California.

"Prosecutors presented the 2017, 2018, and 2019 criminal tax charges to the Central District of California around September 2022 only after President Biden's nominee, Martin Estrada, was confirmed," Shapley told Congress.

A few days later Wolf told the prosecution team that Estrada "will need time to review the charging memo [and] learn to become a US attorney," Shapley wrote in notes on the meeting.

Anyway, Wolf said, Weiss had decided the case won't be charged until after the mid-term elections on November 8, 2022: "Why would we shoot ourselves in the foot by charging before the election?"

Shapley was dismayed. Another needless delay. He messaged his boss,

Director of Field Operations Michael Batdorf, after the meeting: "Big news on Sportsman . . . Bad news. Continued inappropriate decisions affecting timing. i.e. Election . . . I believe their actions are simply wrong and this is a huge risk to us right now."

He followed up with an email to two other IRS supervisors, saying Wolf's "statement is inappropriate, let alone the actual action of delaying as a result of the election. There are other items that should also be discussed that are equally inappropriate."

As for Estrada, he also would end up declining to bring the 2017–2019 tax charges against Hunter in his district.

"For all intents and purposes," Shapley would later testify, "the case was dead, with the exception of one gun charge that could be brought in Delaware . . . The Justice Department [had] allowed the President's political appointees to weigh in on whether to charge the President's son."

The DOJ and its Delaware proxies had banned investigators from asking about Joe during witness interviews, forced them to strip reference to "Political Figure 1" (Joe) from affidavits, withheld evidence from them, excluded them from meetings with Hunter's attorneys, and tipped off defense counsel about pending search warrants.

David Weiss had sat on his hands for so long that the most dangerous charges, implicating then–Vice President Biden in his family's alleged influence peddling operation in Ukraine, had evaporated.

Joe's ousting of Ukraine's Prosecutor General Viktor Shokin was the quid pro quo that would have sunk him. Under Shokin's successor, a man described by Joe as "solid," all legal proceedings against Burisma and Mykola Zlochevsky had been dropped, and Hunter continued to be paid handsomely for another three years, albeit with a 50 percent pay cut once Joe left office.

As Shapley put it, "The purposeful exclusion of the 2014 and 2015 years sanitized the most substantive criminal conduct and concealed material facts."

Whatever happened to Hunter now, Joe was home free. Or so he believed.

CHAPTER 18

REDLINE

October 7, 2022
WILMINGTON, DELAWARE

Two days after Joe Biden's hot mic outburst in Fort Myers, Gary Shapley got the bad news.

The Hunter Biden investigation was effectively nobbled. Their suspicions about their opaque leader, US Attorney David Weiss, were confirmed.

At a meeting of the Sportsman team in Wilmington on October 7, 2022, Weiss dropped the "earth-shattering news," as Shapley would later describe it, that the U.S. attorney in Washington DC, Matthew Graves, had refused to allow him to bring tax charges against Hunter in his district, and Weiss was offering no resistance.

Weiss told the team that he subsequently had requested special counsel authority from the DOJ so he could override Graves, but his superiors refused to grant it.

To make matters worse, the statute of limitations was about to run out on the 2014 and 2015 charges and a passive Weiss was letting it happen. It meant that Joe's role in ousting Ukraine's top prosecutor Viktor Shokin and any potential foreign lobbying charges relating to Burisma would go unexamined.

Weiss' bombshells were the last straw for Shapley. The IRS supervisory agent would later describe the meeting as his "red line."

He gave Weiss a piece of his mind, telling the U.S. Attorney in front of everyone that he held numerous concerns about the way "the case had been handled from the beginning." The meeting turned "surprisingly contentious" and "ended quite awkwardly," he would testify.

He took detailed notes of everything that was said during the three hour confab, which was attended by Weiss; his three top deputies, Lesley Wolf, Shawn Weede and Shannon Hanson; Baltimore FBI Special Agent in Charge Tom Sobocinski and his deputy; and Shapley's boss, Darrell Waldon, Special Agent in Charge of the IRS in Washington.

What Weiss told them contradicted Attorney General Merrick Garland's sworn testimony to Congress that Weiss had "full authority," free of political pressure, to criminally charge Hunter without the permission of anyone else in the DOJ. Garland swore that politics could not possibly affect the case because Weiss was a Trump-appointed U.S. Attorney.

And yet here was Weiss admitting he was powerless to bring criminal charges against Hunter that had been through a rigorous DOJ approval process. Prosecutors called them "slam dunk charges." Here was Weiss admitting that, far from having "ultimate authority" as he repeatedly claimed, he was at the mercy of Biden-appointed counterparts in Washington and California who declined to help him bring charges in their districts.

"Weiss was fishing for 'no's," said a source familiar with the legal maneuvers.

Weiss was preparing to throw away five years of hard work by Shapley's IRS team and give the president's son a free pass that no other taxpayer would get.

"I watched U.S. Attorney Weiss tell a room full of senior FBI and IRS senior leaders . . . that he was not the deciding person on whether charges were filed," Shapley testified. "That was my red line. I had already seen a pattern of preferential treatment and obstruction . . . Weiss was admitting that what the American people believed, based on the Attorney General's sworn statement, was false. I could no longer stay silent."

Straight after the meeting, that Friday night, the eve of Columbus Day weekend, Shapley wrote an email to his bosses summarizing for posterity exactly what Weiss had said.

Waldon emailed him to confirm the summary was an accurate rendition of the meeting: "You covered it all."

Weiss stopped talking to Shapley after that. He was already paranoid about the leak to the *Washington Post* the previous day suggesting charges against Hunter were imminent, that must have come either from the defense lawyers or the Sportsman team.

He informed Waldon that he "would not be communicating with Mr. Shapley anymore and he would be going directly to me," Waldon later testified.

Weiss realized that Shapley had been documenting in great detail in emails to his IRS bosses over two years all the ways in which the investigation was being slow-walked and, in my opinion, mishandled. Shapley's bosses had done nothing about his regular updates, but Weiss understood that these were protected disclosures under the law that could be used at a later date to damage him if Shapley decided to blow the whistle. Shapley's note-taking skills were second to none, and he and his lead investigator Ziegler were seasoned witnesses, expert in marshalling evidence to mount a persuasive case. They would be formidable adversaries.

Weiss immediately moved into damage control. He went to Shapley's bosses to get him taken off the case. Shapley was officially removed on May 15, 2023, but he had been sidelined for months.

Shapley had been having sleepless nights, waking up at 3 a.m., heart racing, padding around his Maryland house trying not to wake his wife and four daughters. He had done his best to protect the integrity of the Sportsman investigation and ensure Ziegler had the tools he needed. But he faced obstruction, cowardice, and flat out deceptions at every stage.

Throughout his career, Shapley had done the right thing. He was respected by everyone up and down the line. He communicated directly with his boss, IRS Chief of Criminal Investigation Jim Lee, who liked Shapley because he reeled in the big cases and made him look good.

But on Hunter Biden, Shapley thought Chief Lee had gone AWOL. He didn't seem to want to know. Nobody did. They all suddenly got amnesia. The Hunter Biden case was a political hot potato that burned anyone that touched it.

Shapley crossed the Rubicon. He researched whistleblower attorneys, and found Mark Lytle, a veteran former federal tax prosecutor, and Tristan Leavitt, president of Empower Oversight, a nonprofit whistleblower group that helped with legal fees. They guided him through the fraught process of exposing what he thought was unethical conduct that had derailed the Sportsman investigation "for the benefit of the President's son."

"When I first started noticing deviations from the normal investigative process around June 2020, I did not run to Congress to air grievances," Shapley later testified. "I tried to give the prosecutors the benefit of the doubt for a very long time . . .

"In this country, we believe in the rule of law and that applies to everyone. There should not be a two-track justice system depending on who you are and who you are connected to. Yet, in this case there was. Based on my experience, I am here to tell you that the Delaware U.S. Attorney's Office and Department of Justice handling the Hunter Biden tax investigation was very different from any other case in my 14 years at the IRS. At every stage, decisions were made that benefited the subject of this investigation."

Shapley made a series of legally protected whistleblower disclosures, first to IRS leadership and then to the DOJ Inspector General and the Treasury Department Inspector General for Tax Administration.

Starting in late May 2023, he testified in multiple closed-door sessions and in public before the House Committee on Ways and Means, which was authorized to accept confidential tax information from whistleblowers.

Ziegler joined him in June, after the entire investigative team was removed from the Sportsman case. Together, the two IRS whistleblowers meticulously backed up their claims with more than 120 exhibits, including documents and messages retrieved from a search warrant of Hunter Biden's iCloud, memorialized conversations of internal IRS and DOJ meetings, and interview transcripts with associates of Hunter Biden.

Their bombshell revelations brought together two strands of the burgeoning Biden scandal. First was the original story of potential political corruption revealed on Hunter's abandoned laptop. Second was the seeming coverup which, like Watergate, had become an even bigger story.

Things changed for the president when the IRS duo came forward. Over the next six months they would place on the record irrefutable evidence of Joe's purported involvement in Hunter and Jim Biden's alleged influence peddling schemes, which augmented mountains of evidence that was piling up in Comer's Oversight committee. The stakes could not have been higher.

"I'm sitting here in front of you right now terrified," Ziegler told the Ways and Means Committee when he first was deposed behind closed doors in June 2023 as Whistleblower X.

"I'm an American, and my allegiances are to my country and my government. I'm also a gay man. I have a husband, two dogs, a home, and a life full of family and friends. But above all else, I'm a human being . . .

"In coming forward, I'm risking my career, my reputation, and the casework that I'm working outside this investigation. I believe that the Delaware U.S. Attorney's Office and DOJ Tax have a clear target on me and my supervisor's back, and I believe that they are waiting for an opportunity to pounce on us . . .

"I did not ask to be in this position, nor do I want to be. My supervisor, who I wholeheartedly respect, decided to blow the whistle on how this investigation was handled because his red line was crossed.

"At the end of the day, I worked on a complex criminal tax investigation over the last 5 years, and the investigative process is 99.9 percent done, and we were in the process of bringing the case to indictment . . .

"This case [was] about access and introductions to high-level government and political officials for wealthy foreign individuals," Ziegler testified at a later committee hearing in December 2023. "[It was] access for individuals in Ukraine, Romania and China in exchange for money to enrich a well-known political family, [one of whom] Hunter Biden, had failed to file and pay his taxes [in a] timely [fashion], as is required by law, on millions of dollars of income and had allegedly willfully filed false tax returns to the IRS.

"And at the end of the day, it appears that Department of Justice attempted to sweep everything under the rug . . . We are bringing evidence forward that justice is not blind, that people are given preferential treatment, [and] we need to learn from that so that this doesn't happen again in the future."

* * *

Democrats in Congress saw the danger when the IRS agents testified. They browbeat and threatened them, and scoffed that they had "nothing new," and "no evidence." They insisted that the president did nothing wrong and always changed the topic to Donald Trump. Allied media outlets followed their lead.

But Ziegler and Shapley held their own. In one notable exchange in December 2023, Georgia Democrat Terri Sewell stepped on a landmine when she asked the knowledgeable pair to point to any evidence they had uncovered "that directly prove[s] that Joe Biden has done something illegal, yes or no?"

Shapley replied: "There is evidence that exists."

Sewell, flustered: "I just—it is yes or no."

Shapley: "Yes, there is."

Sewell forged on: "Direct, direct evidence. Please show me the direct evidence that is not being refuted by your supervisor or by other people that actually proves that Joe Biden did something unlawful, illegal."

Ziegler replied: "Hunter Biden states in his email that his original agreement—"

Sewell cut him off: "Yes or no, sir."

Ziegler ploughed ahead as she tried to talk over him: "—with the [CEFC] director was for consulting fees. Can I respond, Mr. Chairman?"

Sewell: "No. This is my time. I am reclaiming my time."

Ziegler. "That the original agreement with the director—"

Sewell, getting frantic: "I am reclaiming my time."

Mr. Ziegler: "—was for consulting fees, based on 'introductions alone' at a rate of $10 million per year for—"

Sewell interrupted him: "Please . . . You don't come to this body, which is the House Ways and Means Committee, and run over a Member of Congress who simply asked one question."

She then asserted: "I don't see how any of this relates directly to Joe Biden, either as Vice President or as President, doing anything illegal."

Soon enough, Ziegler was allowed to complete his answer, citing three pieces of evidence pointing to Joe's potentially illegal involvement in the bribery scheme.

The first was an email to an executive of Chinese energy firm CEFC, on August 2, 2017, in which Hunter states the original deal "me and my family" had with CEFC was "for introductions alone [at] a rate of $10 million per year for three years [for a] guarantee[d] total of $30 million."

The second was a threatening WhatsApp message three days earlier, on July 30, 2017, in which Hunter demands a CEFC executive pay up, and says: "I am sitting here with my father and we would like to understand why the commitment made has not been fulfilled."

Ziegler's third piece of evidence was an email two months earlier to Hunter from one of his business partners in their joint venture with CEFC on May 13, 2017, suggesting an equity split between the four partners of 20 percent each, with 10 percent going to Hunter's uncle Jim and the remaining 10 percent "held by H for the big guy." H is Hunter and the big guy has been identified as Joe.

Ziegler told Congress: "So those things altogether, when you put them all together, I mean it says a lot . . . Those three things together . . . are kind of painting a picture. [But] we were never able to go down those investigative routes [to Joe]."

Another Democrat congressman, Lloyd Doggett, tried to clean up after his colleague, asserting that the "introductions alone" email does "not show on its face by itself any wrongdoing by Joe Biden, does it?"

Ziegler: "It shows a benefit for Hunter and his family. It says that: and his 'family.'"

Doggett: "I will take your answer as being, no, it does not."

Ziegler's reply prompted laughter in the room: "Joe Biden is a part of Hunter Biden's family."

Doggett pressed on, saying that the eventual contract between a CEFC entity and Hunter and his uncle Jim Biden did not name Joe Biden.

Ziegler agreed but said: "There was a belief in the investigation that James [Jim] Biden was a cover for Joe Biden."

It was one potentially damaging revelation after the other.

Comer had just discovered deposits of $200,000 and $40,000 by Jim Biden into his brother Joe's bank account that corresponded with a 10 percent cut of two deals Jim had just collected on. They were listed as loan repayments on the deposit slips and that is how the White House characterized the payments.

But Ziegler testified that "there was nothing to verify that they were loans in the evidence."

Asked again if there was evidence that Joe was "involved in any way with the Biden family business dealings with foreign governments or entities," both Shapley and Ziegler answered yes. "There is evidence of involvement, yes."

They also testified to the fact that as vice president, Joe may have used at least five alias email accounts such as "robinware456," "Robert L. Peters" and "JRB Ware" to communicate with Hunter and one of his business partners around the time he was travelling to Ukraine.

Hunter's laptop contains 38 emails from White House email accounts to a Joe Biden alias, in which Hunter is copied in on his business email address. In response to a Freedom of Information Act request, the National Archives and Records Administration admitted in 2023 that it was holding nearly 5,400 emails that potentially show Joe using a pseudonym during his vice presidency.

Republican Blake Moore of Utah asked Ziegler about "documents [that] show right around the time of international trips, like those to Ukraine,

Joe Biden was emailing his son and his son's business partner from private email accounts using aliases while Vice President."

Ziegler replied: "Yeah, there is evidence of involvement . . . The thing that I pointed to was the White House call notes. I mean, these are call notes about the upcoming trip of the Vice President to Ukraine, and part of that is reform of the prosecutor's office in Ukraine [and] there were multiple emails that show involvement from administration officials during the time. There was the call from the White House with meeting minutes prior to the Vice President going to Ukraine."

Ziegler provided emails that showed Burisma was getting "access via Hunter Biden to different people in the U.S. administration, and also in Ukraine in order to [get] the CEO of Burisma off of his [corruption] charges in Burisma . . . And ultimately, through Joe Biden's actions, this individual [Viktor Shokin] was fired."

Ziegler also testified to "red flags" he saw linking Joe to potential criminal activity relating to Ukraine and China, such as an email to Hunter from Burisma executive Vadym Pozharskyi spelling out how "high-ranking political officials within the administration in the U.S. . . . can help [Burisma] with their case over in the Ukraine.

"There is Joe Biden admitting that he went over to Ukraine and threatened to withhold money in exchange for firing the prosecutor general . . .

"You move forward to China. There is the WhatsApp message. There is the perception in that message that 'I am sitting here with my father waiting to make a deal.' There is 10 percent 'held by H for the big guy.' There is the financial transactions that we have seen between the associates of Hunter Biden and Joe Biden."

In his testimony, Shapley pointed to evidence that showed Joe "was at least discussing business information with Hunter Biden, to include attending meetings and so on and so forth. You have to understand that someone who is a Vice President, a Senator for years . . . their involvement in a business is not going to be coming up with mission statements and working on Excel spreadsheets. Him coming across to a lunch and having a glass of water would have shown his support for his son Hunter Biden."

Ziegler and Shapley repeatedly testified that all investigative avenues that would lead to Joe had been blocked by Lesley Wolf, under the mantle of Weiss and the DOJ. The aim, in their view, was to ensure that the most serious tax and foreign lobbying charges that implicated Joe would never be laid against Hunter.

At one point, Dan Goldman, New York congressman, heir to the Levi Strauss fortune and novice Democratic attack dog, tried to trip up Shapley with a question about the time Joe dropped into a lunch Hunter was having with his Chinese partners from CEFC.

"Hunter told his dad, according to [Hunter's former associate] Rob Walker, 'I may be trying to start a company or try to do something with these guys,'" Goldman said. "Now let me ask you something. That doesn't sound much like Joe Biden was involved in whatever Hunter Biden was doing with the CEFC if Hunter Biden is telling him that he's trying to do business with them, does it?"

"No," Shapley replied, "but it does show that [Hunter] told his father he was trying to do business and he was talking to his father about the business."

Realizing the exchange had just contradicted Joe's claim he never talked to his son about business, Goldman loudly talked over Shapley: "Well, that is true. Hunter Biden does try to do business," he said.

By the end of the testimony, Goldman and colleagues were forced to retreat from their assertion that there was "no evidence" Joe was "involved" in Hunter's business and start saying there was "no direct evidence" that Joe "profited" from Hunter's business. In fact, there was a small amount of evidence on the laptop that Hunter had paid some of Joe's household bills, including a monthly AT&T bill of around $190, and hefty bills to Wilmington contractors for maintenance and upkeep of his Greenville property.

But as Shapley pointed out, Joe benefited even if he wasn't paid directly. Any money that went into Hunter's pocket, whether from Burisma, CEFC, or a shady oligarch, was money Joe didn't have to find to help out his often in trouble, often indebted son.

As the contents of his laptop reveal, Hunter liked to spend money, as the IRS investigators discovered when they totted up millions of dollars of eye-popping expenditures between 2016 and 2019.

On one months-long bender in Los Angeles in 2018, for instance, Hunter spent $34,400 for 42 nights in a poolside bungalow at the Chateau Marmont. One night he spent $8,000 on an extended callout for a 24-year-old Russian prostitute named "Yanna," an "elite courtesan" with green eyes and brown hair from Emerald Fantasy Girls. He shelled out $1,000 a pop for a sex-cam porn site called STREAMRAY where women with names like "PerfectTits" took off their clothes, and he tooled around L.A. in a $650-a-day Lamborghini Gallardo Spyder rental.

He spent $140,000 on a 14-night bender in Las Vegas for a suite at the Palms Casino Resort, not counting the drugs, hookers and room service pizza.

In New York, he stayed at the Mandarin Oriental in Columbus Circle in a $2,495-a-night suite with views of Central Park and dropped $30,000 on Brunello Cucinelli suits from Riflessi on West 57th Street, Billionaire's Row.

One time he spent $69,000 to fix his teeth at Smile Design Cosmetic Dentistry in Midtown, and $12,000 on an outing to Larry Flynt's Hustler Club in Hell's Kitchen.

There was a sex club membership that cost $10,000 and over $1.6 million withdrawn from cash machines between 2016 and 2019.

"Simply looking at your spending is enough for any judge to be disgusted," Kathleen told him in the middle of their divorce in 2017.

In any case, if there had been "direct evidence" of payments to Joe, Shapley and Ziegler were not allowed to find it. Wolf unremittingly denied them search warrants and blocked any line of questioning that touched on Joe, they testified.

When they tried to interview Hunter's adult daughters about deductions related to them that Hunter had made on his tax returns, allegedly such as a $30,000 Columbia University tuition payment, Wolf told them they would be in "hot water" if they went anywhere near the Biden family.

* * *

From May until December of 2023, in multiple congressional hearings, Shapley and Ziegler placed on the record the myriad ways the investigation had been sabotaged in Delaware and Washington.

Their cool testimony was a masterclass in facts over obfuscation. But it came at considerable personal cost. They were under intense attack, from Hunter's lawyers, the DOJ and the IRS, Democrats in Congress, and a section of the media.

They stayed in their jobs but suffered retaliation and ostracism, while the leaders who abandoned them were rewarded. Shapley's boss, Chief Jim Lee, was honored by Joe with the 2023 Presidential Rank Award as a Distinguished Executive.

Ziegler was genuinely disappointed by the hostility he encountered from Democrat lawmakers. At one point he scolded them in his testimony: "I am a Democrat, and I expected that we would want to work on a bipartisan basis . . . I hope you guys understand, the impact to me and my husband, to our family. It has not been an easy process. We have been attacked and we brought forward the facts . . .

"There is preferential treatment at the hands of the Department of Justice. If you have got money, if you have got political favor, there is preferential treatment there. And I hoped that Congress would have wanted to act on this."

It was tough personally for Shapley, too. His beloved mother, who had brought him up solo when his dad walked out soon after he was born, is an anti-Trump liberal who watches CNN. She was horrified that her son's revelations might damage Joe's electoral prospects.

Shapley described his experience as a whistleblower as "an extremely rude awakening."

"Elected officials who believed my disclosures helped their political party have hailed me as a hero," he testified. "Elected officials who believed my disclosures hurt their political party have obfuscated and spun the evidence, doing virtually everything they can to hide the truth on this issue from the public.

"Worse, members of [Congress] have actively worked to discredit the two career government agents who believed they were honoring the rule of law and their oath to the Constitution by providing this evidence to Congress. This unquestionably deters any future whistleblowers who may ever consider making protected disclosures to Congress."

But he drew comfort from the fact that he knew "what I witnessed was wrong. As a career law enforcement officer with no agenda but the truth, I did my best to right that wrong. This country is the greatest the earth has ever seen, and I will fight for it until my last breath."

Shapley and Ziegler's principled opposition to the apparent coverup changed the course of history. They were called liars and political partisans, and their integrity was questioned. But they remain firm in their belief that they did the right thing for the right reasons.

Judging by the private outpouring of gratitude and praise they received from colleagues, in the process they became role models for every honest public servant.

* * *

By the time Shapley and Ziegler finished unloading, the IRS and the DOJ had been publicly shamed. The Attorney General had been accused of committing perjury (but was never charged and denied any wrongdoing). Weiss had to frantically issue multiple clarifying letters to House Judiciary chairman Jim Jordan trying to explain the discrepancies between what Garland told Congress under oath and what Weiss told Shapley in the "red line" meeting attended by six other witnesses.

Lesley Wolf was off the case and two new killer prosecutors from Baltimore, Leo Wise and Derek Hines, had taken over.

In July 2023, the sweetheart deal Hunter's lawyers had engineered with prosecutors collapsed under questioning from an astute judge, and the two sides went from partners in deceit to bitter adversaries as Hunter's lawyers accused Weiss of reneging on their agreement.

In August, the fallout from Shapley and Ziegler's revelations forced Garland to make Weiss a Special Counsel, to reassure the public that he really did have "full authority" to indict Hunter.

But Shapley was skeptical: "No report written by Mr. Weiss can be taken seriously," he said at the time, "as it will be a document full of self-serving justifications to defend himself against the allegations that he engaged in unethical conduct and allowed Hunter Biden preferential treatment." Instead, an independent special counsel should have investigated Weiss, the DOJ and the IRS's handling of the probe, said Shapley.

Sharing his skepticism, Chairman Comer and two fellow House committee chairmen wrote to Garland asking why Weiss, of all people, had been chosen as Special Counsel in a fox-guarding-the-hen-house scenario.

The Department of Justice "pulled punches in this investigation, handicapping veteran investigators and preventing them from freely pursuing the facts," they wrote. "The Department agreed to an apparently unprecedented plea deal with Hunter Biden after his attorneys threatened to call his father, President Biden, as a witness in the case. Now you have appointed as special counsel an individual who oversaw all the investigation's irregularities, who spent the past two months claiming that he did not need special counsel status, and who was responsible for the plea agreement that collapsed in court."

On September 12, 2023, Kevin McCarthy, then Speaker of the Republican-controlled House, announced an impeachment inquiry into the President, to be led by Comer and conducted by the Oversight, Judiciary, and Ways and Means committees.

By the end of the year, Hunter would face felony indictments in California and Delaware.

Pressure was mounting on the president, and the realization was dawning on his campaign that Hunter had become a big drag on his re-election prospects. The White House began to leak stories about the "heavy toll" on Joe of Hunter's legal woes.

"The White House has long stressed that the president does not interfere in matters before the Justice Department," wrote *Politico*. "But privately, fears about the upcoming campaign and potential criminal trial have become an ever-present weight on the president, according to those close to him. The elder Biden has told friends he worries that his son could even backslide into addiction."

Pathos was added by a confidant of the president: "You can see it in his eyes, and you can see his shoulders slump. He's so worried about Hunter. And we're worried it could consume him."

If they managed to get near him, reporters started asking Joe about his involvement in his family's alleged influence-peddling schemes.

One day in December 2023, the *New York Post*'s White House correspondent Steven Nelson was assigned by the White House Correspondents' Association as the "pool reporter" to represent the rotating "pool" of journalists covering the president.

Nelson made the most of the rare opportunity to buttonhole Joe.

"President Biden, on Ukraine and also China, there's polling by the Associated Press that shows that almost 70 percent of Americans, including 40 percent of Democrats, believe that you acted either illegally or unethically in regard to your family's business interests. Can you explain to Americans, amid this impeachment inquiry, why you interacted with so many of your son and brother's foreign business associates?"

The president's eyes narrowed: "I'm not going to comment on that," he snarled. "I did not. And it's just a bunch of lies."

Nelson followed up: "You didn't interact with any of their business associates?"

Biden spoke over him: "They're lies," he said, before answering: "I did not. They're lies."

CHAPTER 19

GET YOUR DAD ON THE PHONE

December 4, 2015
DUBAI, UAE

Mykola Zlochevsky was living in a white villa on the Palm Jumeirah, a pretty palm-shaped archipelago of artificial islands off the coast of Dubai where his neighbors were other often-investigated oligarchs and wealthy exiles who could live in luxury without fear of extradition.

After prosecutors in Ukraine started turning up the heat, Zlochevsky moved the Burisma board meeting from Monaco to the Burj Al Arab Hotel in Dubai, which is perched on its own artificial island just a few miles up the coast from Zlochevsky's villa.

Decorated with 20,000 square feet of 24-carat gold leaf and billed by travel journalists as the world's only "seven-star" hotel, it looked like a huge billowing white spinnaker teetering on the edge of the Persian Gulf.

Late in the evening of Friday, December 4, 2015, after dinner with the Burisma board, Hunter quietly slipped away to the Four Seasons Resort at Jumeirah Beach, six miles north, where he had opted to stay separately from the rest of the board.

He planned to meet up in the outdoor bar with an old friend, Christian Clerc, formerly the discreet general manager of the Four Seasons Hotel in Georgetown, now running the Dubai resort for the hotel group.

Hunter didn't like to drink in front of Zlochevsky and his right-hand man Vadym Pozharskyi, who were paying him $83,000 a month to do not very much on the board. But he also wanted to escape the unsubtle pressure the Ukrainian hard men had been applying lately. Pozharskyi was becoming increasingly explicit when conveying Zlochevsky's demands that Hunter use his political influence to stop the criminal investigation of Burisma in Ukraine.

Prosecutor General Viktor Shokin was showing no signs of letting up on his pursuit of the company. His office was already working to secure a court order to seize Zlochevsky's assets in Kyiv, including his beloved mansion on the Dnieper River, with its Versailles-like gardens, saunas, cold room, salt room and outdoor hot tubs.

Pozharskyi demanded that Hunter and his fellow board member Archer use their influence to "close down" Shokin's criminal investigation against Zlochevsky. In a November 2, 2015 email found on the laptop, he told them they needed to provide "a list of deliverables . . . a concrete course of actions, incl. meetings/communications resulting in high-ranking US officials in Ukraine (US Ambassador) and in US publicly or in private communication/comment expressing their 'positive opinion' and support of Nikolay [Zlochevsky]/Burisma to the highest level of decision makers here in Ukraine: President of Ukraine, president Chief of staff, Prosecutor General, etc.

"The scope of work should also include organization of a visit of a number of widely recognized and influential current and/or former US policymakers to Ukraine in November, aiming to conduct meetings with and bring positive signal/message and support on Nikolay's issue to the Ukrainian top officials above with the ultimate purpose to close down any cases/pursuits against Nikolay in Ukraine."

Zlochevsky wanted Shokin stopped. He was sick of living in exile, sick of his $23 million still being frozen in London, sick of having visas denied, first for the US, now for Mexico, as Shokin tried to claw back money from the kleptocratic Yanukovych government in which he had been ecology minister. He was sick of hearing from his neighbors that Dubai might cave to international pressure to stop being a haven for dirty money. And he was sick of Hunter fobbing him off.

Blue Star Strategies, who Hunter and Archer had hoped would be a buffer between them and Burisma, just didn't cut it. The one thing Zlochevsky understood was power, and he was not paying $83,000 a month—times two—for an introduction to a lobbying firm. Hunter's father had the power to do, with a flick of the wrist, what Zlochevsky needed. The time had come for Hunter to sing for his supper.

Dinner for the Burisma board was outdoors that balmy Friday evening at a long rectangular table at Rockfish restaurant among the palm trees of the Jumeirah Al Naseem resort, across the bridge from the Burj. There were 16 people, including the other board directors and Burisma senior staff.

Chairman of the board Alan Apter, the former Merrill Lynch investment banker, was there, as was Aleksander Kwasniewski, Poland's former president, Joe's old pal. Every time he saw Hunter, Kwasniewski would joke with him about the Polish cavalryman's sword he had given his father years before, a friend recalls. According to former White House stenographer Mike McCormick, Joe allegedly boasted in 2014 about receiving the precious sword and said it "hangs proudly in my family home," but there did not appear to be any record of the valuable item on the US federal register of foreign gifts.

Hunter vanished before the dinner was over. Zlochevsky and Pozharskyi went in search of him, but he was nowhere to be found. They caught up with Archer in the lobby of the Burj looking for a drink and told him they needed to speak urgently to Hunter. Archer knew where his friend was, and tried to phone him to warn him he was about to have visitors.

He reluctantly hopped in the back of Zlochevsky's white S-Class Mercedes, and the driver took the three of them the short distance up the coast to the Four Seasons.

When they found Hunter at the bar, Pozharskyi immediately told him to phone his father, Archer recounted to a friend, and Hunter obliged, putting Joe on speakerphone, and introducing him to the Ukrainians by name as "Nikolai and Vadym," with words to the effect that the Burisma bigwigs "need our support."

When he testified to Congress in 2023, Archer was more circumspect about the speakerphone call. Now, he said that Pozharskyi had asked Hunter simply to "call DC." Archer also testified that he didn't hear the call, because Hunter and the Ukrainians moved away from him to speak privately.

But in the Mercedes on the way back to the Burj Al Arab, or sometime the next day, Pozharskyi told Archer that it was Joe on the line in Washington, DC, where it was early afternoon Friday.

"Listen, I did not hear this phone call, but he, he called his dad," Archer said in a deposition to the House Oversight committee in July 2023.

Q: "How do you know that?"

Archer: "Because he, because I think Vadym told me. But, again, it's unclear. I just know that there was a call that happened there, and I was not privy to it . . ."

Q: "When Vadym told you this, where were you?"

Archer: "I was, you know, basically what, then we drove back to the hotel I was staying at."

Q: "Who's 'we'?"

Archer: "Me, Vadym, and Mykola."

Q: "Was it during that drive back that Vadym told you that Hunter Biden had called VP Biden at that time?"

Archer: "It would have been at some point there or after. You know, maybe the next day . . . So, the exact time I can't say, but that's what happened."

There was a sudden interruption at this point of the testimony, by Archer's lawyer Matthew Schwartz, from Boies Schiller, the law firm that had paid Hunter $216,000 a year for a no-show job as "of counsel," and whose chairman was long-time Biden donor David Boies.

"He told you expressly he called his father or that he called DC?" Schwartz asked his client.

"DC, DC," Archer hastily replied.

Schwartz had been representing Archer for eight years, pro bono in recent years, through the roller coaster of his conviction for securities fraud in June 2018, which was overturned, then reinstated on appeal.

Facing a one-year prison sentence and more than $15 million in fines and restitution, Archer, 48, was in a delicate position, abandoned by the Bidens, but not willing to expose his wife, Krista, and young children to their wrath. He trusted Schwartz, but he didn't really have much choice.

In May 2024, Manhattan Federal Judge Ronnie Abrams vacated Archer's 2022 prison sentence due to a prosecutorial error that wasn't picked up by Schwartz. He was due to be resentenced, but due to his cooperation with the Oversight Committee and with the SDNY on a non-Biden related case, he was hopeful of leniency.

Archer testified that Hunter put his VP dad on the speakerphone more than 20 times during meetings with foreign clients. The very point of getting Joe on the phone was to demonstrate that his important father was available at a moment's notice to chat with the shady oligarchs in Paris or Dubai or Lake Como who showered Hunter with millions of dollars and lavish gifts.

"You do a favor for me you are my friend; you do a favor for my son, and you are a friend for life" was one of Joe's favorite sayings, according to Archer. He would repeat the phrase time and again to his son's business partners.

It left nobody in any doubt that paying money to Hunter was the equivalent of paying it to Joe, only better.

Introducing his dad on speakerphone was Hunter's party trick. The Ukrainians regularly asked Hunter to get his dad on the phone, said Archer. "The request was made by Vadym [Pozharskyi] a lot."

Congressional investigators noted the context of the Dubai speakerphone call: three days later, on December 7, 2015, then–vice president

Biden flew to Kyiv and demanded that President Petro Poroshenko fire Shokin.

It was on that trip, behind the scenes, that Joe "explicitly linked" $1 billion in US loan guarantees to the Prosecutor-General's removal, according to Colin Kahl, the VP's national security adviser at the time.

Kahl told the *Washington Post* that Biden would have announced the $1 billion aid package if Poroshenko had immediately fired Shokin. But the Ukrainian president dug his heels in so, instead, Joe railed about the evils of corruption, ironically enough.

It took three more months to oust Shokin.

Archer also testified about two dinners Hunter organized at Georgetown's Cafe Milano for his father to meet his benefactors from Ukraine, Russia and Kazakhstan in 2014 and 2015.

The phone calls and dinners were a signal that everybody understood, especially in the most corrupt countries in the world, where a politician's son possibly selling his father's influence is commonplace.

Pozharskyi attended the first dinner, on April 16, 2015, along with Russian billionaire Yelena Baturina and her husband, former Moscow mayor Yury Luzhkov.

The Biden campaign initially denied that Joe had met Pozharskyi, after the *New York Post* reported an email from Hunter's laptop in which the Burisma executive thanked Hunter for introducing him to his father. Safely after the election, the Biden White House eventually admitted to the *Washington Post* in 2021 that Joe had, indeed, met Pozharskyi when he attended the Cafe Milano dinner.

Archer debunked the false narrative, told by the *Washington Post*, which claimed that Joe only popped in briefly to speak to a Greek Orthodox priest there.

"No," Archer replied: It was actually "a regular dinner" and "that's not correct reporting."

Hunter gave contradictory testimony about the dinner, and most everything else, in his deposition to the impeachment inquiry in February 2024.

Texas Republican Pat Fallon asked him about the Cafe Milano dinner that Pozharskyi attended with Joe.

"After [Burisma] hired you, Vadym Pozharskyi had dinner with your father as well?"

Hunter: "He did not have dinner with my father. I said this many times before."

Fallon, puzzled: "He did not have dinner with your father?"

Hunter: "My dad did not come for dinner. He came and sat down at the presentations. He sat down next to Father Alex, who he's known for almost 42 years, who was a close family friend. And I believe that he probably had a Coca-Cola and a bowl of spaghetti, maybe, and then got up and gave Xanthi a hug and Michael a hug, walked out, shook hands to the people that were sitting on the table."

Fallon: "So he ate there. Most people would define that as having dinner."

Hunter's lawyer Abbe Lowell interjected at this point, just to add more obfuscation: "Well, he said he's not sure that he ate."

Fallon: "Okay. Well, he said spaghetti."

Lowell: "He said he might've had a bowl of spaghetti."

Fallon: "So he might've had dinner. Okay."

Hunter broke in: "My bottom line is this, is that, yes, my dad attended, in one form or another, he stopped by, whatever way you want to characterize it, but for nothing other than to say hello to the people around the table and particularly those related to the World Food Program."

Fallon: "Do you see the pattern here, though? I mean, people give money to either you or your business associates and then they have access to your dad?"

Hunter took umbrage: "You're trying to make every single thing in business that I was ever involved in somehow corrupt."

Asked about the speakerphone calls, Hunter adopted the same tone of injured innocence.

"Did you ever place your father on speakerphone with any of your business associates?" he was asked.

Hunter: "Over the course of the last 30 years when speakerphone was invented on a cell phone? I'm certain my dad has called me. My dad calls me like I'm sure a lot of your parents do or a lot of you do with your children, and if I'm with people that are friends of mine, I'll have him say hi."

Q: "By placing him on speakerphone?"

Hunter then pulled out the Biden family sympathy card which his father has used to good effect in the past.

Hunter: "I'm surprised my dad hasn't called me right now, and if he did, I would put him on speakerphone to say hi to you and to Congressman Raskin and everybody else in the room. It is nothing nefarious literally.

"You understand my relationship with my family. When my dad was 29 years old, he woke up one day, went to work, and got a phone call and lost his wife and his daughter. And, in that same accident, he also lost almost my brother and myself. And then, when I was 46 years old, my 47-year-old brother died. And in our family, when you have a call from—I call him or he calls me or I call one of my—his grandkids or one of my children, you always pick up the phone. It's something that we always do. And you can ask anybody that I know; it does not have to do with Devon. If my dad calls me and I'm in the middle of something, I either get up from the table or I answer the phone at the table if it's with people that I have a long-term relationship with."

* * *

Archer described how Joe was "the brand" of his family "business" and was used to send "signals" of power, access, and influence, whether on speakerphone or meeting in person. There were dinners at Cafe Milano, breakfasts at the vice-presidential residence in DC, handshakes on the sidelines of Beijing meetings.

Ultimately, it was this access to VP Biden that apparently sent millions of dollars flowing into Biden family coffers.

"They were calls to talk about the weather, and that was signal enough to be powerful," testified Archer. It wasn't the content of the calls, in other words, but the fact that they were made. That was the "signal."

Archer stated the obvious which was that Hunter's value to Burisma was his access to his father, the VP, and he explained later to Fox News' Tucker Carlson what a "signal" means in a corrupt country like Ukraine.

"It's almost like, you know, the shakedown . . . they're using a common term to them and sending back here to us and say, 'I hope we're protected' kind of thing."

Archer acknowledged in his testimony that Zlochevsky was widely suspected of acquiring Burisma's gas permits corruptly when he was the government minister in charge of handing out permits. Zlochevsky has evaded conviction and denied every accusation.

"There were allegations that some of the . . . deposits or some of the reserves were not, you know, authentically acquired."

This was why Shokin was "taking a close look at Burisma," said Archer. "Shokin was considered a threat to the business . . . You've got to get the signals to the government. I think anyone in government is always a threat and always trying to shake down these businesses that were highly successful."

Archer hedged by saying that he was told by Burisma executives that Shokin himself was corrupt and "there was a big push by European leaders, the Atlantic Council, etc., to fire Shokin because he was corrupt . . . It certainly wasn't made clear to us at the board level . . . that that was a favor to be done . . . I wasn't involved in Shokin or any of this."

But ultimately, Archer concluded, Shokin "was a threat. He ended up seizing assets of Nikolai [Mykola Zlochevsky], a house, some cars, a couple of properties. And Nikolai actually never went back to Ukraine after Shokin seized all of these assets . . .

"And then [Shokin] was fired and then somehow Burisma was let off the hook."

Asked if Burisma executives were trying to leverage Hunter's relationship with his powerful father, Archer said, "Yes, there was constant pressure to send signals to leverage all of his, you know, his dad included . . .

"It was that ability to help on the geopolitical stage, keep them out of trouble, keep them out of investigations, unfreeze assets [and] unsuccessfully, you know, unfreeze visas."

Ultimately, said Archer, "I do believe that, at the end of the day, Burisma wouldn't have stayed in business so long if Hunter was not on the board . . . I think Burisma would have gone out of business if it didn't have the [Biden] brand attached to it."

Archer testified that the Biden "brand" protected Burisma because "people would be intimidated to mess with them."

Hunter's presence on Burisma's board and access to his father gave the company "defensive leverage [and] 'longevity'" because now it had the "capabilities to navigate DC."

He was asked if Hunter talked "about how bringing his dad either to Ukraine or using his dad as Vice President would add value in the eyes of Burisma officials?"

"Yes," replied Archer. "It's pretty obvious if you're, you know, you're the son of a Vice President."

According to Hunter's testimony, Joe possibly made himself available for breakfasts, lunches, dinners, coffees, and pleasant chit-chat on the speakerphone with Hunter's foreign benefactors, all to oil the wheels of the family business—which can be seen as selling access to him, as he should have known.

"Look after my boy," he told Kremlin-backed Baturina and her husband, Luzhkov, when Hunter activated the speakerphone at a Russian restaurant in Brooklyn called Romanoff on May 4, 2014.

Just three months earlier, Baturina had wired $3.5 million to Rosemont Seneca Thornton LLC, the firm cofounded by Hunter, Archer, John Kerry's stepson Chris Heinz, and Jimmy Bulger, nephew of mobster "Whitey" Bulger.

Jason Galanis, a former business partner of Hunter and Archer serving 14 years in jail for his part in the $60 million Burnham securities fraud, testified to the impeachment committee in 2024 from an Alabama jail, to say that he was "stunned" when Hunter put his dad on speakerphone with the Russians.

"Hunter called his father, said hello and 'hold on, Pops,' then put the call on speakerphone and said, 'I am here with our friends I told you were coming to town, and we wanted to say "hello" . . . It was clear to me this was a pre-arranged call with his father meant to impress the Russian investors that Hunter had access to his father and all the power and prestige of his position."

Joe's speakerphone diplomacy on behalf of Hunter's finances was part of a well-established pattern in the Biden family business, as Tony Bobulinski also alleges.

During a meeting by the pool at the Chateau Marmont in LA, Bobulinski recalls Hunter offering to get his father on the phone.

"I am also aware of other Biden family business associates confirming that Joe would take phone calls from Hunter in the middle of business meetings and would weigh in via speakerphone," says Bobulinski.

"Sitting with Hunter at Chateau Marmont before I first met Joe Biden on May 2, 2017, Hunter was adamant that his father takes his calls at any time, no matter what his lawyers say or with gatekeepers like [former Biden spokesperson] Kate Bedingfield playing interference."

Bobulinski also believes that the American people don't fully appreciate yet the key role Joe Biden played in Hunter and Jim's alleged global influence peddling. "I would equate it to a chairman's role in a traditional business structure."

* * *

Back in 2019 in the middle of his legal woes, Archer complained to Hunter about his predicament.

"Why did your dad's administration appointees arrest me and try and put me in jail?" he wrote on March 6, 2019, in a text message found on Hunter's abandoned laptop.

"Why would they try and ruin my family and destroy my kids and no one from your family's side step in and at least try to help me? I don't get it."

Hunter reassured his friend he would not be abandoned by the Biden family.

"Every great family is persecuted . . . you are part of a great family—not a side show, not deserted by them even in your darkest moments. That's the way Bidens are different, and you are a Biden. It's the price of power and the people questioning you truly have none."

If he just sat tight, would Hunter's father make sure he got a pardon after the election? The polls were pointing to a Biden win.

But nothing happened. Hunter stopped taking his calls. An intermediary reached out to see what the prospects were for a presidential pardon. Not good. It was "too political." Maybe during the lame duck period, if Joe lost the 2024 election. But probably not. He was on his own.

Hunter's lawyer Abbe Lowell then started denigrating Archer by referring to him as the "inmate."

The Bidens had abandoned him.

District Judge Ronnie Abrams, an Obama appointee, had declared "an unwavering concern that Archer is innocent" when she overturned his conviction, accepting that he had been taken advantage of by co-defendant Galanis, who used him as a front-man in the scheme to defraud a Native American tribe.

Archer lost millions in the disaster, unlike Hunter, who made $200,000 as vice chairman of Burnham Financial Group, the firm at the center of the scam, but was alleged not to have been involved in the scheme and was not charged by the SDNY.

After the news broke that he was cooperating with congressional investigators in 2023, Archer was bombarded with death threats, and had to move out of his Brooklyn home temporarily.

He told as much of the truth as he could while trying to survive at the center of a brutal tug-of-war between Congress and the White House.

Friends urged him to save himself by using the only currency he had left—his knowledge of Hunter and Jim's alleged influence-peddling scheme, for which he had a front-row seat for four years during Joe's vice presidency.

In return for his cooperation, Archer hoped for a letter from House Republicans to Judge Abrams urging leniency, perhaps in the form of home detention.

But two days before his bombshell testimony to the impeachment committee, the US attorney for the Southern District of New York, Damian Williams, sent an extraordinary letter to Judge Abrams asking her to immediately set a date for Archer to report to prison.

In his letter, Williams explicitly rejected a request he had received from Schwartz to postpone any decision until after Archer had testified.

It was hard not to view the letter as a gratuitous attempt to rattle Archer before his testimony.

This was the same SDNY that turned a blind eye to Jim and Hunter's alleged malfeasance over the years. They never asked Archer a single question about Hunter's involvement with Burnham, for instance, and ignored Gal Luft's disclosures about Hunter and Jim's CEFC payments and the existence of an FBI mole in their ranks.

Oversight Committee Chairman James Comer alleged the SDNY letter as "obstruction of justice."

Bob Costello, former SDNY deputy chief of the Criminal Division, agreed, saying it was "highly unusual" for a US attorney to pressure a judge over a surrender date.

"They want to put pressure on him. They want this to be weighing on his mind."

Costello saw the letter to Abrams as "a psychological operation on Archer to see . . . how it affects his ability to recollect [damning details during his testimony].

"I think what the SDNY has done borders on obstructing justice, by interfering with a congressional witness. While they might technically be allowed to do this, it exhibits bad form at the very least."

As careful as he was, Archer's testimony was devastating to the president's credibility.

Hunter's misdeeds were catching up to him, and they would dredge up the ghosts of Joe's past that he thought were long buried.

CHAPTER 20

POKING THE BEAR

December 11, 2013
MAIDAN SQUARE, KYIV, UKRAINE

Television footage captured Victoria Nuland, Obama's Assistant Secretary of State for Europe, in an odd scene in Kyiv's wintry Maidan Square the day after violent clashes between protesters and riot police.

The Western-backed protests in Ukraine had begun three weeks earlier, after President Viktor Yanukovich, under pressure from Vladimir Putin, backtracked on a major economic deal with the European Union and decided to accept Russia's counteroffer of a $15 billion aid package and cheaper gas.

A rotund figure in a blue puffer jacket clutching a bulging plastic bag, Nuland strides around the square like a union boss on the picket lines, handing out sandwiches and good cheer to bemused protesters and riot police.

"Hello, how are you? Good to see you," she says, beaming as she thrusts her hand out to Ukrainian strangers. "We're here from America. Would you like some bread?"

An elderly woman waves her away, and an elderly man claps his hands politely. Then Nuland barrels up to a row of helmeted young cops in riot gear.

"Some bread for you?" she asks one, who looks at her blankly. "Take some bread. You're hungry. C'mon."

Alongside her is the grim-faced US ambassador to Ukraine, Geoffrey Pyatt, who can be seen in the footage shoving a bread roll into the unreceptive hands of another young policeman.

Nuland would later explain her actions as "a symbol of sympathy with the horrible situation that Yanukovych had put Ukrainians in, pitting them against each other." But the bizarre optics came to symbolize the casual ineptitude of US meddling in Ukraine.

Few policymakers were as influential in Ukraine as Nuland, a Russia hawk who had been national security adviser to former vice president Dick Cheney at the start of the Iraq war. As NATO ambassador, she had urged President George W. Bush to accept both Ukraine and Georgia as NATO members, a failed effort that inflamed Russia for years to come. She went on to be assistant secretary of state, managing Ukraine, in the Obama administration, where she was involved in spinning the Benghazi debacle. She would sit out the Trump administration at the liberal Brookings Institution with her husband Robert Kagan, a leading proponent of the Iraq war, before becoming point woman for Ukraine once again in the Biden administration, an apparent vote of confidence in her performance during the overthrow of Yanukovich.

Nuland represented the Washington foreign policy establishment's lust to move Eastern Europe out of Russia's orbit and integrate it into the West. To that end, she boasted that the US had "invested $5 billion" since 1991 in pro-Europe "civil society" groups in Ukraine.

Her role was to encourage the bloody protests that came to be known as the Euromaidan Revolution, or Revolution of Dignity, that ultimately forced out Yanukovych, although the full extent of US involvement is not known. Foreign policy hawk Senator John McCain would join her to cheer on the protests, which became increasingly violent, culminating in mysterious sniper fire on Maidan Square, which was blamed on both sides.

By the time the government fell, 108 civilians and 13 police officers had died. The slain protesters, aged from 16 to 83, came to be known as the "Heavenly Hundred."

Ukraine's capital, Kyiv, the cradle of Slavic civilization, is one of Europe's most beautiful cities, full of churches with golden domes that serve as an antidote to the hulking Soviet buildings dotting the city. Maidan, or Independence Square, is the majestic heart of the city. A patch of marshy ground when the Mongols invaded in the 13th century, a popular marketplace in the 19th century, a Soviet parade ground in 1922, and a ruin after World War II, it was renamed October Revolution Square in 1977 in honor of the Bolsheviks. After independence in 1991 came a new centerpiece, representing optimism and freedom, a soaring white marble pillar topped with a 30-foot gilded statue of the Slavic goddess Berehynia, surrounded by fountains and sculptures and inviting patches of lawn. The Bolshevik-era granite statue of Lenin survived the 2004 Orange Revolution but was toppled by protesters during Euromaidan ten years later.

A few weeks after their sandwich dispersal, with the protests escalating, a phone call between Nuland and Pyatt was bugged and posted online, reportedly by the Russians. Nuland's wispy voice can be heard outlining her plans for regime change. She wanted to install one of the pro-Western opposition leaders, Arseniy "Yats" Yatsenyuk, as the new prime minister, and so it transpired.

"I think Yats is the guy who's got the economic experience," she tells Pyatt. Later she exclaims: "Fuck the EU," in exasperation at European reluctance to provoke Moscow.

Nuland also refers to Joe in the call, saying that the VP's national security adviser, Jake Sullivan, had just called her directly to tell her: "You need Biden." She told Pyatt, "I said probably tomorrow for an 'atta-boy' and to get the deets [details] to stick. So, Biden's willing."

In the most recent chapters of Ukraine's tragedy, Joe Biden is a central figure. An aspiring statesman, he was designated as President Barack Obama's point man in Ukraine in February 2014, despite being "wrong on nearly every major foreign policy and national security issue over the past four decades," as former Bush-Obama Defense Secretary Robert Gates wrote in his 2014 memoir.

In 2009, at the start of his vice presidency, Joe had struck up a "towel-snapping rapport" with Yanukovich, according to the *New Yorker*, and liked to tell the near six-foot-six former mechanic from Donetsk: "You look like a thug! You're so damn big."

As the political crisis threatened to destabilize the strategically located former Soviet republic, Joe took control of the "delicate diplomatic maneuvering" on behalf of the Obama administration, as the *Associated Press* described it. From December to February 2014, the vice president spoke by phone nine times to Yanukovych, peremptorily issuing impossible demands and making grandiose threats, according to official readouts of the calls that each lasted at least an hour. It was "an unusual level of contact," but Joe was keen to burnish his foreign policy credentials as he contemplated a 2016 presidential run.

After the ninth phone call with Joe, on February 21, 2014, Yanukovych fled the capital in a helicopter bound for Moscow, and the Ukrainian government collapsed. The opulent estate he left behind in Kyiv, with its pet peacocks, fleet of antique cars, and private restaurant in the shape of a pirate ship, came to symbolize his kleptocratic regime.

Russia responded to what it regarded as a Western coup by illegally annexing Crimea on March 18, 2014. Soon after, conflict broke out between Russian-backed Ukrainian separatists and government forces in the gas fields of the Donbas region in eastern Ukraine, which simmered for almost a decade before descending into full-scale war.

John Mearsheimer, a political science professor at the University of Chicago, warned at the time that Russia would destroy Ukraine if the former Soviet state persisted with plans to join NATO. A champion of the "realist school" of foreign policy, Mearsheimer writes in his 2018 book, *The Great Delusion: Liberal Dreams and International Realities,* that American policymakers intent on pushing Ukraine toward Europe had provoked Russia to launch a "preventive war."

"The United States and its European allies are deeply committed to fostering social and political change in countries formerly under Soviet control. They aim to spread Western values and promote liberal democracy, which means supporting pro-Western individuals and NGOs in those countries . . . NATO enlargement, EU expansion, and democracy promotion are a close-knit package of policies designed to integrate Ukraine into the West without antagonizing Russia. But they inadvertently turned Moscow into an enemy, leading directly to the Ukraine crisis."

Russia was already "deeply suspicious of the American-led effort to promote democracy in Eastern Europe through the so-called color revolutions. It is hardly surprising that Russians of all persuasions think Western provocateurs, especially the CIA, helped overthrow Yanukovych."

Joe flew into Kyiv in April 2014 on his first trip after Euromaidan and told the parliament: "Corruption can have no place in the new Ukraine." That same month, Hunter was appointed to the board of Burisma.

* * *

Joe's influence on the world stage began when he was elevated to the Senate Foreign Relations Committee just two years after entering the Senate in 1973. He fast developed a reputation as a pompous blowhard among colleagues but his status as a grieving young widower helped propel his stratospheric rise. He also had a certain boyish charm in his younger days that endeared him to veteran Foreign Relations committee member and sometime chairman, the patrician liberal senator from Rhode Island, Claiborne Pell, one of his earliest and most influential mentors. Pell, with his wife Nuala, had reached out to the newly elected Senator Biden after the death of his wife and baby daughter and sponsored him onto the Senate's most powerful and prestigious committee. Joe's tenure of more than 30 years with the committee, including a decade rotating between Chairman and Ranking Member, placed him at the center of the Senate's dealings with the State Department and the CIA.

When he wasn't pushing for US military intervention in the Yugoslav civil war in the 1990s, and urging NATO's enlargement, Joe was an avid proponent of the 1994 Budapest Memorandum on Security Assurances, which forced a reluctant Ukraine to give up its nuclear arsenal. Coincidentally, the US Ambassador to Hungary at the signing of the Memorandum was Donald Blinken, the father of Joe's future Secretary of State Antony Blinken.

The Budapest Memorandum had its roots in the 1991 START treaty, a nuclear disarmament agreement originally proposed by Ronald Reagan and signed by Presidents George Bush Snr. and Mikhail Gorbachev who each agreed to reduce their nuclear arsenals by one-third. The collapse of the Soviet Union later that year delayed implementation until the former Soviet states Ukraine, Belarus, and Kazakhstan agreed to return their nuclear weapons to Russia.

Ukraine was concerned about being forced to give up what it felt was its only way to deter a future Russian invasion and asked for formal security guarantees from America. But in a June 1992 hearing of the Senate Foreign Relations Committee, Bush's Secretary of State James Baker declared: "We did not think it appropriate to provide" security guarantees. Then-Senator Biden, advocating a tough line for the holdout former Soviet satellite, advised Baker that "one of the quickest ways" to force Ukraine to disarm was to "attach a condition so they know if they do not sign they are going to be faced with a three-to-one superiority of nuclear weapons from Russia as opposed to what they'd be faced with otherwise."

After Russia's post-Euromaidan annexation of Crimea in 2014, Vice President Biden told Ukrainians they were on their own. "We no longer think in Cold War terms," he later explained. In the subsequent election campaign, presidential candidate Poroshenko broke with polite protocol when he said that Ukraine had made a big mistake by surrendering its nukes and had been "influenced by pacifist illusions," presumably of Western leaders like Joe.

Bill Clinton would go on to say, after Putin's 2022 invasion, that he regretted strong-arming the Ukrainians to surrender their 1,900 nuclear warheads in exchange for vague security assurances from the US and the UK, and a promise from Russia's alcoholic puppet president Boris Yeltsin to respect Ukraine's territorial integrity.

"What Will Ukraine Do Without Uncle Joe?" asked *Foreign Policy* in a fawning article at the end of his vice presidency. "No one in the U.S. government has wielded more influence over Ukraine than Vice President Joe Biden."

Regime change in Russia has been on the minds of some senior members of the Biden administration for at least a decade. Nuland told a Congressional committee in 2014: "Since 1992 we have provided $20 billion to Russia to support the pursuit of a transition to the peaceful, prosperous, democratic state its people deserve."

The goal was to weaken Putin by weaning Europe off its reliance on Russian gas. Russia, one of the world's biggest energy producers, supplied almost half of all natural gas imported by European Union states in 2021, before Putin's invasion. The gas was transported to Europe through a series of pipelines, the largest running through Ukraine.

Ukraine also was dependent on Russian gas but had its own rich shale gas deposit, Europe's second-largest known reserves, after Norway, mostly concentrated in the Dnieper-Donets basin in the Russian-speaking east, where civil war raged after Euromaidan. And, unlike most of Europe, Ukraine had not banned fracking.

The Atlantic Council, which operates as NATO's think tank in Washington, theorized that "Ukraine could become the next European energy powerhouse, with enough natural gas reserves to replace Russian exports to Europe." In reality, Ukraine's reserves (38.5 million cubic feet) amount to less than 3 percent of Russia's total (1320.5 million cubic feet), according to BP's 2021 Statistical Review of World Energy, and existing production sites are almost depleted. When the war in Ukraine triggered an energy crisis in Europe, expensive LNG, half of it from the US, would make up most of the shortfall in piped gas from Russia.

Joe was the official American voice evangelizing energy independence in Ukraine, flying into Kyiv in 2009 to tell the Yushchenko government that Ukraine's economic well-being depended on it, at the same time as he championed NATO's expansion to Ukraine and Georgia, despite Russia's vociferous objections. After Euromaidan, on April 29, 2014, Joe gave a keynote speech to the Atlantic Council, emphasizing the need to cut

Russia out of supplying Europe with gas, and promising renewed opportunities for US energy giants like Chevron and Exxon Mobil, who also happened to be Atlantic Council donors, to cash in. "This would be a game-changer for Europe, in my view, and we're ready to do everything in our power to help it happen," he told his audience.

Chevron had signed a $10 billion shale gas production agreement with Ukraine in November 2013 with much fanfare, but pulled out of the deal a year later, citing the risks of the battle raging in the gas fields and a collapse in gas prices. A consortium led by Exxon and Shell also abandoned plans for a $10 billion shale gas project.

Privatizing the Ukrainian state-owned Naftogaz, which accounted for about 75 percent of the country's gas output, and beefing up investment in the private sector were priorities for the US. Burisma was the fastest-growing of about seven private gas companies owned by oligarchs or former government officials that accounted for the remaining gas production. Zlochevsky granted Burisma most of its 39 gas permits while he was Ecology and Natural Resources minister under Yanukovych from 2010 to 2012. They included Ukraine's largest gas field, Sakhalin, in the northeast Kharkiv region, whose reserves are estimated to be worth $4 billion.

* * *

Tass, the Russian state-owned news agency, reported in July 2014 that, under cover of fighting in East Ukraine, Ukrainian soldiers were helping install shale gas drilling rigs in the middle of the Donetsk Republic near the east Ukrainian town of Slovyansk, "which they bombed and shelled for the three preceding months."

The area was controlled at the time by the thuggish Ukrainian oligarch Igor Kolomoisky, suspected to be the alleged real owner of Burisma. In March 2014, he had been appointed Governor of Dnipropetrovsk, in the east, near the industrial city of Donetsk, by the new interim president of the US-controlled Ukrainian government. He reportedly had spent $10 million to create a private army, founding the Dnipro Battalion and allegedly helping fund the neo-Nazi Azov regiment, to fight pro-Russian separatists in the region—and to further his commercial interests.

"Civilians protected by the Ukrainian army are getting ready to install drilling rigs. More equipment is being brought in," *Tass* reported, adding that "the military are encircling the future extraction area." While the story refers to government soldiers, it is just as likely that they were Kolomoisky's mercenaries. After all, Burisma owned the rights to develop the shale gas fields in the Dnieper-Donetsk basin, so it benefited from the sneaky tactic of using the civil war to capitalize on its asset.

Slovyansk locals had been protesting against fracking and wanted a referendum, so before the civil war it had been expected to take years before Burisma could start exploiting its shale gas deposits. "But throw in some civil war, and few will notice, let alone care, that a process which was expected to take nearly a decade, if not longer, while dealing with broad popular objections to fracking, may instead be completed in months!" declared the financial website *ZeroHedge*, citing the *Tass* report.

Burisma chairman Alan Apter forwarded the *ZeroHedge* article to Hunter, without commenting on its suggestion that Ukraine had decided to "let no crisis, (staged or otherwise) including civil war, go to waste." Environmental concerns had stopped countries such as the Czech Republic, the Netherlands, France, and Germany from fracking for shale gas, "which clearly makes Ukraine, potentially the last place with massive shale gas deposits and no drilling ban, quite valuable to those who want to develop a major source of shale gas, one which reduces Europe's reliance on Russian gas even more, yet one whose future depends on one simple question: who controls East Ukraine?"

If Burisma could benefit from the civil war, it would be a key player in the bid to make Ukraine energy independent and allow it to turn its back on Russia. This was how Hunter framed his alleged Ukraine grift as a noble cause. He wasn't there for the money, but to help the Ukrainian people. "Burisma, it was a bulwark against Russian aggression in a moment in time when the single purpose of Vladimir Putin, in his taking Crimea and his incursions into Donetsk and to Donbas, was to take over the natural gas fields, was to take over their energy supply," Hunter testified to the Oversight and Judiciary committees in 2024.

For the Ukrainian people, Western assistance for their looted economy came with costly strings. After Euromaidan, Nuland's handpicked Prime Minister "Yats" Yatseniuk announced that Ukraine's household natural gas prices would rise by a punishing 50 percent from May 1, 2014. The impost was necessary, he explained, to meet the austerity conditions set by the International Monetary Fund for a $14 billion to $18 billion rescue package, including a wage and pension freeze, spending cuts, and the end of heating subsidies.

Unlike other Yanukovych ministers in exile, Zlochevsky was given the green light to operate Burisma remotely and continue to allegedly fill his pockets under the new US-controlled Ukrainian government. While Joe was lecturing the Ukrainians about corruption, one of the country's most corrupt companies was a protected operation. Burisma even entered into a lucrative sponsorship arrangement in 2017 with Joe's favorite think tank, the Atlantic Council, which was worth as much as $250,000 a year.

Everything about Ukraine is smoke and mirrors, so it's hard to know the truth, but there is meaningful evidence to support the theory that Kolomoisky secretly owned Burisma and that Zlochevsky was his puppet. There have also been unproven suggestions that Kolomoisky, Ukraine's second richest man, was working with the CIA.

Burisma Holdings was a subsidiary of Zlochevsky's Brociti Investments Limited, based in Cyprus. He founded the company in 2002 with Mykola Lisin, his former college classmate, and a fellow politician from the pro-Russia Party of Regions. Zlochevsky took full ownership in 2011 after Lisin died in a mysterious car crash while reportedly driving over 100 miles an hour in his Lamborghini Diablo.

According to the Anti-Corruption Action Center (AntAC), a partly Soros-funded Ukrainian NGO, Kolomoisky had a "controlling interest" in Burisma through a company based in the British Virgin Islands. AntAC used company records to trace ownership, through a complicated web of shell companies, to the Burrad Financial Corporation, which was "involved in various financial schemes" of Kolomoisky and his Privat Group companies. AntAC concluded: "Igor Kolomoisky managed to seize the largest reserves of natural gas in Ukraine."

Burisma used the Latvian subsidiary of Kolomoisky's PrivatBank to transfer Hunter's board payments to his accounts in America. But Hunter would allegedly later help cover up a connection between the oligarch and his employer.

Pozharskyi, Burisma's Mr. Fixit, denied to the *New York Times* in 2015 that Kolomoisky owned the company. The question set off a flurry of urgent emails with Hunter and his partners and two crisis consultants employed by Burisma who strategized over the form of words to use in denial.

The consultants' first suggestion was that Zlochevsky "is the owner of the company and has maintained his controlling interest for a number of years."

But Pozharskyi rejected the phrasing: "I think we should sound more decisively . . . they are asking wether [*sic*] Igor Kolomoisky ever started and then sold a company to NZ [Zlochevsky]. This is a well spread absurdity! that keep [*sic*] being repeated. We may use this opportunity to say firmly that that person does not have and never had any relationship to Buriama [*sic*]."

Pozharskyi finally approved a statement saying that Kolomoisky "has never been involved with Burisma and certainly is not today."

Likened to a Bond villain, Kolomoisky kept sharks in his office in a massive aquarium which he reportedly filled with bloody chum by pressing a button on a remote-control box on his desk when he wanted to intimidate visitors. He made his fortune in the wake of the Soviet collapse in the 1990s, when he seized former state-owned assets like steel plants and gas wells and reportedly bribed judges and magistrates so he would never be sanctioned. (As of this writing, Kolomoisky has denied all wrongdoing and his case has not gone to trial.) Described by a judge in a London court as the type of "corporate raider" who takes control of a company "at gunpoint," Kolomoisky cultivated a menacing persona. According to Forbes, he once allegedly brought "hundreds of hired rowdies armed with baseball bats, iron bars, gas and rubber bullet pistols and chainsaws forcibly [to take] over" a steel plant.

He owned steel mills in Ohio, Michigan, Kentucky, and West Virginia, and at one point controlled a reported 40 percent of the world manganese market, with mines in Australia and Ghana.

He also owned the 1+1 Media conglomerate, which had eight Ukrainian television channels which he used to support Euromaidan protesters. He also aired the popular Servant of the People TV series, which made a star of comedian Volodymyr Zelenskyy, playing the role of an idealistic high school teacher who becomes president of a comically corrupt Ukraine.

Kolomoisky would go on to fund Zelenskyy into the real-life role of president in 2019, replacing Poroshenko, who called him "Kolomoisky's puppet." Zelenskyy would later play a role in Donald Trump's impeachment, and invited Kolomoisky into his first cabinet. Four years later, Kolomoisky's Teflon protection would come to an end, with his arrest in Ukraine on charges of fraud and money laundering, after being blacklisted by the US State Department (Kolomoisky has pleaded not guilty and has not been convicted of any charges). Zelenskyy, under wartime pressure from his US paymasters to crack down on corruption, had turned on his patron, or at least made it look that way.

After Euromaidan, Kolomoisky, 51, had ingratiated himself with the US by denouncing Putin and funding Ukraine's militias in the civil war against pro-Russian separatists but with the ulterior motive of controlling the shale gas reserves in the battle zone, not to mention staving off competition from oligarchs across the border, which was dubbed "Kolomoisky's line."

Putin slammed Kolomoisky as a "unique crook," claiming he'd scammed several billion dollars from his friend Roman Abramovich. In turn, Kolomoisky called Putin a "schizophrenic dwarf," after which Putin seized PrivatBank's assets in Moscow and Crimea.

"A large number of people think Kolomoisky's great and the only patriot in the country," Kolomoisky would later boast to the *Washington Post*.

He was a ruthless warlord, and Amnesty International accused his militias of committing "ISIS-style" war crimes on civilians, including "abductions, unlawful detention, ill-treatment, theft, extortion, and possible executions." More civilians than soldiers were dying in the conflict, with cluster bombs raining down on homes in Donetsk.

In one of his angry text streams to a baffled Hallie, Hunter asked: "so you believe ive had children burned alive in DONETSK." He attached a link to an obscure website run by Lyndon LaRouche follower Wesley Tarpley who had just visited Donetsk and mentioned Hunter and Shell in a rant about "NATO-Backed Maidan Nazis" in Kyiv using cluster bombs on civilians.

In any case, Kolomoisky's alleged terror tactics seemed to work, according to the book *Ukraine's Outpost: Dnipropetrovsk and the Russian-Ukrainian War*, edited by Professor Taras Kuzio of the National University of Kyiv. "Kolomoisky's thuggish character proved to be the perfect riposte to Putin's hybrid warfare . . . As a corporate raider, Kolomoisky had tough young 'sportsmen' at his disposal who could be quickly mobilized as vigilantes against a Russian threat to Dnipropetrovsk . . . Patriotic vigilantes came to the small number of poorly attended pro-Russian meetings and broke them up." Witnesses described "comrades when leaving pro-Russian meetings ended up in reanimation [hospital] . . . Some of them had their heads cracked at bus stops, some did not make it to the underpass, and the result was that they concluded it was better to not become involved in these activities."

In April 2014, Kolomoisky offered a $10,000 bounty for each Russian "saboteur" captured, scoring eight scalps in a week. A battalion volunteer is quoted in the book crediting Kolomoisky with saving the country from Putin: "If there had been no Kolomoisky there would be no Ukraine."

Kolomoisky's thugs were blamed for the massacre of 48 people the following month in Odessa, when a group of Russian-speaking Ukrainian separatists were attacked with Molotov cocktails at the Trade Union House where they were trapped inside and burned alive.

The book holds that Dnipropetrovsk, under Kolomoisky's iron fist, halted Putin's "New Russia" ambitions for the region in 2014 and 2015. It "became Ukraine's outpost, preventing a breakthrough of Russian hybrid warfare into Central Ukraine, and Eastern Ukraine outside the Donbas region, which could have threatened Ukraine's independence."

Given Kolomoisky's decisive impact in the war in the east, it is plausible that he would have links to the CIA, although Gal Luft says an Israeli source familiar with the odious oligarch believes his activities in Donetsk were not "under the direction of CIA [but that he may have been] trying to curry favor with the US government so he can get credit toward moving to the US."

Kolomoisky at least benefited from a blind eye, if not a green light, that allowed him to allegedly plunder $2 billion of IMF money that was supposed to bail out the bank he founded, PrivatBank. (This charge has not been proven, and he has denied it.) A London court would hear allegations that Kolomoisky and a partner had siphoned off the money using sham loans via shell companies in the UK and Cyprus.

In March 2015, Kolomoisky tested American patience when he launched a nighttime raid on two subsidiaries of the state-owned Naftogaz using over a dozen armed "lawyers," which Poroshenko took as a direct threat to his authority, reportedly calling on US Ambassador Pyatt to help control Kolomoisky and his private army.

The upshot was that Kolomoisky backed off and relinquished the governorship of Dnipropetrovsk in return for keeping his businesses and getting a one-time US visa that he had previously been denied, and longer visas for family members. "Kolomoisky flew unmolested to the United States, where he is reported to have been spending a lot of time watching basketball games, and with no one asking awkward questions about what happened to all that IMF money," wrote *Harpers Magazine*. His son, 6'5" Gregory Kolomoisky, played basketball at Cleveland State University in 2018 before reportedly signing with Ukrainian pro club BC Dnipro.

Whatever the relationship was early on, Joe was calling Kolomoisky "a pain in the ass and a problem for everyone" by the end of 2016. Six years later the US Department of Justice would file a civil forfeiture complaint against the oligarch and his partner seeking to seize commercial properties in Kentucky and Texas and alleging that they had stolen billions of dollars from PrivatBank which they had laundered in the US and elsewhere. This civil complaint is ongoing.

Poroshenko had nationalized PrivatBank in December 2016, with Joe spending the final days of his vice presidency urgently demanding he get it done before Donald Trump took office. In a leaked phone call on November 16, 2016, Joe can be heard pressuring the Ukrainian president to nationalize the bank immediately because: "I don't want Trump to find himself in a position where he seems willing to circumvent our policies, where the financial system could collapse, and where he's going to block the allocation of money to Ukraine. That's how it will look until you get down to the complicated, unfamiliar details."

By then, the horse had bolted, the IMF billions had allegedly been looted, and Kolomoisky had scarpered for Israel, where he stayed until Zelenskyy's election. The Ukrainian taxpayer was left to plug the hole. "It's not clear that Privat's nationalization hurt Kolomoisky at all," reported the *Kyiv Post*.

* * *

Devon Archer recalls being told by a Washington lobbyist in Ukraine that Kolomoisky would periodically be whisked off in a CIA jet in the middle of the night in his pajamas to parts unknown.

The anecdote bolsters the theory that Kolomoisky and Burisma were collaborating with the CIA. So does the appointment of Cofer Black, the CIA's former Counterterrorist Center Director, to join Hunter on the Burisma board in 2017.

The more you delve into the Biden story, the more you see the fingerprints of US intelligence, including the inordinate resources poured into smearing ousted Ukrainian Prosecutor General Viktor Shokin and seemingly covering up Joe's ulterior motive for having him fired. The cover-up would have worked if it had not been for Hunter's act of Oedipal sabotage when he abandoned his laptop in Delaware.

There was the email showing that the CIA's then-Chief Operating Officer Andrew Makridis had sanctioned the "Dirty 51" letter in 2020.

Then there was the allegation that the CIA was protecting Kevin Morris, according to a congressional whistleblower who claimed the agency blocked IRS investigators from interviewing Hunter's "sugar brother."

Morris told me he had never been a CIA informant and denied Hunter had been, either. But Hunter had an implausible and little-understood role on the Chairman's Advisory Board for the National Democratic Institute (NDI), which is the Democrats' arm of the National Endowment for Democracy (NED). Hunter boasted about his membership of the organization in his 2024 congressional testimony and included the title in his Burisma resume. The appointment before he joined the Burisma board is a flashing neon sign that may explain how he seemingly managed to flout rules with impunity and inspire some of the most powerful former CIA leaders to lie on his behalf.

"Hunter Biden was part of a plausibly deniable CIA operation to swing the gas market towards NATO," alleges Mike Benz, a former Trump State Department official and founder of Foundation for Freedom Online, whose research has been cited in congressional hearings. "That's why Hunter Biden is untouchable by the Justice Department—because he was part of a CIA operation."

NED was founded in 1983 as a bi-partisan, semi-private organization to "promote democracy" overseas and achieve the same aims as the CIA while avoiding the stigma which had attached to the agency since the 1960s. According to its founding president, Carl Gershman, NED was necessary because "it would be terrible for democratic groups around the world to be seen as subsidized by the CIA." After the Senate's Church committee in 1975 had uncovered shocking abuses by the CIA, from domestic spying to alleged assassination plots against foreign leaders, nobody wanted to be associated with the agency. NED helped whitewash its operations. "Promoting democracy" and fostering "civil society" were a soft form of regime change, or at least political change that served the CIA's ends.

Allen Weinstein, a former acting president of NED, told the *Washington Post*'s David Ignatius in 1991: "A lot of what we do today was done covertly

25 years ago by the CIA." Through the late 1980s, while camouflaging its intent, wrote Ignatius, NED "did openly what had once been unspeakably covert—dispensing money to anti-communist forces behind the Iron Curtain."

Since the advent of Putin, NED's strategy for regime change in Moscow has been no secret. In 2013, two months before the Euromaidan protest broke out, Gershman wrote in the *Washington Post*: "Ukraine is the biggest prize. [If it joins Europe] the opportunities are considerable, and there are important ways Washington could help . . . Putin may find himself on the losing end not just in the near abroad but within Russia itself."

When Biden, as president, blurted out in Warsaw, after the 2022 Ukraine invasion, "For God's sake, this man [Putin] cannot remain in power," he was singing NED's tune, although Antony Blinken quickly denied it: "We do not have a strategy of regime change in Russia, or anywhere else, for that matter."

Even with his pedigree, it is curious that Hunter, weighed down by an addiction to crack cocaine and a compulsion for prostitution and pornography, would be appointed to such a sensitive role in an organization many believe is associated with the CIA. The most cursory vetting should have uncovered red flags, such as his mature-age discharge from the Navy Reserve for testing positive for cocaine in his first weekend of service.

At about the same time Hunter joined NED's political affiliate, the CIA approached his partners at Rosemont Seneca, Devon Archer and Chris Heinz.

Archer says the CIA asked them to work for the agency on two occasions, and both times they rejected the offer. (Heinz declined to comment on the approaches.)

According to Archer, the first time was in about 2011 in Santa Fe, New Mexico, when a man and woman who identified themselves as CIA agents "showed up unannounced and uninvited to Rosemont Realty and asked, 'Would you guys be willing to provide intel?' And we declined . . .

"The second bite was more of a prolonged discussion with the agency . . . Chris and I considered taking on a 'plant agent.' They have a program where they give you an agent. The person works for you and does all the normal work, but they pay you. The person travels with you, like a junior analyst or something, but they have a dual duty to report back to the agency and they'd pay his salary and pay the firm $250k a year or something.

"We explored doing it," Archer says. "Our patriotism figured into the thinking, but we decided against it ultimately because we were scared we might get detained overseas or worse . . . It just seemed too dangerous at the end."

Archer asked for advice about the CIA approach from his father, former US Marine Captain Robert Dodson Archer, who had returned disillusioned from the Vietnam War in 1974 and tossed away his medals on the White House lawn as an expression of contempt for the government.

"My dad actually told me 'What, are you nuts?' and we just passed," says Archer.

* * *

The escalation of the CIA's involvement in Ukraine coincided with Hunter's Burisma entanglement. The Aspen Institute's Zach Dorfman wrote that the CIA conducted a "secret intensive training program in the US" in the aftermath of Euromaidan to teach elite Ukrainian special operations forces how "to kill Russians." A former CIA official said: "The United States is training an insurgency."

The *New York Times* has traced the CIA's formal partnership with Ukraine to February 24, 2014, days after Yanukovych fled the country. It claims that was when the new pro-Western interim government's new spy chief, Valentyn Nalyvaichenko, called the local heads of the CIA and MI6 for help rebuilding the Security Service of Ukraine (SBU, the KGB successor) in what the *Times* called a "three-way partnership."

Nalyvaichenko, a pro-Europe former member of parliament, had been accused by political rivals of being a CIA agent, recruited when he worked at the Ukrainian Embassy in Washington in the early 2000s. In September 2013, at the urging of the Communist Party of Ukraine, Prosecutor General Viktor Pshonka filed criminal charges against him for allegedly giving CIA employees access to "state secrets." Nalyvaichenko rejected the charges as "Russian disinformation," and when Yanukovych was overthrown, Pshonka escaped to Russia and the charges evaporated.

In April 2014, CIA director John Brennan flew to Kyiv in an unmarked plane and met with Nalyvaichenko, Prime Minister Yatsenyuk and the soon-to-be-appointed Prosecutor General Vitaly Yarema. Brennan told Nalyvaichenko that to "unlock CIA assistance the Ukrainians had to prove that they could provide intelligence of value" and purge the SBU of Russian spies, according to the *Times*. The result was a new CIA-trained standalone unit inside the SBU dubbed the "Fifth Directorate" that would conduct assassinations against pro-Russian separatists in eastern Ukraine. The CIA also built up the Ukrainian military intelligence agency, HUR, which conducted operations inside Russia.

Poroshenko fired Nalyvaichenko in the summer of 2015, but the US intelligence partnership continued, becoming what the *Times* called the "linchpin" of Ukraine's ability to defend itself against a nuclear-armed Russia after Putin's 2022 invasion.

The US goal of weaning Europe off Russian gas was conveniently advanced in September 2022 when Russia's new Nord Stream 2 pipeline, which would have doubled the supply of natural gas from Russia to Germany under the Baltic Sea, mysteriously exploded. Fingers pointed variously at Russia, the US, and Ukraine for the act of sabotage. Investigations by Sweden and Denmark were closed in February 2024 without naming a culprit. The UN Security Council rejected Russia's request for an independent investigation. The United States government has repeatedly declined to comment on any of the theories, articles, or reports.

Veteran investigative reporter Seymour Hersh alleged, in a 5,000-word self-published Substack article in 2023, that the Biden administration was responsible. On Joe's orders, according to Hersh's anonymous sources, Jake Sullivan had formed a task force of military, CIA, and government officials who met in an office near the White House two months before the Ukraine war began and drew up plans to destroy the pipeline. The job was done by US Navy divers who attached explosive charges to the pipeline under cover of a NATO exercise in the Baltic Sea.

Hersh had made his reputation breaking big stories, from the My Lai massacre to the killing of Osama bin Laden, often relying on anonymous sources, but on this occasion, the one-time hero of the liberal media was written off as a gullible conspiracy theorist or even a Kremlin stooge. Hersh's report was denied by the White House and picked apart by the media.

Seven months before the bombing, the Biden administration had issued ominous warnings about the fate of the pipeline if Russia were to invade Ukraine.

On February 7, 2022, just before the invasion, President Biden declared, "We will bring an end to it [Nord Stream 2]."

He was echoing statements the previous week from Victoria Nuland, by then the administration's Under Secretary of State for Political Affairs: "If Russia invades Ukraine, one way or another, Nord Stream 2 will not move forward." After the explosion, she chortled, "The administration is very gratified to know that Nord Stream 2 is now . . . a hunk of metal at the bottom of the sea."

Secretary of State Antony Blinken called the bombing a "tremendous strategic opportunity," which was not very diplomatic since European gas prices had jumped 12 percent in the aftermath of the attack, and Sweden and Denmark would start complaining about greenhouse gas emissions equivalent to one-third of their annual output.

Radek Sikorski, a member of the European parliament who later became Poland's Minister of Foreign Affairs, tweeted a photograph of the bubbling ocean above the explosion, with the caption: "Thank you, USA." Sikorski is married to Anne Applebaum, the neoconservative Atlantic staff writer who sits on the board of NED, and famously asserted that the Hunter Biden laptop story was "irrelevant."

CHAPTER 21

VIKTOR SHOKIN

April 4, 2014
LAKE COMO, ITALY

Hunter was invited to join the Burisma board at the Italian resort of Lake Como, where he had flown with Archer in April 2014 to a management conference at the Villa d'Este, a sumptuous haunt of Russian oligarchs overlooking the water. It was six weeks after the collapse of the Yanukovych government, and Hunter and Archer joked in emails before they arrived that they were living like the fictional spies, James Bond and Jason Bourne: "Might be very Bond/Bourne to get the 'gharchs [oligarchs] up at the lake for a meeting," wrote Archer.

They had a meeting scheduled with Russia's richest woman, Elena Baturina, who had just wired $3.5 million to their firm, Rosemont Seneca Thornton. The wire was flagged in suspicious activity reports later provided by the Treasury Department to a Senate Republican inquiry (but there were no findings that the payments were improper). Baturina would eventually transfer almost $120 million to an associated company, Rosemont Realty, to invest in office buildings across the US, Archer says.

The next day, Hunter met Burisma owner Mykola Zlochevsky and his right-hand man Vadym Pozharskyi for the first time. According to Archer,

Zlochevsky, 48, asked Hunter to join the Burisma board during a walk by the lake.

"I am strongly leaning towards agreeing to board position. Let's decide this and move on it by Monday," Hunter emailed Archer a few days later.

Archer, already on the board, urged his friend on. "Agreed we should go / no go by Monday AM EST. Spent 60 minutes on the phone with Vadim [Pozharskyi] today. They are in complete agreement in regards to the discrete [sic] nature of your Board role and they actually described the same before I repeated it," Archer replied on April 11, 2014, addressing Hunter's desire that his appointment be kept quiet. "People will discover this though from corporate filings or one way or another so we have to be ready for questions . . .

"My elephant hunt thoughts are that we have a chance to get in on the ground floor of the Gazprom of the U [Ukraine]," he concluded, reflecting Burisma's ambition to become Ukraine's equivalent of the Russian gas giant.

A few days later, Hunter had enlisted New York attorney Clifford Wolff to vet the Burisma director's service agreement. "This is another excellent opportunity for you and your team," Wolff told him.

Hunter wanted the board seat—and the $83,333 a month payment that came with it—but he wanted Burisma to hide his involvement to avoid bad optics for his father. Pozharskyi pushed back firmly in an email on April 17, the day before Hunter formally joined the board: "I do believe that we have to reach reasonable balance here," he told Archer. "Taking into account the political weight of our Directors we have to 'use' their personality carefully and strategically wise, I do realize their vulnerability in this respect.

"Therefore I kindly suggest to indeed now or after his father left our country just put him on our website without going for public camping [fanfare]. And then after we meet in May we agree on joint plan and move forward accordingly, with media campaign or without it, just concentrating on informal talks with relevant interested parties etc. In some sense we cannot 'hide' our directors."

As soon as Hunter joined the board, Pozharskyi wasted no time pressuring him to "use your influence" to combat the Ukrainian government's allegations against Burisma of "misappropriation, embezzlement or conversion of property by malversation."

"Following our talks during the visit to the Como Lake and our further discussions, I would like to bring the following situation to your attention," wrote Pozharskyi the following month. "One or more pretrial proceedings were initiated by the [Ukrainian] Ministry of Internal Affairs with regard to Burisma Holdings companies . . . We urgently need your advice on how you could use your influence to convey a message/signal, etc to stop what we consider to be politically motivated actions."

On April 13, 2014, the day after the White House released a statement announcing Joe would visit Ukraine in ten days to "consult on the latest steps to enhance Ukraine's short- and long-term energy security," Hunter emailed Archer a long and uncharacteristically sophisticated email. It listed 22 points about Ukraine's political situation, with a detailed analysis of the upcoming presidential election, including the likely victory of Petro Poroshenko, and anticipating an escalation of Russia's "destabilization campaign."

Unlike anything else written by Hunter during the nine years covered in his laptop, the email had the distinct flavor of an official briefing, or perhaps even a classified one. The 2023 Special Counsel investigation into Joe's allegedly improper retention of classified material revealed his haphazard storage of classified government documents dating as far back as his Senate days, in his garage and elsewhere. Given Hunter's free rein at his father's home and White House office, he may have had access to secret Ukraine information which would be valuable to his new employer (this has been denied and not proven).

In point 22 of the email, Hunter instructed Archer to buy a "burner phone," presumably to keep their conversations private. "Buy a cell phone from a 7/11 or CVS tmrw and ill do the same."

He also referred to his father's impending trip to Kyiv as "my guys [*sic*] upcoming travels" and talked about leveraging Joe's position as the "public face" of the US administration's policy in Ukraine. "The [Burisma] contract should begin now—not after the upcoming visit of my guy [Joe]. That [contract] should include a retainer in the range of [$]25k p[er]/ m[onth] w/ additional fees where appropriate for more in depth work to go to BSF [Boies Schiller Flexner, the law firm where Hunter was 'of counsel'] for our protection."

Less than two weeks after the Lake Como trip, Hunter and Archer visited Joe's office in the White House, ostensibly for help with a book project for Archer's son Luke. But while they were there, Hunter took a photograph of Archer with his father in front of an American flag that would be posted on Burisma's website the following day, April 17, 2014, as evidence of the corrupt company's powerful friends in the US.

The VP's Chief Counsel, Demetra Lambros, had to contact Hunter's office urgently to get the photo taken down. "Hey. Guys. There is apparently a photo of Devon and the VP on Burisma's website," Hunter's associate Eric Schwerin wrote him and Archer in an email. "Demetra called and asked that we tell Burisma they need to take it down (legally they aren't comfortable with the VP's picture being up on the site as what seems like an endorsement)."

Joe surely was aware of this potentially embarrassing incident that threatened to expose Hunter's apparent Ukraine grift before Hunter even got his first paycheck from a company that stood to profit from the US aid to Ukraine's energy industry being pushed by Joe and his Senate allies.

"I did not know he was on the board of that company," Joe would tell PBS implausibly in 2019. "And, in fact, no one has asserted that it was illegal for him to be on the board or that he did anything wrong . . . No one has established that he's done anything wrong or that I've done anything wrong, period. I have carried out the policy of the United States of America, our allies in the International Monetary Fund, the EU, in dealing with a corrupt prosecutor, period."

Joe's assertion of ignorance about Hunter's Burisma gig contradicted an interview the previous month to CBS: "Do you understand people say: Joe Biden, he's an experienced politician, statesman, knows the issues of

Ukraine, why didn't he just say to his son, 'This is one to take a pass on—it may not look good?'"

Joe replied: "He was already on the board."

A few days after the White House meeting with Hunter and Archer, Joe was winging his way to Ukraine on Air Force Two promising millions in US aid for the energy industry and delivering rousing anti-corruption speeches in Kyiv.

Hunter sent an email to Archer, on April 22, 2014, titled "JRB in UKR," with a quote from Joe's speech to the Ukrainian parliament.

"Mr. Biden spoke of the 'humiliating threats' faced by Ukraine and said the United States was 'ready to assist.' But he also stressed that Ukraine needs to . . . reduce its crippling dependence on Russia for supplies of natural gas."

"Wow," replied Archer. "We need to make sure this rag tag temporary government in the Ukraine understands the value of Burisma to its very existence."

Later, Hunter emailed Archer an article entitled "Joe Biden Lurks Behind Every US Action on Ukraine—and a potential 2016 presidential run hinges on the vice president's success."

There is a "unique timing here in this upcoming opportunity," replied Archer.

At the time that Hunter and Archer joined the board of Burisma, the company was under criminal investigation in the UK and Ukraine. Hunter Biden defended the importance of their work before Congress, saying, "[The president of Poland] called me up and he told me this. He said, if people in the West do not stand up against Vladimir Putin and Vladimir Putin's aggression and they allow for companies like Burisma—whatever you think about Burisma, it was a bulwark against Russian aggression."

* * *

Archer's prowess on the lacrosse field had propelled him into Yale, where he was a charismatic interloper among the moneyed elites he befriended, like Hunter, and John Kerry's stepson, Chris Heinz, heir to the ketchup fortune.

A former Abercrombie & Fitch model who grew up on Long Island, the son of a Vietnam veteran-turned-realtor and a teacher, Archer would come to bitterly regret his association with the Bidens. But until he was arrested over the $60 million Burnham fraud in May 2016, he lived a charmed life in Brooklyn with his wife Krista, a Manhattan podiatrist, and their three athletic kids. They spent summers in the Hamptons, where they had a house in Quogue, and swam at the Swordfish Beach Club in Westhampton. He played golf at the Plandome Country Club in Manhasset, where his big swing and easy manner made him a sought-after playing partner among the well-heeled lawyers who would support him when his world came crashing down.

But the world was at his feet back in June 2009, when he co-founded investment firm Rosemont Seneca Partners with Hunter and Heinz to monetize their powerful connections. Heinz left the partnership in 2014, citing concerns about the taint of Ukrainian corruption with Burisma and the risky nature of their Chinese deals, according to his spokesman Chris Bastardi.

Hunter and Archer had a greater appetite for risk than the Heinz scion, and it was through their attempts to crack the Russian oligarch market that they lucked into Burisma. They discussed setting up a "Rosemont Moscow office" and a "Rosemont Real Estate Acquisition Fund" with Russian investors, and on February 16, 2012, they flew to Moscow to meet with Armenian-born Moscow oligarch Ara Abramyan, a close ally of Vladimir Putin, who had been awarded one of Russia's highest civilian honors by the Russian president, the Order of Merit to the Fatherland.

Breakfast with Abramyan at his $80 million mansion in the upscale Odintsovsky District of West Moscow was one of a whirl of meetings they had over the next two days with oligarchs from Putin's inner sanctum. Two months later they would fly to LA for Abramyan's birthday dinner at the Beverly Hills Hotel.

Abramyan was the founding partner of venture capital firm TriGlobal Strategic Ventures, which offered Western clients assistance in "furthering their business interests in the emerging economies of the former Soviet Union." It was through Abramyan's underling at TriGlobal, Alex Kotlarsky, a New York–based Ukrainian who ran a car-service business, that Archer, and then Hunter, would join the Burisma board. Rudy Giuliani was another of TriGlobal's clients, just one of several overlapping connections in Ukraine between Hunter and the former New York mayor who would become his nemesis.

A month before Lake Como, on March 4, 2014, Archer flew to Moscow, where Kotlarsky introduced him to Zlochevsky at the Ararat Park Hyatt Hotel rooftop "Conservatory Lounge" with its distinctive glass roof and panoramic views over the Kremlin and the Bolshoi Theatre. Over multiple espressos, Archer pitched the Rosemont Realty fund as a potential investment for Burisma. His lasting impression of Zlochevsky was his gold watch, a half million dollar solid gold Ulysse Nardin "Hourstriker Oil Pump" special edition that had a tiny, hand-engraved golden oil rig on the dial, complete with pump jack dipping up and down to chime the hour.

The next day, Kotlarsky told Archer his real estate pitch had been unsuccessful, but that Zlochevsky wanted him to meet with the former Polish President, Aleksander Kwasniewski, Joe's friend who had recently joined Burisma's board. A few days later, Archer flew to Warsaw where he says Kwasniewski raised the prospect of a seat on the board.

Hunter and Archer each would have to pay a "finder's fee" to Kotlarsky for securing them the Burisma roles. Documents on Hunter's laptop show he paid Kotlarsky a total of $277,775, one-third of his Burisma fees for ten months.

Thus, it came to be that, weeks after Joe took control of the Ukraine assignment in 2014, his son and his best friend joined the board of Burisma for an extraordinary $83,333 a month each. Their most arduous task was flying first class to twice-yearly board meetings in glamorous European locales like Monte Carlo and Paris.

In his memoir, Hunter downplays the Burisma board fee as a mere "five figures" and claims it "wasn't out of line with compensation given to board members at some Fortune 500 companies." That's simply not the case. Board members of similarly sized US companies typically are paid no more than $83,000 for an entire year. Even if you were to compare Burisma with Fortune 500 companies, as Hunter insists, in 2014 the total average director compensation was $255,825, according to a report from advisory firm Willis Towers Watson. That's about one-quarter of what Hunter was paid by Burisma.

But it was worth every penny for Zlochevsky to recruit politically connected Westerners to the board at absurdly generous rates in an effort to head off the Ukrainian and international investigations bearing down on him.

* * *

The same day that Joe invited Hunter and Archer into the White House, almost 4,000 miles away in London's Central Criminal Court, Britain's redoubtable Serious Fraud Office (SFO) was granted a court order to freeze $23 million in Zlochevsky's London bank accounts. The exiled former ecology minister had been trying to close his bank accounts and transfer the balance to Cyprus, but a "Suspicious Activity Report" from the London branch of his bank, BNP Paribas, triggered a notification to the SFO.

The SFO launched a money laundering investigation into Zlochevsky in conjunction with the FBI, which had vowed to help repatriate $100 billion that Yanukovych and his kleptocratic ministers were alleged to have stolen from the Ukrainian people.

According to court documents, on April 16, 2014, SFO investigator Richard Gould argued in the Old Bailey criminal court of London that Zlochevsky's wealth "increased when he held public office and the only apparent source of his private wealth was from the exploitation of mineral licenses awarded to his companies when he held public office," facts which suggested a "willful and dishonest exploitation of a direct conflict of interest by a man holding an important public office such as to amount to an abuse of the public's trust in him." Gould convinced a judge that the funds should be frozen because they were the proceeds of crime, but the SFO would need more information from Ukrainian authorities to proceed.

Hunter joined the Burisma board four days later, although the official announcement was delayed almost a month.

At a high-powered international forum in London on April 29, 2014, the British government showcased the Zlochevsky investigation as a textbook case of the first successful seizure of assets stolen by the Yanukovych regime. The Ukraine Forum on Asset Recovery was spearheaded by the ambitious UK Home Secretary (and future Prime Minister) Theresa May, who boasted to assembled delegates about their swift progress in providing "practical guidance and assistance to the Ukrainian government in identifying and recovering assets looted under the Yanukovych regime."

Dominic Grieve QC, the UK attorney general, trumpeted the momentous news that the SFO had already uncovered "corruption linked to the Yanukovich regime [and] obtained a court order to restrain assets valued at approximately $23 million." Sir David Green, the Director of the Serious Fraud Squad, declared the case was in the bag. "We are getting this money."

US Attorney General Eric Holder told the summit that he had created "a dedicated Kleptocracy squad within the FBI" to help Ukrainian investigators claw back the stolen billions. "The squad of about a dozen personnel will consist of case agents and forensic analysts who are capable of unraveling the intricate money laundering transactions commonly employed by kleptocrats."

Zlochevsky's frozen money dominated headlines from the summit and was seen as a feather in the cap of lawmakers from all over the world.

Alas, they all were left with egg on their faces.

Back in Ukraine, something had gone terribly wrong, and according to George Kent, the bow-tie-wearing deputy chief of mission with the US Embassy in Kyiv, it was because "a $7 million bribe was paid." (No bribe was ever proven.)

In December 2014, in the Old Bailey criminal court of London, the SFO asked Judge Nicholas Blake to extend the freeze on Zlochevsky's bank accounts and said they were expecting a letter from the office of Ukraine Prosecutor General Vitaly Yarema, confirming that Zlochevsky was under investigation back home for money laundering and corruption.

However, the letter, signed on December 2, 2014, by a junior investigator in Yarema's office, was sent to Zlochevsky's defense lawyers, and it stated that there was "no active case against their client."

Judge Blake had seen enough. He dismissed the case and unfroze Zlochevsky's funds.

Gould and his SFO team were furious with their American counterparts in Kyiv. The FBI was embedded in the embassy in Ukraine. They were supposed to be in constant contact with the Prosecutor General's office. They had assured the Brits the Zlochevsky case was under control. Instead, the Zlochevsky cases simply faded away.

Kent was one of the few American officials who was as furious as the Brits. In an email to colleagues at the State Department, he expressed his frustration. Prosecutor General Yarema had presided over a "gross miscarriage of justice that undermined months of US assistance," he wrote, "after the FBI and MI5 spent months and arguably millions working to try to put together the first possible asset recovery case involving $23 million frozen in UK accounts under suspicion of bribes paid for licenses issued for gas/oil permits.

"Team Yarema closed the case against Zlochevsky in Dec 2014 just before western Christmas Day by returning it to the MO/Police for further investigation and issuing an immediate letter to Zlochevsky's defense lawyer team that there was no active case against their client; defense lawyers flipped that to the British judge who unfroze assets that were taken out of UK jurisdiction before the UK or US authorities could react.

"When I met with Yarema's right-hand man, the jovially corpulent first deputy prosecutor general Anatoliy Danylenko weeks later during the first week of Feb 2015 I asked him how much the [alleged] bribe was and who took it. Danylenko cheerfully replied 'that's exactly what President Poroshenko asked us last month. I told him $7 million, and it was last May' . . . He then said he'd been a friend of Zlochevsky's for 20 years."

Kent would later testify in the impeachment of Donald Trump: "It was the position of the US when I went into that office on February 3 [2015] that the Prosecutor General should, first of all, prosecute whoever took the bribe and shut the case, and second of all, there was still the outstanding issue of trying to recover the stolen assets."

* * *

This was the mess that Viktor Shokin walked into when he was nominated as Prosecutor General on February 10, 2015, after Poroshenko fired the disgraced Yarema.

In an interview via encrypted voice call with a translator on the line, Shokin, 72, told me he was reluctant to take the job, the Ukrainian equivalent of the Attorney General, because he knew it was a political poisoned chalice. "I had held the position of deputy prosecutor general three times and my results and my work had been reviewed positively. I was very experienced in cases of corruption and related investigations, so I think it's entirely possible that that is why the decision was to hire me. What I think happened was that Poroshenko tried to increase his own credibility by appointing me to be Prosecutor General . . . He literally talked me into becoming Prosecutor General. It was a job that I didn't want."

The powerful post, meant to be for a six-year term, had been a revolving door, with 17 prosecutors general since the Soviet era, and few in the role more than two years.

Shokin said he was never told why Yarema was leaving. "He told me he was tired, that he was a policeman and not prosecutorial material, and the job was ill-suited to him. The true reason was only known by Poroshenko and Yarema."

A twice-married widower and father of three, Shokin lives alone on a pension in a modest house he built himself 25 years ago in a village near a lake outside Kyiv. He prides himself on his integrity and was not regarded as corrupt by ordinary Ukrainians during his decades as a prosecutor, a miracle in a country where nothing is as it seems, oligarchs rule the roost, and prosecuting your political opponents is par for the course. While the Bidens and their defenders continually branded him corrupt, they never produced any evidence (although the Ukrainian parliament voted to remove Shokin from his position).

An Orthodox Christian, Shokin calls the law his "life calling" and describes himself as a "proud citizen of independent Ukraine." He says he always kept "equidistance" from politicians and had an "aversion to PR and a respect for . . . real work, concentrating on results."

When he became Prosecutor General, he told reporters that the rumor that Poroshenko was the godfather of one of his children, or vice versa, was not true and that he just had "regular relations" with the president. He was endorsed by the Opposition parties in the Rada, Ukraine's parliament, and by three of the five parties of Poroshenko's ruling Coalition.

The then-sixty-two-year-old career prosecutor was popular with the public because of his reputation for taking on the powerful and his flair for the dramatic. He had solved several high-profile corruption cases and had been the target of at least one assassination attempt.

One of his most famous cases was the kidnapping and murder in September 2000 of anti-corruption journalist Georgiy Gongadze, the founder of news site Ukrainska Pravda, and a harsh critic of then-President Leonid Kuchma. Gongadze's body was found beheaded outside Kyiv. The murder was a national scandal after audiotapes were released in which Kuchma was heard discussing the need to silence Gongadze with a top aide (Kuchma was never implicated in the murder).

Shokin opened the Gongadze investigation a day after he was first appointed as one of three deputy prosecutor generals. He convicted the killers, four cops, but was determined to find who gave the orders. He was fired before he had the chance.

"Although the actual killers were punished, the case is not over, as the perpetrators who ordered this high-profile crime have not yet been identified," he says. "The main thing left is to expose the customer, who still lives quietly in Ukraine."

On another occasion, he famously went to the Rada and played a clandestine video of a corrupt lawmaker caught red-handed taking a bribe. He played the video to the entire assembly and then theatrically had his deputies arrest the stunned lawmaker there and then, as the other parliamentarians took a quick vote to expel their colleague.

Shokin was born in Kyiv in 1952, months before Stalin's death. His mother was a railway worker, his father a telecom technician and war veteran. They lived in a communal house with five Jewish families. Because his parents were often away doing shift work, Shokin says he was "effectively raised by my Jewish neighbors." He fondly recalls "the Leibovichs, the Wassermans, the old hermit Rosenberg, the Aunt Ida . . . They fed me mostly Jewish cuisine, they taught me manners, about life and society and about how to act. They took care of me . . . I inherited my humanity from them."

After being drafted into two years of compulsory military service, he graduated in 1980 from the prestigious Kharkiv Law Institute and joined the prosecutor's office in Kyiv as an investigator, spending the next 14 years on murder, robbery, rape, and bribery cases. In 1994 he was appointed by the Rada to head up a new organized crime division in Kyiv, called Unit 30. He was elevated to deputy prosecutor general in 2002 under Kuchma, Ukraine's second post-Soviet president, reportedly after lobbying by opposition politicians backed by Poroshenko, known as the Chocolate King after making his fortune acquiring state-owned confectionery enterprises in the 1990s.

Poroshenko became a patron of pro-Western presidential candidate Viktor Yushchenko who was poisoned with dioxin and suffered facial disfigurement in an attempted assassination by suspected Russian agents during the 2004 elections. Poroshenko bankrolled the subsequent "Orange Revolution" protests against the falsification of election results to favor the pro-Russian candidate Yanukovych. In the re-run campaign, he used his television station—Channel 5—to drum up support for the now-pockmarked Yushchenko to win the presidency and then was rewarded with the powerful post of secretary of the National Security and Defense Council of Ukraine, which is responsible for all security, police, and military issues.

In his self-published memoir, titled *True Stories About Joe Biden's International Corruption in Ukraine*, Shokin says that in his new role, Poroshenko tried to pressure him into dropping an investigation into the so-called "White Swan" case. Shokin ignored him and charged Boris Kolesnikov, the head of Donetsk Regional Council and a member of Yanukovych's ousted party, with extortion related to Donetsk's White Swan shopping center in 2005. "Do you even understand that you bought a ticket to the war?" Poroshenko asked.

"I replied that everything was legal, there were grounds for his arrest. In addition, of course, I was aware of the danger—I understood that I could be eliminated or [assassinated]. I was . . . only fired and a criminal case against me was opened. Interrogations, face-to-face threats of arrest. But in the end, I was left alone." The charges against Kolesnikov were later dropped, and he returned to politics.

It was not the only time he was fired. By his own telling, Shokin resigned or was fired four times, and each time was reappointed, serving under three presidents until his final ousting. In 2001, he resigned after refusing to conduct a political prosecution against opposition leader Yulia Tymoshenko, the so-called "Gas Princess" who was backed by Kolomoisky. Then Shokin was fired on Kuchma's orders in late 2003 over the Gongadze murder, after he arrested police chief Oleksiy Pukach, the alleged ringleader. Pukach was released from pretrial detention and disappeared for six years before being convicted of the murder.

In a generally laudatory article on Ukraine's BBC website after he became Prosecutor General, Shokin was described as "a professional who is fully trusted by Petro Poroshenko [and is] a high-class specialist, far from political preferences [who] has always tried to be away from politics despite personal relationships."

The criticism was that he was a relic of the post-Soviet era, "a man from the past [who does not fit] the revolutionary requirements of the time," a reflection of his age and, perhaps, rigidity.

But parliamentarian Alexey Goncharenko told the BBC that in 2005 Shokin "was not afraid and opened [alleged corruption] cases against people such as Boris Kolesnikov [a Yanukovych ally], Yevhen Kushnarev [Kuchma's chief of staff], and Igor Kolomoisky [the powerful oligarch]." (None of them were convicted of corruption or other crimes.)

Shokin is reluctant to talk about Kolomoisky on the phone, under-standably enough, considering his brutal reputation and ties to President Zelenskyy, but it is a matter of public record that he did launch investigations into Kolomoisky's allies.

"Shokin [is] not perfect, but far from the worst choice," said anti-corruption journalist-turned-parliamentarian Sergey Leshchenko after voting for Shokin.

"As a journalist, I remember Shokin as the person who initiated proceedings against Pukach, Kolesnikov, Kushnarev, and Kolomoisky. As a person who communicates with some investigators of the Prosecutor General's Office [PGO], I have insider information of how Shokin performed in this position. Accordingly, he is the best proposal for the post of Prosecutor General over the past 20 years."

(Leshchenko, who soured on Shokin when he fell out of favor with the Americans, is accused by Giuliani of initiating Russiagate when he revealed allegedly illegal payments that Trump campaign chairman Paul Manafort had received from Yanukovych to help him win the 2010 Ukrainian election. After Leshchenko's "black ledgers" bombshell, Manafort had to resign from Trump's campaign and was subsequently jailed in the US on related tax and fraud charges. Manafort served two years of his 7.5 year sentence before being pardoned by President Trump.)

* * *

The Zlochevsky case had been opened in 2012 under one of Shokin's predecessors, Viktor Pshonka, over allegations of money laundering, tax evasion, and corruption. Pshonka's term was cut short when he fled to Russia in 2014 with the rest of Yanukovich's cronies. So, the investigation into Burisma's owner remained dormant until Shokin took office.

One of the first things Shokin did when he became Prosecutor General was to re-open the case: "We started exploring and investigating the Zlochevsky situation and looking into the illegal activities by Burisma, which were highly illegal," he told me. Shokin went on to make additional allegations about Zlochevsky (which have not been proven). "Zlochevsky had been a minister in Yanukovych [*sic*] cabinet and he himself handed out licenses to himself to produce gas in Ukraine . . . They were producing gas illegally. They also stole gas and so on and so forth."

Shokin placed Zlochevsky, who was in exile in Monaco and Dubai, on Ukraine's "most-wanted" list on suspicion of embezzlement.

However, Burisma was not his priority. "Of course, I was well informed about the progress of the investigation, what new facts investigators . . . had discovered [but it] wasn't the biggest anti-corruption case in Ukraine. The reason it received attention was because Zlochevsky brought [Hunter] Biden and Kwasniewski onto the Burisma board. Burisma had a very bad reputation." Zlochevsky has not denied gaining licenses while he was minister.

Shokin's priority was "the affairs of the Maidan and the crimes of Yanukovych and his government officials, and the Donbas. There was an immense amount of work. I worked 24/7 with almost no days off."

The office was in chaos when he arrived, so he held a video conference with all regional prosecutors across the country and began to systematically organize a matrix of crimes relating to the Euromaidan. There were the unsolved murders of the "Heavenly Hundred," including those shot by snipers in Maidan Square, the savage beating of protesters by pro-government forces in February 2014 in Mariinsky Park in front of the Ukrainian parliament, and the killing of 13 Berkut riot police. Then there were the "economic crimes" of Yanukovych and other government officials. All up, Shokin launched more than 2,400 criminal cases. A hotline he set up for Ukrainians to provide information fielded half a million calls. He prepared a trial in absentia of Yanukovich for treason and corruption and began action to recover money stolen by his regime.

He quietly arranged for a prisoner exchange to release 3,000 Ukrainians held captive by Russia. Five years later, Shokin's efforts were acknowledged by General Sergey Krivonos, then deputy secretary of the National Security and Defense Council, who told the website Politika: "Only a few know about the role Mr. Shokin played in the exchange of these hostages, and this is very sad."

By the fall of 2015, Shokin's corruption investigation into Zlochevsky also was gathering pace, and he was planning to interview Hunter and other members of the Burisma board. He describes Hunter as a "wedding general," a Russian term for a well-connected figurehead who has no role to play in the business. The term comes from a 19th-century tradition of bourgeois families in Russia inviting a retired general to a wedding to provide gravitas.

"I think you understand that neither Mr. Kwasniewski or Hunter Biden knew anything about gas production in Ukraine and could not have just simply happened to their positions in Burisma accidentally, for no reason," he said.

"There was a good reason for Zlochevsky to invite Hunter Biden to Burisma. Clearly, it was because he was the son of the Vice President of the United States, Joe Biden. He was in a position to help Zlochevsky because the vice president was handling Ukraine affairs for the United States, and basically, he was in charge of all things domestic and foreign for Ukraine.

"Archer was invited [onto the board], too, and soon photographs of all of them together, Archer, [Hunter] Biden and Kwasniewski appeared in various media outlets in Ukraine in a show of their support for him [Zlochevsky]. We knew that Zlochevsky was using those photographs to prove that he had them as patrons and protectors.

"Zlochevsky, of course, understood that sooner or later, he will be punished for all the evil things and the crimes he committed against Ukraine. And that is why he was trying all these things [to get off the hook]. However, no matter how hard he tried, the investigation was going ahead at full speed and as scheduled . . . The investigation was inexorably moving to the point where all of these individuals, Hunter, Archer, Kwasniewski, and other board members would have to be interviewed. And sooner or later, we would have found out and determined who the culprit was."

Zlochevsky, meanwhile, was telling Hunter and Archer that Shokin was trying to extort money from him by threatening to prosecute him, a charge Shokin denies and for which there is no evidence. Archer testified to the House impeachment inquiry that the board was "fed" a similar story that Shokin was corrupt. But he later said he realized that the Prosecutor General posed "a threat" to Burisma and that Zlochevsky wanted him and Hunter to use their influence with Joe to make it go away.

Burisma was under "pressure from Ukrainian Government investigations into [Zlochevsky], et cetera," Archer testified to the impeachment committee in 2024, "and they [Zlochevsky and Pozharskyi] requested Hunter, you know, help them with some of that pressure."

That pressure was being exerted by Shokin. The pressure is what prompted Pozharskyi to write Hunter and Archer increasingly urgent emails in the fall of 2015, demanding that they use their influence to "close down" the criminal investigation against Burisma. It is what precipitated the phone call to Joe that Zlochevsky and Pozharskyi got Hunter to make the night of the board meeting in Dubai in December 2015.

It is the pressure that the Bidens and their defenders repeatedly ignored, claiming instead that Shokin had let the criminal case against Burisma go dormant because he was corrupt.

The following month, Joe flew to Kyiv and addressed the Ukrainian parliament on December 8, 2015. He slammed the "cancer of corruption" and declared: "The Office of the General Prosecutor desperately needs reform."

Behind the scenes, he was pressuring Poroshenko to fire Prosecutor General Shokin.

CHAPTER 22

SON OF A BITCH, HE GOT FIRED

September 24, 2015
ODESSA, UKRAINE

U S Ambassador Geoffrey Pyatt made the five-hour trip to the Black Sea city of Odessa in September 2015 to give a speech at the stylish fin de siècle landmark, The Bristol Hotel. But his pointed message to the audience of businessmen and investors was aimed directly at the Prosecutor General's office back in Kyiv.

His speech sent shockwaves through Burisma and aimed the finger of blame at Shokin. Pyatt mentioned Zlochevsky by name and criticized "corrupt actors within the Prosecutor General's Office [who] are making things worse by openly and aggressively undermining reform [and who] had undermined prosecutors working on legitimate corruption cases."

In my mind, the ambassador had falsely conflated Shokin's actions with those of his predecessor, Yarema, to imply that it was Shokin's fault that the UK's Serious Fraud Office (SFO) case against Zlochevsky had collapsed in London. To this day, the Bidens and US State Department apparatchiks perpetuate what I believe to be this false narrative.

Pyatt, a 51-year-old Yale graduate and cycling enthusiast in his first ambassadorship, had waited almost two years after the collapse of the UK investigation of Zlochevsky to rail against the Prosecutor General's Office (PGO), as if Yarema and his henchmen had not already been forced out.

Shokin had only been in the job seven months, and his anti-corruption efforts were being praised by US and European officials alike. Yet Pyatt's speech created the impression that Shokin was corruptly protecting Zlochevsky. It was the genesis of a smear campaign that would result in Shokin's removal six months later. By the time Pyatt left Odessa, the Prosecutor General was a dead man walking.

"Officials at the Prosecutor General's office were asked by the UK to send documents supporting the seizure," Pyatt said in his speech. "Instead, they sent letters to Zlochevsky's US attorneys, attesting that there was no case against it. As a result, the money was freed by the UK court, and shortly thereafter, the money was moved to Cyprus. The misconduct by the PGO officials who wrote these letters should be investigated, and those responsible for subverting the case by authorizing those letters should, at a minimum, be summarily terminated."

It was Yarema, not Shokin, who let the Burisma case go dormant. And it was Yarema, not Shokin, who failed to bring a single corruption prosecution in the eight months he was in office, as Kent pointed out. Yet all these sins were unjustly laid at Shokin's feet.

Pyatt knew Yarema had been ousted after the scandal. He knew Poroshenko had appointed Shokin as a safe pair of hands. Pyatt was having regular meetings with Shokin at the time, and their relationship was cordial. Their first meeting was in February 2015, the week after Shokin took office, and Pyatt effusively congratulated him on his appointment.

"Pyatt and I had a very good, almost friendly relationship," Shokin told me. "We met often. I had a very good relationship with Nuland as well who I wrote to and received answers. They both gave me assistance by giving me advice and we worked together in tandem."

The first Shokin knew that the relationship had soured was Pyatt's speech. The investigation into Zlochevsky had reached a stage when witnesses were about to be interviewed, and Shokin came to suspect Joe had intervened to protect his son.

"In September 2015, when Pyatt was in Odessa, all of a sudden he made comments that Shokin is poorly handling the Burisma investigation," Shokin said. "It is the ultimate irony because it was exactly the opposite. We were getting close to interviewing Joe Biden's son and all of a sudden Pyatt lashed out . . . I ask what does Pyatt have to do with Burisma? I see a clear connection with Joe Biden. Out of literally thousands of anti-corruption cases that were being investigated in Ukraine, out of the blue, with no connection whatsoever, Pyatt picked the Burisma case . . . Prior to that Pyatt had never talked about the Burisma case in our meetings and there were a great many anti-corruption cases at the time."

Shokin said their regular meetings stopped after the speech and Pyatt went out of his way to avoid him. "His demeanor changed . . . He knew my personality. He knew I was going to call him out and he understood perfectly well he said something that had no basis in reality."

Shokin was blindsided by Pyatt's attack in Odessa. Only three months previously, on June 11, 2015, Pyatt had personally handed him a congratulatory letter written by Victoria Nuland, the State Department's lead Ukraine official, on behalf of her boss, Secretary of State John Kerry, saying unreservedly what a great job he was doing. "We have been impressed with the ambitious reform and anti-corruption agenda of your government."

Shokin told me that, after Pyatt froze him out, he continued to see ambassadors from Europe and other countries who expressed "a great deal of surprise [about Pyatt's speech]. They all felt mystified. They are very sophisticated professionals and would not discuss the specific aspect with me, but they clearly expressed support for me."

"[Pyatt's speech] was a double shock for all diplomats because the Ambassadors have no right to interfere in the internal affairs of the country," Shokin wrote in his book. "Such a statement by the Ambassador looked like a brazen interference by an authorized representative of a foreign state into the course of a criminal investigation."

Two weeks after Pyatt's speech, a task force of US State, Treasury, and Justice Department officials determined that "Ukraine has made sufficient progress on its reform agenda to justify a third [$1 billion US loan] guarantee," according to an October 1, 2015, Interagency Policy Committee memo obtained by John Solomon of *Just The News*. The IPC was a task force created to advise the Obama White House on Ukraine's progress on corruption reform.

Solomon also obtained memos in which senior State Department officials invited Shokin's staff to Washington for a January 2016 strategy session and sent him a personal note saying they were "impressed" with the progress of reform at the PGO.

This US praise for Ukraine's corruption busting during Shokin's tenure was echoed in reports by influential international bodies in 2015. The Carnegie Endowment for International Peace singled out Shokin's office on Aug. 19, 2015, as among the most active on reforms: "Ukraine has adopted a package of anticorruption laws and established a set of institutions to fight corruption," said Carnegie's Ukraine Reform Monitor report. "The general prosecutor's office has been the agency most active in this agenda."

A positive anti-corruption progress report by the European Commission also contradicts claims by Biden allies that the European Union was clamoring for Shokin's removal. It was published on December 18, 2015, nine days after Joe flew to Ukraine and demanded Poroshenko fire Shokin.

The progress report stated that the European Union was satisfied that Ukraine had achieved "noteworthy" progress, including in "preventing and fighting corruption," and thus was eligible for visa-free travel in Europe. The European Commission noted that Shokin had just appointed the head of a specialized anti-corruption prosecution office, which it described as "an indispensable component of an effective and independent institutional framework for combating high-level corruption." The office would help the newly established National Anti-Corruption Bureau, the report noted. It urged Ukrainian leadership to ensure that both bodies were "fully operational" by the first quarter of 2016.

But Shokin was gone by then. On March 29, 2016, Poroshenko and the Rada finally succumbed to Joe's threats that he would withhold $1 billion in US aid unless Shokin was fired. Shokin is certain Joe pushed him out to protect Hunter.

"The United States is a respectable country, and I like it very much," Shokin told me. "But who gave Biden authority to interfere in the affairs of a sovereign country and act like its handler? A lot of damage was done, and a great deal of people knew about it and that's why the Supreme Council [of the Rada] initially refused to sanction my resignation."

Joe Biden's defense of Hunter's alleged Ukrainian grift relies on Shokin being corrupt. The Democrats impeached Donald Trump on the strength of that uncorroborated allegation.

Shokin has maintained his innocence ever since he was forced out by Joe in March 2016, after just 13 months in the job. He points out that, eight years after his ouster, nobody has produced any evidence of wrongdoing by him.

He says he was not obstructing reforms but attempting to preserve the integrity of his investigations amidst a political turf war between new overlapping anti-corruption bodies imposed by the US State Department and a new anti-corruption unit within his own office that he had created, also at the behest of the US.

He came to view with particular suspicion a presumptuous young prosecutor named Vitaly Kasko, a favorite of Pyatt, who had an eye on Shokin's job.

* * *

In the damage control narrative created by the Bidens and their allies, and laundered through friendly media outlets, it was not just US policy but very much the Europeans—the EU, the IMF, and the European Commission—who wanted Shokin out. In this scenario, Joe had little agency and it was just a coincidence that the removal of Shokin benefited the company that was paying his wayward son $1 million a year.

Nuland, who would become undersecretary of state in the Biden administration, was adamant in her claims that the VP was simply carrying out official US policy and that he was backed by European officials who wanted Shokin gone because they regarded him as corrupt and an obstacle to reform.

"It was a policy that was coordinated tightly with the Europeans, with the International Monetary Fund, the World Bank," she told the Senate's Johnson-Grassley inquiry in 2020. "But not only did we not see progress, we saw the [PGO] go backwards in this period . . . I never saw any influence on policy as a result of Hunter Biden's board seat."

Anders Aslund, a senior fellow at the Atlantic Council in Washington, was equally insistent when he told the *Wall Street Journal* in 2019: "Everyone in the Western community wanted Shokin sacked . . . The whole G-7, the IMF, the EBRD [the European Bank for Reconstruction and Development], everybody was united that Shokin must go, and the spokesman for this was Joe Biden."

However, none of the European bodies cited had ever called specifically for Shokin's removal or even mentioned his name.

Instead, two months after Joe's pressure campaign against Shokin began, bodies such as the IMF issued statements generically criticizing Ukraine's "slow progress" in fighting corruption and repatriating the alleged billions stolen by the Yanukovych regime.

Most Europeans quoted on Shokin's ousting did so anonymously, with one notable exception, Jan Tombinski, then the European Union's ambassador to Ukraine. He was quoted by name in the *Irish Times* as welcoming Shokin's removal the day it happened. The article, on March 29, 2016, claimed in its headline that the EU "has welcomed the dismissal of Ukraine's scandal-ridden Prosecutor General and called for a crackdown on corruption."

And yet Tombinski's actual quotes in the article do not mention Shokin at all. He says, more generically: "This decision creates an opportunity to make a fresh start in the Prosecutor General's office. I hope that the new Prosecutor general will ensure that [his] office . . . becomes independent from political influence and pressure and enjoys public trust. There is still a lack of tangible results of investigations into serious cases . . . as well as investigations of high-level officials within the prosecutor general's office."

When I contacted Tombinski, now an EU adviser on Moldova, he denied "praising Shokin's removal" as Media Matters put it.

"I never asked for the withdrawal of Mr. Shokin because it belonged exclusively to the competencies of the Ukrainian authorities," he said in an email. "We commented [on] work of institutions but refrained from any suggestions regarding personal appointments . . .

"My hope for better work of the Prosecution Office after the dismissal of Mr. Shokin related to the public expectation that three years after the Maidan Revolution people responsible for the abuse of power and offenses against human rights will finally be brought to justice."

In his testimony to the Johnson-Grassley committee, Pyatt claimed that Tombinski's "views on the removal of Shokin were even stronger than mine, and I know he communicated those to the President, to the prosecutor general, and the Ukrainian Government. And I think we actually did so together on a couple of occasions with joint presentations."

Shokin's recollection of his relationship with Tombinski is quite different.

"The fact that under my leadership the Prosecutor General's Office began to produce effective investigations, work, and reforms, became apparent in the summer of 2015," Shokin writes in his memoir. "Jan Tombinski, the then ambassador of the European Union to Ukraine, said in an interview [in April 2015 with now-defunct Ukrainian channel 112]: 'We have not previously seen such reform in Ukraine, as has occurred during the last four months.'

"Ambassadors and heads of law enforcement agencies of Germany, Great Britain, Sweden, Switzerland, Belgium, Latvia, Hungary, and other countries also responded positively to my work."

On one issue, how to staff the new Special Anti-Corruption unit in Shokin's office, Tombinski and Shokin had differing opinions. Tombinski wanted the unit to be completely independent, but Shokin wanted to have a say in the selection process and he was suspicious of Pyatt's golden boy, Kasko, who he believed was going to be appointed to head the unit.

Shokin also was opposed to Georgian nationals being parachuted into crucial positions in his office and into the various new anti-corruption bodies. He claims that in 2014 and 2015, "almost all staffing proposals for the Ukrainian government were approved by Biden and only Georgians were offered to law enforcement agencies." Like Ukraine, Georgia was a former Soviet satellite state on the Black Sea, but the Americans regarded Georgians as more trustworthy—and reliably pro-West.

With a backlog of difficult prosecutions to get through, Shokin's objection to the Georgian interlopers was practical: they were foreigners who didn't understand Ukraine's language or legal system and would be a nuisance in his office.

He complained to Poroshenko when, after he'd been in the top job for less than a week, a Georgian national, David Sakvarelidze, was foisted on him as a deputy.

"I have professional deputies," he complained, "and I'm not going to replace anyone." In the end he created a new position for Sakvarelidze. He gave him the title of "Deputy for Reforms" but privately thought him a fool and called him "Biden's henchman" and a "pseudo-reformer [who] could not read or speak Ukrainian. I do not understand how he was acquainted with our laws and official documents, which were exclusively in the state language."

Shokin describes in his memoir how Poroshenko urged him to accept the Georgians. "The Americans believe that these people are progressive, and they will help us," Poroshenko said, adding that he believed it was a requirement to receive IMF funding.

"Reform of the prosecutor's office, and recruitment is an internal affair," Shokin replied. "Foreigners should not be taken into the law enforcement sphere, because they do not know the Ukrainian language or our legislation, and despite all their probable professional virtues, this alone is already reason enough to doubt their qualifications. Moreover,

Georgia is incomparable with Ukraine, for example, in terms of population it is only slightly larger than Kyiv."

But Poroshenko did not want to listen.

Sakvarelidze's big idea for reforming the PGO was to eliminate the turnstiles at the entrance to the building and install a fancy new all-glass entrance "which should symbolize the transparency of the renewed General Prosecutor's Office," Shokin recalled.

"Do you realize what you are saying?!" Shokin barked at him. "We have investigators working on particularly important cases here. At any moment, anyone can come and kill them. We are a warring country. We are guarded by the police."

On another occasion, Shokin claims Sakvarelidze tried to make himself look important by making up a story "about a bribe of 10 million hryvnias [$250,000], which was allegedly offered to him by a man when Sakvarelidze was running in the morning at the Botanical Garden.

"I laughed: 'Really? Why should anybody give you a bribe, David? You can't do anything, and you don't influence anything." A case was opened to investigate the incident, but Shokin said: "There was no evidence."

The last straw for Shokin was a fiasco with the new recruitment tests for prosecutors. As part of the reform of the PGO there had to be new testing and open recruitment of candidates. Shokin gave Sakvarelidze the job of overseeing the new software for the qualifying exam. "The tests were to be ready by August 15, 2015. The US government has allocated significant funds for its preparation at the expense of taxpayers." But when the new tests were submitted to the National Academy of the Prosecutor's Office, almost a third "contained significant errors," said Shokin.

"Among the questions rejected by experts were surprising: for example, 'what is the distance from Tbilisi [Georgia's capital] to Moscow?'

"Of course, the Academy returned the tests for revision, but a month later, after receiving an updated version, it concluded that these defects had not been corrected, or not corrected in a satisfactory manner. Despite the fact that the test tasks were not approved via professional examination, Sakvarelidze posted them on the [Prosecutor General's Office] website and . . . reported to the donors [Americans] as 'work completed.' Prosecutors on social networks were angry and laughing."

In the end, Shokin got rid of Sakvarelidze by sending him to Odessa, where Joe's friend Mikheil Saakashvili, the former president of Georgia, had been installed as governor. The saga illustrates what Shokin saw as irritating and counter-productive micromanaging of his work by Ukraine's American satraps.

But the situation with another of his deputies, Kasko, was far more serious.

* * *

The maneuvering to oust Shokin picked up pace after Pozharskyi's November 2, 2015, ultimatum to Hunter and Archer.

Three days later, Joe called Poroshenko and "reiterated the U.S. willingness to provide a third $1 billion loan guarantee to Ukraine, contingent on continued Ukrainian progress to investigate and prosecute corruption and ensure that Ukraine's tax reform is consistent with its IMF program," according to a White House readout of the call.

The same day, a document labeled "sensitive but unclassified" laid out the US government's proposed conditions for the $1 billion. The PGO was mentioned in relation to a condition that USAID receive a copy of a regulation governing the independence of the new Office of Inspector General, but there was no criticism of Shokin, nor any suggestion of the aid being linked to his ouster.

On November 12, 2015, Schwerin wrote to Pozharskyi to say that he and Blue Star's co-founder Sally Painter, a former Clinton advisor who was on the board of the Atlantic Council and was about to sign a Burisma contract worth $30,000 a month, had "discussed the potential trip to Kyiv in December." It is not clear if he is talking about an impending official trip by Joe or an "alternative suggestion that Sally made for Blue Star to go alone and do some high-level government meetings in Kyiv."

Pozharskyi gave the latter suggestion short shrift: "I believe that if we aim to reach those deliverables that we had discussed during our meeting . . . we should stick to our original plan to have that delegation trip to Kyiv with somebody heavyweight."

Sure enough, the next day, Joe announced he would make a trip to Ukraine in the week of December 7th, 2015. Pozharskyi emailed Hunter immediately, attaching the White House press release without comment.

An official "Sensitive" but "Unclassified" State Department document dated November 22, 2015, obtained by John Solomon of *Just the News*, lists talking points for Joe to use at his meetings with Poroshenko.

"You will sign our third billion-dollar loan guarantee," it tells Joe. There are no conditions attached. But for the first time, in writing, we see a recommendation to remove Shokin slipped into a section about reforms to the Security Service of Ukraine (SBU), a CIA equivalent: "reforms must include . . . removal of Prosecutor General Shokin, who is widely regarded as an obstacle to fighting corruption, if not a source of the problem."

It now had become official US government policy that Shokin should be removed, and also that Ukraine was to receive the $1 billion aid regardless.

But at some point before Air Force 2 landed in Kyiv on December 7, 2015, Joe decided to force Shokin's removal by tying it to the $1 billion aid.

According to the *Washington Post*'s Glenn Kessler, Biden suddenly changed the plan in midair, en route to Kyiv. According to a person who participated in the conversation, Biden "called an audible"—a football term for when the quarterback changes the play at the last minute.

"The loan guarantee was the main point of leverage with Ukraine, the vice president declared, so he instead should tell Poroshenko the loan would not be forthcoming until Shokin was gone—a suspicious ouster to House Republicans now pushing for President Biden's impeachment," wrote Kessler in 2023.

Joe had the authority to ignore departmental advice and decide on a last-minute change of tactics, but with Hunter's employer Zlochevsky the obvious beneficiary, his conditioning of the aid on Shokin's removal takes on a sinister overtone.

Joe would boast about his chutzpah years later: "I looked at them and said: 'I'm leaving in six hours. If the prosecutor is not fired, you're not getting the money,'" he told an audience at the Council on Foreign Relations in 2018.

"Well, son of a bitch, he got fired. And they put in place someone who was solid at the time."

Something was lost in translation, and Shokin and his family took the vulgar profanity literally. "The fact that he called my late mother a bitch means that nothing is sacred for this man," Shokin told Ukrainska Pravda at the time. "A normal person that has a mother would never say that."

Shokin's American resident daughter, Alina Shokina, then 45, threatened to sue Joe for insulting her family.

"I'm planning to take to court to protect the honor of my relatives," she tweeted on February 4, 2018.

* * *

At the same time as Shokin was investigating Burisma, Blue Star and its powerful Washington friends were lobbying the State Department hard on its behalf. They were knocking on an open door. In December 2015, alone, the lobbyists had meetings with Ambassador Pyatt, with Amos Hochstein—the Obama administration's special envoy on energy policy—and with an official from USAID, the State Department's main foreign aid agency.

To launder its reputation, Burisma had signed a Memorandum of Understanding with USAID the previous year on a so-called Municipal Energy Reform Project (MERP) in the Donetsk region and trumpeted the coup with a press release. The deal appears to have originated with Pyatt. According to a November 2015 email from Pozharskyi to Hunter and Archer, Pyatt had met in October with the Donetsk governor Pavlo Zhebrivsky, who expressed concern that part of the gas network in his region had been destroyed in the civil war. Burisma immediately received a call from USAID asking if they could help. Of course they could, said Pozharskyi.

Seemingly undaunted by Burisma's disrepute, USAID then decided to co-sponsor a clean energy project with Burisma.

The odd partnership drew criticism in the Ukrainian media, causing great consternation for Kent, who seemed to be the only person at the US embassy who cared that Burisma was corrupt.

On July 27, 2016, Kent forwarded a critical news story to eight state Department colleagues that was headlined "American grants go to 'Yanukovychs' and against the Ukrainian army."

"Nasty smear here," he wrote, "against Euro-Optimists, against [Vitaly] Kasko, against potentially USAID . . . Just for our background, did Burisma ever co-sponsor a USAID activity as alleged?

"To remind: someone who joined the Burisma team is Hunter Biden. Zlochevsky is the ex minister of Ecology whose frozen assets were released by PGO perfidy in Dec 2014."

By August 31, 2016, Kent sounded frustrated in an email to colleagues: "Burisma's contribution to upcoming MERP energy efficiency event—how large is the potential reputational risk by association? How much 'know your partner' due diligence was done before this 'public-private' partnership was launched this spring?

"Zlochevsky as a corrupt mal actor was a 2014 story; his control of Burisma, and the very sticky wicket of the Hunter Biden connection on Burisma's board was circulating in 2015. Below [the article] indicates the partnership was rolled out in 2016."

He then asked about the "potential reputational 'guilt by association' risk with public partnering with Burisma? . . . Would we want an article on the front page of the Washington Post (and in this case, the Kyiv Post) commenting about this public-private partnership with Burisma, the link to Hunter Biden, and the link to Zlochevsky?"

When he later testified to Congress, Kent said his intervention had killed the project. "I asked USAID to stop that sponsorship . . . because Burisma had a poor reputation in the business, and I didn't think it was appropriate for the US Government to be co-sponsoring something with a company that had a bad reputation."

No kidding.

Kent, who was a stickler for propriety, didn't just write emails when he was aggrieved. He wrote grand opuses of soaring grievance.

On September 6, 2016, he vented to the new US ambassador Marie Yovanovitch and other colleagues in a long email titled "Bullying, threatening call by Blue Star's Sally Painter (Re Lutsenko)."

The gist of his complaint was that Painter had phoned him in an "aggressive, threatening, bullying" tone and blamed him for Prosecutor General Lutsenko canceling a trip to Washington that Blue Star had been arranging. It was the first time Kent had interacted with Painter: "I am confident it will be the last."

He added the curious addendum that Dan Fried, a former ambassador to Poland, and a Distinguished Fellow of the Atlantic Council, had called in the summer to ask him to talk to Painter. "The subject was Zlochevsky, and allegedly the bad reputational deal he was getting. I warned Dan this was a sticky wicket, that Zlochevsky was viewed as corrupt, not just in Ukraine but by the USG/FBI, that he almost certainly had paid a bribe to the PGO office (Yarema team) to have them close a case against Zlochevsky in December 2014 . . .

"Furthermore, the presence of Hunter Biden on the Burisma board was very awkward for all US officials pushing an anti-corruption agenda in Ukraine.

"Dan then said: 'Sally's apparently been asked to gather information in an attempt to convince Hunter to sever the relationship.'"

There is no evidence of such an attempt on Hunter's laptop—quite the opposite.

In September 2018, Fried was photographed in intense private conversation with Burisma advisor Pozharskyi at an Atlantic Council conference in New York.

A NATO-expansionist, hardline Russia hawk, 40-year veteran of the State Department, and board member of the CIA cutout National Endowment for Democracy [NED], Fried retired four weeks after Trump came to office. He reportedly took a parting shot at the new president in a farewell speech in Washington that was praised by neoconservatives and liberal interventionists alike for its "powerful defense of liberal international order."

In 2021, when the Biden administration slapped Igor Kolomoisky with a visa ban for "significant corruption" during his bloodstained stint as governor of Dnipropetrovsk, the Atlantic Council called on Fried to interpret what the "sanctions" meant for US-Ukraine relations and for President Zelenskyy, who owed his job to the oligarch believed to be the secret owner of Burisma.

Fried congratulated the Biden administration for its "sound . . . move. The penalty on Kolomoisky is visa denial, not full blocking sanctions." In other words, it was a slap on the wrist.

While the blameless Shokin was denied a visa and treated like a pariah in America, his predecessor Yarema was feted by the Atlantic Council in Washington in September 2016, just six months after Shokin was fired. Yarema, who had presided over the UK debacle, was invited for a "round table" with the Atlantic Council on, of all topics, "Anti-corruption and Police reforms in Ukraine." Afterward, there was a ceremony where he placed flowers at the recently opened Holodomor Memorial to Victims of the Ukrainian Famine-Genocide.

The NATO-centric think tank would soon invite Zlochevsky himself to a "Ukraine Strategy Session" at its Washington headquarters in March 2018. The personal invitation was signed by Atlantic Council senior director John Herbst, who had forged a lucrative sponsorship with Burisma a few months after Shokin was fired.

The Atlantic Council had been vocal in calling for Shokin's ouster.

On November 4, 2015, two days after Burisma demanded Hunter use his "influence" to stop Shokin's investigation, an article appeared on the Atlantic Council website titled "Why Poroshenko's Support for Shokin Is Dangerous" that called for the Prosecutor General to be fired. After he was fired, it ran a triumphant article by Anders Aslund slamming the "odious prosecutor."

The Atlantic Council was a shadowy presence across Hunter's ventures in Ukraine and China, at the center of a network of intelligence operatives, foreign policy elites, and fixers who would serve to protect and advance his alleged influence-peddling activities while his father was VP.

Even Franco Nuschese, the owner of Cafe Milano, where Hunter and Joe had dinner with Pozharskyi and other foreign benefactors in April 2015, was on the board of the prestigious think tank.

The Atlantic Council was fingered by Matt Taibbi and Michael Shellenberger, the independent journalists who released the Twitter Files, for secretly working with the CIA and the Pentagon to help censor Americans who strayed from the approved narrative on everything from the Ukraine war and the origins of COVID-19 to Hunter's laptop. In July 2020 the Department of Homeland Security deputized the Atlantic Council, as one of four founding members of the Election Integrity Partnership, to monitor and censor online speech ahead of the presidential election.

A report titled "The Weaponization of Disinformation" from the House Judiciary Committee stated that the EIP was pressuring social media companies to "censor true information, jokes, and political opinions. This pressure was largely directed in a way that benefitted one side of the political aisle: true information posted by Republicans and conservatives was labeled as 'misinformation' while false information posted by Democrats and liberals was largely unreported and untouched by the censors."

The Atlantic Council, which received funding from NED, also boasted seven ex-CIA directors on its board. Three of them, Michael Hayden, Leon Panetta and Mike Morell, signed the Dirty 51 letter in October 2020 which claimed Hunter's laptop was Russian disinformation.

* * *

The Biden narrative that Shokin was corrupt doesn't stand up to scrutiny. But that didn't stop Obama administration officials from pushing it every chance they got.

One of Joe's most strident defenders was Mike Carpenter, his vice presidential foreign policy adviser who became a fellow at the Atlantic Council while it was raking in hundreds of thousands of dollars from Burisma. Carpenter sat out the Trump years alongside Blinken at the Penn Biden Center, where he was managing director, and where Special Counsel Robert Hur would find Joe had improperly stashed boxes of classified documents. He was seated at Biden's side when he made his "son of a bitch, he got fired" boast to the Council on Foreign Relations. When Biden became president, he appointed Carpenter as ambassador to the Organization for Security and Cooperation in Europe. In April 2024, Carpenter would take on a new role as Special Assistant to the President and Senior Director for Europe at the NSC.

Carpenter encapsulated the case against Shokin in an interview with *USA Today*, which claimed that the "international effort to remove Shokin . . . began months before Biden stepped into the spotlight."

According to Carpenter, "Shokin played the role of protecting the vested interest in the Ukrainian system. He never went after any corrupt individuals at all, never prosecuted any high-profile cases of corruption."

But, like everyone in the Biden orbit who told the identical story, he provided no proof, and Shokin's official prosecution record refutes his assertions.

Shokin was prosecutor general for a little over a year but made more progress than his predecessors in pursuing corruption cases and clawing back money from the Yanukovych regime.

On March 11, 2016, his final annual performance assessment was tabled with the Ukrainian parliament, as required by law, and showed his short tenure to have been a stellar success compared to his predecessors.

The document "State of Work of the General Prosecutor's Office of Ukraine" showed that in the year to February 2016, Shokin had conducted 33 prosecutions, including 24 for corruption crimes and nine for "committing crimes against peaceful protesters during the Revolution of Dignity." That compares to a grand total of 8 prosecutions by his predecessors in all of 2013 and 2014; in other words, he was eight times more productive.

What made the achievement all the more commendable was that Shokin had inherited a chaotic office and had to endure heavy meddling from his US overlords.

Another Joe loyalist who falsely blamed Shokin for the collapse of the UK investigation of Zlochevsky was Hochstein, the Obama administration's energy envoy. He flew with Joe to Ukraine on the December 2015 trip, was on the board of the Atlantic Council, and was on the supervisory board of Ukrainian energy company Naftogaz between 2017 and 2020. He joined the Biden administration in 2021, where he rose to the position of Deputy Assistant to the President and Senior Adviser for Energy.

Although Hochstein liked to issue warnings about the perils of Russian disinformation, he seeded some disinformation of his own about Shokin into the public record before the 2020 US presidential election, when he testified to the Johnson-Grassley inquiry.

"There was an active case in the UK that the US Government was supporting against Zlochevsky. Unfortunately, the prosecutor's office in Ukraine did not cooperate with the prosecutor's office in the UK, and that ultimately was a driving factor in dismissing the case."

Hochstein's lawyer, Kelly Kramer, asked him to clarify: "What prosecutor's office was that?

Hochstein replied: "The PGU [Prosecutor General's Office]. Mr. Shokin was the prosecutor at the time."

Again, like Pyatt, Hochstein surely knew that Yarema, not Shokin, was prosecutor general when the UK investigation collapsed.

In his testimony, Hochstein mounted a vigorous defense of Joe: "When somebody says that the vice president wanted to fire Shokin to support his son, I know it's not true. Now I know it because I was there. I was on that trip . . . I know who else was calling for the firing of Shokin. I know that it wasn't the Vice President's view alone. I know that it was called for by other international financial institutions, other governments . . . The removal of Mr. Shokin was being sought not only by Vice President Biden but by the IMF, the EBRD, the World Bank, the Vice President of the EU, the UK government, the German government, the French government, and by several reformists in pro-democracy and pro-governance organizations inside Ukraine."

He also claimed that Shokin's firing "had no material effect on Burisma itself or on Mr. Zlochevsky." But Hochstein must have known that it had an enormously beneficial effect. The charges against Burisma and Zlochevsky were dropped just seven months after Shokin was fired.

Joe lauded Shokin's successor, Yuri Lutsenko, as "solid" when he was appointed. US officials praised the former political prisoner as a reformer who would eradicate corruption in the prosecutor general's office.

Yet a few months after taking office, Lutsenko closed all "legal proceedings and pending criminal allegations" against Zlochevsky and removed him from the "most wanted" list Shokin had placed him on. After paying a fine, the Burisma owner was free to return to Ukraine from exile.

"We won and in less than a year!" Blue Star's Sally Painter crowed in an email to Hunter's partner Eric Schwerin.

CHAPTER 23

SHOWDOWN

August 2015
KYIV, UKRAINE

Tatiana Chornovol stormed into Shokin's office one August day in 2015, full of righteous anger, and accused him of defrauding Ukraine. The heroine of Euromaidan had just been told that the Prosecutor General was blocking the repatriation of money stolen by one of Yanukovych's cronies. When she calmed down, Shokin asked the novice parliamentarian to explain herself.

As soon as she mentioned the name of his deputy, Vitaly Kasko, Shokin rolled his eyes. What was the wretch up to now?

Chornovol described how the Latvian authorities had been trying since early spring to return $80.5 million confiscated from a gas billionaire who had fled Ukraine in February 2014 with Yanukovych. But nobody at the Prosecutor General's office responded to their messages, and the money was about to be deposited into the Latvian treasury.

"On the face of it, this was yet another example of Shokin's alleged corruption, justifying Biden's demand for Shokin's resignation in December 2015, a few months later," Chornovol would write later in Ukrainska Pravda, as translated into English here. How wrong she was.

"I literally broke into Shokin's office [and] began to complain, and stopped when I saw Shokin's reaction—he sincerely did not understand what was being said. And he told me: 'I will call Kasko now, and we will find out everything.'"

Shokin knew that if Kasko were involved there would be trouble. He suspected Kasko was behind the sabotage of the UK's case against Zlochevsky but had to tread carefully because Kasko and his annoying fellow deputy prosecutor general, David Sakvarelidze, the Georgian, were favorites of Ambassador Pyatt. (This allegation was never proven.)

Kasko, once described by the *Guardian* as a lean man "with a sharp chin [and] luxuriant head of black hair," was in charge of the PGO's international section. He was responsible for asset forfeiture and recovery. It was his job to liaise with the 33 Western countries that had gathered at the U.K. summit the previous year and promised to help Ukraine get back its stolen assets. Shokin figured Kasko had to be involved in blocking the Latvians.

When Kasko arrived at Shokin's office and saw Chornovol, he knew he'd been busted. His only defense was offense, so he started shouting at the petite brunette.

"I didn't know Kasko," Chornovol wrote in Ukrainska Pravda. "But I was surprised by the hatred he reacted to me personally, as well as to my natural request to take over the criminal case and money from Latvia . . .

"Kasko is always so polished on television [and here he was] raging, being rude, shouting that there is no money in Latvia.

"From his behavior, it immediately became clear that he himself was blocking the [return of the money from] Latvia, and it was convenient to blame everything on Shokin.

"Then it became unequivocally clear to me why, one and a half years after Maidan, the assets were not being returned and who was sitting on those golden eggs. Something had to be done about it."

From that day on, Chornovol and Shokin became firm allies. Together with a small group of lawyers and anti-corruption crusaders they would manage to retrieve $1.5 billion of the $400 billion estimated to have been stolen from the Ukrainian people. The effort would take two years, continuing under Shokin's successor Lutsenko. It was a good start. But after Shokin was fired, efforts to claw back more of the stolen money ground to a halt.

Chornovol was an unlikely ally for the cynical old prosecutor. The corruption-busting journalist was one of the leaders of Euromaidan and had emerged as an ultranationalist in the new parliament. Then she joined the war against Russia.

Her husband, Mykola Berezovyi, a platoon commander in the Azov battalion, was killed in August 2014 while fighting pro-Russian separatists in southeast Ukraine, leaving her to bring up their two small children alone.

Two weeks after Russia invaded Ukraine in February 2022, Chornovol was one of the citizen volunteers in Kyiv who teamed up with an elite unit of soldiers to "turn the tide in the most consequential European battle since World War II," as the *Wall Street Journal* described the three-hour struggle to repel the Russian army's advance into Ukraine's capital.

A photograph of Chornovol appears with the September 2022 story. Wearing army camouflage, she stands on rubble underneath a destroyed bridge, a khaki bandana holding back thick brown hair, bright red lipstick accentuating a radiant smile. Hoisted on her shoulder is an enormous Stugna anti-tank missile. She had just taken out her first Russian tank when the photograph was shot in March.

In 2023 she was promoted to senior lieutenant and was commander of an anti-tank platoon. She also had learned to operate mini FPV (First Person View) kamikaze drones. At the time of writing, she had just posted a photo of herself on Facebook from a secret location near the frontline. Her hair is in two waist-long braids, and her head is covered in a brown scarf, as she smiles while holding an FPV that looks like a black metal spider, is about the size of a shoebox, and has a red heart affixed to the battery. "I am an FPV pilot," she writes in English. "It's an incredible feeling to fly over the enemy at 15 km depth [distance into enemy territory] and fly straight into the bunker—and in the last frame you can see the orca

[Russian soldier]." The Ukrainian government aimed to make a million FPV drones in 2024, Reuters reported.

Chornovol became famous in 2012 for scaling the walls of Yanukovych's residential compound and photographing his opulent lakefront mansion. On Christmas Day 2013, in the middle of the revolution, she was beaten half to death by thugs in an attack she claimed had been ordered by Yanukovych as payback for her corruption exposes (which was denied and never proven). Her battered face is unrecognizable in news images taken in hospital. Her right eye is black and purple, and swollen shut. Her nose is broken. Her skin is red raw on one side of her face as if it has been grated. Her lips are bloody and puffed up to three times normal size. She also suffered a concussion. The photos caused outrage across Ukraine, but the plucky Chornovol won public admiration when she declared she was "physically beaten but not psychologically broken."

After the revolution, Prime Minister Yatsenyuk appointed Chornovol head of the parliament's National Anti-Corruption Committee.

In early 2015 she teamed up with Olena Tyshchenko, a 38-year-old Ukrainian lawyer who had been appointed Ukraine's Director of the Agency for Asset Recovery.

Tyshchenko is a fascinating figure who could have stepped out of the pages of a Robert Ludlum thriller. The London *Times* described her as "striking, blonde, slim, charming, and hospitable" in a 2022 interview in her mansion in a gated estate in Surrey outside London, where she lived at the time with her five daughters and four female Ukrainian refugees. The anti-corruption investigator was facing prosecution in the High Court of London over allegations that she and her ex-husband had ripped off a Ukrainian bank he owned. "I have become a victim of fraudulent claims," she told the court in 2022, describing the case against her as "like a legal chess game."

A decade earlier, the glamorous Ukrainian unwittingly had led British detectives to the French Riviera hideout of a fugitive Kazakhstani oligarch who was her client—and reputedly her lover. Detectives reportedly saw the diminutive billionaire through the curtains laying lilies on the bed before her arrival. Tyshchenko was then arrested by Russian police on charges of money laundering.

None of the allegations were ever proven, so the scandals did not stop her getting the asset recovery gig for Ukraine. It was Tyshchenko who found the first $80.5 million frozen in a bank account in Latvia. Latvian authorities told her their difficulties trying to contact the PGO.

"The Latvian investigator in this case, when Olena turned to him, immediately pounced," wrote Chornovol in Ukrainska Pravda. "Like, he is glad to hear from Ukraine. [But he] told her the shocking truth that, it turns out, Latvian law enforcement officers have been running around the Ukrainian PGO for a year with a request . . . to take this money."

When Tyshchenko sent the paperwork to the PGO's international division to begin the process of recovering the funds, Kasko told her it was "useless" to try to get the money back because, he claimed, "Shokin is personally blocking Latvia" and had refused to sign the paperwork.

Kasko, "'the beloved of the US embassy,' had undermined all three Prosecutor Generals he worked for," Chornovol would tell the Ukrinform news agency. His "message was always betrayal on the part of prosecutors. The irony was that Kasko himself was often the author of 'betrayal.' However, he skillfully put his failures in the international department of the Prosecutor General's Office onto the leaders."

Shokin ended up sidelining Kasko and sending another prosecutor, Oleksandr Kashulsky, to Latvia to recover the money. But Kashulsky soon left the case. At the same time, a subordinate of Sakvarelidze launched a bogus criminal investigation into Kashulsky's father.

In other words, Shokin's US-backed deputies were preventing him from doing the very thing the US was criticizing him for failing to do: recover the stolen Yanukovych money.

Yet Ambassador Pyatt believed they were "the personification of new Ukraine," as he later testified to Congress. "Vitaly Kasko and David Sakvarelidze . . . were the good guys who were trying to clean up the Prosecutor General's Office."

In his incendiary speech in Odessa, Pyatt singled out his proteges for praise: "We applaud the work of the newly established Inspector General's office in the PGO led by David Sakvarelidze and Vitaliy Kasko. Their investigations into corruption within the PGO, have delivered important arrests and have sent the signal that those who abuse their official positions as prosecutors will be investigated and prosecuted."

Yet, as Chornovol pointed out, during Kasko's tenure as the asset recovery chief at the PGO, "there were no successes in asset recovery, even though Kasko worked under all three Prosecutor Generals after the Maidan."

Kasko's ally, Sakvarelidze, was a protégé of Mikheil Saakashvili, the deposed pro-Western president of Georgia who had now become involved in Ukrainian politics.

Shokin thought Saakashvili was "a poser and a talker" who fooled a lot of Ukrainians. He complains in his book that "when Saakashvili was the head of the Odessa regional state administration, he poured a lot of unfounded accusations against the Prosecutor General's Office."

Apart from getting offside with the Georgians, Shokin became convinced that Kasko was involved in the sabotage of the U.K. investigation into Zlochevsky back in Christmas 2014.

"I am sure that Kasko deliberately procrastinated [and] sent a short reply, knowing in advance that it would not satisfy the British. Instead, Mykola Zlochevsky's lawyers received a certificate from the [PGO] stating 'uncertain legal status and absence of any notifications about suspicions,' which they successfully used [to end the case] during a court hearing in London in December 2014 . . .

"Kasko's [alleged] sabotage cost Ukraine $23.5 million. The [PGO] opened a criminal case on this fact in 2016. After I was forced to resign, this case was probably closed due to Joseph Biden's and the US [embassy's] protection of Vitaliy Kasko." It's unclear if Klosko, or anyone, purposely sabotaged the UK's case.

Running roughshod over Shokin's objections, Biden and Pyatt wanted Kasko to head up the new Special Anti-Corruption unit inside the PGO. However, during the vetting process, a PGO investigation found that Kasko had allegedly corruptly acquired two state-owned apartments.

Kasko denied the allegation and nothing was proven true, but it killed his appointment, and an ally of Shokin won the job. The *Kyiv Post* accused Shokin and Chornovol of "organizing a smear campaign" against Kasko.

Meantime, Chornovol's idea to get back the rest of the stolen Yanukovich money was to have the Rada pass a "special confiscation" law. But her proposal was opposed by US officials and by powerful oligarch-backed factions in the parliament, including those tied to Kolomoisky, and ultimately was defeated. Chornovol complains in her blog about a "sea of dirt and lies . . . The idea of the 'special confiscation' bill was noble and pure—to return what Yanukovych had stolen to the state budget. So why was there so much opposition? How can things so easily turn black in the public eye? It turns out they can when there's money involved."

One of the last things Shokin did before he was ousted was to fire his Georgian deputy Sakvarelidze.

The last straw was Sakvarelidze's attempt to smear Shokin in the "diamond prosecutors case." In July 2015, two prosecutors were busted with cash and diamonds and accused of taking bribes.

Shokin denies any involvement and says he was set up by Sakvarelidze in retaliation for an investigation he had launched into missing grant money earmarked for the PGO, which ended up going to the Odessa Regional State Administration, run by Sakvarelidze's Georgian friends. Shokin opened a similar investigation into the anti-corruption body AntAC, which was partly bankrolled by two foundations funded by controversial Hungarian-American billionaire George Soros.

The two prosecutors were arrested in dramatic scenes that made international news. Under Sakvarelidze's authority, the heavily armed counterterrorist unit of the Ukrainian SBU reportedly broke down office doors in the PGO building.

Later, once Shokin had been removed, the case quietly went away and has never been concluded.

"By the time that U.S. State Department officials were testifying at the 2019 impeachment and 2020 [Johnson-Grassley] hearings, the 'diamond prosecutors' case had more or less totally stalled under Shokin's successors," wrote Stephen McIntyre, the founder and editor of the Climate Audit website, who researched the affair for a report on Substack in May 2024. "But none of the State Department officials reported this."

At the time of the arrests, Shokin was in the U.S. for surgery, and to see his daughter and grandchildren. Returning to Ukraine on July 10, 2015, he was greeted with an article in the *Kyiv Post* calling for his resignation. *USA Today* piled on with a seemingly evidence-free story that Shokin had sabotaged the U.K. case against Zlochevsky: "British authorities had frozen $23 million in a money-laundering probe, but Shokin's office failed to send documents British authorities needed to prosecute Zlochevsky."

AntAC launched a campaign against Shokin, demanding his ouster and sending protesters outside his house in October 2015.

At the same time, Zlochevsky was urging Hunter and Archer to use their "DC" connections to make the Ukrainian investigation of Burisma go away, and Biden was ratcheting up the pressure on Poroshenko to remove Shokin.

In January 2016 four Ukrainian prosecutors, including Shokin's disloyal deputies Kasko and Sakvarelidze, were invited to Washington to discuss corruption with top US officials. Shokin refused permission for Kasko to attend, prompting furious objections from the US Embassy.

An unnamed US official wrote a stern letter to Shokin to say he was "very disappointed that you have refused to allow Deputy Prosecutor General Vitaliy Kasko to join the senior level Ukrainian delegation visiting Washington, DC in January . . .

"Mr. Kasko is responsible for international cooperation, asset forfeiture and asset recovery in Ukrainian PGO. His attendance at these meetings is therefore crucial."

Kasko did end up attending the Washington meeting, on January 19, 2016. The Ukrainian delegation visited the White House and met with US officials including Jeff Zients, who would have at least three meetings the following year with Hunter and would become Joe's presidential chief of staff in 2023.

Also at the Washington meeting was Eric Ciaramella, the CIA analyst who was John Brennan's protégé and had been detailed to the NSC that summer to work closely with Joe on Ukraine issues. He had been on the fateful trip to Kyiv the previous month when Joe conditioned $1 billion in aid on Shokin being ousted.

Three years later, Ciaramella would emerge as a central player in the first impeachment of Donald Trump, in the role of Democrat Adam Schiff's anonymous whistleblower who accused Trump of conditioning aid for Ukraine on a promise that Zelenskyy would investigate the Bidens' involvement with Burisma. In hindsight, the charge looks like an example of the clinical definition of projection practiced by sufferers of narcissistic personality disorder.

Two days after the Washington meeting, Pyatt emailed state department colleagues, including Ciaramella, an article from the Ukrainian media, titled "U.S. loan guarantee conditional on Shokin's dismissal." He added two words: "Buckle in."

"Yikes," Ciaramella responded. "I don't recall this coming up in our meeting."

That same month, in Washington DC, the FBI opened a "205B" Kleptocracy case into Zlochevsky under the Foreign Corrupt Practices Act. It would be quietly closed three years later, in December 2019, just as Trump was trying to defend himself against impeachment.

Kasko resigned as deputy prosecutor general in February 2016, weeks after returning from Washington. He slammed Shokin on the way out.

"My desire to resign is due to the fact that today's top officials of the prosecutor's office have actually turned it into the body saturated with corruption and cover-up," he told the *Kyiv Post*. "It's not justice and law that are in charge here, but arbitrary rule and lawlessness."

Before he was forced out of office, Shokin obtained a court order to seize one of Kasko's apartments, and the PGO charged Kasko in April 2016 with illegally receiving two apartments from the state by fraud and forgery.

Kasko claimed Shokin had trumped up the charges as revenge. He wrote in Ukrainska Pravda that he had received only one service apartment from the PGO in 2008 and privatized it legally in 2014, while another apartment he had received in 2003 was not an "official apartment."

Converting state-owned apartments to private ownership may have been common practice in Ukraine, as the PGO later expanded its investigation into the "abuse of service housing" to other prosecutors. However, the internal register of apartments went missing, and the investigation went nowhere.

Kasko continued to make himself useful to Joe by providing exonerating quotes to Western media: "There was no pressure from anyone from the US to close cases against Zlochevsky," he told Bloomberg News.

But that does not appear to be true.

CHAPTER 24

"JUSTICE WILL COME"

November 2015
WASHINGTON, DC

Through the fall of 2015, Vadym Pozharskyi was leaning on Hunter and Archer to get the Ukrainian investigators off his boss's back, according to an email on the laptop. According to evidence provided to the House Ways and Means Committee by IRS agent Ziegler, Hunter and Archer engaged in a flurry of activity on November 2, 2015, the day Pozharskyi sent his email demand for "a list of deliverables . . . with the ultimate purpose to close down any cases/pursuits against [Zlochevsky] in Ukraine."

Archer messaged Hunter and Eric Schwerin later that day, urging Hunter "to deliver that message" and saying, "I have walked this to the finish (aka starting) line but need some support to close."

The same day, Hunter called Hochstein, the administration's energy envoy, and asked for a meeting four days later at Le Pain Quotidien in Georgetown, near Hunter's office. "I think he wanted to know my views on Burisma and Zlochevsky," Hochstein told the Johnson-Grassley inquiry.

Hochstein said he had raised the issue of Hunter's Burisma role directly with Joe in the West Wing the previous month: "I wanted to make sure that he was aware that there was an increase in chatter on media outlets close to Russians and corrupt oligarch-owned media outlets [about] Hunter Biden being part of the board of Burisma," he testified.

The same day as Pozharskyi's urgent email, Shokin was targeted in what he believed may have been an assassination attempt at his office in Kyiv.

"An unknown assailant shot at the windows of Prosecutor General's office on Riznytska Street. I was saved by the armored glass."

Shokin's instinct was that it was a warning. Years later he wrote in his memoir that he didn't understand what the attack was: "an assassination attempt? threat? warning? Then from whose side? There are more questions than answers. However, obviously, there was a real threat to my life."

It would not be the last attempt to bump him off. He almost died on September 10, 2019, after falling ill with acute mercury poisoning while on holiday in Rethymno on the Greek island of Crete.

He showed me a medical report from the Rudolifinerhaus clinic in Vienna indicating he had five times the normal amount of mercury in his system. He later filed a complaint with the Rethymno Police, who opened a case of attempted murder by poisoning. On June 16, 2020, after Greek investigators sent a request to the Ukraine National Police in Kyiv, he says he sat for an interview in which he named two suspects and requested they be questioned by Greek police. He has heard nothing since.

At the time that his office was shot up in November 2015, Shokin says an "annoyed" Poroshenko was pestering him about the Burisma investigation. Tension between the two men was mounting as Shokin dug in his heels, as he had done throughout his career when faced with pressure from his political masters.

Poroshenko told him: "It is not necessary to force the investigation. Biden is dissatisfied because his son is on the board of directors, and we must understand Ukraine's dependence on America, which means dependence on Biden's support."

Shokin told me: "[Joe] Biden repeatedly demanded that I be removed . . .

Poroshenko told me there were regular ultimatums and discussions about me."

Poroshenko never told Shokin to close the Burisma case. "But I know that Joe Biden made various efforts and conversations with Poroshenko trying to get the case dismissed," Shokin said.

"However, Poroshenko did not wield any influence on me in this regard, because I was following the letter of Ukrainian law very strictly in this matter [and] the case was moving along successfully . . . And sooner or later, we would have found out and determined who the culprit was . . .

"I'm also aware of the fact that Zlochevsky was trying to use the law enforcement agencies in Ukraine to get the case dismissed. But he couldn't do it. He then started looking for opportunities in the West to try and cover up his crimes."

In December 2015, Poroshenko called Shokin and told him that Biden was coming to Kyiv and "will bring data [evidence] of your corruption." Shokin says he "shrugged and said 'Well, let him come.' Because I knew that corruption can be invented, even for me."

But when Joe flew in on Air Force 2 on December 7 he did not bring evidence of what Shokin calls "my mythical acts of corruption."

The next time he met with Poroshenko, Shokin told him: "Petro Alekseevich, Joe Biden is the second person in one of the most influential countries in the world. At his disposal are the FBI, the CIA, and other intelligence services. If he didn't bring any proof of my alleged corruption, then there must be none . . . right?" Poroshenko was silent.

"The only thing Biden brought to me in December 2015 was a dose of political poison," Shokin writes in his memoir, referencing the $1 billion loan tranche that would not be issued to Ukraine unless the President fired him.

The case against Shokin is a sophisticated mirage of disinformation that disappears when you try to look into it. Powerful people treated the Prosecutor General like a disposable patsy, but they didn't anticipate his stubborn refusal to go quietly, despite the attempts on his life.

Shokin maintains that, at the time of his removal, he actively was investigating Zlochevsky, and there is evidence to bolster his claim. On February 2, 2016, eight weeks before Shokin was fired, the Pechersk District Court in Kyiv granted a long-standing petition filed by the Prosecutor General's Office to seize all Zlochevsky's "movable and immovable property," including his mansion on the Dnieper, three other large houses, two plots of land, and a Rolls-Royce Phantom.

A press release from Shokin's office that day stated that the "former Minister of Ecology and Natural Resources of Ukraine, Deputy Secretary of the National Security and Defense Council of Ukraine, M. Zlochevsky is suspected of committing a criminal offense [illegal enrichement]."

"This was the last drop for Zlochevsky's patience when we seized his personal assets," Shokin told me.

"He found a way to complain to Hunter, who must have found a way to complain to his father, and Poroshenko issued an ultimatum for me, demanding my resignation."

Ten days after Zlochevsky's property was seized, Joe phoned Poroshenko, according to official call records.

Poroshenko "growled" at Shokin: "What are you doing again? Why are you forcing this investigation?" The president had run out of patience with his ornery lawman.

"I suppose Petro Poroshenko promised Joe Biden that everything would be OK," recalled Shokin, "but it turned out not OK for them, so [he] was angry."

* * *

Two days after his properties were seized, Zlochevsky sent Hunter an expensive Hublot watch for his 46th birthday on Feb. 4, 2016. "Dear Hunter," he wrote in a flowery note. "In the short time that I've known you I have seen that you are a smart decent person which believe me is a rare quality in the world of business, and even more so, with my background as a minister, in the world of politics. Today, on your birthday with all my heart I am wishing you to remain true to yourself, regardless of the circumstances, and give yourself some credit now and then!!"

Hunter thanked him for the "far too extravagant" gift.

Poroshenko asked Shokin to resign on February 16, 2016, although the Ukrainian parliament did not ratify his ousting until the end of March.

"'Victor Nikolaevich, you have to go,' the President said calmly . . .

"Honestly, it was annoying. The bitter taste of injustice, the same as that day, does not leave me all these years.

"On the same day . . . President Poroshenko, for the Bidens' pleasure, without even waiting for my letter of resignation, made a televised address to the Ukrainian people regarding my dismissal as a fait accompli."

Poroshenko publicly declared: "Victor Shokin has implemented the reforms that Prosecutor General's Office has resisted for decades, [but] unfortunately has not been able to gain the public's trust, and that is why the issue of the Prosecutor General's resignation is on the agenda."

Poroshenko's popularity plummeted after Shokin was ousted. The American public might have been fooled by the Biden smokescreen, but Ukrainians knew the score.

In a leaked recording of a conversation between Poroshenko and Joe on February 18, 2016, believed to have been hacked by the Russians, the Ukrainian president says he has "good news for you . . . I went to meet with [Shokin] and, in spite of the fact that we don't have any corruption charges, we don't have any information about him doing something wrong, I especially asked him . . . to resign his position as a state person, and despite the fact that he has support in the public. And as a finish of my meeting with him, he promise me to give the statement of resignation, and one hour ago he bring [sic] me the written statement of his resignation."

Joe lets out a sigh and says: "Great."

On May 13, 2016, Joe tells Poroshenko: "Congratulations on getting the new prosecutor general. . . . It's going to be critical for him to work quickly to repair the damage Shokin did, and I'm a man of my word, and now that the new prosecutor general is in place we're ready to move forward in signing that new one-billion-dollar loan guarantee."

Poroshenko: "Thank you very much indeed for these words of support. Believe me that it was a very tough challenge."

* * *

Yuriy Lutsenko, Shokin's "solid" successor, as Joe would later describe him, had been a key figure in Ukraine's 2004 Orange Revolution and was feted as a hero in the West after he was thrown in prison. He was one of the leaders of the Maidan Revolution, and claimed to have spoken to Joe on the phone during the protests.

But after he took over from Shokin, he faced the same turf battles with competing anti-corruption agencies and fell out with Pyatt's successor, Ambassador Marie Yovanovitch, who would later be removed by President Trump.

Lutsenko's discontent led him to a meeting in New York with Trump's lawyer Rudy Giuliani, who was seeking evidence of Ukrainian collusion with the Clinton campaign in 2016. Lutsenko handed over evidence from the Burisma investigation, including invoices for millions of dollars of payments to Hunter Biden. The encounter ultimately led to Trump's impeachment.

Zelenskyy fired Lutsenko in August 2019. The following month, Democrat Speaker Nancy Pelosi announced an impeachment inquiry into President Trump's call with Zelenskyy, and Lutsenko walked back his criticism of the Bidens, telling NBC that neither Joe nor Hunter Biden had committed "any possible violation of Ukrainian law."

After the 2022 Russian invasion, Lutsenko joined the Armed Forces of Ukraine as a platoon commander on the frontlines before retiring injured in July 2023.

In 2022, Blue Star Strategies retroactively registered as a foreign agent under the Foreign Agents Registration Act [FARA] for its lobbying efforts on behalf of Zlochevsky and Burisma, after the DOJ reportedly opened an investigation and then closed it without finding wrongdoing.

In January 2024, the prestigious law firm Cravath, Swain & Moore also retroactively registered as a foreign agent for work done for Burisma by its litigation partner John Buretta, a former deputy assistant attorney general in the Obama administration. He met several times with Lutsenko before all criminal proceedings were dropped against Zlochevsky and Burisma in January 2017. (Neither firm ended up facing a full probe.)

* * *

For a guy widely dismissed as nothing but a corrupt prosecutor, a lot of effort by a lot of powerful people has been put into discrediting Shokin.

In the fall of 2020, the CIA tried to suppress Shokin's book by warning Twitter that it might be connected to Russian intelligence, as Matt Taibbi revealed in the Twitter Files. "We have information that indicates that the book is intended to reveal corruption allegedly perpetrated by the U.S. in Ukraine," read the message from the CIA to Twitter's content moderation team.

"While it is unclear at this time how involved Russian intelligence might be in the creation or promotion of this book . . . we wanted to highlight the potential nexus . . . and we suspect that the book could be promoted online via foreign-controlled or inauthentic accounts."

In August 2023, Shokin gave a rare on-air interview to Brian Kilmeade of Fox News: "Poroshenko fired me at the insistence of the then Vice President Biden because I was investigating Burisma," he said.

When asked about Devon Archer's testimony that he was a threat to Burisma, Shokin agreed he was, "because [Archer] understood, and so did Vice President Biden, that if I had continued to oversee the Burisma investigation, we would have found the facts about the [allegedly] corrupt activities that they were engaging in. That included both Hunter Biden and Devon Archer and others."

When Kilmeade asked Shokin: "Do you believe that Joe Biden or Hunter Biden got bribes?" Shokin replied, "I do not want to deal in unproven facts, but my firm personal conviction is that, yes, this was the case."

Soon after the interview, Shokin started to express concerns for his own safety and sent me photographs of rocket debris in his backyard to illustrate how easy it would be to take him out and make it look like an accident.

"In the conditions of a full-scale war in Ukraine and the approaching elections of the President of the United States, Biden can use the capabilities of Russia or of Ukrainian law enforcement agencies, to discredit or destroy Shokin," he told me.

Shokin's TV interview had caught the attention of his old boss Poro-shenko, who was facing charges of treason over his business dealings in separatist-controlled areas of Ukraine and was not allowed to leave the country. After the Russian invasion, he appeared on TV, ostentatiously posing with a Kalashnikov rifle alongside soldiers in Kyiv, and announced plans to run for president again once the war was over.

Poroshenko denounced Shokin as a "completely crazy person," in an interview with Kilmeade in September 2023. "This is something wrong with him. Second, there is not one single word of truth [in Shokin's al-legations about the Bidens]. And third, I hate the idea to make any com-ments and to make any intervention in the American election. We have very much enjoyed the bipartisan support [during the war]. Please do not use such a person like Shokin to undermine the trust between bipartisan support and Ukraine."

Then, in April 2024, an obscure NGO with an official-sounding name, the "Anti-Corruption Bureau of Ukraine in the City of Kyiv and Kyiv Re-gion," sent a letter to the Ukrainian parliament alleging that Shokin's pub-lic comments had the potential to "undermine cooperation with Ukraine's international partners" and requesting that Shokin's assets be seized.

According to the letter, Shokin "committed actions aimed at under-mining Ukraine's state security, disseminating unverified information intended to complicate and undermine cooperation with Ukraine's international partners, seeking consequences such as reducing trust in Ukraine as a country overall and preventing fruitful cooperation with international partners."

In other words, by publicly defending his reputation, Shokin was ac-cused of risking US support for Ukraine's war.

Shokin has pursued justice for himself in the Ukrainian courts. Accord-ing to the *Kyiv Post*, in April 2020, Kyiv's District Court ordered that pros-ecutors open a case into Joe's alleged unlawful interference with Shokin's work. In November 2020, the criminal probe was closed, having found no evidence of wrongdoing.

In a May, 2022 letter to Attorney General Garland, Senators Johnson and Grassley questioned whether the lobbying firm had "failed to disclose at least nine other meetings it had with US government officials—including two meetings with sitting US ambassadors to Ukraine—regarding Burisma and Mr. Zlochevsky" when it belatedly filed for FARA.

For instance, Blue Star CEO Karen Tramontano told the Johnson-Grassley Senate inquiry in December 2019 that her firm had held two Burisma-related meetings with Biden energy adviser Hochstein, on December 10, 2015, and March 24, 2016.

Shokin still burns with the injustice. "I do not pursue any political goals," he writes. "I want to debunk [alleged] international corruption in the person of Joe Biden . . .

"He put pressure on me, the President, and other leaders of Ukraine. My warring country needed help, and I was well aware of that, so I put the interests of the state above my own and wrote a letter of resignation. But the truth must be told: it was pressure and [I believe] blackmail . . .

"The President of the United States, the leader of the democratic world, cannot be a person who does not respect and love the people of his country or other peoples [while lecturing them about] international corruption. This is a problem . . . for the whole world.

"I saw a lot of evil. And I know that justice will come."

* * *

In testimony to the Biden impeachment inquiry in 2024, parts of which have been disputed by Archer, his fellow former Burisma director, Hunter was adamant that the removal of Shokin was a European project. He denied emphatically that Shokin was investigating Burisma.

"No, that's the exact opposite of the truth. And I think you can go to, I don't know, maybe 15,000 public reports. And you can talk to the IMF, and you can talk to the World Bank. And you can talk to the E.U., the E.U. Commission on Energy, and the E.U. Commission as it related to democracy . . . There is not a single person other than Alexander Smirnov who says that Shokin was fired because I was on the board of Burisma. It's literally the exact opposite, and that has been a fact now since it was first claimed. It is a fact. I'm telling you. It is a fact."

He told lies about Shokin: "Viktor Shokin was prosecuted inside of Ukraine because he was found with cash and diamonds and his chief of staff, who was formerly his driver, were both prosecuted. And so, Viktor Shokin was the problem, and the entire world community was asking for his removal."

Hunter said he did not know if Burisma wanted Shokin removed. "I never involved me in any of that. I didn't have any discussions whatsoever about Viktor Shokin. It was not on my radar at the time. I had no involvement. But the one thing also to make absolutely clear is I never spoke to my dad about it. Never had any discussions with him about it, because the only honest, the only thing that would be of value here would be for Viktor Shokin to stay in place, not the opposite . . . I do not know whether he was investigating Zlochevsky."

Archer told me it is "false" that Hunter didn't know about Shokin's investigation because it "was common knowledge among the board."

In turn, Hunter denied Archer's testimony that he called his father in Dubai: "That never happened, okay," he testified. "100 percent never happened. I never called my dad . . . And my point is, is that, number one, this is Devon talking about a call that I made to DC. And I never would have called, and never did my father on behalf of Burisma with Vadym Pozharskyi to ask for anything. It never happened."

Q: "Okay. Who did you call?"

Hunter: "I have no idea whether the call ever took place. If I called DC, most likely I called back to my office. Most likely, I called back to my, my wife. Most likely I called back to one of my daughters who were in high school. But that's who I would call. I wouldn't, in any way ever, you know, call my dad to get him to do something that is business, which I think is made, you know, clear by the evidence."

When asked if he agrees that, after Shokin was fired, "Zlochevsky was never investigated again, and he was charged with no crimes," Hunter replies: "Yes."

Q: "Do you see how that could be viewed as a conflict of interest?"

Hunter: "As I pointed out before, is that one of the things that, in everything that I do, every area that my father has influence over, which is almost ubiquitous, is that I try to minimize the conflict that there could possibly be.

"And the way that I did that was, number one, making certain that I never had any discussions with my father or anyone in his administration or asking them to do things on my behalf . . . for the benefit of anyone that I was working for or any board that I was serving on."

Hunter would try to erase any lasting perception of a conflict of interest by resigning from the Burisma board in April 2019, the month his father announced his run for president. It was also the month Hunter abandoned his laptop at John Paul Mac Isaac's repair shop in Delaware.

Five weeks later he married Melissa Cohen in LA. He was ready to start a new life, but the old one wasn't ready to let him go.

CHAPTER 25

BABY MAMA GOES POSTAL

September 2022
BATESVILLE, ARKANSAS

Lunden Roberts' heart sank. She'd had to fight to get child support from Hunter for their out-of-wedlock daughter, Navy Joan, in 2019. Now he was reneging on the deal, and she was back at square one.

According to her lawsuit, she'd endured the hardship of being thrown off his payroll three months after the birth, and the humiliation of dragging him into court to have a paternity test, when he knew perfectly well that he was the father. It was only to avoid the ugliness affecting his father's campaign that Hunter had agreed in 2020 to pay $20,000 a month.

And now, just two years on, Hunter was crying poor and trying to slash the payments. Roberts, 31, knew from the media that he was living in another mansion in Malibu that cost $20,000 a month to rent. Wasn't he selling his paintings for half a million dollars each? Flying around in a private jet? He sure didn't seem poor.

As far as Roberts was concerned, it was more of the same disrespect and dishonesty Hunter, 53, had shown her since the day in 2018 that he ghosted her when she texted to say she was pregnant.

He lied about their relationship in his memoir *Beautiful Things*, claiming he had "no recollection" of their "encounter," and refusing to acknowledge Navy's existence.

"Hunter Biden is . . . the father of three daughters [and a] son," he wrote on the jacket flap of the 2021 memoir, erasing the fourth of his five children.

In truth, their steamy affair had gone on for months behind Hallie's back. Hunter used to smuggle Roberts into his office through a back door after hours, and boasted to his building manager that she was his youngest daughter Maisy's "basketball mentor" and coached Maisy's friend, Sasha Obama, as well. Roberts had been a star basketballer at Southside High School in Batesville, graduating with honors, and going on to play for the Red Wolves at Arkansas State.

She met Hunter in 2017 at his favorite strip joint in Washington, DC, the Mpire Gentlemen's Club. But she did not like being described in the media as a "stripper" or "lap dancer," insisting she was just a waitress earning money while studying for her master's in Crime Scene Investigations at George Washington University, although she never completed the degree after falling pregnant.

Hunter wanted nothing to do with her or their blonde, blue-eyed little girl. But Roberts would make sure he lived up to his financial responsibilities, and she wanted Navy to know her Biden pedigree.

Roberts' petition for child support stated that she and Hunter were "in a relationship" and that a baby was born in August 2018 "as a result of that relationship."

In January 2020, within a few weeks of Kevin Morris getting involved in Hunter's affairs, his lawyers told the court that he would start paying child support.

The generous settlement saved Hunter from potentially being thrown in a jail cell in Arkansas, after Independence County Circuit Judge Holly Meyer threatened that she would hold him in contempt of court.

Now Roberts had to lawyer up again, with Little Rock family attorney Clint Lancaster, a former US Marine, facing off against Hunter's four high-powered "super lawyers."

After she was interviewed in 2021 by Delaware FBI and IRS investigators on the "Sportsman" case and testified to the grand jury in Wilmington in February 2022, Roberts gave federal prosecutors "a significant amount of Hunter's financial records," said Lancaster.

"Just based on what I saw in his financial records, I would be surprised if he's not indicted," the lawyer told CNBC a few weeks after Roberts' testimony.

The left-wing research group Facts First USA tried to paint Roberts as a political operative who was cynically exploiting her daughter to damage Joe at the polls. As "evidence" of the nefarious plot, they dug up a photo of her dad, Rob Roberts, posing with Donald Trump Jr. after delivering him a custom-made Benelli rifle, complete with American flag and "USA" stamped on the barrel.

"Proud to have delivered a custom build to a man that needs no introduction," her dad posted in 2022 on his company Instagram page, "Rob Roberts Custom Gun Works."

Facts First USA, funded with more than $10 million of Democrat donations, was founded by self-described former "right-wing hit man"-turned Democratic activist David Brock as a "SWAT Team to Counter Republican Congressional Investigations" into Joe and Hunter.

The group was part of an elaborate strategy by Biden donors to protect Joe, including a legal defense fund for Hunter, and extensive dirt digging on witnesses such as Tony Bobulinski and John Paul Mac Isaac. Brock laid out his plans in a fundraising memo in October 2022. He would target witnesses, journalists and members of Congress investigating the Bidens, weaponize social media and suppress the story, or as Brock put it: "limit the reach of the right-wing rage machine—to keep it within their own echo chamber rather than allowing it to become part of the mainstream media coverage . . . putting the mainstream reporters on notice that they will be held accountable if they simply buy into Republican propaganda . . .

"Facts First will win the war of public opinion by controlling the narrative—not just by defending against the partisan witch hunt, but by aggressively turning the tables on the attackers with offensive maneuvers and strong counter narratives that reveal their motivations and misconduct and tell our side of the story."

They were as good as their word, but the weight of the evidence against the Bidens denied them a narrative victory. By the end of 2023, an AP-NORC poll showed more than two-thirds (68%) of Americans believed Joe had at the very least acted unethically in his handling of his son's overseas business dealings, including a third who thought he did something illegal. Only one third thought he had done nothing wrong. Forty percent of Democrats thought the president had behaved unethically or illegally, compared to 96 percent of Republicans.

For Roberts, trying to bring up her daughter alone, Hunter's effort to reduce child support was personal, not political. She worked part time at her dad's gun store, Rob Roberts Custom Gun Works, and wasn't looking for a handout. She bore no animus to the Bidens, and she wanted her daughter to carry her father's name.

To that end, in December 2022, three months after Hunter applied to slash his payments, she asked Judge Meyer to allow their daughter to take the Biden name, claiming it is "now synonymous with being well educated, successful, financially acute and politically powerful."

The name will open opportunities for little Navy, "just like it has for other members of the Biden family," Roberts said in a court filing. Navy's "estrangement" from the First Family and Hunter's "neglect" of his daughter "can be rectified by changing her last name to Biden so that she may undeniably be known to the world as the child of the defendant and member of the prestigious Biden family."

Hunter tried to block the move, telling the judge the Biden name would rob the child of a "peaceful existence," and that Roberts' motivation was "political warfare."

Navy was simply ignored by the Bidens. While Joe always boasted about his "six grandchildren" he never mentioned her. But by the time she was four, Navy knew her paternal grandfather was the president of the United States, and her mother had plastered her Instagram with photographs of the two of them in Washington DC. In one April 2022 photo in front of the Jefferson Memorial, Navy wore an Air Force One "presidential crew" baseball cap.

"To the little girl that made me a mama, Navy Joan, I hope one day when you look back you find yourself proud of who you are, where you come from, and most importantly, who raised you," Roberts captioned another photo of Navy.

Hunter flew into Batesville, Arkansas (population 7202), in April 2023, on Morris' $6 million private jet and drove to the courthouse in a six-car motorcade, with a police escort and his Secret Service detail. Bomb-sniffing dogs swept the courtroom ahead of his appearance and a phalanx of sheriff's deputies provided security.

One of the high-powered Washington attorneys accompanying Hunter was Abbe Lowell, who "charges a rate of $855 per billable hour," Lancaster noted, and whose retention was "indicative of the defendant's influence, prestige, and importance."

Lancaster told the court Hunter was pretending to be "nothing more than a Yale educated attorney/artist who is somewhat financially destitute and needs his child support adjusted.

"However, for an artist living on meager means, Mr. Biden is living lavishly . . . He travels the world on the safest and most comfortable airplane in existence—Air Force One. He also has some of the most expensive attorneys on planet Earth."

Hunter, on the other hand, argued that he had paid Robert $750,000 already and had suffered "a substantial material change" in his income so could no longer afford the payments.

Roberts, supported in court by her parents and sister, demanded voluminous discovery of Hunter's financial affairs, covering everything from his Burisma payments in Ukraine to the BHR and CEFC deals in China, to the identities of the buyers of his pricy paintings.

To twist the knife further, Lancaster enlisted Hunter's nemesis Garrett

Ziegler as an expert witness for the trial. No relation to the IRS agent, Ziegler was a 27-year-old former Trump adviser, and the Illinois-based founder of nonprofit research outfit Marco Polo, who published a 644-page analysis of Hunter's laptop in 2022, alleging he had found hundreds of crimes.

During the case, Ziegler revealed that Hunter had offloaded his 10 percent stake in Chinese equity fund Bohai Harvest RST (BHR) to Morris. Board papers on Hunter's laptop showed that the fund had accumulated assets under management of $2.5 billion as of January 2019, had fourteen shell funds in the tax haven of the Cayman Islands, and would deliver lucrative "future distributions" from companies it owned shares in, including Henniges, Sinopec, and Face++.

Author Peter Schweizer estimated the value of Hunter's share to be as much as $20 million, although Archer, who also owned a 10 percent share, claimed it was worth far less, because adverse publicity had scared off Chinese investors.

Hunter's lawyers did their best to get Ziegler thrown off the case, to no avail. They maligned the devout Lutheran father of two as an unhinged "zealot" and wrote letters to the Delaware Attorney General, the DOJ's National Security division, and the LA County District Attorney, urging he be investigated.

Hunter also sued Marco Polo and Ziegler, claiming they had "hacked into" and spent "countless hours accessing, tampering with, manipulating, altering, copying and damaging" his computer data, and "scouring" a hard drive copy of "what they claim to be [Hunter's] 'laptop' computer." Hunter would continue to cling to the fiction that the laptop he left at Mac Isaac's Delaware computer repair store was not his.

Hunter also sued Rudy Giuliani and Bob Costello for alleged breach of privacy, Trump donor Patrick Byrne for defamation, and the IRS for allegedly breaching his privacy.

Mac Isaac sued Hunter for defamation, and Hunter countersued Mac Isaac, alleging he had breached his privacy and stolen his data. To manage all the lawsuits and criminal defense work, Hunter had 18 lawyers, running up millions of dollars in fees.

Hunter's pricy lawyers refused to agree to a settlement with Roberts in Arkansas that might avoid his opening the kimono on his financial secrets. By Easter, 2023, Lancaster was asking Judge Meyers to jail Hunter for failing to hand over his records, as required.

Despite the courtroom travails and the five-year criminal investigation heating up in Delaware, Hunter was even more conspicuously at his father's side during this time.

He spent a lot of time living at the White House in April, popping up at Easter activities and joining his father for the holiday long weekend at Camp David, before tagging along with Joe to Ireland on Air Force 1 on a multi-day official visit, where he held his father's umbrella and stood next to him as he met dignitaries.

"I'm here with my sister, Valerie, and my younger son, Hunter Biden," Joe said at one event. "Stand up guys, I'm proud of you."

A week later, career IRS criminal supervisory special agent Gary Shapley came forward to Congress with claims that the fix was in on Hunter's case. He said federal prosecutors were preventing tax charges being brought against then president's son.

Shapley's attorney, Mark Lytle, alleged in a letter to House Judiciary Chairman Jim Jordan and eight other House and Senate committee chairs that "preferential treatment and politics [are] improperly infecting decisions and protocols that would normally be followed by career law enforcement professionals in similar circumstances if the subject were not politically connected . . .

"Despite serious risks of retaliation, my client is offering to provide you with information necessary to exercise your constitutional oversight function and wishes to make the disclosures in a nonpartisan manner to the leadership of the relevant committees on both sides of the political aisle," said the letter.

Under law, the Ways and Means Committee was allowed to request and receive any tax returns from the IRS, notwithstanding privacy concerns.

Shapley already had blown the whistle internally at the IRS and to the Justice Department's inspector general about the corruption of the "Sportsman" investigation into Hunter.

A week later, on April 25, 2023, aged 80, Joe officially announced he was running for re-election, having promised during the 2020 campaign that he would only serve one term, due to his advanced age.

The next day, Hunter's attorneys, including Chris Clark, went to DOJ headquarters in Washington DC to meet with US Attorney Weiss and Associate Deputy Attorney General Bradley Weinsheimer and the DOJ tax division attorneys. According to leaks to the *Washington Post*, Weiss was "nearing the end of his decision-making process."

On May 5, 2023, Joe interfered with deliberations by giving a rare sit-down TV interview to declare Hunter's innocence.

"My son has done nothing wrong," he told MSNBC. "I trust him. I have faith in him, and it impacts my presidency by making me feel proud of him."

The timing was shocking. The president was sending a public signal to his subordinates at the DOJ, including Attorney General Garland, that his son should not be charged with any crime.

"That's a highly inappropriate message from a President," the *Wall Street Journal* editorial board declared at the time. "He's essentially telling prosecutors that they are wrong to bring an indictment because Hunter is innocent of any criminal behavior. Some might think it's only natural for a father to defend the son he loves, but the Justice Department is part of the executive branch that he runs. Mr. Garland and his prosecutors work for the President."

The optics never concerned Joe. He would do whatever it took to extricate his family—and himself—from legal jeopardy. He'd had close calls all his life. This was no different, except he had more power than ever.

* * *

Hunter had always wanted to be an artist or a writer, but Joe had assigned him the role of Biden bagman. According to the laptop, Hunter was paying the bills for the rest of the family (a claim he now disputes) through lucrative grace-and-favor jobs and sweetheart deals facilitated by benefactors looking for favor with his powerful father.

But in Los Angeles, newly married, he took up a career as a painter, blowing droplets of alcohol ink with a metal straw onto Japanese Yupo paper.

The art was a form of therapy his former shrink Keith Ablow had long recommended for him. Ablow saw the blown ink artworks as a way to re-process the pain of losing his mother and sister at an early age.

"You can't drug yourself into oblivion after you've experienced that . . . Hence the suggestion to be an artist, if that is where your passion is, and don't drug yourself.

"Artists are often reprocessing pain but productively. They are alche-mists. They take pain and they turn it into meaningful images."

Which was all very well, but it was the reported prices he was charging—$75,000 to $500,000—for a first-time artist with no formal training, which made Hunter's hobby an ethical nightmare for the White House.

The weight of dealing with the ethics of Hunter cashing on his father's name fell on George Berges, the affable Manhattan gallerist dragooned into representing the president's son. He had been persuaded to show Hunter's work by none other than the Joe Biden's LA socialite fundraiser Lanette Phillips, who also had connected Kevin Morris with Hunter back in 2019.

Berges testified about his dealings with Hunter in a deposition to the House impeachment inquiry in January 2024. "I flew in, and I looked at his art," Berges remembered of his first meeting with Hunter at the end of 2019 at his house in the Hollywood Hills. "I liked the potential, what I saw. I also liked his personal narrative for a variety of reasons."

In July 2021, Berges hit the headlines, when the *Washington Post* re-ported that the White House was grappling with the "ethics of Hunter Biden's pricey paintings."

The White House claimed it had put an agreement in place with Berges' gallery that would keep the art buyers' identities a secret from Hunter, the president, the White House, and the public.

White House press secretary Jen Psaki told reporters in July 2021 that, "after careful consideration, a system has been established that allows for

Hunter Biden to work in his profession within reasonable safeguards. Of course, he has the right to pursue an artistic career, just like any child of a president has the right to pursue a career . . . The gallerist will not share information about buyers or prospective buyers, including their identities, with Hunter Biden or the administration, which provides quite a level of protection and transparency."

It won't surprise you to learn that wasn't how it turned out.

Bergès later would say that he was "surprised" by claims of a "system" to create a firewall between Hunter and his buyers, because he never had any communication with the White House about a so-called "ethics agreement" governing the sale of Hunter's art.

As Hunter's art dealer testified, it was a sham. Far from the blind purchases promised by the White House, Hunter knew the identities of the individuals who purchased roughly 70 percent of the value of his art, including Democrat donors Kevin Morris and Elizabeth Hirsh Naftali.

In fact, in his initial contract with Berges, Hunter demanded that the "gallery will give artist list of names of purchasers of work with prices . . . on a quarterly basis," Berges testified.

Hunter asked Berges to remove the clause in September 2021, after Psaki's claims that the buyers would be anonymous.

"The Biden White House appears to have deceived the American people," Oversight Committee Chairman James Comer said after Berges' testimony.

"Hunter Biden's amateur art career is an ethics nightmare. The vast majority of Hunter Biden's art has been purchased by Democrat donors, one of whom was appointed by President Biden to a prestigious commission after she purchased Hunter Biden's art for tens of thousands of dollars."

Naftali bought a painting for $42,000 in February 2021 and later paid $52,000 for a second piece. In July 2022, eight months after Hunter's first art show in Hollywood, she was appointed to the Commission for the Preservation of America's Heritage Abroad, the same gig Hunter secured for his old partner Eric Schwerin. She also visited the White House at least a dozen times.

Morris bought most of Hunter Biden's art: paying $875,000 for 11 paintings in January 2023.

The other Hunter art aficionado was Bergès' gallery co-owner William Jacques who bought three paintings, paying $40,000 in December 2020, $25,000 in February 2021 and $32,500 in November 2021.

The art, itself, drew mixed reviews: "Generic Post Zombie Formalism" was the verdict of Jerry Saltz, *New York* magazine critic.

"I guess it's important that wounded men of a certain age and privileged background have the opportunity to find themselves creatively," critic Scott Indrisek snarked to Artnet News. "It's just too bad that everyone else is expected to pay attention."

Sebastian Smee, the Pulitzer Prize–winning art critic for the *Washington Post*, described Hunter as "a cafe painter . . . a bit of a dabbler. His work has the feeling of an afterthought. It doesn't feel like it needed to be made, except perhaps as a therapeutic exercise."

Berges spoke on the phone and met Joe while representing his son and used to wear a Camp David cap Hunter had given him around Soho, although he said he had never been to the presidential retreat.

But like mostly everyone who helped Hunter, he got stiffed, finding himself out of pocket for a lot of unpaid bills.

"I'm still bitter about a lot of that stuff," he told the House Oversight Committee.

He'd had to pay about $60,000 for Hunter's October 2021 art show in Hollywood. "I had to do all the framing. I had to do all the shipping. I had to expedite it," he said.

He was out of pocket for the show in New York a couple of weeks later, as well. "I have my natural overhead. I pay tens of thousands a month in rent and staffing, insurance. At the time I had, like, three, four people working on it. So it's a considerable expense.

"I took a gamble, and it didn't really pay off, but so that's one of the reasons I haven't really renewed the contract." He ended his agreement with Hunter at the end of 2023.

"It hasn't been a lucrative business decision on my part. I think he wants to obviously work with me, and but, you know, I also have to make business decisions. I have my own family to support."

* * *

Hunter was back in Batesville, Arkansas for the child support case in June 2023. Roberts was in the deposition room, listening to him. They talked privately during a break about 45 minutes in. He worked his charm, and she had a change of heart, giving Hunter pretty much everything he wanted.

She settled the case by agreeing to a vastly reduced monthly support, less than $5,000 a month, one quarter of what he had originally agreed.

"We set aside our differences and came together for the sake of our adorable little girl," Roberts would later write.

"As someone who has been lucky enough to have the unwavering support of an incredible father throughout my own life, I know that Navy Joan deserves the same opportunity . . . That's why I'm 100 percent behind Hunter's recovery and his determination to become the loving father figure that all five of his children deserve."

As part of the deal, she asked Hunter to give Navy a number of his paintings and commit to building a relationship with his daughter. In return she dropped her request to have Navy's last name changed to Biden.

"Lunden is a great mom and little Navy is going be fine," Lancaster told me after the settlement. "The kid has lots of love on the maternal side of the family in Batesville. They are a very, very close family. They adore her and are always going to support her . . . But I think everybody is disappointed that there's not more contact [with the Biden family].

"It's not lost on anybody that Jill Biden wrote a children's book and [dedicated it] to her grandchildren. She could have kept it at that, but she named every child except Navy. They hung stockings for the dog at Christmas but not for Navy. That is one of the saddest things."

News of the settlement came on the same day federal prosecutors in Delaware said Hunter had agreed to plead guilty to misdemeanor counts of willful failure to pay federal income tax, as part of a deal with the DOJ to keep him out of jail. He also would agree to enter a pre-trial diversion on a felony gun possession charge.

The next month, Joe and Jill Biden finally publicly acknowledged Navy Joan Roberts as their 7th grandchild in a statement to People Magazine.

"Our son Hunter and Navy's mother, Lunden, are working together to foster a relationship that is in the best interests of their daughter, preserving her privacy as much as possible going forward," Joe said in the July 28, 2023, statement.

"This is not a political issue, it's a family matter. Jill and I only want what is best for all of our grandchildren, including Navy."

But that was the only grudging acknowledgment Navy received from her paternal grandparents.

That Christmas, the Bidens broke with their tradition of the past two years of hanging personalized festive stockings embroidered with the names of each of their grandchildren and even their pets over the mantle in the State Dining Room at the White House. Navy had been left out of every First Family Christmas display and then, in 2023, when Roberts expected that her daughter would be included, there was no display at all.

Dark clouds hung over the Bidens that Christmas. The IRS whistleblowers had delivered their payload and Hunter's sweetheart plea deal with David Weiss in Delaware had collapsed, so he was now facing twin indictments on tax and gun charges.

On December 13, 2023, the Republican-controlled House of Representatives had voted to formalize the impeachment inquiry into Joe for political corruption, abuse of power, and obstruction. To top it all off, Joe was running for re-election.

There was a lot to discuss at Camp David over the holidays.

CHAPTER 26

NEMESIS

July 26, 2023
WILMINGTON, DELAWARE

O n the flight east from Los Angeles on Kevin Morris' private jet the
night before he had to appear in court in Delaware, Hunter rehearsed
the speech he planned to give to the media after the judge rubber-
stamped his sweetheart plea deal.

Ever the showman, Morris had a documentary crew accompanying
them on his nine-seater luxury Dassault Falcon 50. He had planned every aspect of what he expected to be the grand finale in the Hunter Exoneration Project. Morris saw himself as the ringmaster of Hunter's life,
overseeing a team of more than 20 lawyers who were not just defending
Hunter but aggressively suing his adversaries.

This court appearance would be a triumph of vindication for Hunter.
He wanted the world to know that the nearly five-year effort by the IRS,
the FBI, and the US Attorney's office in Delaware to investigate him for tax
fraud, money laundering, foreign agent violations, and sex trafficking was
politically motivated and had come to nothing. Or virtually nothing—he
would agree to plead guilty to just two tax misdemeanors and, in a separate side deal, prosecutors would drop a felony gun charge as long as

Hunter kept his nose clean for two years. Sweeping immunity would protect him from prosecution of any further charges connected to his business dealings.

His long legal odyssey was almost at an end—or so he thought.

Morris had organized for a podium and a microphone stand outside the courthouse, and friendly media outlets had been alerted that Hunter would be speaking once proceedings were wrapped up. He would proclaim his innocence, speaking with emotion about the toll on his family of the lengthy prosecution, and insisting that his father was not involved in any way whatsoever with his get-rich-quick projects around the world.

But Hunter would have to wait almost six months to give that speech, and it would be in gloomier circumstances.

All of Morris' carefully laid plans were about to unravel. The consequences of the Hunter and Jim's alleged decades-long grift were about to rain down on Hunter and jeopardize the president's re-election prospects the following year. And Hunter only had himself to blame. His hubris and reckless sense of entitlement, not to mention his lawyers' cocky overreach, had brought them all undone.

It had been a long time coming, but Hunter would meet his nemesis in courtroom 4A in the J. Caleb Boggs Federal Building in Wilmington, Delaware.

The drab Soviet-style building was named after the former Republican governor and two-term senator whom the allies of a 29-year-old Wilmington councilman named Joe Biden had allegedly narrowly maneuvered out of office in 1972. According to a biography of the late mob hitman Frank "The Irishman" Sheeran, who was then the president of Teamsters Local 326 in Wilmington, a union-organized newspaper strike was orchestrated on election eve to stop voters from seeing a damaging Boggs campaign ad attacking Joe.

Now, as Hunter walked inside the building on that fine summer's day 51 years later, you could imagine the ghost of Boggs reaching out from the grave to avenge the sins of the father. According to Irish folklore, vengeful shades from a lifetime of walking over "chumps" like Boggs must one day come back to haunt Joe's descendants.

It felt ominous as soon as he got into U.S. District Judge Maryellen Noreika's courtroom just before 10 a.m. with his Secret Service detail and large team of lawyers. The confident demeanor slipped, and Hunter regressed to the schoolboy called to the headmaster's office. He addressed the judge with exquisite deference and politely shook hands with new prosecutor Leo Wise, a razor-bald 6-foot-4 tall pit-bull lawyer, who had just taken over the case after joining U.S. Attorney Weiss' Delaware office in March.

Weiss' top deputy, Assistant US Attorney Lesley Wolf, the architect of the sweetheart plea deal, sat in court quietly behind Hunter that morning, but only as an observer. She had moved on, along with the entire Sportsman team, when the IRS whistleblowers' allegations of obstruction, interference, and political favoritism started to burn not just Weiss, but Attorney General Merrick Garland.

Though she denies that she had to, Wolf gave up a 20-year career in the DOJ, most of it at the U.S. Attorney's office in Delaware, and her dream of a big promotion to Main Justice, for a job in the Philadelphia office of Democratic law firm Ballard Spahr, which she officially joined in November 2023. The consolation was a nicer salary and a shorter commute from her suburban Philadelphia home, but she didn't enjoy the media attention or the fact that she appeared to be taking the rap for her boss David Weiss for the Hunter debacle.

Before she left, Wolf nailed down details of the sweetheart plea deal with Hunter's main lawyer Chris Clark, with whom she had developed a rapport through the course of the investigation.

Emails obtained by *Politico* and the *New York Times* give a glimpse of the unrelenting pressure over 15 months placed by Clark on prosecutors not to charge Hunter, and the lengths that the Delaware US attorney's office was willing to go to accommodate the president's son.

Clark buttonholed Weiss in Wilmington, telling him his "legacy" would be defined by how he handled this decision, the *Times* reported. He wrote him scathing letters, accusing the U.S. Attorney of caving into "the relentless political pressure from the opponents of the current President of the United States."

He went over Weiss' head to seek meetings with Garland, Deputy Attorney General Lisa Monaco, the head of the DOJ Criminal Division, the head of the Tax Division, the Office of Legal Counsel, and the Office of the Solicitor General.

At one point, Clark threatened to put the president on the witness stand if Hunter were charged, and dramatically predicted that the move could spark a constitutional crisis and destroy the reputation of the Justice Department.

"President Biden now unquestionably would be a fact witness for the defense in any criminal trial," Clark wrote in a 32-page letter to the DOJ, reported by *Politico*.

"This of all cases justifies neither the spectacle of a sitting President testifying at a criminal trial nor the potential for a resulting Constitutional crisis."

Undoubtedly a criminal trial would be damaging, not least to the president himself. The evidence presented in court would be devastating to a candidate seeking reelection, and both the felony gun charge and the tax evasion carried the real risk of prison time for Hunter. Even with a presidential pardon in his back pocket, would Joe want to use it to free his son if it cost him the presidency? Time was running out to bring an end to the case and avoid disaster.

IRS Supervisory agent Gary Shapley was preparing to testify to Congress about obstruction and slow-walking in the "Sportsman" investigation, and about Weiss deliberately allowing the statute of limitations to run out on serious tax charges. Shapley had lodged a complaint with the DOJ watchdog two months earlier.

On April 26, 2023, five days after news broke about Shapley's plans to testify, Clark finally secured a meeting with Associate Deputy Attorney General Bradley Weinsheimer, which Weiss attended.

After that meeting, according to Shapley's later testimony, Weiss insisted that Hunter could not skate free without pleading guilty to at least a misdemeanor. Negotiations between Clark and Wolf took on a sense of urgency. On May 15, 2023, the same day that Shapley and lead IRS investigator Joe Ziegler were removed from the "Sportsman" case, Wolf made a firm offer to Clark: a deferred prosecution agreement. She knew then that her days on the case were numbered.

Clark agreed but wanted much more, according to emails leaked to the *New York Times* after the plea deal collapsed. He wanted Hunter to receive blanket immunity not only for all potential federal crimes investigated by the Delaware US Attorney's office but for "any other federal crimes relating to matters investigated by the United States" he might have ever committed.

Wolf negotiated Clark's ambit claim down to "a narrower promise" not to prosecute Hunter for any of the offenses "encompassed" in a statement of facts that would be presented to court, and included his Chinese, Ukrainian, and Romanian deals from 2015, his "willful" failure to pay tax on millions of dollars in income in 2017 and 2018, and his crack cocaine use and "nonstop debauchery." The felony gun charge would be dealt with in a diversion agreement that is usually applied to first-time non-violent misdemeanors and allows a case to be dismissed if an offender fulfils requirements set by the court.

On May 19, 2023, Wolf agreed to the final terms, and Clark flew to California to clear the deal with Hunter in a meeting in the garage-turned-studio of his Malibu rental, according to the *Times*.

The following week, in a CBS interview, Shapley went public with his allegations that Hunter had received "preferential treatment" throughout the investigation. On May 26, he testified behind closed doors before the House Ways and Means Committee. Ziegler testified on June 1.

Now, in Judge Noreika's courtroom, eight weeks later, Leo Wise's signature was on Wolf's plea agreement, and he would be expected to defend it, even though he had not been involved in any of the negotiations.

Wise, 46, a New Jersey native with a resolute jaw, a law degree from Harvard, and a master's degree from Johns Hopkins University, was a commissioned officer in the United States Navy Reserve Intelligence Program. An aggressive trial attorney in the DOJ Criminal Division, he had spent nearly two decades in the Baltimore U.S. attorney's office, where he headed the Fraud and Public Corruption unit. He was involved in some of the biggest cases the Justice Department had run in the past ten years, prosecuting Enron, Big Tobacco, drug dealers, corrupt cops, and Democratic politicians. Now he had been handpicked to take over one of the most explosive political cases in DOJ history.

Wise and his 6-foot-6 prosecuting partner Derek Hines were described in the Baltimore Sun as a killer team. "Like the Terminator, they just never stop coming" and are "hardliners" who pursue harsh sentences. "Anybody who committed wrongdoing, they're going to search them out."

The pair had been quietly detailed to Delaware to conduct damage control, but the convoluted form that would take would only start to take shape over the next year.

It didn't take long after Judge Noreika entered the courtroom on the morning of July 26, 2023, to realize that things were not going to go to plan.

For almost three hours, Noreika peppered Hunter's lawyers and the prosecutors with questions about the unorthodox two-part plea deal that she found troubling. Hunter's lawyers reacted with shrugs, exasperated exhales, "frantic glances," and other expressions of discontent, according to reporters in the courtroom.

Noreika raised concerns about the opaque link between the tax misdemeanor plea agreement and the gun felony diversion agreement, describing the arrangement as "atypical" and "not straightforward," and repeatedly informed both sides that she would not provide a "rubber stamp."

"I have concerns about the agreement, and that's why I'm asking these questions," she told the exasperated lawyers on both sides. "I'm trying to exercise due diligence."

She asked Wise if he had ever seen a diversion agreement "so broad that it encompasses crimes in a different case." He agreed there was no precedent.

Then she asked if the agreement gave Hunter blanket immunity or if he could face any future related charges. "There are references to foreign companies, for example, in the facts section. Could the government bring a charge under the Foreign Agents Registration Act?"

"Yes," said Wise, suggesting the government may have been considering potential charges against Hunter for allegedly failing to register as a foreign agent in countries like China and Ukraine where his father had played a role in his enrichment activities.

Hunter's main lawyer, Chris Clark, interjected. "I don't agree with what the government said."

Wise responded: "Then there is no deal."

"Where does that leave us?" asked Noreika.

A "visibly frazzled" Clark replied: "As far as I'm concerned, the plea agreement is null and void."

The courtroom erupted with audible gasps.

Hunter was reported to be "visibly agitated" standing up and motioning to his lawyers to explain what was going on. Morris appeared to jolly him along, making him laugh at one point amid the whispering, and exchanging a friendly "gimme-five" hand slap with him. On the opposite side of the court, David Weiss looked unsettled.

Clark then asked the judge for some time to "see whether we can somehow make any headway on this."

During a 20-minute recess, both sides negotiated and whispered among themselves as they tried to find a way to defend their agreement to a skeptical Noreika.

Reporters heard snatches of conversation as Clark approached Wise at one point with arms stretched wide, saying "I don't know what you're trying to accomplish."

"You can't get around that," Wise replied.

"Then we'll rip it up!" retorted Clark. "Does anyone want to talk about this? [It's] really bad for everyone . . . no good."

Hunter's new high-priced Washington attorney, Abbe Lowell, who had been sitting quietly at the back of the court with three lawyers from his firm, approached Weiss and introduced himself.

"Looks like I'm going to be involved in the fray now," he said, shaking Weiss' hand. "I was hoping not to be."

When Judge Noreika returned to the bench, both sides presented her with a revised plea deal in which Hunter would face no new charges for tax, drug and firearm offenses between 2014 to 2019.

She questioned Hunter to make sure he understood what he was agreeing to. Then she asked about a discrepancy in his sobriety dates, since he had told her he hadn't used drugs since May 2019, but had given his formal "sober date" as June 1, 2019.

He explained that, after going to rehab six times in 20 years, "I was married on May 17th of 2019, and that is my sobriety date [but] to be technically and completely honest from the day that I got married until June 1st, I did have a drink or two."

Noreika then asked him about his tax liabilities in October 2019. "You were sober at that time. But you didn't file your taxes."

Hunter replied: "Yes, Your Honor, in putting my life back together, it was a flood, an enormous amount of problems and, by the time I was able to find someone to be able to help me, I was already past the deadline in which I should not have gone past."

Noreika continued to go through the statement of facts: "It says that in 2020, during the process of putting together your 2017 and 2018 tax returns, you mischaracterized certain personal expenses as legitimate business expenses. What's that referencing?"

Clark jumped in at this point. "Your Honor, it may be better if I explain it because Mr. Biden is actually not that close to the facts. In essence, in a very compressed time frame, Mr. Biden was asked to identify for all of these tax years that were being done from his credit cards and other bank accounts what's a business expense and what is a personal expense. And he was asked to go through charts and mark them. And there are situations in which he made an error with regard to marking business expenses or personal expenses . . .

"So, we concede that he made mistakes, erroneous mistakes in categorizing some of these business and personal expenses."

Leo Wise summarized the prosecution case: "Despite his addiction issues, he was able to generate significant amounts of income and made financial decisions about how to spend that money [and] those decisions did not include meeting his obligations to pay his taxes."

Noreika asked Wise to explain the diversion agreement on the felony gun charge which she described as "a bit unusual."

Wise explained that the agreement required that Hunter be supervised by a probation officer, "that he continue to actively seek employment; that he refrain from unlawfully possessing controlled substance; that he refrain from using alcohol; that he submit to substance abuse testing and participate in substance abuse treatment . . . and that he not commit a violation of any federal, state or local law."

Noreika remained wary of approving a deal that would obligate her to impose no prison sentence. She said that in other cases she had presided over involving drug addicts buying guns, "we usually see a felony charge for false statement. The Defendant has admitted that his statement was false, but he wasn't charged.

"I'm not trying to get into the purview of the prosecutor . . . but I just want to ask, does the government have any concern about not bringing the false statement charge."

"No," said Wise.

But Noreika smelled a rat: "You all are telling me just rubber stamp the agreement . . . But it seems like the argument you're making is form over substance . . . These agreements are not straightforward, and they contain some atypical provisions. I am not criticizing you for coming up with those, I think that you have worked hard to come up with creative ways to deal with this. But I am not in a position where I can decide to accept or reject the Plea Agreement, so I need to defer it."

"We're not asking the court to rubber-stamp anything," Wise said defensively.

Noreika answered: "It certainly sounds like it."

Then she turned to Hunter: "Without me saying I'll agree to the plea agreement, how do you plead?"

"Not guilty, Your Honor," he said.

Hunter was silent as he left the courthouse, ignoring the shouted questions of reporters.

The ghost of J. Caleb Boggs had finally taken his revenge.

* * *

The somber reality dawning on Hunter and his entourage as they left court was a far cry from the hubris they exhibited a month earlier, when the cozy plea deal was announced on June 20, 2023 and they all laughed at the cries of outrage from Republicans.

Hunter had walked into the court expecting a swift and painless end to his legal ordeal. He walked out facing possible indictments on further charges and even prison.

Hunter moved back into the White House with Melissa and their three-year-old son, Beau, the following day. The next night he effectively had his coming out party, parading around a state dinner for Indian Prime Minister Narendra Modi.

He was all smiles, handsome in his tuxedo, gladhanding and rubbing shoulders with the good and the great, who included none other than Attorney General Garland.

Garland was careful not to be photographed anywhere near the First Son, but the optics were appalling, as numerous critics pointed out.

"Hunter and Merrick hanging out at Joe's place?" Tennessee Republican congressman Andrew Ogles tweeted, "Classic Biden Crime Family."

Political rivalries had hardened since the Republicans had taken control of the House that January and started investigating Hunter and Jim's corruption. The Russia-Ukraine war which had erupted the previous year had placed the alleged Burisma grift in a grave new light.

Joe wanted to rub Hunter's impending exoneration in the faces of his detractors. I'll show you, he seemed to say. No one fucks with a Biden.

But Hunter's presence at the Modi dinner (and another state dinner for the president of Kenya, also attended by Garland) was frowned upon even by Joe's allies as needlessly provocative, not to mention premature. They fretted that the plea deal still had to be ratified by a judge in Delaware, and nothing was certain until then. And as it turned out their fears were well founded.

Nobody knew how long Hunter had been living at the White House, but numerous sightings over the previous nine months of him and his family on the grounds lent credence to rumors in Washington and New York that he was at least a part-time resident.

During that period, he was photographed numerous times strolling across the White House lawn with his father to Marine One to jet off for weekends at Delaware or Camp David, or for longer vacations at the borrowed homes of billionaires. He flew with his father on Air Force 1 on a state visit to Ireland. He was spotted hanging out on the Truman Balcony to watch the Fourth Of July fireworks. Adding to the impression of a resident young family was an elaborate swing set suitable for toddler Beau that had popped up on the White House grounds.

Hunter's eldest daughter, Naomi, and her fiancé also had reportedly moved in with "Pops" for a few weeks before their wedding on the South Lawn the previous November. The Executive Residence of the White House has 16 guest bedrooms and 35 bathrooms on the second and third floors, as well as a private guest kitchen, an in-house gym, bowling alley and private cinema. Plenty of room for the entire Biden clan, who can come and go as they please without signing the visitor log, making it difficult to verify their presence.

When a bag of cocaine was found by the Secret Service on a Sunday night, July 2, 2023, in a quiet corner of the West Wing near the Situation Room, fingers were pointed at Hunter, being the White House's most famous cocaine aficionado, but White House press secretary Karine Jean-Pierre slapped down that line of questioning from reporters as "incredibly irresponsible." She also misleadingly claimed that the president and his son were not at the White House two days before the cocaine was found.

"They were not here Friday. They were not here Saturday. They were not here Sunday."

But Hunter and Joe were indeed at the White House on Friday, until 6:34 p.m., when they flew off for a long weekend at Camp David.

The Secret Service closed its investigation after 11 days, saying they had found no fingerprints or DNA evidence on the plastic bag of cocaine and, in a complex bristling with security cameras, there was no surveillance video footage because the baggie was located in a "blind spot." Further, Secret Service spokesman Anthony Guglielmi told NBC that it was not possible to conduct interviews of potential cokeheads known to be in the vicinity of where the drugs were found because that would infringe on their civil rights.

Hunter's Teflon protection had once again proved impenetrable. But there was more peril to come in the next two weeks before his court appearance.

* * *

An indication that all was not well between Joe and his Attorney General appeared on July 21, 2023, in the form of an extraordinary memo from Merrick Garland officially limiting contacts between the White House and the Justice Department relating to investigations in order to "protect the norms of Departmental independence and integrity."

Garland said that the DOJ "will not advise the White House concerning pending or contemplated criminal or civil law enforcement investigations or cases unless doing so is important for the performance of the President's duties and appropriate from a law enforcement perspective."

Coming a few days before Hunter's sweetheart plea deal was set to be heard in court, the memo carried an extra sting.

The White House responded the same day with its own memo, cautioning its staff not to contact any department or agency about any specific investigations unless approved by the White House Counsel's Office. Whatever behavior behind the scenes had prompted the dueling memos, they came in a week of high drama for Hunter and his father.

Just two days earlier, on July 19, 2023, IRS whistleblowers Shapley and Ziegler had testified to Congress for the first time and contradicted Garland's sworn testimony about the independence of the investigation of the president's son. Ziegler dropped his anonymity and said he was a Democrat who felt he had to do the "right thing" by exposing what he described as "the corrosion of ethical standards and the abuse of power that threaten our nation."

The next day, July 20, Senator Chuck Grassley released the FBI FD-1023 document that the bureau had been fighting to keep hidden. It was a three-year-old report from a long-term "highly credible" confidential FBI informant who had alleged that Hunter and Joe had each been paid a $5 million bribe by Ukrainian Mykola Zlochevsky, the Burisma founder. Within weeks, the informant would be charged with making false statements to the FBI, but the allegation could not have come at a worse time for Hunter.

The night before his appearance in Noreika's court six days later, Hunter's lawyers panicked. It's hard to explain their antics any other way.

In an apparent dirty trick that did not dispose Noreika kindly towards Hunter's legal team the next day, a mystery caller got an amicus brief taken down that had been filed by the Republican-controlled House Ways and Means committee. The filing contained the IRS whistleblowers' congressional testimony claiming that Hunter had benefited from "political interference which calls into question the propriety of the investigation" and urged the court to consider the allegations in light of Hunter's cozy arrangement with prosecutors.

According to a letter sent to Noreika by the committee's counsel, Theodore Kittila, someone from Hunter's legal team had persuaded court officials to seal his damning amicus brief by impersonating someone from his office.

"At approximately 1:30 p.m., we received word that our filing was removed from the docket," Kittila wrote to the judge. "We promptly contacted the Clerk's office, and we were advised that someone contacted the Court representing that they worked with *my office* [his emphasis] and that they were asking the Court to remove this from the docket. We immediately advised that this was inaccurate. The Clerk's Office responded that we would need to re-file. We have done so now."

When he re-filed, Kittila included an email in which a court official told him that the person who had phoned to ask that his filing be removed was Jessica Bengels, director of litigation services at the law firm Latham & Watkins, where Hunter's lawyer Chris Clark had recently been a partner.

Late that night, a panicked Bengels submitted an affidavit in which she denied impersonating anyone and blamed the fiasco on a misunderstanding by court officials.

"I am completely confident that I never indicated that I was calling from Mr. Kittila's firm or that I worked with him in any way," she wrote. "The only mention of his name was when [the clerk] asked me if the filings had been entered by Mr. Kittila's firm and I answered that I believed that to be the case."

When Kittila confronted Clark, Hunter's lawyer claimed the filing improperly revealed confidential tax information, even though the whistleblower testimony has been public for more than a month.

"Your attempts to publicly file my client's personal financial information with no protections [are] improper, illegal, and in violation of applicable rules," Clark said in an email to Kittila. "We will seek all appropriate sanctions in response to your actions."

But the only sanctions considered by the furious judge were those she threatened against Hunter's lawyers that night.

She gave them until 9 p.m. to "show cause as to why sanctions should not be considered for misrepresentations to the Court."

"We have no idea how the misunderstanding occurred," Clark replied in a letter to the judge, "but our understanding is there was no misrepresentation."

Hunter's lawyers could not have found a better way to shine a spotlight on Shapley and Ziegler's allegations. To seemingly resort to such lengths to hide the committee's amicus brief spoke volumes about the damning nature of the IRS whistleblowers' testimony.

Added to Devon Archer's testimony, and ongoing damaging revelations from Comer's Oversight Committee, the pressure on the Attorney General forced him to give Special Counsel powers to Weiss, the man he had insisted under oath had "ultimate authority" to pursue charges against Hunter.

In a brief statement on August 11, 2023, Garland said he had agreed to Weiss' request to be elevated to Special Counsel due to "the extraordinary circumstances relating to this matter." According to IRS whistleblower Shapley, Weiss had previously asked for the extra authority in 2022 and been been denied by his DOJ superiors.

The move was intended to confer the appearance of independence in what was still an ongoing investigation of Hunter, and to answer Shapley's criticism that Weiss had been prevented from bringing charges in California and Washington by his Biden appointee counterparts.

House Oversight Committee Chairman Comer was suspicious that Weiss' new status was designed to "stonewall congressional oversight."

On the same day as Weiss elevation, a new filing from his office with the Wilmington US District Court said talks with Hunter's legal team about a potential guilty plea were "at an impasse . . .

"The Government now believes that the case will not resolve short of a trial," wrote Leo Wise.

Weiss would go on to indict Hunter in Delaware over the gun charge and in California over the tax charges. When Hunter stood trial in Delaware in June 2024, the prosecution case relied heavily on his abandoned laptop—government exhibit 16—and the witnesses and evidence that Joe Ziegler had managed to gather, against all odds.

Even so, the indictments were effectively a "limited hangout," a damage control tactic to protect Weiss, the attorney general, and, of course, the president.

The successful obstruction of the IRS financial investigation of Hunter meant that the most serious charges from 2014 and 2015 were excluded and nobody would be held legally accountable for the Biden family's global influence-peddling operation during Joe's vice-presidency, or for the government-wide cover-up.

But, without the IRS whistleblowers coming forward, it's likely that Hunter would not have been indicted for anything at all. Shapley and

Ziegler had put their careers on the line to testify about alleged wrong-doing they had seen at the highest levels of the DOJ, that had ultimately destroyed their five-year criminal investigation into Hunter. For their effort, they would be retaliated against by the IRS, abandoned by the DOJ watchdog and sued by Hunter's well-funded legal attack dogs.

But the evidence they continued to provide Congress would lead to great peril for Hunter, Joe, and Joe's brother Jim Biden.

It also finally put the nail in the coffin of Joe's repeated claims that he knew nothing about Hunter's overseas business dealings.

EPILOGUE

"They who cannot be wise are almost always cunning."

—SAMUEL JOHNSON

Eight days before his son was due to go to trial on felony gun charges before Judge Noreika in Delaware, President Joe Biden made a surprise nighttime visit to the Wilmington home of his daughter-in-law Hallie Biden, the trial's star witness. Joe made the unscheduled stop with his motorcade en route home to Washington from his nearby home at around 8 p.m. on Sunday, May 26, 2024.

Hallie, the widow of Beau Biden, was Hunter's lover in October 2018, when he allegedly lied on a federal background form while buying a Colt Cobra 388PL revolver.

In the indictment, she was described as having "observed the defendant using crack cocaine frequently—every 20 minutes except when he slept." Prosecutors said she and her children had discovered drugs and drug paraphernalia when they searched Hunter's belongings in the fall of 2018.

Hallie's testimony about Hunter's drug addiction at the time was crucial to the case, so naturally eyebrows were raised about her private 15-minute discussion with Joe.

The White House denied any impropriety, claiming that Joe did not discuss the trial with Hallie and that the visit was simply to mark the impending ninth anniversary of Beau's death.

It was a classic Biden tactic, citing a family tragedy as an excuse for apparently unseemly behavior.

When Hallie did testify for the prosecution on June 6, 2024 she had to run the cold-eyed gauntlet of Biden family and friends packed into the rows behind Hunter and his lawyers.

Joe's sister, Valerie Biden Owens, never a fan of Beau's widow, had taken Jill Biden's prominent seat in the front row while the first lady flew to France for 24 hours for D-Day commemorations. Jill was back in court the following day for a few hours before returning to Paris for a state dinner. The round trip on Air Force 1 was estimated to have cost the taxpayer upwards of $250,000. After an outcry, the Democratic National Committee announced it would reimburse the government the price of a first-class return ticket to Paris.

Jill was a conspicuous presence in the courtroom the rest of the week, sitting in the public gallery behind Hunter wearing brightly colored suits.

Nobody, least of all the jurors, could miss the power of the presidency emanating from the first lady and her oppressive Secret Service detail. When prosecutor Leo Wise summed up his case he gestured toward her and the rest of the Biden entourage sitting in the front rows of the public gallery.

"All of this is not evidence," Wise said. "People sitting in the gallery are not evidence. You may recognize some of them from the news or from the community. In the course of this trial, you may have looked at them and they may have looked at you. You may have seen them reacting to the testimony or the photographs, or something that one of the lawyers said. But respectfully, none of that matters."

The jury took three hours to convict Hunter of all three gun felonies on June 11, 2024.

Despite all the efforts of Kevin Morris, the CIA, the FBI and the DOJ to clean up Hunter's messes, his problems had become a liability for his 81-year-old father's re-election campaign.

By the spring of 2024, Morris was crying poor, declaring that he was "tapped out," and Abbe Lowell was complaining about a lack of resources.

As Joe continued to sink in the polls through the summer of 2024, Hunter's looming tax fraud trial in California in September 2024 threatened to dredge up ghosts of the past that the Bidens thought long buried.

Even though Special Counsel Weiss had allowed the statute of limitations to run out on the 2014 and 2015 charges against Hunter, the Californian indictment referred to those dangerous years.

Thus, less than eight weeks before the election, the trial placed on the table for public consumption a period that covers Joe's role in ousting Viktor Shokin and any potential foreign lobbying charges related to Burisma.

The pressure on Hunter to take a plea and avoid going to trial was immense. But the First Son knows he has the trump card: his father's pardon power.

ACKNOWLEDGMENTS

This book would not have been possible without the support of my terrific editors at the *New York Post*: Keith Poole, Steve Lynch, and Col Allan, who believed in the story from the start.

At HarperCollins, I am grateful to my editors Eric Nelson and James Neidhardt, for their ideas and expertise.

To my colleagues, past and present, thank you for your friendship, solidarity, and great reporting: Emma-Jo Morris, Jon Levine, Steve Nelson, Kelly Jane Torrance, and all the other Posties who played it straight on a tough story.

Special mention to Sohrab Ahmari, who encouraged me to write *Laptop from Hell* back in 2020.

Thanks to the stalwarts at Fox who have so warmly welcomed me, including Suzanne Scott, Sean Hannity, Jesse Watters, Laura Ingraham, Maria Bartiromo, Brian Kilmeade, Liz MacDonald, Stuart Varney, and the Fox Nation team. Special mention to Tucker Carlson for his early camaraderie.

Thanks to the wonderful David Limbaugh for taking the pain out of the book contract and Anthony Ziccardi for having the courage to publish the first book.

My gratitude and admiration go to the whistleblowers and other sources who trusted me, without whom this story would never have been told. Some must remain nameless.

John Paul Mac Isaac was the first of these American patriots. He was the computer repair shop owner who recognized the national security implications of Hunter Biden's laptop, forced the FBI to take it, and then ensured it could not be buried. I am grateful for his help.

Rudy Giuliani, America's mayor, who has suffered enormously for being right, and attorney Bob Costello, who entrusted me with the story back in October 2020. I value the friendship we have forged in the tumultuous years since. You never steered me wrong.

IRS investigators Gary Shapley and Joe Ziegler stepped out of the shadows to do the right thing at great cost to themselves. They are heroes. The lawful disclosures they made to Congress form an invaluable record of wrongdoing by bad actors within the federal government. They ensured that Hunter did not get off scot-free and provided evidence to pursue others in the future.

Another man of integrity, courage, and patriotism is Tony Bobulinksi, whom I would trust with my life. He has been relentless in exposing the national security dangers of the Biden family's Chinese ventures. Another of Hunter's former business partners, Devon Archer, deserves praise for his courage and resilience in bringing the truth to the American people. A fine father, husband, and friend, he was burned by his association with Hunter, like so many others.

Special thanks to Viktor Shokin, the honest Ukrainian former prosecutor-general, for the hours he spent patiently explaining how Joe Biden railroaded him. In the middle of a war, after multiple assassination attempts, it took enormous courage not to be silenced.

Thanks also to Gal Luft, the Israeli-American professor turned fugitive whose knowledge of CEFC's inner workings and insights into the Chinese hierarchy were invaluable. He was generous with his time and expertise, and I hope he finds justice.

Chris Tigani, the Delaware businessman who went to jail for the Bidens, has been an essential source of local knowledge.

To James Comer, Republican chair of the House Oversight Committee, thank you for your candor and tips, dogged pursuit of the truth, and hard work that most Americans don't see. You do Kentucky proud. Thanks also to committee staff, especially Jessica Collins and Russell Dye, Chairman

Jim Jordan's House Judiciary Committee, Senators Ron Johnson and Chuck Grassley, and staff.

To Mike Benz and Lee Smith, thank you for the geopolitical insights.

Thanks to the RealClearPolitics team for honoring the story by giving me the inaugural Samizdat Prize. Thanks also to the good people at the Media Research Center for the Bulldog Award.

Thanks to Matt Taibbi and Michael Shellenberger for their work exposing the Censorship Industrial Complex. It's been nice finding common ground.

Tristan Leavitt and Jason Foster at Empower Oversight, thanks for the tipoffs and dedication to whistleblowers.

Thanks to John Solomon for his comradeship and advice.

To John Catsimitidis, Sid Rosenberg, and Rita Cosby at WABC, thanks for welcoming me on board.

To Nina, Mimi, Heather, Terry, Melanie, Alexandra, Stephanie, James, Rusty, Johnny, and Dave, for your friendship and hospitality. Thank you for making New York home.

ABOUT THE AUTHOR

Miranda Devine is a *New York Post* columnist, Fox News contributor, and author. Born in Queens, New York, she grew up in Japan and Australia, and attended Northwestern University in Chicago. A reformed mathematician and mother of two, she lives in New York City with her husband. Her last book, *Laptop from Hell*, was a national bestseller.